DEFENDING THE KING JAMES BIBLE

A fourfold superiority:

- Texts
- Translators
- Technique
- Theology

God's Words Kept Intact in English

Third Revised Edition

Pastor D. A. Waite, Th.D., Ph.D.
Director, The Bible For Today, Inc.

Published By

THE BIBLE FOR TODAY PRESS
900 Park Avenue
Collingswood, New Jersey 08108, U.S.A.

Copyright, 1992, 1993, 1994, 1995, 1996,
1998, 1999, 2002, 2004, 2006

ISBN #1-56848-012-1

First Printing: October, 1992
Second Printing: August, 1993
Third Printing: August, 1994
Fourth Printing: May, 1995
SECOND EDITION
Fifth Printing (hardback): December, 1996
Sixth Printing (hardback): June, 1998
Seventh Printing (hardback): December, 1999
Eighth Printing (hardback): January, 2002
Ninth Printing (hardback): April, 2004
THIRD EDITION
Tenth Prining (hardback): September, 2006

SEPTEMBER, 2006

DEFENDING THE KING JAMES BIBLE
A FOURFOLD SUPERIORITY

GOD'S WORDS KEPT INTACT IN ENGLISH

By Pastor D. A. Waite, Th.D., Ph.D.
Director, THE BIBLE FOR TODAY, INCORPORATED
900 Park Avenue, Collingswood, New Jersey 08108
Phone: 856-854-4452; FAX: 856-854-2464; Orders: 1-800-JOHN 10:9
E-Mail: BFT@BibleForToday.org; Credit Card Orders Welcomed
Web Pages: **www.BibleForToday.org** and **www.BFTBC.org**

****

Published and Copyrighted
1992, 1993, 1994, 1995, 1996, 1998, 1999, 2002, 2004, 2006 by
THE BIBLE FOR TODAY, INCORPORATED
ALL RIGHTS RESERVED

****

THIRD EDITION

B.F.T. #1594-P

THE BIBLE

Majestic, eternal, immutable BOOK,
Inspired, inerrant, complete.
The Light of my path as I walk on life's way,
The Guide and the Lamp to my feet.

Its writings are holy and verbally true,
The unalterable Statute of Light,
For profit, for doctrine, for correction, reproof,
Infallible Guide to the right.

My Treasure, my Comfort, my Help, and my Stay,
Incomparable Measure and Rod,
Each page is replete with its textual proof,
The BIBLE, the exact WORD OF GOD!

By Gertrude Grace Barker Sanborn
(The author's mother-in-law)
September, 1979

DEDICATION
September, 2006

This book is affectionately and lovingly dedicated to my wife, Yvonne Sanborn Waite, who has been by my side now since August 27, 1948-- fifty-eight years as of last month.

She has encouraged me, prayed for me, assisted me, and stood with me for the things of the Lord and in the defense of His precious and inerrant Words.

Through her help and willingness, this book has now been published to the glory of God and **"IN DEFENSE OF TRADITIONAL BIBLE TEXTS,"** including the incomparable KING JAMES BIBLE.

"THE ANVIL OF GOD'S WORDS"

Last eve I passed beside a blacksmith's door
And heard the anvil sing the vesper chime;
Then, looking in, I saw upon the floor
Old hammers, worn with blasting years of time.

"How many anvils have you had," said I,
"To wear and batter all these hammers so?"
"Just one," said he; and then, with twinkling eye,
"The anvil wears the hammers out, you know."

And so I thought, the anvil of God's Words
For ages, skeptic blows have beat upon.
Yet tho' the noise of falling blows was heard
The anvil is unharmed--the hammers gone.

By John Clifford

ACKNOWLEDGMENTS

I wish to thank those who helped in the production of this book, including: Ruthe Baker who typed the original seminar from the cassettes; Dr. Galen Gavel who designed the cover; and Yvonne S. Waite, Mr. D. A. Waite, Jr., and Phyllis B. Detwiler who proofread the manuscript and gave valuable suggestions.

A special word of thanks goes to Dr. Kirk DiVietro. Pastor DiVietro, in my estimation, is a computer genius. He set up my new IBM-compatible computer two different times; he helped smooth out the text in Word Perfect 5.1 and later in 6.0 format; and he has graciously assisted me in many computer questions. Without his aid, this book could not have been published in its present form.

A final word of appreciation goes to Daniel Stephen Waite for securing from the internet the names of scores of printers; for finding the best printing prices; for getting our fifth and sixth printings in hardback; and for marketing the book successfully to many active distributors.

The copy has been gone over many times in an effort to bring to the reader the most effective tool possible in *DEFENDING THE KING JAMES BIBLE*. Though others have assisted in this process, the author accepts the responsibility for any oversights in form or content that we might have overlooked.

FOREWORD

This study on *"DEFENDING THE KING JAMES BIBLE--A Fourfold Superiority--God's Words Kept Intact In English"* is the product of over twenty-eight years of the author's thinking, researching, writing, publishing, and speaking on this most important theme.

There is no more important subject in all the Christian Faith than the BIBLE. One vital question is: Which English Bible are we to read, study, memorize, preach from, and use today?

A second important question is: Which English Bible can we hold in our hands and say with great confidence, "These are the WORDS OF GOD in English"?

It has been the purpose of this study to answer BOTH of the above questions by pointing to **THE KING JAMES BIBLE**, proving its **superiority** in four areas: (1) its superior **TEXTS**; (2) its superior **TRANSLATORS**; (3) its superior **TECHNIQUES**; and (4) its superior **THEOLOGY**. In all **FOUR** of these areas, the KING JAMES BIBLE has no equal!

The study is to be viewed as a suggestive outline of this theme rather than being in any sense exhaustive. There is really no end to this important discussion, due to the almost inexhaustible information available on it. Throughout the book, we have cited many helpful volumes for further study. We have also included (at the end of this book) a Bibliography which, at the time of publication, consisted of over 900 titles. This Bibliography lists books, tapes, videos, and other valuable materials on this theme which the reader might want to secure for his own library. More titles are being added monthly. For the latest up-to-date list of materials, we suggest you write THE BIBLE FOR TODAY and request **BROCHURE #1**.

Though much has been added to this present volume, the bulk of material contained was delivered at a seminar on the KING JAMES BIBLE given at GRACE BAPTIST CHURCH, Cortland, New York, on February 13 and 14, 1988. The original seminar is available in both five, two-hour audio cassettes and/or two video cassettes. (**BFT #1594/1-5**)

To the original three chapters have been added CHAPTER V, APPENDICES A and B, the INDEX, and the ADDITIONAL REFERENCES. APPENDIX C contains thirty-nine questions and answers that were asked during the original seminars. We hope that the answers to these questions which pertain to the defense of the KING JAMES BIBLE might be helpful to the readers.

See p. xxxi for the THIRD EDITION's important changes.

THE N.T. GREEK TEXTUAL BATTLEGROUND	
TEXTUS RECEPTUS	**W/H CHANGES IN T.R.**
Has 140,521 Greek wds.	Changes 5,604 places in the N.T.
Has 647 pp. in Greek Text	Changes include 9,970 Greek wds.
Has 217 Greek wds. per page	Changes 15.4 Greek wds. per page
Has 100% of the Greek wds.	Changes 7% of the Greek wds.
Has all 647 pp. unchanged	Changes total 45.9 pp. in Greek text

From the above chart, you can see the real **GREEK TEXTUAL BATTLEGROUND** between the Westcott and Hort Greek text and the *Textus Receptus* Greek text of the New Testament. You can see that the **additions, subtractions,** or **changes** include **almost 10,000 Greek words!**

To get a picture of just how many Words are involved (if they were together in one place) consider what **10,000 English words** would amount to. It would be the equivalent of either: (1) the entire book of Romans **(9,447 words)**; or (2) the entire book of 1 Corinthians **(9,489 words)**; or (3) the books of 2 Corinthians and Galatians **(9,190 words)**; or (4) the books of Ephesians, Philippians, Colossians, and 1 Thessalonians **(9,096 words)**; or (5) the books of James, 1 Peter, 2 Peter, 1 John, 2 John, 3 John, and Jude **(10,088 words)**; or (6) the books of Colossians, 1 Thessalonians, 2 Thessalonians, 2 Timothy, Philemon, 2 Peter, 2 John, 3 John, and Jude **(9,819 words)**.

This represents the total number of *Received Text* Greek Words that have either been **added** to God's Words, **subtracted** from God's Words, or **changed** from God's Words by the Westcott and Hort Greek text. I think you will agree with me that there is much at stake in this **BATTLE** for our Bible! Isn't it time to **CONTEND for the BOOK?!**
Sincerely for the Defense of God's Words,

D. A. Waite

Pastor D. A. Waite, Th.D., Ph.D.
Director, THE BIBLE FOR TODAY, INCORPORATED
"FORT 900"
900 Park Avenue, Collingswood, New Jersey 08108
Phone: 856-854-4452
September, 2006

TABLE OF CONTENTS

CHAPTER II

THE KING JAMES BIBLE IS GOD'S WORDS KEPT INTACT IN ENGLISH BECAUSE OF ITS SUPERIOR ORIGINAL LANGUAGE TEXTS

CHAPTER III

**THE KING JAMES BIBLE IS GOD'S WORDS KEPT
INTACT IN ENGLISH BECAUSE OF ITS SUPERIOR
TRANSLATORS**

A. THE SOURCES ABOUT THE KING JAMES

CHAPTER IV

THE KING JAMES BIBLE IS GOD'S WORDS KEPT INTACT IN ENGLISH BECAUSE OF ITS SUPERIOR TECHNIQUE 83

CHAPTER V

THE KING JAMES BIBLE IS GOD'S WORDS KEPT INTACT IN ENGLISH BECAUSE OF ITS SUPERIOR THEOLOGY

APPENDIX C

The Reasons For This THIRD EDITION

September, 2006

In this **THIRD REVISED EDITION (2006)**, I have revised over 82 pages of this book. I have also revised the subtitle of the book from "God's **Word** Kept Intact in English" to "God's **Words** Kept Intact in English." I have made hundreds of changes in these 82 pages. The principle changes have been made whenever "God's **Word**" has been found. I have changed all these references, where applicable, to "God's **Words**" or the "**Words** of God."

The reason for this is what I consider to be a clever, sly, secret, deceptive, and surreptitious re-definition, by some Fundamentalists, of the term, "**Word** of God." This re-definition has been found in the books, booklets, other writings, and speeches from the faculty, graduates, and/or sympathizers of such leading Fundamentlist schools as Bob Jones University, Detroit Baptist Seminary, Central Baptist Seminary, Calvary Baptist Seminary, Maranatha Baptist Bible College and Seminary, Northland Baptist College, and others who follow this serious error.

The Bible uses "**Word of God**" as a synonym for the "**Words of God**." (See Psalm 119:9, 11, 16, 17, 25, 28, 38, 41, 42, 43, 43, 49, 50, 58, 65, 67, 74, 76, 81, 82, 89, 101; 105, 107, 114, 116, 123, 133, 140, 147, 148, 154, 158, 160, 161, 162, 169, 170, 172 *et al.*) Their modern re-definitions restrict their terms "**Word** of God" and "**Bible Preservation**" exclusively to the "*message, thoughts, ideas, concepts, truth, doctrine, or revelation*" of the Bible, rather than to the Bible's original Hebrew, Aramaic, and Greek **Words**. This is a Fundamentalist travesty on God's **Words** and on the entire doctrine of **Bible Preservation**!

INTRODUCTION

A. DEFINITIONS OF TERMS.

When we say the KING JAMES BIBLE is "GOD'S WORDS KEPT INTACT," what do we mean by *"intact"*? The word "intact" comes from the Latin word *intactus*, which, in turn, comes from *in* (meaning "not") and *tactus* (meaning "touched"). It means "not touched." It means "not harmed." Nothing harms or defiles it. That is what we mean when we say "GOD'S WORD KEPT INTACT." If we really want to know what the Hebrew in the Old Testament says and what the Greek in the New Testament says in the English language today, the KING JAMES BIBLE--in my studied opinion--is the only translation that completely and **accurately** reflects, in English, the original Hebrew/Aramaic and Greek. This brief study will attempt to convince the reader of the truth of this statement, and--failing of this-- will at least show clearly why I believe it.

When we use versions other than the KING JAMES BIBLE, we cannot be absolutely certain that in every verse, sentence, and word, they **accurately** translate the Hebrew and Greek words God has given us. Instead, we have man's words all mixed up in them throughout. This is done by their use of "DYNAMIC EQUIVALENCY" which permits them to ADD, SUBTRACT, and/or CHANGE God's Words. You say, "Well, the KING JAMES BIBLE was translated in 1611. That is over three hundred eighty-one years ago. That is quite a long time. Doesn't that time span make the KING JAMES BIBLE difficult to understand?"

B. HELP FOR 618 UNFAMILIAR WORDS IN THE KING JAMES BIBLE.

If you come across some words used in our KING JAMES BIBLE that have changed their meaning since 1611, there's a *Bible Word List* published by the TRINITARIAN BIBLE SOCIETY of London, England, that lists them all with a brief definition of each. [B.F.T. #1060] There are only about 618 of these words out of 791,328 in the KING JAMES BIBLE. Using this little booklet will save you the time of looking these words up in a dictionary (although all of them are in a good dictionary). They are right there, with a brief explanation of what they mean. I've looked at all these 618 and have come up with only 257 words that I would really have to look up if I were not familiar with the KING

JAMES BIBLE. Maybe you would have to look up more than that, but all 618 are listed. For instance, "draught" which would be "drain," or "sewer." The word "fan" is "a winnowing fan." "Press vat" is a "vat of a wine press." "Ossiphrage" is a "vulture which breaks the bones of its prey." There may be a few other words you don't understand, but the meaning can be found by a dictionary or a small pamphlet like this one which you can keep in your Bible.

In 1992, we first began to think seriously about bringing out a special study edition of the KING JAMES BIBLE which would give accurate definitions for all these 618 words (and more). A friend of mine began thinking about this project, and worked at it with some of his assistants for a while, but finally, I believe, he came to the conclusion that it was far too complicated a task for him to complete. I think he has laid aside this project for many other projects he is working on.

In 1996, THE BIBLE FOR TODAY, in cooperation with Dr. S. H. Tow of Singapore, began working on a similar KING JAMES BIBLE. Dr. Tow is a world-renowned gynecologist and also the Pastor of the Calvary Bible Presbyterian Church in Singapore. My oldest son, Mr. D. A. Waite, Jr., has completed our *Defined King James Bible* and has inserted footnotes which define words that may not be clear. Dr. Tow, raised funds for 4,000 of these *Defined Bibles* and has distributed them. He drafted some introductory and editorial remarks, explaining the history and background of the textual battle which now rages concerning our Bible. He has a burden to place this King James Bible into the hands of many third world countries such as the Philippines and India. This 12-point large print Bible (7½ by 10") is in genuine leather, either black or burgundy. It is for a gift of **$40 + S&H. Order at 1-800-JOHN 10:9.**

C. THE MANIFOLD DEFICIENCIES OF THE NASV, THE NKJV, AND THE NIV.

Let me tell you what the difficulty is in trying to find the Words of God if you are not using the KING JAMES BIBLE. You don't know which English words are actually found in the Hebrew or the Greek. Unlike the KING JAMES BIBLE, most of the modern versions don't use italics to tell us what has been supplied for sense, though NOT in the original languages.

The NEW AMERICAN STANDARD VERSION uses italics occasionally where they depart from the Hebrew or Greek, but there are so many other words added, subtracted, or changed, that you just don't know what the original words are. What you have to do is what I had to do. I read the entire NASV, from Genesis to Revelation, listening to the KING JAMES BIBLE on a cassette tape recording, while looking at the NEW AMERICAN STANDARD VERSION and underlining in red some of the significant alterations and changes. Then I compared these changes with the Hebrew and Greek texts that underlie the KING JAMES BIBLE (which I accept as the true and accurate original language texts). I found **over 4,000 examples** of addition, subtraction, and change regarding the Words of God. [**B.F.T.** #1494-P]

To be certain of the accuracy of any version other than the KING JAMES BIBLE, you would have to check every Hebrew and Greek word. This is much more difficult than using this simple word list to look up the mere **618 words** with which you might not be familiar. This little pamphlet is an accurate guide. There are only a few words to look up.

You have the same lack of accuracy, though in not as many places, in the NEW KING JAMES VERSION. I found **over 2,000 examples** of DYNAMIC EQUIVALENCY in that version, where the editors had **added to, subtracted from,** or **changed** God's Words. As I did the research, I indicated in red, on the version I used, the changes from the KING JAMES BIBLE, and, in many instances, from the Hebrew and Greek. There are changes in the footnotes also. There are many problems in the NEW KING JAMES VERSION. You wonder which words are accurate and which ones are not. [**B.F.T.** #1442]

The same is true for the NEW INTERNATIONAL VERSION. In 2 Samuel, for example, I have all kinds of red marks indicating changes. The major differences I put on a tape recording and said, "The Hebrew or the Greek or the KING JAMES says this and here's what the NIV says." I ended up with **over 6,653 examples** of additions, omissions, or changes plus departures from the proper Hebrew and Greek original language texts in the NEW INTERNATIONAL VERSION. It took me two years and eight months to complete, and then there were hundreds and hundreds of examples that were left out due to space and time factors. I came up with a computer printout like we have for the NEW KING JAMES or the NEW AMERICAN STANDARD VERSION. [**B.F.T.** #1749-P] It is 284 large pages, and is available from THE BIBLE FOR TODAY.

D. **THE KING JAMES BIBLE OF 1611 HAS ONLY 421 CHANGES OF SOUND FROM OUR PRESENT KING JAMES BIBLE.**

Because people often say that the present KING JAMES BIBLE is so very different from the original 1611 KING JAMES BIBLE, I looked into this question carefully. Nelson Publishers put out the 1611 KING JAMES BIBLE in regular Roman type script that we can read. They let it go out of print, and then brought it back into print. The original 1611 KING JAMES BIBLE was in German script. I have photographic copies of the original KING JAMES BIBLE in the German script. It is difficult to read. The "s" is different, for example. But Nelson put it into our kind of script. They did that on a page by page basis.

I have heard through the years (and perhaps you have also) that all the NEW KING JAMES VERSION was going to do was take the 1611 and make one more edition and bring it up to date. It was said that the KING JAMES BIBLE had undergone thousands of serious changes from 1611 to 1979, when the NKJV first came out. I said to myself, "Is that true?" So I examined the Old Scofield Reference KING JAMES BIBLE of 1917, by listening to it as I read that edition of the KING JAMES BIBLE on cassette recording. While listening to the KING JAMES BIBLE, I compared it diligently, word for word, from Genesis through Revelation, with the A.V. 1611 as published by Nelson. There were very few changes that I could hear with my ear. There are many spelling changes; they spelled words differently in the original KING JAMES BIBLE than they do today. For instance in Deuteronomy 31:1, *"Moses went and spake these words to all Israel."* In the original KING JAMES the word *"words"* is spelled *"wordes."* All I noted were the differences between sounds. Comparing the 1611 KING JAMES BIBLE to the KING JAMES of today I found very few changes of sound. We printed up all the details, just the way they are. The sound differences were minor.

There are **only 421 changes** affecting the sound throughout the entire Old and New Testaments. Do you know how many words there are in the KING JAMES BIBLE? There are **791,328 words**. Out of that total, there are only **421 words** in the 1611 KING JAMES BIBLE which have a different sound from the words of the KING JAMES we have today. Of these 421 changes, **285** are minor changes of "form" only. There are only **136** changes of "substance," such as an added "of" or "and." Some examples of minor changes are as follows: I can hear the difference and so can you between "towards" and "toward." So, if I could hear it, I put it down. Fourteen times that happened. I could hear the difference between "burnt" and "burned" thirty-one times, so I put that down. As long as you could hear the difference, I recorded it as a change in this list of **421 changes.** For instance, "amongst" and "among." There were thirty-six of those changes. "Lift up" instead of "lifted up" was used fifty-one times. "You" was changed to "ye" eighty-two times. You can see that these are extremely minor changes. That totals 214 of these kinds of minor changes. There were 71 other minor changes which total 285 changes of form only. In summary, then, I found there were **285 changes of FORM ONLY,** and only **136 changes of SUBSTANCE,** making a **total of 421 changes in all to the ear.** This research is available as **B.F.T. #1294.**

E. THE KING JAMES BIBLE OF TODAY IS VIRTUALLY IDENTICAL TO THE KING JAMES BIBLE OF 1611.

Don't let people say what we have today really isn't the KING JAMES BIBLE. It most certainly IS! It is a lie to imply that there are 30,000, 40,000 or 50,000 important differences. If they mean differences in spelling, that is one thing; but spelling is not important as far as listening or meaning are concerned. **So God's Words are still kept intact by our present KING JAMES BIBLE.**

CHAPTER I

"GOD'S WORDS KEPT INTACT" IS BIBLE PRESERVATION
(THE BIBLE'S TIMELESSNESS)

A. GOD PROMISED BIBLE PRESERVATION.

In a very real sense, the Bible is a **TIMELESS BOOK**, that is, it will never have an end. It will never cease to exist. There will never be a year or a century, either now or in the future, when it can be accurately said, "The Bible is no more. It has disappeared. It has evaporated." In the first chapter of this book, let us look at fifteen of the many verses in God's Word having to do with what we refer to as the **preservation** of the Words of the Bible, or **"Bible preservation."** You may be asking yourself, "Do we have the Words of God today?" or, "Are the Words of God *intact* today?" I believe every one of the Words of God has been preserved or kept right down to the present.

There are two strong reasons for this. (1) The first reason why I believe in **Bible preservation** is that God has repeatedly promised in both the Old and New Testaments, that He would preserve and keep every one of His Words that He originally gave in the Hebrew and Greek languages. (2) The second reason I believe in **Bible preservation** is that God has always kept His promises in the past, and we assume that He will keep up this perfect record in the present and on into the future.

1. Psalm 12:6-7: *"The words of the LORD are*
pure words: as silver tried in a furnace of earth, purified
seven times. Thou shalt KEEP them, O LORD, Thou shalt
PRESERVE them from this generation FOR EVER."

The word "them" in verse seven refers back to *"the words of the LORD."* That is a promise of Bible preservation. God has promised to *"PRESERVE"* His "PURE WORDS." This promise extends *"from this generation* [that is, that of the Psalmist] *FOR EVER."* That is a long time, is it not? God is able to do this, and He has done it! He has kept His Words even more perfectly, if that is possible, than He keeps the stars in their course and the sun, moon, and all the other heavenly bodies in their proper place.

2. Psalm 78:1-7: *"Give ear, O my people, to My law: incline your ears to the **Words of My mouth**. (2) I will open My mouth in a parable: I will utter dark sayings of old: (3) Which we have heard and known, and our **FATHERS** have told us. (4) We will not hide them from their **CHILDREN**, shewing to the **GENERATION TO COME** the praises of the LORD, and His strength, and His wonderful works that He hath done. (5) For He established a testimony in Jacob, and appointed a law in Israel, which He commanded our **FATHERS**, that they should make them known to their **CHILDREN**: (6) That the **GENERATION TO COME** might know them, even the **CHILDREN** which should be born; who should arise and declare them to their **CHILDREN**:"* [Here are the Words preserved from generation to generation.] *(7) "That they might set their hope in God, and not forget the works of God, but keep His commandments."*

These verses certainly indicate that God intended to *preserve* His Words for all time.

3. Psalm 105:8: *"He hath remembered His covenant **FOR EVER**, the **WORD** which He commanded **TO A THOUSAND GENERATIONS**."*

If a "generation" is twenty years, this would be **20,000 YEARS**. If a "generation" is thirty years, it would be **30,000 YEARS**! God wants us to see clearly His promise of **Bible preservation**.

4. Psalm 119:89: *"FOR EVER, O LORD, Thy WORD is settled in heaven."*

God's Words are not in doubt. It is permanent. It is unconfused and plain. God has settled this. If it has been settled, that means it has been preserved, kept pure. Nothing has been lost. Something which is settled is determined and even more solid than steel or concrete. Some people say, "Well, it is settled in Heaven but not on earth." But God needs it less than we do; He knows His Words. We are the ones who need it. He is using this verse, Psalm 119:89, to show us that God has given us Words that are settled. He hasn't given us everything He knows; He certainly hasn't given us everything that took place, but what He has put down in His Words is what He wants us to know and have and use. It is true that God's Words are not only preserved and settled *"in heaven,"* but they are also preserved by Heaven's Omnipotent God.

> **5. Psalm 119:111:** *"Thy TESTIMONIES have I taken as an heritage FOR EVER: for they are the rejoicing of my heart."*

If you take God's Testimonies as a *"heritage for ever,"* they must be preserved if we are to keep them.

> **6. Psalm 119:152:** *"Concerning Thy TESTI-MONIES, I have known of old that Thou hast founded them FOR EVER."*

Here again is a promise that the *Testimonies*, the Words of God, will be preserved *for ever*.

> **7. Psalm 119:160:** *"Thy WORD is true from the beginning: and every one of Thy righteous Judgments ENDURETH FOR EVER."*

"Endureth forever"--that is **Bible preservation!**

> **8. Proverbs 22:20-21.** *"(20) Have not I WRITTEN to thee excellent things in counsels and knowledge, (21) That I might make thee know the CERTAINTY of the WORDS OF TRUTH; that thou mightest answer the WORDS OF TRUTH to them that send unto thee?"*

Here is a clear statement by the Lord that He has given us things in WRITING so that we might have *"CERTAINTY"* about them. The only way we can have that certainty today is for God to have PRESERVED every one of His *"WORDS OF TRUTH."* This truly is a promise of **Bible preservation.**

> **9. Ecclesiastes 3:14:** *"I know that, whatsoever God DOETH, it shall be FOR EVER: nothing can be put to it, nor anything taken from it: and GOD DOETH IT, that men should fear before Him."*

If God has done anything or given us anything, it is perfect. He has given us His Words, therefore His Words are perfect. We can't add to it or take away from it. It has been preserved exactly.

> **10. Matthew 4:4:** [Satan was tempting the

Lord as He was in the wilderness for testing and temptation. Here is His answer] *"But He answered and said, IT IS WRITTEN, Man shall not live by bread alone, but by EVERY WORD that proceedeth out of the mouth of God."*
When Jesus said, *"It is written,"* that referred to the Old Testament. There are two things I want you to see from this verse.

(1) How can a man or woman live by **every Word of God** that proceeds out of the mouth of God unless God has preserved these Words to listen to? It is impossible. And you and I who speak English and may not know Greek or Hebrew, how will we know God's Words unless He has preserved it to the present day, and then we have it accurately and faithfully translated (as in the KING JAMES BIBLE) into English. What the Lord Jesus Christ was telling Satan was that the Old Testament has been preserved. He's quoting from Deuteronomy. The Old Testament had been preserved right down until His day and man should live by those very Words. That is a number of years, about 1500 years from Moses until Jesus' day. He kept, guarded, and preserved **"EVERY WORD."**

(2) The second thing I want to show you from that verse is that the word **"written,"** which is recorded scores of times in the New Testament, is in the perfect tense in the Greek. It is *gegraptai.* The root verb means "to write." Our English word, "graphite," comes from this word, as well as the word, "mimeograph." *GraphO* is the Greek word for "write" and *gegraptai* is the perfect tense of that verb. There are three main past tenses in Greek. (1) There is the imperfect past tense, which is the progressive past, "was writing." (2) There is the aorist past, which is a spot or point action, "wrote." (3) Then you have another past tense, the perfect tense which is used here.

According to *The Intermediate Grammar of the Greek New Testament* by Dana and Mantey, pages 200-205, the perfect tense indicates that an action has begun in the past and the results of that act continue right on down to the very present.

This is the tense that the Lord Jesus Christ used when He said, *"It is written."* It means that the verse He quoted to Satan had been written down in the past in the Hebrew language by Moses and those very Hebrew words were preserved to the very day and hour when the Lord was quoting them to the Devil. Every time *gegraptai* is used or some other form of the perfect tense of that verb (and we have it scores of times in the New Testament) that is a proof of the **Bible's preservation. God's Words stand just as they were written down.**

I didn't see the significance of that word in the perfect tense for many years. I taught the Greek and Hebrew language in our home in our BIBLE FOR TODAY Baptist Seminary and Institute for four years. We had some seminary students who wanted to learn first year Greek. The classes on tape are being used in various parts of the country and in some foreign countries as well. The classes were on a seminary level with regular hours, credits and everything else that is proper. We taught a first year Greek class, a second year Greek class, and then a first year Hebrew class. After that, we taught another first year Greek class. So we have the first year Greek and second year Greek classes on tape and also the first year Hebrew. During our second year Greek class, we went through the whole Gospel of John. We translated every verse in John and also went through the entire Greek grammar of Dana and Mantey. It was while we were going through John, that the significance of this word *gegraptai* jumped out at me.

> **11.** **Matthew 5:17-18**: *(17) "Think not that I am come to destroy the law, or the prophets* [those are two divisions of the Old Testament canon: Law and Prophets. Psalms is the third, but sometimes "Law and Prophets" are used to include all three divisions of the Old Testament.]: *I am not come to destroy, but to fulfill. (18) For verily I say unto you, Till heaven and earth pass,* **ONE JOT** *or* **ONE TITTLE** *shall* **IN NO WISE PASS** *from the law, till all be fulfilled."*

Not *"one jot"* nor *"one tittle"*--**that is Bible preservation,** isn't it? Now, He's talking about the Old Testament, and I'm sure by extension we can carry that on to the New Testament as well. Let us take a look at what He means by *"one jot or one tittle."* A "jot" is like our apostrophe or comma (only at the top of the line). It is the Hebrew *yodth*. The sound is like "ya." The "tittle" represents a tiny difference between two Hebrew letters. I want you to notice two letters in Psalm 119. In most of our KING JAMES BIBLES we have at the beginning of verse 9 the word "beth." The Hebrew letter is to the left of the word *beth*. Compare at verse 81. Above that verse you have the word *caph*. Notice those two letters. What is the difference? *Caph* is more rounded. The little extension at the bottom right of the *beth* is a tittle--a little jutting foot. That is what the Lord meant. Look above verse 73 where it says *jod* (yodth), the little apostrophe is a jot. Look above verse 25 at the *daleth*. Look at the Hebrew word *resh* above verse 153. What is the difference between them? The same small extension, only on the top right of the *daleth*, and the *resh* is rounded. Those are examples of the tittle, the smallest distinguishing characteristic between two letters in the Hebrew language. The Lord Jesus said that not one jot or tittle would pass away until all would be fulfilled. So the Lord Jesus believed in **Bible preservation**, didn't He? There is good evidence that a tittle is the smallest Hebrew vowel which is a dot. This view is even better than the other view.

12. Matthew 24:35: [The Lord Jesus speaking again] *"Heaven and earth shall pass away, but MY WORDS shall not pass away."*

The Lord is talking of **His** *Words*, the New Testament. Not the Masoretic Hebrew Old Testament only, but His **Words** will not pass away. That means the promise extends to the New Testament. I believe, personally that the Lord Jesus was the Source and Author of every word of the Hebrew Old Testament text. He was the Revelator. He is the Word of God. In a very real sense, therefore, His *Words* include the entire Old Testament. He is also the Source and Author of all the New Testament books. Though we had human writers, the Lord Jesus Christ is the Divine Author and SOURCE of it all.

a. Christ's Authorship of the Gospels. In John 14:26 Jesus said that the Holy Spirit would *"bring all things to your remembrance, whatsoever I have said unto you."* This includes the four Gospels: Matthew, Mark, Luke, and John. John 14:26 says:

*"But the Comforter, which is the Holy Ghost, whom the Father will send in My name, He shall teach you all things, and bring all things to your remembrance, **whatsoever I have said unto you.**"*

He was talking to His disciples in the Upper Room. This includes **everything** He *said* in the four Gospels. His *Words shall not pass away.* The Holy Spirit of God will bring to these Apostles the exact *words* so that nothing is forgotten. The Holy Spirit was the MEANS.

b. Christ's Authorship of the Acts of the Apostles. Let us take a look at John 15:26-27:

*"But when the Comforter is come, whom I will send unto you from the Father, even the Spirit of truth, which proceedeth from the Father, He shall testify of Me: (27) And ye **also shall bear witness**, because ye have been with Me from the beginning."*

The Apostles bearing *"witness"* is written about in the Acts of the Apostles. The Holy Spirit of God bore *witness* through the Apostles, and the book of Acts is the record of their *witness*. When the Lord Jesus said that the Holy Spirit would *bring all things* to their remembrance, His statement included the book of Acts.

c. Christ's Authorship of the Epistles. Let us turn to John 16:12-13. The Lord Jesus said:

> *"I have yet many things to say unto you* [He's talking to His disciples], *but ye cannot bear them now.* [They couldn't understand them] *(13) Howbeit when He, the Spirit of truth, is come, He will guide you into all truth: for He shall not speak of Himself* [from Himself, Himself being the SOURCE]; *but whatsoever He shall hear, that shall He speak."*

The guiding *into all truth* includes the Epistles." Notice also that it is clear that the Holy Spirit is not the Source and Author of the Words of God, but it is the Lord Jesus Christ Who is both Source and Author.

d. Christ's Authorship of Revelation. In John 16:13b, the Lord Jesus continued,

> *". . . and He will shew you things to come."*

Although it refers to other New Testament prophetic books, the phrase *"things to come"* certainly refers also to the book of Revelation. So you have the book of Revelation, the Epistles, the Acts of the Apostles, all the Gospels written by the Lord Jesus, working through the Holy Spirit, using human writers.

When He says, *"My Words shall not pass away,"* the Lord Jesus is including the Gospels, Acts, Epistles, and Revelation. All of them are His *Words*. The whole New Testament is tied up in a bundle and can be held in your hand. He has promised to **preserve** the *Words* of the New Testament as well as the Old Testament. I want you to notice also in John 16:14. Jesus says:

> *"He* [the Holy Spirit] *shall glorify Me; for He shall receive of Mine, and shall shew it unto you."*

That certainly is an answer to the Charismatic Movement which glorifies the Holy Spirit instead of glorifying Christ.

In Matthew 24:35, the Lord Jesus Christ said: *"Heaven and earth shall pass away . . . ."* What could be more stable than the heavens and earth? Now, we do have earthquakes, but we think of the earth as being solid. We call it *terra firma*. That means "firm earth." But the Lord Jesus said that *heaven and earth shall pass away.* Look at the unbelievers and Christians who do not believe in God's preservation of His Words. They take the earth for granted. We all do. We walk on it. We assume it won't give way when we walk on it. It is a solid thing. But Jesus said, *"Heaven and earth SHALL pass away, but My Words shall not pass away."* There will be a new heaven and a new earth, but the Words of God will continue. They are *forever settled in Heaven;* they are **preserved** Words. They are even more preserved and more settled than either the heaven or the earth!

> **13. John 10:35.** [Jesus is talking about the Old Testament judges and the translation of the word *elohim* which is sometimes used for "judges." He's referring to Psalm 82:6.] *"If he called them gods, unto whom the Word of God came, and the Scripture cannot be broken. . . . "*

The word for "broken" is the Greek word *luO* and *luthEnai* is the word in the aorist tense. Strong defines it as follows:

> *"3089. luo {loo'-o}; a primary verb; to "loosen" (literally or figuratively): -break (up), destroy, dissolve, (un-)loose, melt, put off. Compare 4486.*

From this root we get the English word, "analysis." The Lord Jesus Christ Himself is saying that the Words of God cannot be "loosened, broken up, destroyed, dissolved, melted, or put off." It is permanent and preserved by God. **The Lord Jesus certainly believed in Bible preservation.**

> **14. Colossians 1:17.** [Speaking of Christ]: *"And He is before all things, and by Him all things CON-SIST."*

Now that word "consist" didn't mean much to me until some time ago, when I was asked to have a summer Bible conference on the book of Colossians. I studied my Greek New Testament, as usual, in preparation for the study. I looked all the words up. I found that one of the meanings of the word "consist" is "to hold together or **preserve.**" When you think of the phrase, *"by Him all things consist,"* you usually think of the worlds that do not fly apart. They are held together. But it also means "**to preserve.**" What are some of things that are preserved? Not only the things in the heavens and the earth which are going to pass away, but His *Words.* He has preserved them, and by Christ all things are preserved. You may ask how He preserved them, but that is not our problem. That is His problem. He's able because He's the omnipotent God, the omnipresent God, and the omniscient God. He has all power. He said, *"All power is given unto Me in Heaven and in earth."* (Matthew 28:18).

So He holds things together and preserves them.

> **15.** **1 Peter 1:23-25:** *(23) "Being born again, not of corruptible seed, but of incorruptible, by the WORD of God, which liveth and abideth FOR EVER."*

That is a reference to **Bible preservation,** isn't it? The Word of God is *incorruptible.* Strong defines this word as follows:

> *"862. aphthartos {af'-thar-tos}; from 1 (as a negative particle) and a derivative of 5351; undecaying (in essence or continuance): -not (in-, un-)corruptible, immortal."*

God's Words cannot be corrupted, corroded, or decayed like our bodies. When we die and are put into the earth, our bodies see corruption. They are decayed and vanish away into dust, but the Words of God are incorruptible. They live and abide forever. That is a promise of God's preservation. The illustration of that is given in verse 24:

> *(24) "For all flesh is as grass, and all the glory of man as the flower of grass. The grass withereth, and the flower thereof falleth away: (25) But the Word of the Lord ENDURETH FOR EVER. And this is the Word which by the gospel is preached unto you."*

This teaches preservation, the opposite of what happens to the flower of the grass. You know full well what happens to pretty flowers when it begins to snow. They perish. They go away. The Words of God do not go away. They do not perish. They endure *for ever.*

God promised to preserve His Words. We must believe that God keeps His promises in general. He has never broken a single promise He has made. His track record is perfect. We must also believe that He has kept His promise to **preserve** His exact Bible Words, right down to the present, in the Hebrew and Greek languages in which they were written.

B. GOD KEPT HIS PROMISES FOR BIBLE PRESERVA-TION.

Does God keep His promises? No one would question that He is able to keep His promises. Consider God's ability. He flung the universes and the hundreds of thousands of galaxies into being with millions and millions of stars. He made the tiniest speck on earth, the tiniest little amoeba, and the unseen, yet powerful atom. He created Adam and Eve, and from them came on other human beings with such complex and wonderfully constructed bodies. Yes, our God is able to keep every promise He ever made, including those promises concerning the **preservation** of His Words!

Let us look at four verses, out of many others, showing that God keeps His promises:

1. 1 Kings 8:24. [King Solomon is speaking. He's built the temple and is speaking of the Lord:

". . . Who **HAS KEPT** with thy servant David my father **THAT THOU PROMISEDST** him: thou **SPAKEST** also with thy mouth, and **HAST FULFILLED IT** with Thine hand, as it is this day."

God promised and *fulfilled* with His hand. He promised the temple. It was built by Solomon who praised God for His faithfulness in keeping His promises.

2. Romans 4:20-21. [Speaking of Abraham]:
"He staggered not at the promise of God through unbelief; but was strong in faith, giving glory to God; (21) And being fully persuaded that, **WHAT HE HAD PROMISED, HE WAS ABLE ALSO TO PERFORM.**"

Here, the capability of God is exalted, as well as the fact that God keeps His promises. Though both Abraham and Sarah had passed the age of being parents, God told Abraham that he would have a son by Sarah. He was "fully persuaded" to believe "the promise of God."

3. Titus 1:2: "In hope of eternal life, which GOD, **THAT CANNOT LIE, PROMISED** before the world began."

Here is a promise-keeping God, One who has not lied, One Who *cannot lie,* and One Who keeps His promises.

4. Hebrews 10:23: "Let us hold fast the profession of our faith without wavering: (For **HE IS FAITHFUL THAT PROMISED**)."

Yes, God is *faithful* and He keeps His promises.

C. THE HISTORIC CREEDS TAUGHT BIBLE PRESERVATION.

There are many historic Confessions of Faith. These confessions alluded to **Bible preservation.** We don't hear a lot about **Bible preservation** today. I have not found many church statements of faith that even mention the subject. But in the years gone by they did make mention of it. I'll give you some of the historic Confessions of Faith that mention **Bible preservation** in them and then I'll quote from one. They say about the same thing.

The London Baptist Confession of 1677, 1689.

The Philadelphia Baptist Confession of about 1743.

The Presbyterian Westminster Confession of Faith 1646.

The Savoy Confession of 1652.

Let me quote from the Westminster Confession of Faith on Bible preservation:

*"The Old Testament in **Hebrew**, (which was the native language of the people of God of old,) and the New Testament in **Greek**, (which at the time of the writing of it was most generally known to the nations,) being immediately inspired by God and by His singular care and providence **KEPT PURE IN ALL AGES**, are therefore authentical; so as in all controversies of religion the Church is finally to appeal unto them."*

That is **Bible preservation.** They believed God's Words were **"KEPT PURE IN ALL AGES."** It is a strong testimony to the **preservation** of the Hebrew and Greek original Words of the Bible.

This same Confession makes an important statement directly following this one concerning the need for proper translation of these **preserved** original Hebrew and Greek Words of God into the languages of "every nation":

*"But because these **original languages** are not known to all the people of God who have right unto and interest in the Scriptures, and are commanded, in the fear of God, to read and search them, therefore **they are to be translated into the vulgar language of every nation** unto which they come, that the Word of God dwelling plentifully in all, they may worship him in an acceptable manner, and, through patience and comfort of the Scriptures, may have hope."*

This is a strong appeal to the accurate and proper translation from the providentially **preserved** Hebrew and Greek Words into the languages of all people. For the English speaking people, this has been done in a superior manner by the KING JAMES BIBLE.

D. THE RELATIONSHIP OF BIBLE PRESERVATION IN OUR ENGLISH LANGUAGE TO THE KING JAMES BIBLE

1. The Relationship Outlined. I believe that God has carried forward **Bible preservation** in our English language through our KING JAMES BIBLE. This is not to refer Bible preservation to the English translation in the absolute sense, but only in the sense that our KING JAMES BIBLE accurately preserves the proper Hebrew and Greek Words in the English language and accurately translates those divinely preserved Words. In this sense, we have a "preserving" of God's Words in English. There are four reasons why I believe this:

a. **First,** because of the **SUPERIORITY** OF THE KING JAMES BIBLE'S ORIGINAL LANGUAGE **TEXTS**, that is, the Hebrew and Greek on which it is based.

b. **Second,** because of the **SUPERIORITY** OF THE **TRANSLATORS** of the KING JAMES BIBLE. The men who translated the KING JAMES were superior in every way to any men who lived before or who live today. The men who live today are pygmies, Lilliputians, and tiny ants in comparison to the scholars who translated the KING JAMES BIBLE from the original Hebrew and Greek. We will be more specific on this later in the study.

c. **Third,** because of the **SUPERIORITY** OF THE **TECHNIQUE** of translating the KING JAMES BIBLE. It is different from the other versions. They haven't used the same techniques.

d. **Fourth,** because of the **SUPERIORITY** OF THE **THEOLOGY** of the KING JAMES BIBLE.

2. The Relationship Illustrated. These four areas are illustrated in 1 Corinthians 3. It doesn't say anything about Bible translation or preservation there, but it does give an illustration of building. I think the process of building is a good analogy of the process of Bible translation. Notice this statement about building:

1 Cor. 3:9-11: (9) *"For we are labourers together with God: ye are God's husbandry, ye are God's **building**."*

[I realize it is not talking about versions or preservation, but I think it is a good illustration.] (10) *According to the grace of God which is given unto me, as a wise **masterbuilder**. I have laid the FOUNDATION, and ANOTHER BUILDETH thereon. But let every man take heed HOW HE BUILDETH thereupon. (11) For other **foundation** can no man lay than that is laid, which is Jesus Christ.* " [This is speaking of Christ, the Foundation of the Church.] Let us take a look at Bible translation, comparing it to a building.

    a. The FOUNDATION Used for a Building Is Like the Hebrew and Greek TEXTS of a TRANSLATION. First of all, he talks about a *foundation*. Paul says he is a *masterbuilder* and has laid the *FOUNDATION*. The foundation of a building is important, isn't it? If you d on't have a good foundation, no matter what you have as far as builders, or structural techniques, it will fall. The same with our Bible. The foundation of our Bible is the Old Testament Hebrew text and the New Testament Greek text from which it is translated. There must be a proper foundation for an English Bible, a Spanish Bible, an Italian Bible, or any Bible that you translate. It must come from the proper Hebrew Old Testament text and the proper Greek New Testament text.

    b. The BUILDERS Used for a BUILDING Are Like the TRANSLATORS Used for a TRANSLATION. The second thing you notice about the building trade in verse 10 (even though I realize it is talking about Christ) are the words: *". . . I have laid the FOUNDATION and ANOTHER BUILDETH thereon."* Someone is building on that foundation. The builder is important. Is he able to build? Does he know how to build? Does he have the materials with which to build? Suppose you have the best foundation possible but the builder is NOT a builder but a musician, or a theologian, or a Bible teacher, or a hockey player, or a football player; BUT, I repeat, NOT a builder. I don't care if the foundation is perfect, on the proper soil, using proper cement; if the man doesn't know what he's doing as far as building is concerned, it will not be done right! The same with the Bible. The builders are like the translators. If they don't know what they're doing, if they are not supremely skilled in Hebrew/Aramaic, Greek, and English (or whatever language they are translating into), then they're not going to do a proper job and are not the ones to use.

    c. The METHOD Used for a BUILDING Is Like the TECHNIQUE Used for a TRANSLATION. The third thing Paul mentions here in verse 10 is: *". . . but let every man take heed HOW HE BUILDETH thereupon."* That is the "how" of it, the method he uses. He may be a good builder. He may have the best track record as a builder. He may have built thousands of churches, amphitheaters, large buildings, huge cathedrals, and/or even skyscrapers; but when he comes to build your building on your foundation, HOW does he do it? HOW? That is like the translating TECHNIQUE. **What TECHNIQUE does the translator use?** He may be the best translator, have a lot of skill and expertise, but how is he going to do it in this particular instance when he takes the Old Testament Hebrew or the New Testament Greek over into English? This is very important.

      d. The MATERIALS Used for a BUILDING Are Like the THEOLOGY Used in a TRANSLATION. The fourth thing is also found in Paul's words in verse 10: *". . . but let every man take heed HOW HE BUILDETH thereupon."* This is not only the "how" or technique of building, but it also includes the materials used in the building. The materials of a building are like the theology of a translation. Is the theology sound? Is it proper? Is anything left out? Is anything that is included faulty or improper?

NOTE:

      In this **THIRD REVISED EDITION (2006)**, I have revised over 82 pages of this book. I have also revised the subtitle of the book from *"God's **Word** Kept Intact in English"* to *"God's **Words** Kept Intact in English."* I have made hundreds of changes in these 82 pages. The principle changes have been made whenever "God's **Word**" has been found. I have changed all these references, where applicable, to "God's **Words**" or the "**Words** of God."

      The reason for this is what I consider to be a clever, sly, secret, deceptive, and surreptitious re-definition, by some Fundamentalists, of the term, "**Word** of God." This re-definition has been found in the books, booklets, other writings, and speeches from the faculty, graduates, and/or sympathizers of such leading Fundamentlist schools as Bob Jones University, Detroit Baptist Seminary, Central Baptist Seminary, Calvary Baptist Seminary, Maranatha Baptist Bible College and Seminary, Northland Baptist College, and others who follow this serious error.

      The Bible uses "**Word of God**" as a synonym for the "**Words of God**." (See Psalm 119:9, 11, 16, 17, 25, 28, 38, 41, 42, 43, 43, 49, 50, 58, 65, 67, 74, 76, 81, 82, 89, 101; 105, 107, 114, 116, 123, 133, 140, 147, 148, 154, 158, 160, 161, 162, 169, 170, 172 *et al.*) Their modern re-definitions restrict their terms "**Word** of God" and "**Bible Preservation**" exclusively to the *"message, thoughts, ideas, concepts, truth, doctrine, or revelation"* of the Bible, rather than to the Bible's original Hebrew, Aramaic, and Greek **Words**. This is a Fundamentalist travesty on God's **Words** and on the entire doctrine of **Bible Preservation**!

CHAPTER II

THE KING JAMES BIBLE IS GOD'S WORDS KEPT INTACT IN ENGLISH BECAUSE OF ITS SUPERIOR ORIGINAL LANGUAGE TEXTS

The first reason why God's Word is kept intact best in the KING JAMES BIBLE is because of the **SUPERIOR TEXTS** on which it was built. The TEXTUAL FOUNDATIONS of the KING JAMES BIBLE are the best FOUNDATIONS of any English Bible that exists today.

A. THE KING JAMES BIBLE IS GOD'S WORDS KEPT INTACT IN ENGLISH BECAUSE OF ITS SUPERIOR OLD TESTAMENT HEBREW TEXT.

The KING JAMES BIBLE is translated from a **superior** Old Testament text. It is translated from what we call the Traditional Masoretic Hebrew Old Testament text. These other versions that are translated today, such as the NEW AMERICAN STANDARD VERSION of 1960, the NEW INTERNATIONAL VERSION of 1969, or even the NEW KING JAMES VERSION of 1979, have big question marks as far as the foundation of their Old Testament text. There are many things that are changed when compared to the text of the KING JAMES translators, who used the Old Testament Masoretic Hebrew text. The word, "Masoretic," comes from *masor,* a Hebrew word meaning "traditional." The Masoretes handed down this text from generation to generation, guarded it and kept it well, as we will see.

1. The Inferior Old Testament Texts of the New Versions.
a. The NEW AMERICAN STANDARD VERSION Old
Testament Text. Take a look, for instance, at the NEW AMERICAN STANDARD VERSION. They admit, in their Preface (p. viii), the following:

> *"Hebrew Text: In the present translation the latest edition of [1] Rudolph Kittel's BIBLIA HEBRAICA has been employed together with the most recent [2] light from lexicography, [3] cognate languages, and [4] the Dead Sea Scrolls."*

You can see from this that the NASV does not use only the Masoretic

Hebrew Text (the right one), but makes use of other sources as well. The Hebrew text they use is Kittel's *BIBLIA HEBRAICA*. That would be the 1937 edition, the same one we used when I studied Hebrew under Dr. Merrill F. Unger at Dallas Theological Seminary (1948-53). This edition has about fifteen to twenty suggested changes in the Hebrew text placed in the footnotes on each page. If you multiply this by the 1424 pages in this Kittel Bible, it comes out to between 20,000 and 30,000 changes in the Old Testament. They could be major changes, or they could be minor changes. Does that sound like a "preserved" Bible to you? Does that sound like the fulfillment of not *"one jot nor one tittle?"* I don't like the way these men dealt with the Old Testament text. My Savior said that every word, every letter, and every part of every letter has been preserved by the power of God (Matthew 5:18). Evangelicals and even Fundamentalists are using and recommending the NEW AMERICAN STANDARD VERSION, the NEW INTERNATIONAL VERSION, and even the NEW KING JAMES VERSION, all of which use inferior Old Testament texts.

     b. The NEW INTERNATIONAL VERSION'S Old Testament Text. The NEW INTERNATIONAL VERSION has the same thing to say as to the Old Testament foundation they are using for their translation. On pages viii-ix of the NEW INTERNATIONAL VERSION of 1978, the editors wrote:

> *(p. viii) "For the Old Testament, the standard Hebrew text, the Masoretic text, as published in the latest editions of [1] BIBLIA HEBRAICA* [which is the same Kittel Bible I mentioned before] *was used throughout. The [2] DEAD SEA SCROLLS contain material bearing on an earlier stage of the Hebrew text.* [So they're going to use the Dead Sea Scrolls. They're going to change it when the Dead Sea Scrolls say change it in various places]. *They were consulted as were the [3] SAMARITAN PENTATEUCH* [that is another text that is different from the Hebrew] *and the [4] ANCIENT SCRIBAL TRADITIONS relating to [p. ix] textual changes* [that is a tradition, maybe, in some places, and they're going to use that perhaps over the Masoretic Hebrew text for textual changes]. *Sometimes a [5] VARIANT HEBREW READING IN THE MARGIN of the Masoretic text was followed instead of the text itself. . . .* [Now they're going to use mar-

ginal readings instead of the actual text]. *In rare cases,* *[6] WORDS IN THE CONSONANTAL TEXTS WERE DIVIDED DIFFERENTLY from the way they appear in the Masoretic Text. . . . The translators also consulted the more important [7] EARLY VERSIONS*--[that is] *the [8] SEPTUAGINT;* [so here's the Old Testament translated into Greek and they're going to use that as their basis and foundation] *[9] SYMMACHUS and [10] THEODOTION* [they had a translation from the Old Testament Hebrew into Greek]; *the [11] VULGATE* [there's your Latin translation]; *the [12] SYRIAC PESHITTA; the [13] TARGUMS and for the Psalms, the [14] JUXTA HEBRAICA of Jerome. Readings from these versions were occasionally followed. . . . Some words were read with a [15] DIFFERENT SET OF VOWELS. These instances are usually NOT indicated by footnotes."* [My words are in brackets]. *[NIV, Preface, pp. viii-ix].*

The NIV editors have very honestly and very boldly altered the foundations of our Old Testament text in the above fifteen DIFFERENT WAYS, whenever it suited their fancy! You don't know at what point they've used one document to contradict the Masoretic Hebrew text, and at what point they used another document. It is like not being sure whether they've used cement or sand for a foundation. They may have used a little cement, but all of a sudden there is much sand. You don't know whether it will hold up as a building or whether it will fall flat. The foundation is different. It has been altered.

      c. The NEW KING JAMES VERSION Old Testament Text. But you might say, "The NEW KING JAMES VERSION translators, are more fundamental people. They wouldn't dare change the Old Testament text, would they?" Let us take a look and see what they say about their Old Testament text. The Preface of the NEW KING JAMES VERSION on Page vi says,

      ". . . the text used was the [1] 1967/77 STUTTGART EDITION of BIBLIA HEBRAICA."

This is not Kittel's *Biblia Hebraica* but a new edition. I have that Hebrew text also. It is called *"Biblia Hebraica Stuttgartensia"* (which is from Stuttgart, Germany). This is similar to Kittel's edition. The date, however, is not 1937, but 1967/77. That is the Hebrew text they are using in all the schools now, I am told. It is the one now available on computer. In fact, THE BIBLE FOR TODAY carries it from the LOGOS Bible Study Software for Microsoft Windows. The *Biblia Hebraica* from Rudolf Kittel is abbreviated **BHK** (*Biblia Hebraica Kittel*). The one used by the NKJV is abbreviated **BHS** (*Biblia Hebraica Stuttgartensia*). The **BHS** has a similar arrangement as Kittel's. The Hebrew text (though not the same Hebrew text as that which underlies the KING JAMES BIBLE) is printed at the top of each page. The same things hold true for this Hebrew text as for Kittel's, that is, there are still about fifteen to twenty suggested changes in the Hebrew text placed in the footnotes on each page. This amounts also to about 20,000 to 30,000 suggested changes throughout the Old Testament. In addition to this woefully and tragically **inadequate** Hebrew text, the NEW KING JAMES BIBLE preface says (p. vi):

> ". . . *with frequent [2] comparisons being made with the* **BOMBERG EDITION** *of 1525* [which was the basis of the KING JAMES, by the way] *the [3]* **SEP-TUAGINT** *version of the Old Testament and the [4]* **LATIN VULGATE**, *in addition referring to a variety of [5]* **ANCIENT VERSIONS** *of the Hebrew Scripture and manuscripts from the [6]* **Dead Sea Scrolls**."* [My words in brackets].

Here are at least six admitted foundations consulted and possibly used for the NKJV as a Hebrew text foundation.

So you have, in all three of these Bibles that fundamental Christians are using today, a Hebrew text and Old Testament foundation that is **different** from that of the KING JAMES BIBLE. So, if you have a **different** foundation, how can the building, the Words, be the same? They can't be the same. They are not the same. They are **different**.

2. **The Old Testament Hebrew Text Was Accumulated by the Jews.** Let us take a look at the Old Testament of the KING JAMES BIBLE and why it has a superior text. First, it was **accumulated** by the Jews, and secondly, it was **authorized** by Jesus.

a. **Romans 3:1-2--The Jews Were Named by God to Be the Guardians of the Old Testament.** A Scripture text we ought to use to prove that the Jews were the **God-appointed custodians** of the Old Testament is Romans 3:1-2. No Gentile was to put his unclean hands upon God's Old Testament. Even the New Testament (with the possible

exception of one book) was written by Jews, God's ancient earthly people
Israel, who one day will be restored to faith when they see their Messiah
and they will look upon Him "Whom they have pierced." (Zechariah
12:10).

> *Rom. 3:1-2: "What advantage then hath the Jew? or what
> profit is there of circumcision? (2) Much every way: chiefly,
> because that UNTO THEM WERE COMMITTED THE
> ORACLES OF GOD."*

Strong gives this information about the word, "oracles":

> *"3051. logion {log'-ee-on}; neuter of 3052; an utter-
> ance (of God): -oracle.*

The *"oracles of God"* are the very "utterances" or Words of God. Unto
them (the Jews) "were committed the oracles of God." This is why we
place so much confidence in the traditional Masoretic Hebrew Old
Testament text that those Jews guarded and kept for us. That is why the
KING JAMES translators used this text as the basis for their Bible rather
than the Latin Vulgate (which was not Hebrew at all) or the Septuagint
Greek (which is not Hebrew), or Symmachus, or Theodotion (all these are
Greek), or an ancient tribal tradition, or any other source which is not the
Masoretic Hebrew text. None of these other things should ever have a say
in how the text should read, nor should any of them be used to contradict
the traditional Masoretic Hebrew text that underlies the KING JAMES
BIBLE.

     b.   The Methods of the Old Testament Guardians. Let us
take a look at how the Jews fulfilled this Biblical promise by their strict
rules in copying the Hebrew Old Testament. This is from *General
Biblical Introduction* by H. S. Miller written in 1960, pages 184-185. He
lists eight rules the Jews used in the copying of the Synagogue Rolls of
the Old Testament Scriptures. These rules are mentioned in the Talmud:

> *"1.   The parchment must be made from the
> skin of clean animals; must be prepared by a Jew
> only, and the skins must be fastened together by
> strings taken from clean animals.*
>
> *2.   Each column must have no less than 48
> nor more than 60 lines. The entire copy must be
> first lined. . . .*
>
> *3.   The ink must be of no other color than
> black, and it must be prepared according to a
> special recipe.*
>
> *4.   No word nor letter could be written from*

memory; the scribe must have an authentic copy before him, and he must read and pronounce aloud each word before writing it. [For instance "In the beginning God created the heaven and the earth" You would have to pronounce the word "in the beginning" in Hebrew, (*b'reshith*); "God," (*Elohim*); "created," (*bara*); "the heavens" (*eth hashamaim*); "and the earth" (*wa eth ha arets*). He had to pronounce every word before he wrote it down, with an authentic copy before him. He had to pronounce it aloud, not just see it in his mind. This was to avoid any errors, duplications, omissions, etc.].

5. *He must reverently wipe his pen each time before writing the word for "God"* [which is *Elohim*] *and he must wash his whole body before writing the name "Jehovah"* [which is translated "LORD" in our KING JAMES BIBLE] *lest the Holy Name be contaminated.*

6. *Strict rules were given concerning forms of the letters, spaces between letters, words, and sections, the use of the pen, the color of the parchment, etc.*

7. *The revision of a roll must be made within 30 days after the work was finished; otherwise it was worthless. One mistake on a sheet condemned the sheet; if three mistakes were found on any page, the entire manuscript was condemned.* [What if the man got from Genesis all the way through to Malachi and found three mistakes? He would have to start from Genesis and go all the way to Malachi again. You see the meticulousness with which the Jews were ordered to guard the Words of God? Those men believed that the Words they were copying were God's holy Words. Because of this, they guarded them, unlike men today who add, subtract, and change at will such as has been done in the NKJV, NASV, NIV, and in other new versions. To that extent, they are perversions of truth and Scriptures.]

8. *Every word and every letter was*

counted. Think of counting all the letters on every page of the Hebrew Old Testament. Talk about exactness. Yet that was the method God used to preserve the Old Testament.] *and if a letter were omitted, an extra letter inserted, or if one letter touched another, the manuscript was condemned and destroyed at once." [Miller, op. cit., pp. 184-185]* [My comments in brackets.]

These are historic rules the Jews used. Miller also added these words which we should bear in mind:

"Some of these rules may appear extreme and absurd, yet they show how sacred the Holy Word of the Old Testament was to its custodians, the Jews (Rom. 3:2), and they give us strong encouragement to believe that WE HAVE THE REAL OLD TESTAMENT, THE SAME ONE WHICH OUR LORD HAD AND WHICH WAS ORIGINALLY GIVEN BY INSPIRATION OF GOD." [Miller, op. cit., p. 185]

c.   A Brief History of the Traditional Hebrew Masoretic Old Testament Text. Let us take a brief look at the history of the Hebrew Old Testament text. The word, *"Masoretic,"* is from the Hebrew *masar* ("to hand down"). It means to hand down from person to person. The Masoretes were "traditionalists" who guarded the Old Testament Hebrew text. There were families of Hebrew scholars in Babylon, in Palestine, and in Tiberius. According to most students of these matters, these Masoretes safeguarded the consonantal text. According to some fundamentalist writers, the vowels were present in the Hebrew language right from the start. All the Masoretes had to do was to guard both consonants and vowels. They may very well be correct in this. I agree with this position. Dr. Thomas Strouse has written extensively proving that the vowels were a part of original Hebrew Old Testamen.

For instance, in our English language, if we use the word *"WATER"* the vowels are *"a"* and *"e."* By analogy, if it were a Hebrew word, all they would have had would have been *"WTR."* They knew what the word meant. We would have recognized it, but with other vowels, it might have been *"WAITER."* So, to safeguard the words, to be certain what the Word of God was saying and teaching, God put in the vowel markings. Underneath the consonants, for example, you might find a small *"t"* which is the sound *"ah"*; you might find three dots which is the sound *"eh"*; or you might find two dots which is the sound *"ay"*; one dot is *"ee."* These are called *matres lectiones*, ("mothers of reading") which enabled Gentiles (and other Jews who were not as familiar with the text) to read those Hebrew words with the vowels in there and know exactly what word it would be. So it would be, for instance *"WATER"* instead of *"WAITER."* These Masoretes guarded the consonantal text and later put in these vowels. They wanted to make sure we knew what those words were, especially for the benefit of those of us who are not Jews, and who would not understand the history of it. The Masoretes flourished from about 500 to 1000 A.D. They were supposed to have standardized the Hebrew Old Testament in about 600-700 A.D. by putting in the vowel pointings to aid in the pronunciation of the consonantal text. Their text is called the Masoretic Text or "M.T." if you want to abbreviate it. Some people spell the word "Massoretic," some "Masoretic." I prefer "Masoretic" with only one "s."

d. The Hebrew Text Used by the KING JAMES BIBLE. What about the Hebrew text used by the KING JAMES BIBLE translators? Here's some background on it. The **Daniel Bomberg edition**, 1516-1517, was called the *First Rabbinic Bible.* Then in 1524-25, Bomberg published a second edition edited by Jacob Ben Chayyim (or Ben Hayyim) iben Adonijah. This is called the **Ben Chayyim edition** of the Hebrew text. Daniel Bomberg's edition, on which the KING JAMES BIBLE is based was the **Ben Chayyim Masoretic Text.** This was called the *Second Great Rabbinic Bible.* This became the standard Masoretic text for the next 400 years. This is the text that underlies the KING JAMES BIBLE. For four hundred years, that was the Old Testament Hebrew text. Nobody translated the Old Testament except by using this text. [This is from *Biblical Criticism Historical, Literal, Textual* by Harrison, Walkie and Guthrie, 1978, pages 47-82.]

The **Ben Chayyim Masoretic Text** was used even in the first two editions of *Biblia Hebraica* by Rudolf Kittel. The dates on those first two editions were 1906 and 1912. He used the same Hebrew text as the KING JAMES BIBLE translators.

The edition we used when I was a student of Dr. Merrill F. Unger at Dallas Theological Seminary (1948-53), was the 1937 edition of the *Biblia Hebraica* by Kittel. All of a sudden in 1937, Kittel changed his Hebrew edition and followed what they called the **Ben Asher Masoretic Text** instead of the **Ben Chayyim.** They followed, in that text, the

Leningrad Manuscript, (B19a or "L.") The date on it was 1008 A.D. This was not the traditional Masoretic Text that was used for 400 years and was the basis of the KING JAMES BIBLE. They changed it and used this Leningrad Manuscript. **So even the main text used by the NKJV, NASV, and NIV in the Hebrew is different from that used for the KING JAMES BIBLE.** In addition to the various changes in the Hebrew text at the top of the page, the footnotes in Kittel's *BIBLIA HEBRAICA* suggest from 20,000 to 30,000 changes throughout the whole Old Testament.

The reason that most of the Hebrew departments (in colleges, universities, and seminaries who teach Hebrew) use the **Ben Asher Hebrew Text** instead of the **Ben Chayyim Hebrew Text** is the same reason these same people use the critical Greek text in the New Testament. They believe the "oldest" texts, either in Hebrew or in Greek, must always be the best. Not necessarily. These so-called "old" texts of the New Testament, such as "B" (Vatican) and "Aleph" (Sinai) and their some forty-three allies, were corrupted, I believe, by heretics within the first 100 years after the original New Testament books were written. Therefore, even though these might be the oldest, they were doctored by heretics and therefore are not the "best." Other texts, even though they might be later, if they follow the words of the original must therefore be the ones to use. Those texts which agree with the original documents are those which the KING JAMES BIBLE has followed.

Then there was a revision of Kittel's *Biblia Hebraica*. It was called the *Biblia Hebraica Stuttgartensia*, the Stuttgart edition of 1967/77, based also on the same **Ben Asher** text. That is based on the **Leningrad Codex** which is the same one the revised Kittel Bible of 1937 used.

    e.   Nineteen Erroneous Documents Used to "Correct" the Masoretic Hebrew Text. Not only are the texts that the new versions are taken from based on the *Biblia Hebraica Stuttgartensia* or the *Biblia Hebraica Kittel* (which is the wrong Hebrew base, with a lot of erroneous footnotes) but the NIV and other modern versions also make corrections based upon nineteen other spurious criteria.

I will be quoting in part from *ASV, NASV, and NIV Departures from the Traditional Hebrew and Greek Text*, which I wrote some time ago. [**B.F.T. #986**] In this study, we have listed a total of 103 examples of changes from the Hebrew text and twenty-three Greek examples. We print the Masoretic Hebrew text with the Bomberg Edition as the basis of the KING JAMES BIBLE; then we print what the AMERICAN STANDARD VERSION of 1901 has, the NEW AMERICAN STANDARD

VERSION of 1960 has, and what the NEW INTERNATIONAL VERSION of 1969 has. We also show what the KING JAMES BIBLE has. The Masoretic text and the KING JAMES BIBLE agree with each other but these other versions depart from the Masoretic text in these examples. We could have picked from hundreds of other examples. In this study, we list on page A-9, at the bottom, some of the other ways of departing from the Hebrew text, including the following eleven together with eight more sources listed in the NIV's Preface, pages viii-ix: (Cf. section 1-b above).

(1) **The Septuagint, LXX, the Greek Old Testament**. The AMERICAN STANDARD VERSION, NEW AMERICAN STANDARD VERSION, and the NEW INTERNATIONAL VERSION departed in the Old Testament seventy-three times (35% of the 103 departures we have listed in here) preferring the Septuagint over the Hebrew. Now that Greek Old Testament is a very deficient translation from the Hebrew into the Greek. In many books and places, it is just like the LIVING VERSION. It is a paraphrase, a **perversion**. In fact, in the beginning of this document [**B.F.T.** #986] we have an analysis of the Septuagint, showing how bad it is as a translation. There are quotations from the *International Standard Bible Encyclopedia* and comments as to why the Masoretic text should be followed instead of the Septuagint.

(2) **Conjecture, No Reason Given**. In sixty-seven examples out of the 103 (32% of the time) the Masoretic Hebrew text is scuttled merely because of **conjecture**. In other words, these editors don't even have a Hebrew text, Greek text, or Latin text. They don't have any sources at all. They just say, "Well, we want it to read this way." When I was studying Hebrew at Dallas Theological Seminary, (1948-53), as I mentioned before, our teacher was Dr. Merrill F. Unger (who wrote *Unger's Bible Dictionary*, etc). We were reading in the book of Isaiah, using the Kittel Bible (*Biblia Hebraica* by Rudolf Kittel) and of course it has all these footnotes. Dr. Unger read the word in a way different from the Masoretic text. He used one of the footnotes as a basis for the change. I raised my hand and said, "Dr. Unger, why did you change this text?" He replied, "It just reads better that way." That is because down in the footnotes, every time they want to change it, with no evidence whatever, the footnotes read *"L"* which stands for the Latin word *legendum*. It means "which read." When they are following the Septuagint, or some other version, or the Latin Vulgate, the footnote reads, "with the Latin Vulgate," etc. But sometimes they just have an *"L."* In fact, in Genesis 1:9, there's an *"L."* After the *"L,"* it says "probably this." In other words,

there's no evidence, no document. It is just conjecture and guesswork. How Bible-believing Christians can allow guesswork and conjecture to determine their Bible is beyond me, but they do.

        (3) The Syriac Version. In twenty examples out of the 103 (10% of the time), they used the Syriac instead of the Masoretic Hebrew text.

        (4) A Few Hebrew Manuscripts. Sometimes, just a "few" Hebrew manuscripts, not the Masoretic text, but a few manuscripts were used to correct the Masoretic text.

        (5) The Latin Vulgate. Sometimes the Latin Vulgate (the Latin translation of the Bible), was used to correct the Masoretic text.

        (6) The Dead Sea Scrolls. In eight examples out of the 103 (4% of the time) the Dead Sea Scrolls were used instead of the Masoretic text. When Mrs. Waite and I visited Israel in 1982, we went into the Qumran caves where they found the so-called Dead Sea Scrolls. They were preserved by the Essenes. Among other things, they have the Book of Isaiah. There is very little difference from the Scripture. These Essenes fled from Jerusalem to this place and took some of the Hebrew Bible scrolls they had. But, why would we use the Dead Sea Scrolls instead of the Masoretic Text which the Hebrews in Jerusalem had so carefully guarded? These Essenes left the Hebrew synagogue in Jerusalem. They left the Jewish beliefs their fathers had. They were an offshoot and a false, heretical cult. There are two reasons for questioning these Dead Sea Scrolls where they might differ with the Masoretic Hebrew text: (1) They might have had corrupt Hebrew texts that they began with, at least in some places; (2) They might have been careless in the transmission of these texts. These are both unknown, hence, they should never be used to replace the Masoretic Hebrew text. They could have changed the text in a hundred different ways. I don't know why any version should take a Dead Sea Scroll reading over the Masoretic traditional text, the historical text which had been guarded so meticulously. Yet in some instances this is done.

        (7) Aquila. Sometimes Aquila, a Greek Old Testament translation, was used to correct the Masoretic text.

        (8) The Samaritan Pentateuch. Sometimes the Samaritan Pentateuch was used to correct the Masoretic text. This contains the first five books of Moses which the Samaritans used. The Samaritans were a mixed people who had a different translation of the Old Testament.

        (9) Quotations from Jerome. Sometimes quotations

from Jerome, who translated the Latin Vulgate, were used to correct the Masoretic text.

(10) Josephus. Sometimes Josephus, a Jewish historian, and not even a saved man, was used to correct the Masoretic text.

(11) An Ancient Hebrew Scribal Tradition. Sometimes an ancient Hebrew scribal tradition was used to correct the Masoretic text.

(12) The BIBLIA HEBRAICA of Kittel or Stuttgartensia. These are false Hebrew texts which are improper bases for the Hebrew Old Testament.

(13) A Variant Hebrew Reading in the Margin. This is also an unreliable source to challenge the Masoretic Hebrew text.

(14) Words in the Consonantal Text Divided Differently. There is nothing wrong with the way the Hebrew consonants are presently divided. They need not be divided differently.

(15) Symmachus. This Greek translation of the Old Testament should not be permitted to set aside the Masoretic Hebrew text.

(16) Theodotion. This Greek translation of the Old Testament should not be allowed to contradict and bypass the Masoretic Hebrew text.

(17) The Targums. These documents, once again, should never be taken as authoritative Old Testament Scripture. They were never meant to supplant the Masoretic Hebrew text.

(18) The Juxta Hebraica of Jerome for the Psalms. Again, this is not the Scripture of the Old Testament, no matter how it may be regarded as information about the Psalms.

(19) A Different Set Of Hebrew Vowels. Just as we do not need any different consonants in the Masoretic Hebrew text, so we do not need any different sets of vowels for that text. Just leave it alone, and let it be! God has preserved it just as it is.

f. My Conclusion on the Hebrew Masoretic Text. My conclusion on the Masoretic Hebrew text is this: There may be some places in the text of the Daniel Bomberg Hebrew edition of the Masoretic text where there are seeming contradictions. For instance, the king may be eighteen years old or eight years old. Even if there are seeming contradictions, I feel it is imperative to go by what the Traditional Masoretic text has as its reading and let the Lord figure out what may seem contradictions to us. **Keep what God has given and preserved through the ages and let the Lord figure out why.** It could be both eight and eighteen and have a harmonization we don't know anything about. The editors of these new versions, have footnotes that depart from the Masoretic text. They often decide the issue on the basis of **pure guesswork!** But how do you know their decision is the correct one? Just leave the Hebrew text as it is. **The KING JAMES translators came along and saw what the Hebrew Masoretic text said and simply translated it right over into the English. They didn't quibble with it; they didn't try to harmonize it.** For instance, you'll find in Isaiah 9:3 that there is a *"not"* [LO] which has been completely eliminated by the new versions. The Scripture says, *"Thou hast multiplied the nation, and not increased the joy . . ."* and these new versions have just taken it out because they think it makes more sense. But the Hebrew says "not" and the KING JAMES translators simply wrote it down, faithfully as they ought to have done.

Never be ashamed of the traditional Masoretic Hebrew text that underlies the KING JAMES BIBLE!! It was accumulated by the Jews in fulfillment of Romans 3:1-2. We agree with Dean John William Burgon who wrote of "the **INCREDIBLE FOLLY OF TINKERING THE HEBREW TEXT.**" [from a letter April 8, 1885, appearing in the *Guardian* as quoted in *JOHN WILLIAM BURGON, LATE DEAN OF CHICHESTER--A BIOGRAPHY,* 1892, by Edward Mayrick Goulburn, Vol. II, p. 241. **[B.F.T. #1619]** It truly is an "**INCREDIBLE FOLLY**" for anyone who is "guilty" of "**TINKERING THE HEBREW TEXT.**" We should LEAVE IT ALONE just as it is!

3. The Old Testament Hebrew Text Was Authorized by Jesus. Not only was the Scripture **accumulated** by Jews, but it was **authorized** by Jesus. Jesus Christ authorized the traditional Masoretic Hebrew Old Testament text. Though we have looked at some of these verses under the subject of **Bible preservation,** we will look at them once more from a slightly different aspect.

      a. Verses Teaching This Position.

         (1) Matthew 4:4. Jesus was speaking to the devil and refuting him with Scripture:

> *"But He answered and said, **IT IS WRITTEN,** Man shall*
> *not live by bread alone, but by **EVERY WORD** that*
> *proceedeth out of the mouth of God."*

As we said before, *"it is written"* is in the perfect tense, meaning it has been written in the past and stands written now, preserved until the present time. **So the Lord Jesus Christ AUTHORIZED the Old Testament He had in His hand.** The first books of the Old Testament were originally written by Moses around 1500 B.C. The Old Testament Hebrew Words were preserved for 1,500 years and the Lord Jesus said, *"it is written."* This means that the **WORDS OF GOD** have been written down in the past and these very **WORDS** have been preserved down to the present time, and they stand written NOW as they were at the first. This is the very essence of BIBLE PRESERVATION!

(2)   **Matthew 5:17-18**. Jesus speaks about the *"law or the prophets."* This is a technical term referring to the traditional Masoretic Hebrew Old Testament text. There are three divisions in the Old Testament: the Law, the Prophets, and the Writings. Sometimes the expression, "law and prophets," refers to all three divisions. The Law (the *torah*) refers to the first five books; the Prophets (the *naviim*) refers to both the former and the latter Prophets; and the Writings (the *kethuvim*) refers to the Psalms and the rest of the books. Here in verses 17 and 18 Jesus said,

> *"(17) Think not that I am come to destroy the LAW, or the PROPHETS: . . . (18) For verily I say unto you, Till heaven and earth pass, one jot or one tittle shall in no wise pass from the Law, till all be fulfilled."*

Jesus said of the words, letters, and even parts of the letters found in the Hebrew Bible in His day, that no jot or **tittle** would be eliminated, effaced, or changed in the slightest manner until all was fulfilled. So He put His AUTHORIZATION on the traditional Masoretic Hebrew text He had in His day.

(3)   **Luke 24:27**. When the Lord Jesus Christ talked to the disciples on the road to Emmaus, He taught them:

> *"And beginning at Moses and all the prophets, He expounded unto them the things concerning Himself."*

Here is the phrase *"Moses and all the prophets."* It leaves off the "writings," but again, this was referring to the threefold division of the Hebrew Bible: Law, Prophets and Writings. That is AUTHORIZATION by the Lord Jesus of the traditional Masoretic Old Testament Hebrew text that was present in His day.

(4)   **Luke 24:44**.

> *"And He said unto them, These are the words which I spake unto you, while I was yet with you, that all things must be fulfilled, which were **written** in THE LAW of Moses, and in THE PROPHETS, and in THE PSALMS, concerning Me."*

The Greek word *"written"* is *gegrammena*, the perfect participle: that which was written in the beginning and is continuously being preserved and stands written today.   The phrase *"in the Psalms"* makes it the complete threefold division of the Hebrew canon: the law of Moses (Torah); the prophets (Naviim); and the Psalms or Writings (Kethuvim). It is called the *"TANACH"* today by the Jews, taking the *"TA"* for *"TORAH,"* the *"NA"* from *"NAVIIM,"* and the *"CH"* for *"KETHUVIM."* This is the one abbreviation for the entire Masoretic Hebrew Old Testament. **He put His hand on the entire Masoretic Hebrew Old Testament text that existed then and AUTHORIZED it.** Many people may ask, "Didn't the Lord Jesus Christ use the Septuagint Version of the Old Testament?   Wasn't He referring to that?"   No, he was not.   He referred to the Law of Moses, the Prophets, and the Psalms. The Septuagint did not have that division at all.   In fact, aside from the Apocrypha contained in the Septuagint, the order is LAW, PSALMS, and PROPHETS instead of, as the Hebrew, LAW, PROPHETS & PSALMS. As you can see, the Septuagint has the order of books much as we have in our Bibles today.   The Hebrew does not have the same order; it ends with the book of 2 Chronicles.

      b.   Quotations Explaining This Position. Christ appealed unreservedly to the traditional Hebrew text.

      (1)   A Quotation from Dr. Edward Hills. Here is a quotation from Dr. Edward Hills, who has written extensively on the subject of the Bible.

> *"During His earthly life, the Lord Jesus appealed unreservedly to the very words of the Old Testament text (Matthew 22:42, John 20:44 ff), thus indicating His confidence that this text had been accurately transmitted. Not only so, but He also expressed this conviction in the strongest possible manner, `. . . till heaven and earth pass, one jot or one tittle shall in no wise pass from the law till all be fulfilled,' (Matthew 5:18.) . . . Here our Lord Jesus assures us that the Old Testament in common use among the Jews during His earthly ministry was an* ***ABSOLUTELY   TRUSTWORTHY REPRODUCTION OF THE ORIGINAL TEXT WRITTEN BY MOSES AND OTHER . . . WRITERS."*** *[BELIEVING BIBLE STUDY, by Dr. Edward Hills, pp. 5-6].*

The Lord Jesus Christ never refuted any text, any word, or any letter

in the Hebrew Old Testament. He didn't say, "Now Moses was misquoted here, it should have been this." He offered no textual criticism whatever. Had there been any changes, I'm sure He would have corrected it, but He didn't. It stands written! His stamp of approval is on the Masoretic Hebrew text. It is AUTHORIZED by Jesus. He did not authorize the Septuagint, the Latin Vulgate, some scribal tradition, Josephus, Jerome, the Syriac version, or any other document!

(2)   A Quotation from Dr. Robert Dick Wilson. Here is a quotation from Dr. Robert Dick Wilson, a Presbyterian, and a teacher there at Princeton Seminary before the flood of Modernism came in. Henry Corey reflected on the life of Dr. Robert Dick Wilson, a man who had mastered some forty-five languages and dialects and who was a staunch defender of the doctrine of verbal inspiration of Scripture. Corey affirmed that Wilson accepted as **accurate** the Masoretic Hebrew text. Corey, quoting Wilson, wrote:

> *"The results of those 30 years' study* [that is what Wilson wrote of his own study of Scripture in the Hebrew] *which I have given to the text has been this: I can affirm that there's not a page of the Old Testament in which we need have any doubt. We can be absolutely certain that substantially we have the text of the Old Testament that Christ and the Apostles had and which was in existence from the beginning." [WHICH BIBLE, 1st edition, by Dr. David Otis Fuller, pp. 80-81].*

Here is a man who studied, and studied, and found the Masoretic Hebrew text to be accurate and solid. So I see no reason why we should have any other foundation for the Old Testament than the Masoretic Hebrew text that underlies the KING JAMES BIBLE, the **Daniel Bomberg edition,** edited by **Ben Chayyim--the 2nd Rabbinic Bible of 1524-25.**

   c.   **Alternative to Believing This Position?** You might say, what is the alternative? What if you do not accept the **Daniel Bomberg edition** of the **Masoretic Hebrew** text on which the KING JAMES BIBLE is based as the **authoritative** Hebrew text from which to translate? The alternative, quite logically, would be to accept some other basis. What other basis are you going to use? Are you going to use the Kittel *Biblia Hebraica* (**BHK**) which was based upon the same text as the KING JAMES BIBLE in 1906 and 1912, and then was revised and scrapped for another Hebrew text in 1937? Or are you going to use the 1967/77 *Biblia*

Hebraica Stuttgartensia (**BHS**) which is a revised Kittel? If you're not going to use the base that is printed in the **defective** Hebrew text at the top of the page in either **BHK** or **BHS**, are you going to use some of these changes in the footnotes--20,000 to 30,000 of them? If so, which ones are you going to use? Are you going to use only the ones they used in the NEW KING JAMES VERSION? Only the ones they used in the NEW AMERICAN STANDARD VERSION? Only the ones they used in the NEW INTERNATIONAL VERSION? Are you going to use 25% of them? 50% of them? Or are you going to use all of them? Or are you going to become a doubter, thinking that we don't really know what the Old Testament is? Are you going to take the position that "We can't be certain of the Hebrew Old Testament, so we must doubt all of it"? **Satan is the master of deceitful doubting and he is the author of all this confusion.** Once you forsake a standard, you're adrift in a sea of doubts. There's nothing to take its place. Young Christians and people in the pews that have not been saved too many years might say, "If there's all this bickering and fighting among the theologians and pastors as to the right Hebrew Old Testament text to use, I give up and throw up my hands." The devil wins if he can plant the seeds of confusion and doubts into the hearts of men and women as well as boys and girls.

After much study, thinking, and praying about this subject, I have personally arrived at a **strong conviction** that I will not budge from the traditional Masoretic Hebrew text on which our KING JAMES BIBLE is based. That is it. I'm not going to move. I don't want to change anything. We're going to stand right there. Somebody's got to stand. **Martin Luther said, "Here I stand; I can do no other."** He wasn't going to move from salvation by faith (*sola fide*), salvation by grace (*sola gratia*) and salvation only by the Scripture (*sola scriptura*). He wasn't going to follow the Pope. He wasn't going to follow the decrees of the Church Councils. He was standing on the Words of God alone! Though we might not be Lutherans like Martin Luther, we must not budge either. If we do, we are like a wave of the sea, driven by the wind and tossed.

d. Illustration of Rejecting This Position. Let me point out an illustration about the Old Testament text. *The NIV Interlinear Hebrew-English Old Testament* (1979) has four volumes. It is edited by John R. Kohlenberger, III, and published by Zondervan. Zondervan is supposed to be a Bible-believing, evangelical publishing house. I want to show you what they have done to the Old Testament text. Rudolf Kittel, who wrote this *Biblia Hebraica*, the two editions earlier and then the edition of 1937, was an apostate German rationalist. He was a

believer in the Graf-Welhausen documentary hypothesis of the Pentateuch. It is called the JEDP theory. He did not believe in the inerrancy of Scripture. He was all he shouldn't be. This man, although we don't believe in the Hebrew text he used (he used the **Ben Asher** instead of the **Ben Chayyim** text), at least he put the Hebrew text on the top of the page. He kept the changes separate and distinct by putting them in the footnotes, so you could read his Masoretic text as it was. The same method was followed later in the *Biblia Hebraica Stuttgartensia.*
What did the NIV and Zondervan do, though? Any time they wanted to change the Masoretic Hebrew text, **they put it right up in the text,** instead of in the footnotes. Let me illustrate: Genesis 4:9 says in the KING JAMES BIBLE, and in the Hebrew Masoretic Text:

> *"And Cain talked with Abel his brother: and it came to pass, when they were in the field, that Cain rose up against Abel his brother, and slew him."*

In the NIV it says,

> "Cain said to Abel, his brother, **'Let us go out to the field. . .'"**

There's nothing in the Hebrew text to justify this. All the other Hebrew versions leave it out, but Kohlenberger puts it right into the text. He has a footnote on it in very small type which says,

> *"This Hebrew reading and translation is **conjectured** on the basis of the early versions listed above in Note 1."*

So they conjecture it and put the Hebrew into the text, if there's anything they want to add to it. A devout Jew would NEVER do such a thing! All these unbelievers, like Kittel and the German Stuttgart editors, at least put any suggested changes from the Hebrew text into the footnotes. But Kohlenberger and Zondervan, **who are supposed to be believers in Christ,** put the **conjecture** right into the Hebrew text. It is a sad day when a supposedly Bible-believing evangelical will emend the traditional Masoretic Hebrew text itself.

As we've pointed out before, the Old Testament basis of our KING JAMES BIBLE is the traditional Masoretic Hebrew text, the **2nd Rabbinic Bible, Daniel Bomberg Edition, edited by Ben Chayyim** in 1524-25. The date of the 1st Bomberg Edition was 1516-1517. It was called the First Rabbinic Bible. During this time they came up with a standard Masoretic Hebrew Old Testament text and it lasted 400 years. That standard was used even in Kittel's first two editions, 1906 and 1912. Let us stick to it firmly!

B. THE KING JAMES BIBLE IS GOD'S WORDS KEPT INTACT IN ENGLISH BECAUSE OF ITS SUPERIOR NEW TESTAMENT GREEK TEXT.

We believe the KING JAMES BIBLE is based on a **superior** New Testament text. We believe this for two reasons: (1) The first is that the *Textus Receptus* that underlies the KING JAMES BIBLE was **accepted by the churches**. (2) Secondly, the *Textus Receptus* that underlies the KING JAMES BIBLE is **attested by the evidence**. Before taking up these two main divisions, let us look at a little background information.

1. The Chief Opponent of the *Textus Receptus* Today. The text which is used today in most colleges, universities, and seminaries (even conservative and/or fundamental ones) is the *Nestle/Aland Greek New Testament, 26th edition*. It has gone through twenty-six editions thus far. Nestle began his critical Greek edition in 1898, following the basic text of Westcott and Hort and three other editions of his day. The Greek-English edition I have is dated 1981. I believe the 26th Greek edition came out in 1979. From 1898 to 1979, is about eighty-one years. If you divide eighty-one by twenty-six, you can see that they have come out, on the average, with one new, updated, changed, **different edition of the Greek New Testament every 3.1 years!** What does that tell you as to the certainty these editors have in **God's preservation** of His New Testament Words? It tells you that these men really don't know what the Greek New Testament is. This is basically the same as the Westcott and Hort text, 1881 edition, with changes here and there. The history of this text is an interesting history. The edition of *Nestle/Aland Greek New Testament 26th Edition* that I have has with it, in parallel columns, the English of the REVISED STANDARD VERSION, which is copyrighted by the NATIONAL COUNCIL OF CHURCHES, the apostate-led Council.

2. The Editors of the *Nestle/Aland* Greek Text. This *Nestle/Aland* Greek text was named for Eberhard Nestle, a German, and Kurt Aland, also a German. It was made up by a committee consisting of Kurt Aland (who is an unbeliever), Matthew Black (an unbeliever), Carlo M. Martini (a Cardinal of the Roman Catholic Church), Bruce Metzger (who is from Princeton, a man who demonstrated his apostasy as editor of the *Reader's Digest Bible*), and Alan Wigren (from Chicago, an apostate also). All these were editors of the 26th edition of the *Nestle/Aland*

Greek New Testament Text.

3. This Text Underlies the Modern English Versions. This Greek New Testament text, or one like it, is the basic text that underlies the modern versions: the ENGLISH REVISED VERSION (ERV) of 1881, the AMERICAN STANDARD VERSION (ASV) of 1901, the NEW AMERICAN STANDARD VERSION (NASV) of 1960, the NEW INTERNATIONAL VERSION (NIV) of 1969, the NEW ENGLISH VERSION (NEB) of 1961, and most of those listed in APPENDIX B. This Greek text is what the so-called scholarly world as well as New Evangelicals and many Fundamentalists (sad to say) use. The fact that there have been **TWENTY-SIX EDITIONS IN EIGHTY-ONE YEARS (a new edition every 3.1 years)** would give you the DISTINCT impression that these men, and their followers, who put confidence in their editions, have **NO ASSURANCE WHATEVER** of what **ARE** and what **ARE NOT** the very and the exact **GREEK WORDS OF GOD** in the New Testament! I certainly wouldn't want to be in their shoes! I have CONFIDENCE in the *Received Text* that underlies our KING JAMES BIBLE, and I have CONFIDENCE in our KING JAMES BIBLE as the most **accurate** English translation of that text. For this reason, I believe the KING JAMES BIBLE is the **WORDS OF GOD IN ENGLISH!**

4. The Greek Text That Underlies the KING JAMES BIBLE. The KING JAMES BIBLE used a text (which the Trinitarian Bible Society has reprinted) called *HE KainE DiathEkE* (The New Covenant or Testament). This was copied from the Greek text produced by Dr. Frederick H. A. Scrivener and published by the Cambridge University Press in 1894, originally. This *Textus Receptus* that underlies the KING JAMES BIBLE New Testament, was basically **Beza's 5th edition of 1598.** Dr. Frederick H. A. Scrivener, in his *NEW TESTA- MENT IN GREEK ACCORDING TO THE TEXT FOLLOWED IN THE AUTHORISED VERSION TOGETHER WITH THE VARIATIONS ADOPTED IN THE REVISED VERSION* of 1881, lists about 190 places where the KJB editors departed from Beza's 5th edition in favor of eight other sources (Cf. pp. 648-656). [B.F.T. #1670] This Greek text is the exact text which underlies the KING JAMES BIBLE. **It is a text that hasn't changed. It hasn't had a revision in the last 381 years.** I don't believe it needs any revising. It is called the Traditional *Received Text,* or the Byzantine Text, or the Syrian text, or the *Textus Receptus.* It is the best, and the only foundation as far as I can see, to use to translate the

New Testament from the Greek language into English or any other language. This is the text I want to talk about, the *Received Text* which has been handed down from generation to generation by the church.

5. The *Textus Receptus* Has Been Accepted by the Churches. As mentioned before, there are two reasons why we believe the *Received Text* is **superior**: (1) First, it has been **accepted by the churches**. **It is traditional.** It has been handed down by the people who knew what they were talking about. (2) Second, it has been **attested by the evidence**. There is evidence that this is a superior text. We don't have to take it only by faith. There is strong **evidence** to indicate that this is the text that should be used, and that it is **historic**.

I will be giving a total of thirty-seven links in the historical chain of evidence. I will show how, through the history of the Christian church, various churches, groups, organizations, and documents have accepted this text, the *Textus Receptus*, as the true Greek text which we should accept as our New Testament and from which we should translate. The translation of the New Testament should be based upon the *Greek Received Text.* These Greek words, we believe, go all the way back to the original manuscripts of the Greek New Testament. They have been accepted ever since they were written down.

6. Westcott and Hort Refused to Accept the *Textus Receptus* Greek. Though there was some scattered opposition to the *Received Text* in years before, the **concerted** effort against the *Received Text* came in 1881, and after. In 1881, two theological heretics (**posing as conservatives**) from the Anglican Church (Church of England), Westcott and Hort, published their Greek text that rejected the *Textus Receptus* in 5,604 places by my actual count. This included 9,970 Greek words that were either **added, subtracted,** or **changed** from the *Textus Receptus.* This involves, on the average, 15.4 words per page of the Greek New Testament, or a total of 45.9 pages in all. It is 7% of the total of 140,521 words in the *Textus Receptus Greek* New Testament.

Westcott was a bishop of the Anglican Church; Hort was a teacher at Cambridge University. I've written a little booklet entitled, *The Theological Heresies Of Westcott And Hort* [**B.F.T. #595**] In this study, I quote from their writings extensively and show from five of their books that they are **apostates, liberals, and unbelievers.** And yet, they are the ones that altered this text. Hort was worse than Westcott. He wrote an *INTRODUCTION* to this revolutionary text. **If we don't understand the part of Westcott and Hort in this, we won't understand why there was** the change from the *Textus Receptus* to the new Westcott-and-Hort-type text. Why was it? Because Hort, writing the *INTRODUCTION* in 1882, propounded a totally erroneous theory (530 pages). We've reprinted it so that people who are interested in it can see what Hort wrote, his contradictions, and that which was false. [**B.F.T.** #1303] Hort swayed the whole scholarly world on his side of the Atlantic Ocean including England, Scotland, and Germany, as well as on this side of the Atlantic. B. B. Warfield and his Presbyterians followed him. Baptist institutions, such as A. T. Robertson's Southern Baptist Seminary at Louisville, followed him. They just threw out the New Testament that had been in our hands for hundreds of years. **Westcott and Hort concocted a new Greek text and changed the *Received Text* that had been used in the Church from the beginning of the writing of the New Testament.**

7. The Westcott and Hort Text Changes the *Textus Receptus* in Over 5,600 Places. Do you know how many changes they made? My own **personal count**, as of August 2, 1984, using Scrivener's *GREEK NEW TESTAMENT* referred to above, was **5,604** changes that Westcott and Hort made to the *Textus Receptus* in their own Greek New Testament text. Of these 5,604 alterations, I found **1,952** to be OMISSIONS (35%), **467** to be ADDITIONS (8%), and **3,185** to be CHANGES (57%). In these **5,604** places that were involved in these alterations, there were **4,366** more words included, making a total of **9,970** Greek words that were involved. This means that in a Greek Text of 647 pages (such as Scrivener's text), this would average **15.4 words per page** that were CHANGED from the *RECEIVED TEXT*. Pastor Jack Moorman counted 140,521 words in the *Textus Receptus*. These changes would amount to 7% of the words; and 45.9 pages of the Greek New Testament if placed together in one place. Here's what it would be like in a table format. I entitle it **"THE BATTLEGROUND"** between the two different kinds of Greek New Testament: *"T.R."* stands for the *Textus Receptus*. *"W/H"* stands for Westcott and Hort's Greek Text of 1881.

THE N.T. GREEK TEXTUAL BATTLEGROUND

TEXTUS RECEPTUS	W/H CHANGES IN T.R.
Has 140,521 Greek wds.	Changes 5,604 places in the N.T.
Has 647 pp. in Greek Text	Changes include 9,970 Greek wds.
Has 217 Greek wds. per page	Changes 15.4 Greek wds. per page
Has 100% of the Greek wds.	Changes 7% of the Greek wds.
Has all 647 pp. unchanged	Changes total 45.9 pp. in Greek text

Dr. Jack A. Moorman, in December, 1988, wrote a book entitled: *MISSING IN MODERN BIBLES--IS THE FULL STORY BEING TOLD?* It was published by THE BIBLE FOR TODAY in April, 1989. Rev. Moorman counted every word of the *Received Greek Text* and also every word of the *Nestle/Aland Greek Text* and, on a chapter by chapter count, came up with the *Nestle/Aland* text being **SHORTER** than the *Received Text* by **2,886** words. This is 934 words more than were omitted from the Westcott and Hort text. (1,952 vs. 2,886). The omitting of 2,886 Greek words is the equivalent, in number of English words involved, of **DROPPING OUT THE ENTIRE BOOKS OF 1 PETER AND 2 PETER!** Pastor Moorman's book is eighty large pages. **[B.F.T. #1726]**

People say, "Well, they don't make any difference. There isn't any doctrine in the changes." But there are doctrines that are changed. We will see this in CHAPTER V of this book. Do you see that if you were taking an English Bible based on the foundation of the *Nestle/Aland* 26th edition instead of the *Received Text,* you could not possibly make them equal? There's a theorem in geometry and mathematics, that states: "Things equal to the same thing are equal to each other." These things cannot be equal. No matter how you try to translate--the NEW INTERNATIONAL VERSION, let us say, or the NEW AMERICAN STANDARD VERSION, since they're based in the New Testament on the *Nestle/Aland text* that differs from the *Received Text* in over 5,600 places, involving almost 10,000 Greek words--there's no way in the world you could make them equal to the KING JAMES BIBLE which is based on the *Received Text.* The NIV and NASV are perversions of the Words of God because they are based upon a Greek text that is false to the truth and improper in every way. The FOUNDATION is faulty.

8.   The Two Greek Texts Have Irreconcilable Differences. The foundational New Testament and Old Testament texts in question are fundamentally and irreconcilably different. It is impossible that they can come up with anything but **confusion.** Talk about doctrinal changes! In our booklet **[B.F.T. #83]** *THE CASE FOR THE RECEIVED TEXT OF HEBREW AND GREEK UNDERLYING THE KING JAMES VERSION-- A Summary Of the Evidence & Argument,"* [Available from the Bible For Today] I analyzed three books that summed up the argument and put it as clearly as I could in 1971. In the back of this **B.F.T. #83,** *"THE CASE FOR THE KING JAMES VERSION OF THE BIBLE,* page thirty-nine, we have listed some very important verses, Greek texts, and

English translations that eliminate parts of them, using forty-four different versions of the New Testament. There are 162 key verses to compare in these Greek texts. In each of these translations you have a number of verses or parts of them that are omitted. For instance, the Revised Standard Version omits some or all of 158 of the 162 test verses, or 97%; Nestle's Greek text omits some or all of 155 of the 162 test verses, or 96%.

9. Many Doctrinal Differences in the Two Greek Texts. Though CHAPTER V will take up the doctrinal errors in the versions more in detail, in **B.F.T.** #83, I took these key verses, listed them and then classified them as to doctrines that are omitted. For instance, the deity of Christ: I give three verses on that. Now, that is a doctrinal difference. There are a total of sixteen verses on this. The second is the omission of Christ's full title, the Lord Jesus Christ. In addition, there are changes regarding the matters of Christ's Virgin Birth as well as the omission of "begotten" which alters His eternal Sonship and His relationship with the Father. These are doctrines. There are omissions of "Alpha and Omega" involving His eternal generation and eternal future, omission of Christ's omnipresence, His eternal future state, His part in creation, the fact that salvation is only through Jesus Christ and faith in Him, weakening of the fact of Christ's bodily resurrection, His bodily ascension, His bodily return, and His great commission. There are omissions. Here is what the argument is. People usually say: "The Westcott and Hort text has a few omissions but no major doctrines are involved." Well, **major** doctrines **are** involved. Secondly they say: "If they take a doctrine out here, it is found somewhere else in the New Testament." Well, I don't care if they leave it in 100 other places; if they take it out any place it is a defective, deficient Greek version and a defective, deficient English version based upon it.

10. The Early Heretics Polluted the Westcott-and-Hort-type Text. You know why the heretics took out some things but not all of them? They wanted the Bible to agree with them. The heretics who flourished in the first hundred years after the Bible was written did not have every New Testament book in their possession, so they couldn't rip out, change, recopy, or forge various verses throughout the New Testament. They could only do such things with the books they had in their hands. So some books escaped the heretics' knife. **But, if you take out anything, it is defective.** How many words of God have to be left out of your Bible before it is no longer 100% God's Words? Just one? That would be enough for me. But when you have over 5,600 changes involving almost 10,000 words, you have serious trouble.

11. Why the NIV & NASV and Others Are NOT the Words of God. Can I hold up the NEW INTERNATIONAL VERSION and say it is the Words of God in English? No, I can't because there are almost 10,000 reasons why it isn't the Words of God in English. Can I hold up the NEW AMERICAN STANDARD VERSION and say it is the Words of God in English? No, I can't. Can I even hold up the NEW KING JAMES BIBLE and say it is the Words of God in English? No, I can't. **Can I hold up the KING JAMES VERSION and say it is the Words of God in English?** Yes. **All the words are there, accurately translated by master translators.**

12. This Writer Was Trained in the Westcott and Hort Camp. *The Case for the King James Version* [**B.F.T.** #83] was the first paper I wrote on the subject of the superiority of the KING JAMES BIBLE. It was written in 1971. I was trained to prefer the Westcott and Hort Greek text (now called the *Nestle/Aland* text) at Dallas Theological Seminary. The *Received Text* had been, almost without question, the text in use up until 1881, when this change took place. For almost 1,800 years the church accepted the *Received Text*. Suddenly many people threw it out. Something that had lasted for 1,800 years is now, all of a sudden, no good. These days, you are looked down on and almost thought of as an ignoramus if you stand for the *Textus Receptus* for which Christian churches down through the centuries have stood. If you don't use the *Nestle/Aland* text, many think something must be wrong with you. This is a serious situation. That is why the DEAN BURGON SOCIETY (of which I am now president) was raised up in 1978. And this is why THE BIBLE FOR TODAY has been emphasizing this issue ever since 1971. These organizations and others have been seeking to put the truth of this issue before the people and to defend the *Received Greek text* and the *Masoretic Hebrew text* that underlie our KING JAMES BIBLE.

13. The Thirty-Seven Historical Evidences Supporting the *Textus Receptus*. Here are the thirty-seven links in the chain of historical evidence to support the *Received Text*.
      a.   Historical Evidences for the *Received Text* **During the Apostolic Age (33--100 A.D.)**

> (1) *All of the Apostolic Churches used the Received Text.*
>
> (2) *The churches in Palestine used the Received Text.*
>
> (3) *The Syrian Church at Antioch used the Received Text.*

b. Historical Evidences for the *Received Text* During the Early Church Period (100--312 A.D.). Dr. Scrivener and Dean Burgon both agree that, during the first 100 years after the New Testament was written, the greatest corruptions took place to the *Received Text* used by the early church. The B (Vatican) and Aleph (Sinai) manuscripts and the approximately forty-three allies which underlie the Westcott-and-Hort-type text were, I believe, the result of such corruptions. Some of the heretics which operated in this period were Marcion, (160 A. D.); Valentinus, (about 160 A. D.); Cyrinthus, (50-100 A. D.); Sabellius, (about 260 A. D.); and others.

> (4) *The Peshitta Syriac Version*, (150 A. D., the second century.) This was based on the *Received Text*.
>
> (5) *Papyrus #66 used the Received Text.*
>
> (6) *The Italic Church in Northern Italy (157 A. D.) used the Received Text.*
>
> (7) *The Gallic Church of Southern France (177 A. D.) used the Received Text.*
>
> (8) *The Celtic Church in Great Britain used the Received Text.*

Why did all these have their Bibles based on the Received Text?--the churches in Italy, France, and Great Britain--why? Because that was the true Word of God, **and they knew it**. That was the *Received Text*. They lived in 150 A. D. The Bible was completed in 90-100 A. D. They had the originals right there in their hands and they based it on that which was pure, accurate, and preserved by God and by the Lord Jesus Christ Who preserves everything. These churches used this text and not any other. The heretics made most of the changes in the *Received Text* during this time; the greatest proportion of which, according to both Dr. Scrivener and Dean Burgon, were made during the first 100 years after they were originally written.

> (9) *Church of Scotland and Ireland used the Received Text.*
>
> (10) *The Pre-Waldensian churches used the Received Text.*

(11)   The Waldensians (120 A. D. and onward) used the Received Text.

c.   **Historical Evidences for the *Received Text* During the Byzantine Period (312--1453 A.D.)**

(12)   The Gothic Version of the 4th century used the Received Text.

(13)   Codex W of Matthew in the 4th or 5th century used the Received Text.

(14)   Codex A in the Gospels (in the 5th century) used the Received Text.

(15)   The vast majority of extant New Testament manuscripts all used the Received Text. This includes about 99% of them, or about 5,210 of the 5,255 MSS.

(16)   The Greek Orthodox Church used the Received Text.

We don't agree with many of their doctrines or practices, but that entire church for over 1,000 years has used the *Received Text.* Why? **They know the Greek language. They're Greeks.** Even though they are **modern** Greeks, they use the New Testament that is based upon the *Received Text* because it is the Word of God, and they know it.

(17)   The present Greek Church still uses the Received Text. When Mrs. Waite and I were in Israel, we visited the church which is supposed to be on the place where Jesus was born, the Church of the Nativity. They have a big Church built on the site. It doesn't look anything like the original place, I am certain. I don't even think it is on the proper place. They have commercialized it. In Jerusalem, they have Christ born in various places, crucified in various places, and buried in several places. In the Church of the Nativity, Christ's supposed birth place, we met a Greek Orthodox priest. I said to him, "You're a member of the Greek Orthodox clergy, is that right?" He said, "Yes," and then told us his name. I said, "You have a New Testament you use, don't you?" "Oh, yes," he said. I asked, "Which text do you use? Are you familiar with the so-called Westcott-and-Hort-type-text?" "Oh, yes," he said,

"We use the Received Text; we have no confidence at all in the Westcott and Hort text."

That was interesting. **The Greek Orthodox Church still goes back to this text that underlies the KING JAMES BIBLE.**

d.   **Historical Evidences for the *Received Text* During the**

Early Modern Period (1453--1831 A.D.)

(18) The churches of the Reformation all used the Received Text.

(19) The Erasmus Greek New Testament (1516) used the Received Text.

(20) The Complutensian Polyglot (1522) used the Received Text. A Roman Catholic Cardinal named Ximenes, edited it, yet it was based, **not** on the texts which most Roman Catholic Bibles used, the Westcott and Hort text, but on the *Received Text.*

(21) Martin Luther's German Bible (1522) used the Received Text.

(22) William Tyndale's Bible, (1525), used the Received Text. Tyndale was a great Bible translator who was martyred because of his Bible translation.

(23) The French Version of Oliveton (1535) used the Received Text.

(24) The Coverdale Bible (1535) used the Received Text.

(25) The Matthews Bible (1537) used the Received Text.

(26) The Taverners Bible (1539) used the Received Text.

(27) The Great Bible (1539-41) used the Received Text.

(28) The Stephanus Greek New Testament (1546-51) used the Received Text.

(29) The Geneva Bible (1557-60) used the Received Text.

(30) The Bishops' Bible (1568) used the Received Text.

(31) The Spanish Version (1569) used the Received Text.

(32) The Beza Greek New Testament (1598) used the Received Text. **That is the Greek text that the KING JAMES BIBLE was based on, using the 1598, 5th edition of Beza.**

(33) The Czech Version (1602) used the Received Text.

(34) The Italian Version of Diodati (1607) used the Received Text.

(35) The KING JAMES BIBLE (1611) used the Received Text.

(36) The Elzevir Brothers' Greek New Testament (1624) used the Received Text.

(37) The Received Text in the New Testament is the Received Text--the text that has survived in continuity from the beginning of the New Testament itself. It is the only accurate representation of the originals we have today!

In fact, <u>it is my own personal conviction and belief, after studying this subject since 1971, that the WORDS of the Received Greek and Masoretic Hebrew texts that underlie the KING JAMES BIBLE are the very WORDS which God has PRESERVED down through the centuries, being the exact WORDS of the ORIGINALS themselves</u>. As such, I believe they are **INSPIRED** WORDS. I believe they are **PRESERVED** WORDS. I believe they are **INERRANT** WORDS. I believe they are **INFALLIBLE** WORDS. This is why I believe so strongly that any valid translation MUST be based upon these original language texts, and these alone!

14. The Radical Text of Westcott and Hort. The *Received Text* was "received by all" until German Rationalism began to doubt it late in the 1700's and early in the 1800's. In 1881, Westcott and Hort came along with a new Greek text for the English Revised Version (ERV) of 1881. The *Received Text* was certainly accepted by the churches down through the corridor of history. But all at once, these two men had a powerful influence by means of Hort's *INTRODUCTION* to the Greek New Testament. This book, though based on pure untested hypothesis, swayed most people of the so-called scholarly world. Everything had to change. **The Received Greek Text was under fire**. At first, all the preachers **studied out of this false Greek text,** the Westcott-and-Hort-type text, or *Nestle/Aland* text but **preached out of the KING JAMES BIBLE** which was based on a different Greek text. This was a little **hypocritical**, but it didn't seem to bother those who practiced it. They'll do anything to keep the money and support of the fundamentalists who favor the KING JAMES BIBLE, perhaps.

But after a while the publishers began to get itchy palms. They wanted to make a little money, so they had to change that KING JAMES BIBLE. Also, some of the ones who were professors, teachers, preachers, and theologians said, in effect,

> *"Isn't it a little inconsistent to use this Westcott and Hort Greek text and still cling to the KING JAMES BIBLE which is not based on the same Greek text?"*

For many years I was told by various teachers at the Dallas Theological Seminary where I attended from 1948-53, to use the AMERICAN STANDARD VERSION of 1901 (not the NEW AMERICAN STANDARD VERSION of 1960, but the AMERICAN STANDARD VERSION of 1901). They pushed it and said it was the best version to use. I never got it through my head why it was better. They said, "Oh, it is better, for the KING JAMES is not as good, not as accurate." The reason they told me to use the AMERICAN STANDARD VERSION of 1901, was because it was based on the Westcott and Hort text. They were beginning to throw out the *Received Text,* and the KING JAMES. The AMERICAN STANDARD VERSION of 1901, never really got off the ground. People never really bought it. It was almost a dead issue from the start.

First, there was the ENGLISH REVISED VERSION of 1881 in England. Then there was the AMERICAN REVISED VERSION of 1898 (see APPENDIX B). After that, as an outgrowth of the ENGLISH REVISED VERSION OF 1881, this same Committee arranged for the AMERICAN STANDARD VERSION of 1901, in this country. It followed the Westcott and Hort text. But after a while other versions came out. The one that really began to shock and shake the world of the Evangelical Bible believers and fundamentalists was the NEW AMERICAN STANDARD VERSION of 1960. That is when everybody got into the act and said, in effect:

> *"Well, I guess the time has come to be logical and reasonable, to put the Greek text into the English and let us have the NEW AMERICAN STANDARD VERSION."*

But the way they sold it was **not** to admit they were changing the Greek in over 5,600 places, involving almost 10,000 words in the *Received Greek text* of the New Testament, **nor** to admit they were changing the *Masoretic Traditional Hebrew Text* and using something else. They didn't sell it on that basis. They sold it on the basis that you couldn't understand the KING JAMES BIBLE.

As far as READABILITY INDEX is concerned, here are some levels for the KING JAMES BIBLE based on the computer English program "RIGHT WRITER."

For Genesis 1	Readability = 8.13	8th Grade
For Exodus 1	Readability = 7.94	8th Grade
For Romans 1	Readability = 9.74	10th Grade
For Romans 3:1-23	Readability = 5.63	6th Grade
For Romans 8	Readability = 7.72	8th Grade

For Jude 1   Readability = 10.11   10th Grade
This certainly puts the lie to the charge that the KING JAMES BIBLE is too difficult to understand. This "RIGHT WRITER" readability index can be found out for any chapter or verse in the KJB.

The man who led me to the Lord Jesus Christ was a custodian in my High School, Uncle Charles Allen, who never went through the fifth grade. He understood the KING JAMES BIBLE and led me to Christ by using it when I was a High School senior. I know hundreds of people whose intelligence and educational levels have not reached as high as some of these high and mighty people who say they can't understand this KING JAMES BIBLE, yet these people do understand it. How do you figure that out? They say you can't understand it, that it is outmoded. Can't you understand John 3:16? Listen to it:

> *"For God so loved the world, that He gave His only begotten Son, that whosoever believeth in Him should not perish, but have everlasting life."*

What is difficult about that? I observed last Christmas-time that the retarded children from the SHEPHERD'S HOME, during their presentation of "*CHRISTMAS IS,*" memorized all of their Bible verses from the KING JAMES BIBLE. Why can't the rest of us understand it who go to grade school, elementary school, high school, college, graduate school, and/or seminary? But that was the way it was sold. Publishers said that the new translation makes the Bible so much easier to understand. Remember 1 Corinthians 2:14 which states:

> *"But the NATURAL MAN receiveth NOT the things of the Spirit of God: for they are FOOLISHNESS unto him: neither can he know them, because they are SPIRI-TUALLY DISCERNED."*

This verse is still true, regardless of which TRANSLATION is used!

15. How I Got the Thirty-seven Links of the *Textus Receptus* Together. There is an interesting background story of how I got together the thirty-seven historical links for the *Textus Receptus*. One of the deacons from a church in Michigan asked me to find this out for him. The pastor wanted to have a man who could represent the Received Text and the KING JAMES BIBLE, because his church was in the midst of a controversy over what Bible they should use. Some of the intelligentsia there wanted to introduce the NEW INTERNATIONAL VERSION into the church. The pastor had been there about twenty-three years and always preached from the KING JAMES BIBLE. He didn't want to change. These NIV people, who were teachers in the Christian school, began to foment trouble. So the Pastor said to the deacons, in effect:

"I don't often do this as pastor, but in this one instance I will do this: You can bring a man, whomever you want from Grand Rapids Baptist Seminary [which is a GARBC-approved school] *or wherever you want. He can talk to you deacons about the NEW INTERNATIONAL VERSION. Then I'll bring a man to talk about the Textus Receptus which underlies the Greek New Testament of the KING JAMES BIBLE. You deacons can listen to these men and then make up your minds and decide what this church is going to do."*

They agreed to that. Whatever the deacons would decide, that would be the way the church would go. There would be unity. So the pastor asked me to speak. I said I would be very glad to speak. There were about eight to ten deacons in the meeting. I talked to them for a while, and then opened up the meeting for questions and answers. They had some tough questions, but I gave them the answers as well as I could. First, they were going to get a man to precede me so I could be the last word (which I would rather have had). Do you know, with one excuse after another, the men from Grand Rapids Baptist Seminary refused to appear. They found out I was going to be the other side of the coin and some refused to speak. Finally, I spoke first. When their side was to show up, not one seminary man arrived, but two men. It took two of them to defend the NEW INTERNATIONAL VERSION and the Westcott and Hort Greek text. When I asked them for a tape so we could see what they said, what their reasons were, they wouldn't give me a tape. These two men from GRAND RAPIDS BAPTIST COLLEGE AND SEMINARY didn't want me to have a tape of anything they said. Do you suppose I could have answered all their arguments? I would hope so! When all was said and done, the deacons recommended that the church use only the KING JAMES BIBLE in all of its meetings, including the Sunday School classes. Praise the Lord! The truth (and that is what I believe we gave them) won out, at least for a while.

We're going to have battles like this all over the country. Some churches have been splitting over what Bible to use. There are many preachers who don't know what to do. They are in a quandary. They are divided between one version or another. Their church can't read a Scripture verse in unison. They have to go to the hymnbook to get something they can read together, because one will read one version and another read a different one. A lot of pastors are sweeping it under the rug, hoping it will go away. It won't go away. The issue is before us. **The KING JAMES BIBLE is the Word of God in English and the other versions are not. That is the simple truth.**

16. The *Textus Receptus* Is Attested by the Evidence. Let us see how the *Textus Receptus* is attested by the evidence. We've said that it was accepted by the churches, but what about the evidence? What evidence do we have that we can trust that this is the preserved Greek New Testament text from which we should translate our New Testament Bibles? The evidence is divided into three groups: (1) Manuscripts, (2) Ancient Versions, and (3) Church Fathers' writings.

a. The Evidence of the MANUSCRIPTS. As of 1967, the Greek manuscripts which have survived numbered 5,255. Kurt Aland, who is an apostate German, working in Munster, Germany, doesn't believe in the *Received Text*. His name is on the *Nestle/Aland text*. He was the chairman of the editors. He has copies of many manuscripts, most of them in microfilm, (about 90% of the total available, according to one source). But every time Aland comes to a manuscript that goes along with the *Received Text,* he disregards and says it is just a copy of some other text and is not to be counted as a separate witness or as valuable. That is how Aland and his followers deal with evidence. They don't take things at face value. When they find a manuscript that agrees with the *Received Text,* they say it has been doctored, "mimeographed," or duplicated. Therefore, the number of texts that agree with this are not 500, 1,000, or over 5,000, but just **one** witness.

Aland and his followers accept the false explanation of Hort and Westcott to the effect that there was a meeting in the early church (250-350 A.D.) of all the church leaders then living. They believe, though there is not one shred of historical evidence to support this hypothesis, that these church leaders made up a revision or recension of the Greek text in which, allegedly but falsely, all the Greek manuscripts that went along with the Westcott-and-Hort-type text were thrown out and all that went along with the *Textus Receptus* were kept. They say that everything from then on was a repetition, just like a mimeographed copy. With the result that the *Received Text* manuscripts that have survived are thought to be, NOT independent witnesses (which, in fact, they are), but only carbon copies of but ONE witness. This theory has one problem, that is, it is just a THEORY. There is **no proof** that such a meeting or recension ever took place. Something that stupendous, where they would have called all the bishops and church fathers from all areas of the then-known world to a meeting in 250 A.D. or 350 A.D., should have left a record.

But that is the concoction Hort dreamed up. He had to account for the fact that in upwards of 99% or more of the 5,255 manuscripts that we have in our hand, the evidence points to the *Received Text,* not to either the Westcott-and-Hort-type of text or the *Nestle/Aland 26th-Edition-type Greek Text.* Hort would have to say to himself in effect:

"How are we going to counter that? How are we going to account for the fact that just a mere 45 documents out of 5,255, or less than 1% of the evidence now in our possession conforms with our text, while all the other evidence agrees with the Received Text? Let us concoct a theory with no proof necessary. Let's say the church leaders got together and made up a recension, a text that is made to our specifications. After making it, let us say these church leaders threw out all the others and just kept their own, thus making but one recension or revision of the Greek New Testament."

That is the gist of what Hort wrote in his *INTRODUCTION.* It is just as false as the day is long, but people bought it. In the back of this *Nestle/Aland text* there is a list of manuscripts and documents that are cited in my copy of their 26th edition, on page 711. There are about 562 manuscripts on this page. A footnote at the bottom of the page says, in Latin, **"and many others."** All of them, since they go along with this *Received Text,* are counted by Westcott and Hort and Aland as only one witness since they believe there was this special recension and all the manuscripts that agree closely are merely carbon copies of that one recension. Again, there is NO evidence whatsoever in the history of the church that this ever took place! It must be considered false, therefore. It is a mere theory and hypothesis.

What about the manuscripts? What kinds are there? There are four kinds of Greek manuscripts that we have in our possession today: (1) papyri, (2) uncials, (3) cursives, and (4) lectionaries.

(1) **Papyrus Fragment Manuscripts.** The first kind of manuscript is the papyrus fragment. These are small pieces of papyrus. Papyrus is a kind of paper made out of the papyrus plant which grows plentifully in Egypt. It is brittle. Most papyri don't have many verses on

them. There were eighty-one of them as of 1967. Now they have eighty-eight. Of the eighty-eight, according to an estimate by Pastor Jack Moorman in his book, *Forever Settled*, only about thirteen (15%) go along with "B" and Aleph, the Westcott and Hort text; about seventy-five (85%) of the eighty-eight go along with the *Received Text.* [B.F.T. #1428]

(2) **Uncial Manuscripts.** Uncials are Greek manuscripts written in capital letters which run together. There are no punctuation marks and no spaces between the letters. There are some old uncials and there are some more recent ones. They are also called majuscules. Uncials means "large or inch-long letters." There are 267 uncials. Only nine of these 267 go along with the Westcott and Hort text (only 3%). But 258 of the 267 (97%) go along with the *Received Text.* By the way, when Westcott and Hort saw that only nine of the 267 uncials lined up with their text, they decided to use only the old uncials, *A, B, Aleph, C* and *D.* These are called old uncials, from the 4th century up to the 6th century. What about the others? They left them out completely because they didn't prove their point or support their Greek text.

(3) **Cursive Manuscripts.** Cursives (or minuscules) are Greek manuscripts written in longhand, or cursive. Their letters flow together as our own "cursive" writing does today. There are 2,764 of them preserved for us today. Only twenty-three of those go along with the Westcott and Hort text (1%). 2,741 (99%) go along with the *Received Text* that underlies our KING JAMES BIBLE. That is a huge number of documents favoring the *Received Text.* That is why Hort had to make up his "recension" theory, which was a tissue of lies that has no historical support behind it. He had to account for this discrepancy, even if it meant resorting to colossal deception and falsehood!

(4) **Lectionary Manuscripts.**   There are 2,143 lectionaries.   "Lection" comes from a Latin root meaning "to read." Lectionaries were portions of Scripture in the Greek and Latin Bibles, that were read in the churches on certain days. All (100%) of them go along with the *Received Text* which underlies the KING JAMES BIBLE. There are none that support the Westcott-and-Hort-type text. In the Roman Catholic Church and the Greek Orthodox Church they do the same today. They read a certain portion from the Gospels, and a certain portion from the Epistles on specific days. In those days, they took the Bibles they had, and marked them up to make the lections, the exact portion which should be read for that day. Those lectionaries are good evidence to show what manuscripts they had at that time. They either put together a lectionary

themselves or they had a whole Greek New Testament and marked off these special portions to show which should be read on what day. So the 2,143 lectionaries are powerful evidence for the *Received Text*.

THE LAST TWELVE VERSES OF MARK, is the title of a book by Dean John William Burgon, written in 1871. It contains over 350 pages, and has been reprinted by the BIBLE FOR TODAY. [B.F.T. #1139] We have reprinted almost 3,000 pages of books by or about Dean Burgon. He was a scholar who defended the Traditional Text which underlies our KING JAMES BIBLE. This book contains overwhelming evidence, from manuscripts, lectionaries, ancient versions, and the church fathers, proving that the last twelve verses of Mark (Mark 16:9-20) are genuine. These verses have been taken out of the Westcott and Hort text. That is one of the 5,604 places (involving almost 10,000 words) that are changed. A black line is put between this section and the foregoing verses in the NEW INTERNATIONAL VERSION with a note reading:

"[The two most reliable early manuscripts do not have Mark 16:9-20.]"

They also put in a footnote in the NEW AMERICAN STANDARD VERSION which questions the authenticity of these verses. But these twelve verses are a lection, one of the Scripture portions that was read by the "Melchite Syrian Christians as well as by the Greeks" on the 2nd Sunday after Easter. Burgon goes into that and proves beyond any question that this was the reason a few manuscripts dropped this section out. He also shows that the portion before Mark 16:9-20 (verses 1-8) was also a lection or a reading. At the beginning of verse 9 there is the word, *telos*, meaning "end." Some people took this to mean that was the end of Mark's Gospel. It doesn't mean that at all. It meant that was the end of the lection portion. In this case, it was the reading from Mark 15:43 through 16:1-8. This lection was read on the second Sunday after Easter [cf. Burgon, *THE LAST TWELVE VERSES OF MARK*, pp. 226, 238. [See page 238 for the other times these verses were read as a lection]. So lectionaries bear strong testimony in favor of the *Received Text*. In chart form, here is the manuscript evidence for the *Received Text* (TR) and for that of Westcott and Hort's or the *Nestle/Aland's* text (WH):

	TOTALS	# of MSS WH/TR	% of MSS WH/TR
Papyrus Fragments	81(88)	13/75	15%/85%
Uncials	267	9/258	3%/97%
Cursives	2764	23/2741	1%/99%
Lectionaries	2143	0/2143	0%/100%
TOTALS:	5255	45/5210	1%/99%

b. The Evidence of the Ancient Versions. The ancient versions are translations of the Greek Bible from the early days. For instance, the Peshitto Syriac, second century, about 150 A.D., is mostly based on the *Received Text.* The Curetonian Syriac, third century, is basically the *Received Text.* The Old Latin, or *Vetus Itala*, second century A. D. is from the *Received Text.* In the other versions we have, some take the *Received Text,* some do not. **But these are evidences.**

c. The Evidence of the Church Fathers. The Church Fathers were old church writers such as bishops and pastors who wrote letters to the churches in the early days of the church. In the course of their writings, they often alluded to verses of Scripture that were found in their Greek or Latin New Testament, They either quoted the verses verbatim, or made reference in some way to the verses. From some of those allusions, you can tell what kind of Bible text they had in their hand. Was it the Westcott and Hort reading, or was it the *Received Text?*

Dean John William Burgon, is the author of these five books which we have reprinted: (1) *REVISION REVISED* [B.F.T. #611], (2) *THE LAST 12 VERSES OF MARK* [B.F.T. #1139], (3) *THE TRADITIONAL TEXT OF THE HOLY GOSPELS* [B.F.T. #1159], (4) *CAUSES OF CORRUPTION OF THE HOLY GOSPELS* [B.F.T. #1160], and (5) *INSPIRATION AND INTERPRETATION* [B.F.T. #1220].

In these books, Burgon goes into great detail on the matter of the Church Fathers. Before he died in 1888, Dean Burgon and his staff amassed more then 86,000 quotations or allusions to Scripture by the Church Fathers. This documentation still exists today in the British Museum Library. The research is contained in sixteen large folio volumes. One of the members of our Dean Burgon Society Executive Committee, Dr. Jack Moorman, a missionary in England, gave me a report on these volumes in his letter of January 10, 1992. He wrote that each of the sixteen volumes was about ten inches by twelve and one half inches in size. They are five inches to seven inches thick. You can well imagine the hundreds of hours that went into that research on the part of Burgon and his staff to produce sixteen volumes of that size. It is unfortunate that these were not published in a more permanent manner. They are in handwritten form only. Dr. Moorman wrote:

> "They are . . . an _index_ to quotations in _other_ works, mainly that of J. P. Migne. The volumes are all references: there are no quotations from the Fathers. . . . The references are handwritten on small slips and pasted on the pages in Biblical order under a given Father. Each slip contains the chapter and verse of the Scripture, followed by the volume and page in a patristic edition where that text is quoted. I assume that there are some 86,000 slips in the sixteen volumes. . ."

This letter was a valuable report on the present status of this research on the Church Fathers and their allusions to the New Testament Scriptures.

The quotations showed what kind of Greek text the Church Fathers were using. There were many allusions made to the Received or Traditional Text. From 100-300 A. D. there were approximately 100 Church Fathers who wrote extensively and referred in some way to the New Testament verses. From 300-600 A. D. there were approximately 200 Fathers who wrote extensively. So there are 300 Church Fathers who wrote from 100 A.D. to 600 A.D. You can quite often look at the writings and see which text they had in their hands, whether the _Received Text_ or the so-called Neologian text of B and Aleph favored by Westcott and Hort.

Edward Miller edited Burgon's work, because Burgon died before he could complete his massive study on the New Testament text. In 1896, Miller published two of Burgon's books, one of which was _THE TRADI-TIONAL TEXT OF THE HOLY GOSPELS._ In it is a list of Church Fathers who quoted different portions of the _Received Text_ and a list of those who quoted from the Westcott-and-Hort-type text. This list (pages 99-100) is of seventy-six writers who died before 400 A. D. and shows the impressive number of quotations from the Traditional Text. Miller found that not only (1) there **WERE** quotations from the Traditional Text (_Received Text_) from Church Fathers who died in 400 A.D. or before; but also (2) the Traditional Text quotations were **IN THE MAJORITY** over those favoring the "neologian" (Westcott-Hort-type) text; and also (3) the Traditional Text quotations were in the **RATIO OF 3 TO 2** in their favor! Of a total of 4,383 quotations from the seventy-six Church Fathers who died before 400 A.D., there were 2,630 (60%) of the quotations from the Traditional or *Received Text* and only 1,753 (40%) of the quotations from the neologian or Westcott-Hort-type of text. This is a ratio of 3 to 2 or 1.5 to 1 in favor of the Traditional or *Received Text*. Today, writers of the Westcott and Hort school frequently make the false statement that there are NO references to the Traditional or *Received Text* before the fourth century. These figures certainly prove them in error.

Dr. Moorman's sixth book on the subject of the New Testament text was entitled *Early Church Fathers And The Authorized Version--A Demonstration--Companion Volume To Early Manuscripts And The Authorized Version.* [B.F.T. #2136] This is an excellent book that our readers will want to acquire. He used a more recent reference source for both the Nicene and Post-Nicene Church Fathers. He examined eighty-six different works from Church Fathers who died from 110 to 397 A.D. (before 400 A.D.). He compared 401 Scripture quotations cited in the Digest source. He found 279 to refer to the *Textus Receptus* and only 114 or 122 to refer to the B and Aleph (or Westcott/Hort or *Nestle/Aland)* type of text. This is a ratio of 2.3 to 1 as over against 1.5 to 1 found by Burgon and Miller--a much higher ratio! We appreciate Pastor Moorman's excellent scholarship in New Testament textual matters.

17. An Evaluation of Manuscripts "B" and "Aleph." The big two manuscripts that the Westcott and Hort people rely upon are *B* and *Aleph. B* is the Vatican manuscript; *Aleph* is the Sinai manuscript. These are presumably fourth century uncials which had very little, if any, use by their owners. I believe this was true because the owners recognized them to be perverted texts, having been defaced and polluted by heretics and others. Westcott & Hort and their followers say B and Aleph are superior merely because they are the oldest and therefore purest. Well, they are neither the best nor the purest. They were corrupted by the heretics. One reason they were preserved is they were in Egypt where the climate was conducive to their survival. The second reason they were preserved is that they were not used by the church because they realized they were full of heretical changes. These copies happened to escape the burnings and persecutions in the early church, perhaps, by being hidden away through disuse and not out in the open. **If they had been used, they would have been worn out like my Bible, which is just about in tatters.** My wife gave it to me in 1947, the year before we were married. I'm using it, and have had it rebound several times. When you use a book constantly, it tatters and tears.

The Vatican manuscript (B) was stored in the Vatican library. The Sinai manuscript (Aleph) was found in the wastepaper basket at St. Catherine's Monastery. They were getting ready to burn it to keep warm for the winter. There was a very comical expression that my fellow debater used when we were debating Dr. Stuart Custer of Bob Jones University on the Greek manuscripts. Dr. James Qurollo had a very interesting way of putting it. Tischendorf was the one who bought this manuscript from St. Catherine's Monastery. He was a German apostate scholar who was working on the New Testament. He bought it for hundreds and hundreds of dollars from the monks who were getting ready to burn it. Dr. Qurollo said,

"I don't know which of them had the truer evaluation of its worth--Tischendorf, who wanted to buy it, or the monks, who were getting ready to burn it!"

He had to pay for the trash. It really was that, because of all the heretics' changes. After he found this Sinai or Aleph manuscript in the wastebasket, Tischendorf went back and altered his old editions of the Greek New Testament in hundreds of places, completely revolutionizing it after he had completed it. Burgon's *Revision Revised* has an excellent analysis of the defects both of B (Vatican) and Aleph (Sinai). Another excellent analysis of the defects of B and Aleph can be found in a book by Cecil J. Carter entitled *The Oldest And Best Manuscripts--How Good Are They?* [B.F.T. #1733] He cites Tischendorf as reporting that Aleph contained "**15,000 changes made by contemporary or later hands**" (p. 10). Consider the defects that must have abounded in Aleph to need 15,000 changes by various correctors!

Hort, in his *INTRODUCTION* to their new Greek text of 1881, said that the readings of B and Aleph, where they agreed, were the true readings of the New Testament. If they did not agree, then any binary (or combination of two) readings of B with one other manuscript would be the true reading. If they could not find any other manuscript to agree with B (Vatican), then B alone would be sufficient to establish the true reading. It is quite evident that they had a strong prejudice in favor of B. H. C. Hoskier's two volume book on *CODEX B AND ITS ALLIES* has been reprinted by the BIBLE FOR TODAY. [B.F.T. #1643] Hoskier's very technical comparison of B with Aleph showed these two corrupt manuscripts to be in contradiction one with the other in **over 3,000 places in the Gospels alone!** In other words, if B is right, Aleph is wrong. If Aleph is right, B is wrong. It is quite possible, in these instances, that

NEITHER B nor Aleph is correct.

It is mainly the Vatican manuscript (B) which Westcott and Hort relied upon. It was supposedly written in 350 to 375 A. D. They just about worshiped that manuscript. Burgon and Miller came along, with over 86,000 quotations from the Church Fathers, many of which antedated either B or Aleph. Dr. Moorman did further research along the same lines, as mentioned above. If indeed the "oldest is the best," Westcott and Hort are beaten at their own game. The Church Fathers thereby demolish the arguments of B and Aleph of the 4th century because the Fathers go back before even the 4th century and bear witness to a much earlier text than either B or Aleph. As mentioned above, Burgon and Miller cited seventy-six Church Fathers who wrote and who died before 400 A.D. Irenaeus, for example, lived around 150 A. D. Pastor Moorman cited eighty-six Church Fathers who wrote and died before 400 A.D. Ignatius, for example, died in 110 A.D. All three of his quotations were from the Traditional or *Textus Receptus* type of text. The Westcott and Hort people say a manuscript is bad because it is not old enough. They also erroneously boast that there are no *Textus Receptus* readings before 400 A.D. Yet the above evidence proves this to be in error. Not only were readings found from the Traditional Text, but they were found to be in the MAJORITY of cases. In other words, more than half were from the *Received Text* rather than the Westcott-and-Hort-type text. Not only did they find the Traditional Text readings to be in the MAJORITY, but to be in a PREPONDERANCE of cases, either 1.5 to 1 (Burgon & Miller) or 2.3 to 1 (Moorman) in favor of the Traditional Text rather than just a simple majority! So this is a powerful argument.

Of course Hort had an argument explaining **why** the Church Fathers quoted the *Received Text* more than their preferred text of B and Aleph. He claimed falsely that the editions of the Church Fathers were altered also, just like he claims the Greek manuscripts were altered in the years of about 250 to 350 A. D. As in the case of the false recension of the Greek New Testament, so in the case of the Church Fathers' recension, there is not a particle of evidence to prove that this ever took place! It is pure hypothesis and speculation on his part. Hort had an answer for everything, however spurious, erroneous, and bereft of a single shred of evidence or proof. The leaders of the Baptists, Presbyterians, Southern Baptists in Louisville, and many others, fell hook, line, and sinker for Hort's specious arguments. They were thoroughly deceived by a master deceiver and apostate. They apparently did not know enough to check out the evidence for themselves. They just accepted what Westcott and Hort dogmatically asserted with no proof whatever. They accepted this fanciful theory uncritically, and the entire church has been suffering for it ever since.

Basically, I would like to say that the New Testament foundation or basis for our Greek New Testament which underlies our KING JAMES BIBLE was definitely authorized and accepted by the churches down through the centuries, attested by the evidence, and therefore absolutely worthy of being trusted and believed by us today or in any future age!

CHAPTER III

THE KING JAMES BIBLE IS GOD'S WORDS KEPT INTACT IN ENGLISH BECAUSE OF ITS SUPERIOR TRANSLATORS

A. THE SOURCES ABOUT THE KING JAMES TRANSLATORS.

Now, let us look at the SUPERIOR TRANSLATORS of the KING JAMES BIBLE. As 1 Corinthians 3:9 says in part: ". . . let every man take heed **HOW HE BUILDETH** on that foundation." On the back of the paper on *HOW AND WHEN WOULD DEAN BURGON REVISE THE TEXTUS RECEPTUS AND THE KING JAMES BIBLE,* [**B.F.T.** #804] we have a partial analysis of the linguistic qualifications of some of the KING JAMES translators. We based this analysis on the book by Alexander McClure, *TRANSLATORS REVIVED.* It is the history of the KING JAMES translators, with biographical notes. The book has been out of print for a long time, but we have reprinted it. [**B.F.T.** #1419]

THE MEN BEHIND THE KING JAMES VERSION by Gustavus S. Paine, put out by Baker Book House, is also a good book on how the KING JAMES BIBLE came about. [**B.F.T.** #584] It gives a good background of our KING JAMES BIBLE. It has gone out of print, been put back in print, gone out of print, and then returned to print several times. Each time I call Baker Book House and request that it be put back into print. So far, we have been successful. It is in print as of now.

B. THE SPIRITUAL INSIGHT OF THE KING JAMES TRANSLATORS.

Frequently, as I have been in various churches speaking about the "FOURFOLD SUPERIORITY OF THE KING JAMES BIBLE," when we come to the division of the "SUPERIOR TRANSLATORS," I have been asked about the spiritual qualification and insight of the King James translators. Because of this, I want to quote from a firsthand source on this, namely, *THE TRANSLATORS TO THE READER,* being the introductory remarks to be found in the original 1611 KING JAMES BIBLE. Though it was written by one of the translators, it had the approval of them all. [**B.F.T.** #1121] I will cite the page references as put out in our Life Tract edition (forty-five pages in all), but will use the spelling of Dr. Scrivener's edition.

1. The Need for Reading the Scriptures. The KING JAMES BIBLE translators believed people needed to read the Bible. They wrote:
> "But now what piety without truth? What truth (what saving truth) without the word of God? What word of God (whereof we may be sure) without the Scripture? The Scriptures we are commanded to search. (John 5:39; Isaiah 8:20) They are commended that searched and studied them. (Acts 17:11 and 8:28-29) They are reproved that were unskilful in them, or slow to believe them. (Matthew 22:29; Luke 24:25) They can make us wise unto salvation. (2 Timothy 3:15) If we be ignorant, they will instruct us; if out of the way, they will bring us home; if out of order, they will reform us; if in heaviness, comfort us; if dull, quicken us; if cold, inflame us. Tolle, lege; tolle, lege. Take up and read, take up and read the Scriptures. . . ." (p. 10)

2. What the Scriptures Are and What They Can Do. The KING JAMES BIBLE translators had insight as to what the Bible is. They wrote:
> "Well, that which they falsely or vainly attributed to these things for bodily good, we may justly and with full measure ascribe unto the Scripture for spiritual. It is not only an armour, but also a whole armoury of weapons, both offensive and defensive; whereby we may save ourselves, and put the enemy to flight. It is not an herb, but a tree, or rather a whole paradise of trees of life, which bring forth fruit every month, and the fruit thereof is for meat, and the leaves for medicine. It is not a pot of Manna or a cruse of oil, which were for memory only, or for a meal's meat or two; but as it were a shower of heavenly bread sufficient for a whole host, be it never so great, and as it were a whole cellar full of oil vessels; whereby all our necessities may be provided for, and our debts discharged. In a word, it is a panary of wholesome food against fenowed

[mouldy] *traditions; a physician's shop (Saint Basil calleth it) of preservatives against poisoned heresies; a pandect of profitable laws against rebellious spirits; a treasury of most costly jewels against beggarly rudiments; finally, a fountain of most pure water springing up unto everlasting life. And what marvel? the original thereof being from heaven, not from earth, the author being God, not man; the inditer, the Holy Spirit, not the wit of the Apostles or Prophets; the penmen, such as were sanctified from the womb, and endued with a principal portion of God's Spirit; the matter, verity, piety, purity, uprightness; the form, God's word, God's testimony, God's oracles, the word of truth, the word of salvation, etc.; the effects, light of understanding, stableness of persuasion, repentance from dead works, newness of life, holiness, peace, joy in the Holy Ghost; lastly, the end and reward of the study thereof, fellowship with the saints, participation of the heavenly nature, fruition of an inheritance immortal, undefiled, and that never shall fade away: Happy is the man that delighteth in the Scriptures, and thrice happy that meditateth in it day and night."* (pp. 11-12).

3. The Need for Proper Translation of the Scriptures. The KING JAMES BIBLE translators saw the need for proper translation of the Bible. They wrote:

"Translation it is that openeth the window, to let in the light; that breaketh the shell, that we may eat the kernel; that putteth aside the curtain, that we may look into the most holy place; that removeth the cover of the well, that we may come by the water; even as Jacob rolled away the stone from the mouth of the well by which means the flocks of Laban were watered. (Genesis 29:10) Indeed without translation into the vulgar tongue, the unlearned are but like children at Jacob's well (which was deep) without a bucket or something to

draw with: (John 4:12) or as that person mentioned by Isaiah, to whom when a sealed book was delivered with this motion, Read this, I pray thee, he was fain to make this answer, I cannot, for it is sealed. (Isaiah 29:11)." (pp. 12-13)

4. **The Urgency of Reading and Heeding the Scriptures.** The KING JAMES translators closed their notes "TO THE READER" by writing:

"It remaineth that we commend thee to God, and to the Spirit of his grace, which is able to build further than we can ask or think. He removeth the scales from our eyes, the vail from our hearts, opening our wits that we may understand his word, enlarging our hearts, yea, correcting our affections, that we may love it above gold and silver, yea, that we may love it to the end. Ye are brought unto fountains of living water which ye digged not; (Genesis 16:15 and Jeremiah 2:13) do not cast earth into them, with the Philistines, neither prefer broken pits before them, with the wicked Jews. Others have laboured, and you may enter into their labours. O receive not so great things in vain: O despise not so great salvation. Be not like swine to tread under foot so precious things, neither yet like dogs to tear and abuse holy things. Say not to our Saviour with the Gergesites, Depart out of our coasts; (Matthew 8:34) neither yet with Esau sell your birthright for mess of pottage. (Hebrews 12:16) If light be come into the world, love not darkness more than light: if food, if clothing, be offered, go not naked, starve not yourselves. . . . It is a fearful thing to fall into the hands of the living God; (Hebrews 10:31) but a blessed thing it is, and will bring us to everlasting blessedness in the end, when God speaketh unto us, to hearken; when he setteth his word before us, to read it; when he stretcheth out his hand and calleth, to answer, Here am I, here we are to do thy will, O God. The Lord work a care and conscience in us to know him and serve him, that we may be

acknowledged of him at the appearing of our Lord Jesus
Christ, to whom with the Holy Ghost, be all praise and
thanksgiving. Amen." (p. 28)

Certainly, it must be agreed that these men who translated the KING
JAMES BIBLE had spiritual insight and depth. They were far from cold
intellectuals without a heart for the Words of the Lord and the Lord of the
Words.

C. THE GROUPINGS AND LOCATIONS OF THE KING JAMES TRANSLATORS.

Here's the way the men who translated the KING JAMES BIBLE
were grouped according to *THE MEN BEHIND THE KING JAMES*
VERSION, pp. 184-185. There were a total of six companies. They met
in the three cities of Cambridge, Westminster, and Oxford. The
translators began their work in 1604, and finished it in 1611, a total of
seven years. They had an Old Testament and a New Testament company
at Westminster. In Oxford they had a company for the Old Testament
and one for the New Testament. In Cambridge they had a company for
the Old Testament and one for the Apocrypha. Though they translated
the twelve to fourteen books of the Apocrypha in the original KING
JAMES BIBLE, the translators did NOT believe these were inspired.
They translated them only as history between the Old and the New
Testament. In fact, a clear statement about the Apocrypha is in the Creed
of the Anglican Church, the *Thirty-Nine Articles*. That church does not
believe the Apocrypha is canonical Scripture nor inspired by God.

Dr. John Reynolds was the one who addressed KING JAMES to
ask him to begin the KING JAMES BIBLE. He said:

"May your Majesty be pleased . . . to direct that the
Bible be now translated, such versions as are now
extant [still in existence] *not answering to the origi-*
nal."

They wanted one that did answer to the original Hebrew and Greek.
Reynolds was a Puritan. There were other Puritans also who worked on
the committee in addition to John Reynolds. Most of the translators,
however, were non-Puritan members of the Church of England.

There were up to fifty-seven men altogether that worked in six
companies or groups. Not all of the men were present at all times during
the translation. On an average, there were about seven or eight men per

group. Some of the men died before they finished the translation. But the question we want to take up is why do we believe the KING JAMES TRANSLATORS were superior? McClure gives us a good history of these men together with a brief synopsis of their linguistic superiority and ability. I would like to show you some of the linguistic qualifications of three of the men who translated the Old Testament, two who translated the New Testament, and a few highlights about some of the other translators. For more information about many of the other KING JAMES TRANSLA- TORS and their linguistic qualifications that fitted them supremely for their translation task, see McClure's book, or our summary found in our **B.F.T. #804,** *WHEN AND HOW WOULD DEAN BURGON REVISE THE TEXTUS RECEPTUS AND THE KING JAMES BIBLE,* beginning at p. 40.

D. THREE SUPERIOR KING JAMES OLD TESTAMENT TRANSLATORS.

    1. The Accomplishments of Lancelot Andrews. First we will consider the Old Testament translators of the KING JAMES BIBLE and the accomplishments of Dr. Lancelot Andrews. He was the president or director of the Westminster group that translated twelve books altogether, from Genesis to 2 Kings. That was the task of Company One.

    a. **First** of all, he acquired most of the modern languages of Europe at the University of Cambridge. He gave himself chiefly to the Oriental tongues and to divinity [this is from *TRANSLATORS REVIVED* by Alexander McClure, p. 78].

    b. **Second,** Lancelot Andrews' manual for his private devotions, prepared by himself, is wholly in the Greek language. You can see the man was accomplished. Many Christians today don't even have private daily devotions. Of those who do, how many do you know who have made up private devotions manuals? And of the people who have made up private devotions manuals, how many do you know who have written them wholly in the Greek language? This most certainly indicates a linguistic **superiority.** [*op. cit.,* p. 86]

    c. **Third,** "Such was his skill in all languages, especially the Oriental, that had he been present at the confusion of tongues at Babel, he might have served as *interpreter-general."* [*op. cit.,* p. 86] That is a great statement, isn't it?

    d. **Fourth,** "In his funeral sermon by Dr. Buckeridge, Bishop of Rochester, it is said that Dr. Andrews was conversant with

FIFTEEN LANGUAGES." [*op. cit.*, p. 87] Certainly he was a respected and superior translator. I don't know of any of these modern translators of the AMERICAN STANDARD VERSION, NEW AMERICAN STANDARD VERSION, NEW INTERNATIONAL VERSION, NEW ENGLISH VERSION, etc. who are conversant with as many as fifteen languages, do you?

2. The Acumen of William Bedwell. Dr. William Bedwell was also in Company One, the Westminster group translating the books of Genesis through 2 Kings from the Hebrew into the English. Let us note a few things about him:

a. **First,** he was justly reputed to be "an eminent Oriental scholar."

b. **Second,** his fame for Arabic learning was so great that scholars sought him out for assistance. To him belongs, as McClure stated:

> *"the honor of being the first who considerably promoted and revived the study of the Arabic language and literature in Europe." [op. cit., p. 101]*

c. **Third,** in Antwerp, in 1612, he published in *quarto* an edition of the Epistles of St. John in Arabic with a Latin version. Now, I don't know anything about Arabic, but to have an edition of 1, 2, and 3rd John with Latin and Arabic would take a tremendously capable scholar, a capable BUILDER of this building, the KING JAMES BIBLE.

d. **Fourth,** he also left many Arabic manuscripts in the University of Cambridge, with numerous notes and a font of types for printing them.

e. **Fifth,** for many years he was engaged in compiling an Arabic lexicon in three volumes [a lexicon is a dictionary]. [*op. cit.*, pp. 100-101]

f. **Sixth,** as McClure wrote:

> *"Some modern scholars [in 1857 when McClure wrote his book] have fancied we have an advantage in our times over the translators of the KING JAMES days of 1611 by reason of the greater attention which is supposed to be paid at present [in 1857] to what are called the 'COGNATE' and 'Shemitic' languages, especially the Arabic, by which much light is thought to be reflected on Hebrew words and phrases. It is*

evident, however, that Mr. Bedwell and others among his fellow laborers, were THOROUGHLY CONVERSANT in this part of the broad field of sacred criticism."

g. **Seventh,** Dr. Bedwell also began a Persian dictionary, which is among Archbishop Laud's manuscripts still preserved in the Bodleian Library at Oxford. [*op. cit.*, pp. 101-102]

This William Bedwell, with his Arabic, Persian, and other Oriental languages, was greatly **superior** to our modern translators. Many modern "translators" come up to a word, and in a footnote somewhere. or in an index at the bottom of the page, they'll say the meaning of this Hebrew word is uncertain; so they have some other rendition of it. Well, the meaning of it is uncertain, perhaps, to these men who were living in 1960, when the NASV came out, in 1969, when the NIV came out or in 1979, when the New KING JAMES came out; but these men who translated the KING JAMES BIBLE knew their cognate languages well. They understood these references and there was no question in their minds about what most of these words meant. It is a strange thing; yet people doubt and question the authenticity, **superiority,** and the knowledge of these KING JAMES TRANSLATORS. Cognate languages are simply sister languages related to Hebrew like Arabic, Persian, Syriac, Aramaic, Coptic, and so on. They are related like brother and sister.

A word may not be clear, or maybe the word is what they call a *hapaxlegomenon*. *Hapax* means "once" and *legomenon* means "spoken or written." This particular word was used only once in all the New Testament Greek or Old Testament Hebrew. So it is difficult to tell sometimes what these *hapaxlegomena* (in the plural) mean. They go to other sources to try to understand the meaning. The translators of the KING JAMES, who knew Arabic, Persian, Aramaic, Coptic, and all the various cognate languages, could go to these languages and understand very clearly. But the men living today, because they don't know these cognate languages as well [they don't know fifteen languages like Andrews for example], just throw up their hands and say the meaning of the Hebrew is not certain.

3. The Acceptability of Miles Smith. Dr. Miles Smith was in Company Three, the Oxford Group. That group translated a total of seventeen books, from Isaiah through Malachi. Here is some of the background on Dr. Smith:

a. **First**, he was one of the twelve translators selected to revise the work after it was referred to them for the final examination.

b. **Second**, Dr. Smith was employed to write that most learned and eloquent preface to the KING JAMES BIBLE.

c. **Third**, he went through the Greek and Latin Fathers, making his annotations on them all. There were 100 Church Fathers that wrote extensively from 100 to 300 A. D. There were 200 more who wrote from 300 to 600 A. D. He read through all of them in Greek and Latin and made his own comments on each of them.

d. **Fourth**, he was well acquainted with the Rabbinical glosses and comments. These are marginal comments in the Hebrew language.

e. **Fifth**, so expert was he in the Chaldee (which is related to the Hebrew), the Syriac and the Arabic, that they were almost as familiar as his native tongue.

f. **Sixth**, Hebrew, he had at his finger's ends. An extremely proficient man, and certainly SUPERIOR in his qualifications to translate our KING JAMES BIBLE. [*op. cit.*, pp. 141-43]

D. TWO SUPERIOR KING JAMES NEW TESTAMENT TRANSLATORS.

Let us take a look at the **superiority** of two of the New Testament translators of the KING JAMES BIBLE.

1. The Activities of Henry Savile. Sir Henry Savile was in Company Four, the Oxford group. That group had the task of translating six books: the Gospels, Acts, and Revelation. Here is some of the background on Henry Savile:

a. **First**, he became, very early, famous for his Greek and mathematical learning.

b. **Second**, he became tutor in Greek and Mathematics to Queen Elizabeth.

c. **Third**, he translated the histories of Cornelius Tacitus and published the same with notes. Tacitus was a Latin historian, and Savile translated his work into English. The translators of these new versions, I'm sure, wouldn't be able to translate anything this complicated in Latin. In our country, Latin used to be required in the lower grades. In many schools it was a requirement for graduation from High School. Years ago that was the case; but now, in some schools, you don't have to take any foreign language at all. Some require you to take one--maybe French, German or Spanish. I took a year of Latin in college, but didn't have to take it in High School. I took Spanish there, and French in college. Of course I studied Hebrew and Greek in Seminary.

d. **Fourth,** Henry Savile published, from the manuscripts, the writings of *Bradwardin against Pelagius*, the *Writers of English History Subsequent to Bede*, and *Prelections on the Elements of Euclid*. Euclid was concerned with geometry and wrote in Greek. Savile translated that, and other learned works in English and Latin. He certainly had to have tremendous skill in order to do so. Some of the works in Greek are most difficult.

e. **Fifth,** he is chiefly known, however, for being the first to edit the complete work of Chrysostom, the most famous of the Greek Fathers. John Chrysostom had many pages that he wrote to the people to whom he ministered, and Savile was the first to completely edit his work. His edition of 1,000 copies was made in 1613, and makes eight immense folios. A folio is the size of a large dictionary or encyclopedia. That was a monumental task. I don't know any of the modern translators of the new versions (or perversions) who come anywhere near the **superiority** and skill of this man.

f. **Sixth,** Sir Henry Savile was one of the most profound, exact, and critical scholars of his age and "meet and ripe" [as McClure noted] to take a part in the preparation of our **incomparable** version. [Cf. McClure's *TRANSLATORS REVIVED*, pp. 164-69].

2. **The Academics of John Bois.** One more New Testament translator, John Bois, was in Company Six, the Cambridge group, which translated all the books of the Apocrypha.

a. **Why We Do NOT Accept the Apocrypha.** Since we have brought up the Apocrypha, the doubtful books, that the Roman Catholic Church has added to their Old Testament, I want to repeat that the Church of England in their *Thirty-Nine Articles*, clearly stated that the Apocrypha had no Scriptural standing. It is not the Words of God. It is not inspired. But the 1611 KING JAMES BIBLE **did** contain the Apocrypha. They translated it as history between the Old and New Testaments. Modern versions of the KING JAMES do not use the Apocrypha. Let me quote from McClure's, *TRANSLATORS REVIVED-- BIOGRAPHICAL NOTES ON THE KJB TRANSLATORS*, concerning the Apocrypha.

[Page 185]: *"The sixth and last company of KING JAMES BIBLE translators met in Cambridge. To this company was assigned all the Apocryphal books, which, in those times were more read and accounted of than now, though by no means placed on a level with the canonical books of Scripture."*

Then there's a footnote:

"The reasons assigned for not admitting the Apocryphal books into the canon, or list of inspired Scriptures are briefly the following:

1. Not one of them is in the Hebrew language, which was alone used by the inspired historians and poets of the Old Testament. [All but one are in Greek. The other one is in Latin].

2. Not one of the writers lays any claim to inspiration. [Not one says, "The Lord spoke through me," or "These are the words of God."]

3. These books were never acknowledged as sacred Scriptures by the Jewish Church, and therefore were never sanctioned by our Lord.

4. They were not allowed a place among the sacred books during the first four centuries of the Christian Church.

5. They contain fabulous statements [in the sense of being fables] *and statements which contradict not only the canonical Scripture but themselves; as when in the two books of Maccabees Antiochus Epiphanes is made to die three different deaths in as many different places.*

6. It inculcates doctrines at variance with the Bible, such as prayers for the dead, [that is why the Roman Catholic Church prays for the dead] *and sinless perfection.*

7. It teaches immoral practices, such as lying [it couldn't be the Words of God and say it's okay to lie], *suicide, assassination and magical incantations.* [God is against that in His Words--necromancers, those with familiar spirits, and wizards that "peep," as the Bible says, all are forbidden in Scripture].

For these and other reasons, the Apocryphal books which are all in Greek, except one which is extant only in Latin, are valuable only as ancient documents, illustrative of the manners, language, opinions and history of the East." [My words in brackets].

b.   Background of John Bois.

(1)   **First**, John Bois was carefully taught by his father. That is a good thing, isn't it? Fathers should teach more things to their children instead of leaving it up to the schools or Sunday School teacher. Talk about a child prodigy--at the age of **five** years he had read the Bible--**IN HEBREW**. Think what kind of people in our day have anything even approaching the background of this man, John Bois. These men were giants compared to the scholarly "pygmies" walking the earth today. The reason it makes me provoked is that men are ridiculing the KING JAMES BIBLE as being old fashioned, outdated, inadequate, inferior-- heaping up adjectives against this precious Book. They say the KING JAMES BIBLE TRANSLATORS were inferior and didn't have the privilege of all the learning we have today. The truth is absolutely the reverse. We don't have the privilege of all the learning that they had. **Ask if any of the translators of the modern versions have read the Bible through at the age of five!** They probably couldn't even **read** at five. Then put those other two words on the end--"**IN HEBREW**" and see what they say to that. They probably won't believe you. But this is found in McClure's book, *TRANSLATORS REVIVED* (p. 200).

(2)   **Second**, by the time Bois was six years old he not only wrote Hebrew legibly but in a fair and elegant character. If any of you know anything about Hebrew, it's not always easy to make the letters. He was writing them in a fair and elegant character at the age of six. [*TRANSLATORS REVIVED* , p. 200].

(3)   **Third**, he soon distinguished himself by his great skill in Greek, writing letters in that language to the Master and Senior Fellows at his college. If you know anything about the Greek language, you don't usually write letters in Greek. It's difficult enough to translate from the Greek into the English without composing letters, or talking in

New Testament, or Classical Greek. This man was a skilled man, not only in the Hebrew but also in the Greek. [TRANSLATORS RE*VIVED*, p. 200].

(4) **Fourth**, in the chambers of Dr. Downe, the chief university lecturer in the Greek language, Bois read with him twelve Greek authors in prose--the hardest that could be found both for dialect and phrase. It was a common practice for this young man to read and study in the University Library at four a.m. and stay without intermission until eight in the evening, a total of sixteen hours straight. [*op. cit.*, p. 201]

The Classical Greek language has a number of divisions as far as its history. You go way back in the early Greek and you have the Homeric Greek. I studied Homeric Greek while majoring in Classical Greek and Latin at the University of Michigan. We studied Homer's *Iliad* and *Odyssey*. Now that is an entirely different Greek and hard to understand. Then Classical Greek is a little different in spelling, dialect, rules, and grammar. The Classical Greek had **Ionic, Doric, and Attic**. The Attic Greek was the branch that became what we call the Koine Greek. But before that was the Byzantine Greek. The Septuagint Greek was Koine Greek. The Koine period was roughly from 300 B. C. to 300 A. D. The Koine Greek, the common Greek, used in everyday language, was the Greek of the New Testament. Then we have modern Greek which is somewhat different and pronounced differently. But Bois used the Classical Greek and had twelve of the hardest authors in prose and poetry.

I remember when I studied Classical Greek at the University of Michigan. I was first of all majoring in Science and Math and was in the Pre-Medical major, intending to be a medical doctor. Then the Lord called me to His service, and changed my direction. I had to go to Seminary, so I changed my major. The seminary I was intending to enter (Dallas Theological Seminary), at that time, required eight hours of Greek before you could enter. So I majored in Greek and Latin, taking thirty hours between them. Before that, I had not had any language at all of a technical nature. I knew Spanish, but Greek was difficult at first. I took the beginning Classical Greek and took the advanced Classical Greek from Dr. Warren E. Blake who was head of the Classical Department at the University of Michigan at Ann Arbor. He was a scholar and very competent in his understanding of the Greek language. I remember we had to translate various authors in Attic Greek, especially Plato's *Apology*, the life of Socrates which told how he would refute all those who would argue with him. It was difficult Greek! I would look at English translations and then look at the Greek. The trouble was the translations weren't literal translations like the KING JAMES BIBLE is, so it was hard to figure out what the Greek was actually saying.

I remember many a time the Professor would give a deep sigh as I was trying to translate, making no sense whatever out of the Greek words, but I did the best I could. So I think of John Bois, and twelve of the most difficult authors his teacher could find as Bois went flying successfully through them.

(5) **Fifth,** John Bois' library contained one of the most complete and costly collections of Greek literature that had ever been made. So, he was not only skilled as to his ability, but also had an extensive library to go with it. [*TRANSLATORS REVIVED* , p. 203].

(6) **Sixth,** he was **equally** distinguished for his skill in Greek and Hebrew.

(7) **Seventh,** he was one of the twelve translators who were sent, two from each company, to make the final revision at Stationer's Hall in London. This lasted nine months. If there were a problem in Hebrew or Greek, he had the answers.

(8) **Eighth,** he took notes of all the proceedings of this committee. He was the secretary. His notes, by the way, are some of the only evidences we have today telling us how they went about things. [*TRANSLATORS REVIVED* , p. 204].

(9) **Ninth,** he left at his death as many leaves of manuscript as he had lived days in his long life. I looked up his age, and he lived eighty-three years and eleven days. That totals 30,306 days. Imagine leaving over 30,000 pages of writing. A voluminous writer, scholar, reader, and worker.

(10) **Tenth,** he was so familiar with the Greek Testament that he could, at any time, turn to any word that it contained. [*TRANSLATORS REVIVED* , pp. 199-208].

So we have some translators here that certainly are superior by any standard you can think of or imagine. For the other translators, consult **B.F.T.** #1419, #584, or #804 referred to above. **We never need to be ashamed of the men who gave us the KING JAMES BIBLE.** They were skilled builders, building on the proper foundation with every tool at their disposal. They knew English, Greek, Hebrew, and the cognate sister languages. They applied their skills and did the job in a **superior** fashion.

E. BRIEF LINGUISTIC HIGHLIGHTS OF SOME OF THE

OTHER KING JAMES BIBLE TRANSLATORS.

It is in order here simply to list a few other KING JAMES BIBLE translators with a brief highlight about some of their linguistic qualifications.

I'll just give the man's name, the highlight, and the page reference in McClure's book, *THE TRANSLATORS REVIVED: BIOGRAPHICAL MEMOIR OF THE AUTHORS OF THE ENGLISH VERSION OF THE HOLY BIBLE.*

1. John Overall. Dr. Overall received his doctor's degree at Cambridge University. He was celebrated for the appropriateness of his quotations from the Church Fathers. He had spoken Latin so long, it was troublesome to him to speak English in a continued oration. His long familiarity with other languages made him well fitted to discern the sense of the sacred original. He was on the Old Testament Westminster group. [McClure, *op. cit.,* pp. 88-93]

2. Hadrian Savaria. Dr. Savaria received his doctor's degree in 1590. He published several Latin treatises against Beza, Danaeus, and other Presbyterians. He was educated in several languages, especially the Hebrew. He was also on the Old Testament Westminster group that translated the twelve books from Genesis through Kings. [McClure, *op. cit.,* pp. 93-96].

3. Robert Tighe. Dr. Tighe was characterized as "an excellent textuary and profound linguist." He was also assigned to the Old Testament Westminster group of translators. [McClure, *op. cit.,* p. 98]

4. Geoffry King. He was the Regius Professor of Hebrew at Cambridge University. He was in the Old Testament Westminster group. [McClure, *op. cit.,* p. 99]

5. Edward Lively. He was "one of the best linguists in the world." He was the King's Professor of Hebrew at Cambridge University. He had surpassing skill in the oriental tongues. Edward Lively was the author of a Latin exposition of five of the Minor Prophets as well as a work on chronology. Dr. Pusey of Oxford, stated that Lively was, "next to Pococke, the greatest of our Hebraists." He was the chairman of the Old Testament Cambridge group that translated the ten books of 1

Chronicles through Ecclesiastes. [*op. cit.*, pp. 103-4]

6. John Richardson. Dr. Richardson was a "most excellent linguist." He often debated various scholars, as the custom was in those days, entirely in the Latin language at the University of Cambridge. He later became Vice Chancellor of that university. He was also on the Old Testament Cambridge group under Edward Lively. [*op. cit.*, pp. 104-7]

7. Lawrence Chaderton. "He made himself familiar with the Latin, Greek, and Hebrew tongues, and was thoroughly skilled in them. . . . His studies were such as eminently qualify him to bear an important part in the translating of the Bible. . . . He was a scholar, and a ripe and good one." He was a member of Old Testament Cambridge group. [McClure, *op. cit.*, pp. 107-16]

8. Francis Dillingham. He often took part in a "Greek Act" which was a "debate carried on in the Greek tongue." He was called the "Great Grecian" because of his skill and knowledge of that language. He was a part of the Old Testament Cambridge group. [McClure, *op. cit.*, pp. 116-17]

9. Thomas Harrison. "Because of his exquisite skill in the Hebrew and Greek idioms, he was one of the chief examiners in the university [Cambridge] of those who sought to be public professors of these languages." He was a part of the Old Testament Cambridge group. [McClure, *op. cit.*, p. 118]

10. Robert Spaulding. Dr. Spaulding succeeded Edward Lively as the Regius Professor in Hebrew at Cambridge University. He was a part of the Old Testament Cambridge group. [McClure, *op. cit.*, p. 119]

11. Andrew King. Dr. King also became Regius Professor in Hebrew at Cambridge University. He was Dr. Spaulding's successor in that post. He was a part of the Old Testament Cambridge group. [McClure, *op. cit.*, p. 119]

12. John Harding. He had been Royal Professor of Hebrew in Oxford University for thirteen years. Dr. Harding was chairman of the Old Testament Oxford group that translated the seventeen books of Isaiah through Malachi. [McClure, *op. cit.*, pp. 120-21]

13. Thomas Holland. Dr. Holland "had a wonderful knowledge of all the learned languages, . . . He was mighty in the Scriptures; and so familiarly acquainted with the Fathers, as if he himself had been one of them. . . ." He was in the Old Testament Oxford group. [McClure, *op. cit.*, pp. 134-37]

14. Richard Kiley. "He was considered so accurate in Hebrew studies, that he was appointed the King's professor in that branch of literature [at Oxford University] . . . Dr. Kiley was a man of so great learning and wisdom, and so excellent a critic in the Hebrew tongue, that he was made professor of it in this university [Oxford]; and was also so perfect a Grecian, that he was by King James appointed to be one of the translators of the Bible. . . ." He was part of the Old Testament Oxford group. [McClure, *op. cit.*, pp. 138-41]

15. Richard Brett. "He was skilled and versed . . . in the Latin, Greek, Hebrew, Chaldee, Arabic, and Ethiopic tongues. He published a number of erudite works, all in Latin." He was a member of the Old Testament Oxford group. [McClure, *op. cit.*, p. 144]

16. George Abbot. "In 1598, Dr. Abbot published a Latin work which was reprinted in Germany." He was a member of the New Testament Oxford group that translated the six books of the Gospels, Acts, and Revelation. [McClure, *op. cit.*, pp. 152-61]

17. John Peryn. "He was the King's Professor of Greek in the university [that is, Oxford University]." He was a member of the New Testament Oxford group. [McClure, *op. cit.*, pp. 169-70]

18. John Harman. "He was appointed King's Professor of Greek in 1585, . . . He stood high in the crowd of tall scholars, the literary giants of the time. He published several learned works, among them, Latin translations of several of Chrysostom's writings, . . . The master of an excellent English style, and adept in the difficult art of translating. . . . He was a most noted Latinist, Grecian, and divine. . . He was always accounted a most solid theologist, admirably well read in the Fathers and schoolmen. . . ." He was a member of the New Testament Oxford group. [McClure, *op. cit.*, pp. 170-72]

19. John Spencer. "He was elected Greek lecturer for that college [that is, Corpus Christi College, Oxford University] being but nineteen years of age. . . . Of his eminent scholarship there can be no question. He was a valuable helper in the great work of preparing our common English version." He was part of the New Testament Westminster group that translated the twenty-one books of Romans through Jude. [McClure, *op. cit.,* pp. 177-180]

20. William Dakins. "He became bachelor in Divinity in 1601. The next year he was appointed Greek lecturer [that is, at Trinity College, Cambridge University]. . . . He was considered peculiarly fit to be employed in this work, on account of his skill in the original languages." He was a member of the New Testament Westminster group. [McClure, *op. cit.,* pp. 183-84]

21. John Duport. Dr. Duport was a "distinguished Greek professor and divine." He was the chairman of the Apocrypha section of the Cambridge group. [McClure, *op. cit.* pp. 186-9]

22. Andrew Downes. For full forty years he was Regius Professor of Greek in that famous university [that is, Cambridge University]. . . . This venerable professor is spoken of as `one composed of Greek and industry.'" Dr. Downes was a member of the Apocrypha section of the Cambridge group. [McClure, *op. cit.,* pp. 198-199]

23. Leonard Hutten. "He was well known as an `excellent Grecian,' and an elegant scholar. He was well versed in the Fathers, the Schoolmen, and the learned languages, which were the favorite studies of that day. . . ." Dr. Hutten helped as a translator, but was not assigned to any one group. [McClure, *op. cit.,* pp. 210-14]

24. Thomas Bilson. Dr. Bilson was "so complete in divinity, so well skilled in languages, so read in the Fathers and Schoolmen, so judicious in making use of his readings, that at length he was found to be no longer a soldier, but commander in chief in the spiritual warfare." He also helped as a translator, but was not a part of any one group. [McClure, *op. cit.,* pp. 214-16]

F. McCLURE'S ASSESSMENTS OF THE SUPERIORITY OF
   THE KING JAMES BIBLE TRANSLATORS.

1. **The Superiority of the Translators Themselves.** McClure, after researching the superior abilities of the KING JAMES BIBLE translators, gives this final assessment of them:

> *"As to the capability of those men, we may say again, that, by the good Providence of God, their work was undertaken in a fortunate time. Not only had the English language, that singular compound, then ripened to its full perfection, but the study of Greek, and of the oriental tongues, and of Rabbinical lore, had then been carried to a greater extent in England than ever before or since. . . . It is confidently expected that the reader of these pages will yield to the conviction, that all the colleges of Great Britain and America, even in this proud day of boastings, [about 1857 A.D.] could not bring together the same number of divines equally qualified by learning and piety for the great undertaking. Few indeed are the living names worthy to be enrolled with those mighty men. It would be impossible to convene out of any one Christian denomination, or out of all, a body of translators, on whom the whole Christian community would bestow such confidence as is reposed upon that illustrious company, or who would prove themselves as deserving of such confidence." [McClure, op. cit., pp. 63-64]*

I would have to agree with McClure on his assessment of the superiority of these men who gave us the Authorized Version of 1611.

2. **The Inferiority of Those Who Try to Compete With the KING JAMES BIBLE Translators.** McClure has some interesting comments on those who might attempt to compete with the work of the KING JAMES BIBLE translators. He wrote:

> *"And what has not been done by the most able and best qualified divines, is not likely to be done by obscure pedagogues, broken-down parsons, and sectaries of a single idea, and that a wrong one,-- who, from different quarters, are talking big and loud of their `amended,' `improved,' and `only correct' and reliable re-translations, and getting up*

*'American and Foreign Bible Unions' to print their
sophomorical performances. How do such shallow
adventurers appear along side of those venerable
men whose lives have been briefly sketched in the
foregoing pages! The newly-risen versionists, with
all their ambitious and pretentious vaunts are not
worthy to 'carry satchels' after those masters of
ancient learning. Imagine our greenish
contemporaries shut up with an Andrews, a
Reynolds, a Ward, and a Bois, comparing notes on
the meaning of the original Scripture! . . . Let tinkers
stock to the baser-metals; and heaven forefend that
they should clout the golden vessels of the
sanctuary with their clumsy patches. . . ." [McClure,
op. cit., pp. 233-34]*

Certainly McClure had a right to arrive at a conclusion such as this after
devoting so much time in researching his subject on the qualifications of
these translators.

3. **The Superiority of the Product of the KING JAMES
BIBLE Translators.** One final comment by McClure should round out
this chapter on the translators of the KING JAMES BIBLE. What of the
superiority of the product? McClure wrote, quoting the assessment of a
man who had himself attempted a re-translation of the Bible into English.
He is Dr. Alexander Geddes, who was a "minister of the church of
Rome." Though I would not agree with his theology, his words about the
accuracy of the KING JAMES BIBLE are sound. He said:

*"The highest eulogiums have been made on the
translation of James the First, both by our own
writers and by foreigners. And, indeed, if accuracy,
fidelity, and the strictest attention to the letter of the
text, be supposed to constitute the qualities of an
excellent version, this of all versions, must, in
general, be accounted the most excellent. Every
sentence, every word, every syllable, every letter
and point, seem to have been weighed with the
nicest exactitude; and expressed, either in the text,
or margin, with the greatest precision. Paganinus
himself is hardly more literal; and it was well
remarked by Robertson, above a hundred years*

ago, that it may serve as a Lexicon of the Hebrew language, as well as for a translation." [McClure, op. cit., pp. 238-39]

This statement shows the utter confidence expressed by its author in the superiority in the product of the KING JAMES TRANSLATORS. I concur wholeheartedly with this statement.

CHAPTER IV

THE KING JAMES BIBLE IS GOD'S WORDS KEPT INTACT IN ENGLISH BECAUSE OF ITS SUPERIOR TECHNIQUE

The KING JAMES BIBLE is God's Words kept intact not only because of (1) SUPERIOR **TEXTS** of the Old and New Testaments, not only because of (2) SUPERIOR **TRANSLATORS**, but also because of the (3) SUPERIOR **TECHNIQUE** that was used in their work. They did not use the technique used by the present day translators. There are two parts to the discussion of their technique: (1) SUPERIOR **TEAM TECHNIQUE**, and (2) SUPERIOR **TRANSLATION TECHNIQUE**.

A. SUPERIOR TEAM TECHNIQUE.

It's important to know that the KING JAMES BIBLE was translated differently from the other versions that are being sold today, such as the NEW AMERICAN STANDARD VERSION, the NEW INTERNATIONAL VERSION, the NEW ENGLISH VERSION, NEW KING JAMES VERSION, and the other modern versions.

1. Each Translator Had to Translate the Books on His Own. First of all, the books were assigned to each translator to translate on his own. That is not being done today. They have a few men who are skilled in some books and a few men who are skilled in others. But many others on the committee are bystanders so far as any actual translation or paraphrasing is concerned. They don't do anything except, perhaps, check other versions, or smooth out some of the English style. But there is a relatively small group of people on the staff of these modern translating teams who do the actual "translating." They are the "brains" of the committee. That was not the case when the KING JAMES BIBLE was translated. **Every man** on the six companies, some fifty-seven of them in all, had to be so skilled in the Hebrew books or Greek books that were assigned to him that he had to translate all of them **by himself.** Some died before the task was finished, but even if they only had fifty left, each had to translate. They couldn't fake it because they had to come in with the translation of those books from the Hebrew or Greek in their own handwriting. This was one of the rules they followed, as mentioned below.

2. **The Westminster Group.**
    a. **Old Testament Section.** Company One, for instance, the Westminster Group, Old Testament section, [Cf. Gustavus S. Paine, *THE MEN BEHIND THE KING JAMES VERSION,* **B.F.T. #584,** pp. 184-185], had to translate from Genesis through 2 Kings--that is twelve books. If you know anything about translating from Hebrew into English, you know it might take you months before you would get beyond Genesis. It would take some people years--unless you knew Hebrew the way you know English, or Spanish, or one of the more familiar languages. These men had to go through Genesis, Exodus, Leviticus, Numbers, Deuteronomy, Joshua, Judges, Ruth, 1 Samuel, 2 Samuel, 1 Kings, and 2 Kings--every book. This could not have been done in the time they had before them unless they had known the language well. You can't fake it. They had to write it out, bring it in, and defend it. Translating the Old Testament [Paine, *loc. cit.*] from Genesis through Kings were: Chairman Dr. Lancelot Andrews, William Bedwell, Francis Burleigh, Richard Clarke, Jeffrey King, John Layfield, John Oberall, Hadrian Saravia, Robert Tigue, and Richard Thomson. Every one of those men had to translate on his own.
    b. **New Testament Section.** The Westminster Company Two, in the New Testament section, [Paine, *loc. cit.*], had Romans through Jude--twenty-one books. Their task was not just reading through them from the Greek, but translating from the Greek into the English. That meant they had to translate the books of Romans, 1 Corinthians, 2 Corinthians, Galatians, Ephesians, Philippians, Colossians, 1 Thessalonians, 2 Thessalonians, 1 Timothy, 2 Timothy, Titus, Philemon, Hebrews, James, 1 Peter, 2 Peter, 1 John, 2 John, 3 John and Jude--all twenty-one of those books. The members of this team were chairman Dr. William Barlow, William Dakins, Roger Fenton, Ralph Hutchinson, Michael Rabbett, Thomas Sanderson, and John Spenser. In addition, Thomas Bilson was the editor for this company.

3. **The Oxford Group.**
    a. **Old Testament Section.** The Oxford Group Old Testament section [Paine, *loc. cit.*] had to translate seventeen books in the Old Testament, from Isaiah to Malachi inclusive. There were eight men on that committee. Each man had to translate all seventeen of these books by himself. The men were chairman Dr. John Harding, Richard Brett, Daniel Featley, Thomas Holland, Richard Kilby, John Reynolds (he was the Puritan that initiated the KING JAMES BIBLE), Miles Smith, and

William Thorne.

b. New Testament Section. In the New Testament section, they had to translate six books: the Gospels (Matthew, Mark, Luke, John) then Acts and the Apocalypse. The translators were: [Paine, *loc. cit.*] Chairman Dr. George Abbot, John Aglionby, John Harmer, Leonard Hutton, John Perin, Thomas Ravis (Chairman), Henry Savile, and Giles Thomson.

4. The Cambridge Group.

a. Old Testament Section. The Old Testament Cambridge Group had to translate ten books, [Paine, *op. cit.*, p. 185] from 1 Chronicles to Ecclesiastes. All eight of those men had to bring their own translation. The translators were chairman Edward Lively, Roger Andrews, Andrew Bing, Laurence Chaderton, Francis Dillingham, Thomas Harrison, John Richardson, and Robert Spalding.

b. The Apocrypha Section. The Apocrypha section from the Cambridge Group translated the entire Apocrypha (as history only, and NOT as inspired Scripture). The translators were: [Paine, *loc. cit.*] Chairman Dr. John Duport, John Bois, William Braithwaite, Andrew Downes, Jeremy Radcliffe, Samuel Ward, and Robert Ward.

These forty-eight names are listed in the British Museum. To these should be added (49) William Thorne, (50) Richard Edes, (51) George Ryves, (52) William Eyre, (53) James Montague, (54) Arthur Lake, (55) Nicholas Love, (56) Ralph Ravens, and (57) Thomas Sparke whose names appear on some lists as having worked on the KING JAMES BIBLE. [Paine, *THE MEN BEHIND THE KING JAMES VERSION*, p. 185]. This makes fifty-seven men in all.

5. Some of the Rules Governing the KING JAMES Translation.

How do I know they had to bring their own translation? Because on pages seventy and seventy-one of this book, *THE MEN BEHIND THE KING JAMES VERSION*, there is a list of the fifteen rules that KING JAMES insisted upon. Now, KING JAMES had nothing to do with the translation itself other than making the rules. You don't have to defend KING JAMES. He wasn't "Saint" James. There's a good article entitled "It's KING JAMES Not Saint James" by Pastor E. L. Bynum in *The Plains Baptist Challenger*. [**B.F.T.** #1364]. I know Pastor Bynum well and love him in the Lord. A lot of men take great delight in pointing out alleged defects in KING JAMES (for which the KING JAMES BIBLE is named). He wasn't a perfect person in many ways. But he had nothing to do with the translating. He wasn't one of the fifty-seven who did the work. He just commissioned it because he agreed that it ought to be done.

Dr. John Reynolds had asked KING JAMES to permit the KING JAMES BIBLE to be undertaken, to have men to do it, and to provide for the funds to take care of it. James had an interest in the translation, having a knowledge of many languages himself. He just happened to be the king at the time the translation was made. It's a foolish argument people use, trying to drag in something that isn't relevant.

The six translating companies had before them a total of fifteen rules to govern their work. Here are five of those rules:

        a. Rule #8. One of the rules governing the translation was found in Rule #8:

> *"**Every particular man** of each company to under-take the same chapter or chapters, and having translated or amended them severally **by himself** where he thinketh good, all to meet together to confer when they have done, and agree for their parts what shall stand." [Paine, The Men Behind The King James Version, op. cit., p. 71]*

So, if I take Company one that has to translate from Genesis through 2 Kings (twelve books) and an average of seven men on that committee, each had to translate every book, every chapter, every verse himself. That was seven different times the portions were looked over. Then they had to meet together and go over it once more--that is the eighth time.

        b. Rule #9. Then Rule #9 stated:

> *"As any one company has dispatched any one book in this manner they shall send it to the rest to be considered of seriously and judiciously, for His Majesty is very careful in this point." [Paine, The Men Behind The King James Version, op. cit., p. 71]*

So when the seven men looked at it, and then all together, making eight times, then the first Company sends it to Companies 2, 3, 4, 5, 6. This makes five more times. They interchanged their work. Here you have the material gone over thirteen times; and then at the end they have a final joint meeting of two men from each of the six companies, twelve men. This makes **fourteen times** the Bible from Genesis to Revelation was translated, analyzed, and corrected. **That is a team technique that is unequaled by any modern translators.**

        c. Rule #10. Here is Rule #10:

"If any company upon the review of the book so sent doubt or differ upon any place, to send them word thereof with the place and withal send the reasons; [why they differed, what was wrong] *to which if they consent not* [if they're hard-headed about it and won't budge] *the difference to be compounded at the general meeting which is to be of the chief persons of each company at the end of the work. (Thus in the end they all had to agree enough to let all readings pass.)"* [My words in brackets]. *[Paine, The Men Behind The King James Version, op. cit., p. 71]*

At the end, the final company, including John Bois, that expert who read the Hebrew Bible all the way through at the age of five, would take care of any problems.

   d. Rule #11. Rule #11 stated:

"When any place of special obscurity be doubted of, letters to be directed by authority to send to any learned man in the land for his judgment of such a place." [Paine, The Men Behind The King James Version, op. cit., p. 71]

They made use of the many other "learned men" not on the translating committees. This was an excellent team technique.

   e. Rule #12. Rule #12 mentioned:

"Letters to be sent from every bishop to the rest of his clergy admonishing them of his translation in hand and to move and charge as many as being skillful in the tongues [Hebrew, Greek and others] *and having taken pains in that way* [diligently studied the language, not just knowing it] *to send his particular observations to the Company either at Westminster, Cambridge or Oxford. (This indicates that many must have aided in the work.)"* [My words in brackets]. *[Paine, The Men Behind The King James Version, op. cit., p. 71]*

The translators were **a team** and worked as a team, after having worked first of all individually. They were superior translators. They had to be in order to do that. I know enough about the Hebrew and Greek languages to know that I could not qualify to be one of these translators. But these men could be included, because they knew these languages as well as, or better than, we know English. It was a simple thing for them, just like it's a simple thing for some mathematicians to solve difficult mathematical problems. It is similar to the skill of a man who knows engineering and has the ability to build a bridge, or a large building. It is similar to the skill of an architect, or the skill of any specialized technician. These translators knew what they were doing. We ought to praise God for them and the technique they used which was different from and **superior** to that used for the modern versions.

6. Summary of Superior Team Technique. The team technique used by the KING JAMES translators was far different from that used by the translators of the modern versions. Each man had to translate all the books that were on his schedule to translate--twelve books, for instance, in Company One. They were Hebrew books, difficult books. The first company took Genesis to Kings; the Oxford group took Isaiah through Malachi. Every one of these men had to translate from the Hebrew to the English himself, **unaided by anyone else.**

The men who translated the NEW AMERICAN STANDARD VERSION, the NEW INTERNATIONAL VERSION, and the NEW KING JAMES VERSION, didn't have that qualification. In these versions, you had a great deal of window-dressing. You had people on the committees with degrees, "scholars" who may know many things. Many of them were on the committee in order to induce people to buy their version, so the publisher could make a lot of money on it. Some of these individuals wrote promotions at the beginning of the book, the end of the book, and in advertising, "Dr. So-and-so thinks this is a tremendous version." But **each and every man** on each of the committees for the above versions (and other versions as well) did **not** have to translate from the Hebrew or Greek to English by themselves. If any of our readers have absolute and positive documentation to the contrary, we would be happy to know about it! I am quite certain that no one can prove me wrong in this matter. They had a relatively few "scholars" who did most of the work for the whole group. But **each man** who translated the KING JAMES BIBLE was highly skilled. After they had translated their own work, they got together and decided which translated words would stand.

Seven separate times the original book was translated; one time they went through it together. Then they sent it to the other companies. So there were five other companies that worked on the book. They interchanged their translations. It was a team effort. So there were the seven original individual translations, one time as a group, five more times by the other groups. Then, at the end of the work, two men from each of the six groups got together and made a final revision as to what wording should stand. No less than **fourteen different times** the translation for each book was gone over "from stem to stern" (as we say in the Navy). This is an unusual, and so far as we know, a never before and never afterward team technique that was used. It is certainly superior!

B. SUPERIOR TRANSLATION TECHNIQUE.

1. The KING JAMES Translators Adopted the Verbal Equivalence and the Formal Translation Technique. The superior translation technique of the KING JAMES translation employed what we call both the **verbal equivalence** and formal equivalence. They avoided what we call dynamic equivalence.

We believe, and the KING JAMES translators believed, that what God wants is for His people to have His Words and to *"desire the sincere milk of the Word that ye may grow thereby."* WE NEED GOD'S WORDS. **APPENDIX A,** at the end of this study, gives some of the more important verses that stress the importance of God's Words. We suggest you look them over carefully. In our Bibles, we don't need man's words in place of God's Words for the translation. Commentaries, preachers, and teachers are helpful, but primarily, we need the pure, sincere milk of the Words of God so we will grow up in Christ. Peter also says, *"Grow in grace and in the knowledge of our Lord Jesus Christ."* The method of growth is by the use of the Words of God so it is very important for us to know what God's Words are, to grab on to them, to believe them, to let them sink into us, to practice them, and to live by them so we can be mature, grown-up, able to witness, and do God's will.

Now, the problem with all these other versions (including the NIV, NASV, NKJV, and the rest) is that they have purposefully selected a non-verbal equivalence type of translation, a non-formal equivalence type of translation, and a non-literal equivalence type of translation. Instead, to a greater or lesser extent, they have purposefully adopted a dynamic equivalence type of translation. *"Dynamic"* implies *"change"* or *"movement."* These various versions take a sort of **idiomatic rendering** from Hebrew or Greek into English. It is idiomatic in the sense that they didn't take a word-for-word method (even when it made good sense), trying to make the words in the Hebrew or Greek equal to the words in English. They **added** to what was there, **changed** what was there and/or **subtracted** from what was there. If it was a question they might have made a statement, left out words, and so on. **They didn't care. Paraphrase** is another word for it. Of course, the LIVING VERSION is in the lead as far as paraphrase is concerned.

2. The KING JAMES Translators Rejected the DYNAMIC EQUIVALENCE Translation Technique. We want to talk about the diabolical nature of what is called DYNAMIC EQUIVALENCE. The KING JAMES translators adopted a method of **verbal equivalence;** and **formal equivalence,** that is, the words from the Greek or Hebrew were rendered as closely as possible into the English. The same is true for the forms of those words. This is called formal equivalence. We have verbs in English. We have nouns, adjectives, prepositions, participles, and so on. If the structure in the Hebrew language was such that it could be brought into the English in the same way, with the same forms, that is what they did. If you have a verb, they brought it over as a verb instead of changing it or transforming it into a noun. There is a whole area in the field of English called **Transformational Grammar,** where **everything is changed** from one form to another. This is the real seed plot of the so-called DYNAMIC EQUIVALENCY where you don't have the words brought over into English (or another language) word for word. **So the KING JAMES translators' method was superior because it adopted verbal and formal equivalence translation and avoided DYNAMIC EQUIVALENCE.**

     a.   DYNAMIC EQUIVALENCE Is Diabolical. Let's look at the whole subject of DYNAMIC EQUIVALENCE. **It is diabolical because we believe that Satan is at the root of it.** God is very clear about the way He wants His Words to be believed by us. **Every Word of God is important.** *"Man shall not live by bread alone but by EVERY WORD that proceedeth out of the mouth of God."* We believe that words are important. The dynamic equivalency people do not believe this. **Once again, we refer you to APPENDIX A at the back of this book for some very important verses showing the impcrtance of God's Words.**
     b.   The Chronology of DYNAMIC EQUIVALENCE. Let's take a look at the chronology of the DYNAMIC EQUIVALENCY development.
          (1)   Satan Began DYNAMIC EQUIVALENCE. Satan began DYNAMIC EQUIVALENCE in the Garden of Eden. If you'll notice in Genesis 3:1, the serpent was the agent Satan used to defeat Eve, and then Adam. He was, and is, a very clever deceiver and manipulator. And he used the DYNAMIC EQUIVALENCE method

of understanding and translating the Words of God. That is, he made a loose paraphrase of what God's words were to Eve and Adam.

(a) The Diabolical Principle of SUBTRAC-TION. Now the first principle is the principle of SUBTRACTION--SUBTRACTING from the Words of God.

*Genesis 3:1: "Now the serpent was more subtil than any beast of the field which the LORD God had made. And he said unto the woman, Yea, **hath God said**, Ye shall not eat of every tree of the garden?"*

Satan, through the serpent, asked: *"Yea, hath God said, Ye shall not eat of every tree of the garden?"* Now if you take that as it is, it would mean, "Isn't it true that God said you could eat of **every tree** of the Garden?" He subtracted something from the Words of God because that wasn't what God had said at all. In Genesis 2:16, 17, here's what God said to Adam:

"(16) And the LORD God commanded the man, saying, Of every tree of the garden thou mayest freely eat:"

Now, that is so far so good. That is what Satan quoted. But in verse 17, God said:

*"**BUT** of the tree of the knowledge of good and evil, **thou shalt not eat of it**: for in the day that thou eatest thereof thou shalt surely die."*

God went on beyond verse 16 to verse 17. Satan comes up in Chapter 3:1, and says, in effect, "Now, didn't God say you could eat of **every tree?**" **Yes, God did say that, but Satan left something out--he subtracted.** DYNAMIC EQUIVALENCE is diabolical because it follows the Devil's method of subtracting from the Words of God.

We have included in **APPENDIX B** a chronological listing of every complete English Bible and New Testament for the last 612 years through 1991. You'll notice that there are listed 135 complete English Bibles and an additional 293 complete English New Testaments. This makes a total of 428 Bibles or New Testaments. It is our contention that we do NOT need any more English Bibles or New Testaments! Are not 428 more than enough? We are interested, in this book, primarily in those versions used by Fundamentalists or Evangelicals, though our remarks could be applied to many other versions as well.

The versions we're talking about here, NEW AMERICAN STANDARD VERSION, NEW INTERNATIONAL VERSION, even the NEW KING JAMES VERSION, all show this paraphrasing to one degree or another. We have examples and illustrations of what we're talking about. We have examined every verse of this version in detail.I. We have a computer printout of the analysis of the NEW KING JAMES

VERSION comparing it to the Hebrew and Greek; and we give **over 2,000 examples,** chapter and verse, of where the editors have **added** to, **subtracted** from, or **changed** the Words of God by paraphrase. [B.F.T. #1442] We've done the same for the NEW AMERICAN STANDARD VERSION, comparing it to the underlying Hebrew and Greek. We give chapter and verse for **over 4,000 examples** of where the editors have **added** to, **subtracted** from, or **changed** the Words of God by paraphrase. [B.F.T. #1494-P] We've done the same for the NEW INTERNATIONAL VERSION, comparing it to the underlying Hebrew and Greek. We give chapter and verse for **over 6,653 examples** of where the editors have **added** to, **subtracted** from, or **changed** the Words of God by paraphrase. [B.F.T. #1749-P] This methodology was sanctioned by the Devil himself in the Garden of Eden. That is why we call it diabolical. God does not want you and me to tamper with His Words, did you know that? We have no right to subtract anything from the Words of God. God has not given us that privilege. We're not God. When God says something, He expects us to follow it exactly, precisely, and not to go to the right hand or left hand.

      (b)   The Diabolical Principle of CHANGE. Now I want you to see a second principle: the CHANGING of the Words of God. Subtraction is a change, but this is changing God's Words without necessarily subtracting anything God has said. Notice in Genesis 3:4. There's a changing of God's clear Words. In this case this change is a direct denial of God's Words. The Bible reads in Genesis 3:4:

> *"And the serpent said unto the woman, YE SHALL NOT SURELY DIE."*

But, notice, God had said in Genesis 2:17:

> *". . . for in the day that thou eatest thereof THOU SHALT SURELY DIE."*

Would you not agree that this is a change? Death was the penalty: physical death and spiritual death; both deaths were the penalty of disobedience. It really wasn't the eating of the fruit of the tree that killed them; it was the disobedience. The disobedience was evidenced by the taking and eating of the fruit. But the serpent said in Genesis 3:4: *". . . ye shall NOT surely die."* God had said in 2:17: *". . . ye SHALL surely die."* Now, Satan's changing the Words of God. He's absolutely denying what God has specifically said. He is calling God a liar. **This is DYNAMIC EQUIVALENCE.   It's diabolical because it not only subtracts from, but changes the Words of God.**

      (c)   The Diabolical Principle of ADDITION.

Now a third reason we call DYNAMIC EQUIVALENCY diabolical is because it **ADDS** to the Words of God. Notice Genesis 3:5, the serpent, talking to Eve said:

> *"For God doth know that in the day ye eat thereof, then your eyes shall be opened, and ye shall be as gods, knowing good and evil."*

Now, this is an ADDITION to the Words of God. **Did God ever say anything about their eyes being opened?** He didn't say a word about that in Genesis 2:17. He just said, *". . . in the day that thou eatest thereof thou shalt surely die."*

Notice in Verse 2:

> *"And the woman said unto the serpent, We may eat of the fruit of the trees of the garden: (v. 3) But of the fruit of the tree which is in the midst of the garden, God hath said, Ye shall not eat of it, neither shall ye touch it, lest ye die."* **[Now, Eve added to the Words of God "neither shall ye touch it."]**

These three things, **subtracting, changing,** and **adding** to the Words of God, are the essence and heart of DYNAMIC EQUIVALENCY in its approach to translation. **It's not translation, but changing the Words of God. It is pure paraphrase.**

> c. **The History of DYNAMIC EQUIVALENCE.** The modern history of DYNAMIC EQUIVALENCE began with **Eugene Nida.** He was the man who was with the Wycliffe Bible Translators, the American Bible Society, and the United Bible Society. He popularized this DYNAMIC EQUIVALENCE method which now is used throughout the world. From the time Eugene Nida began introducing this poison of DYNAMIC EQUIVALENCE into the translation system, all the versions--using this system, to a greater or lesser degree--have been perversions. This man is the expert perverter of the Scriptures and **the perversion is DYNAMIC EQUIVALENCE.** IT IS DIABOLICAL TO THE CORE, ADDING TO THE WORDS OF GOD ALL OVER THE WORLD, CHANGING THE WORDS OF GOD ALL OVER THE WORLD, AND SUBTRACTING FROM THE WORDS OF GOD ALL OVER THE WORLD IN EVERY LANGUAGE YOU CAN THINK OF BECAUSE HE SAYS, "LET'S CHANGE IT."

Even Bible-believing Fundamentalists have accepted DYNAMIC EQUIVALENCE and have adopted it as their own, instead of translating God's Words properly. Here are some of the published works by Nida and others using the DYNAMIC EQUIVALENCE method:

(1) **In 1947**, Eugene Nida wrote the book, *BIBLE TRANSLATING*, published by the United Bible Society [UBS, hereafter] of London.

(2) **In 1950**, Nida wrote an article, *"TRANSLATION OR PARAPHRASE"* which appeared in "The Bible Translator." [TBT, hereafter].

(3) **In 1952**, Nida wrote *"A NEW METHODOLOGY IN BIBLICAL EXEGESIS"* by TBT.

(4) **In 1955**, Nida wrote *"PROBLEMS IN TRANSLATING THE SCRIPTURES"* by TBT.

(5) **In 1959**, Nida wrote *"PRINCIPLES OF TRANSLATING AS EXEMPLIFIED BY BIBLE TRANSLATING"* by TBT.

(6) **In 1960**, Nida wrote *MESSAGE AND MISSION* published by Harper Brothers.

(7) **In 1961**, Nida wrote "NEW HELP FOR TRANSLATORS " By TBT. It's not a help; it's a hindrance; it's a disgrace.

(8) **In 1964**, Nida wrote *"TOWARD A SCIENCE FOR TRANSLATING"* published by E. J. Brill in the Netherlands.

(9) **In 1966**, Nida wrote *"THE BIBLE TRANSLATOR'S USE OF RECEPTOR LANGUAGE TEXTS"* published by TBT.

(10) **In 1969**, Nida wrote *"THEORY AND PRACTICE OF TRANSLATION"* also published in the Netherlands.

(11) **In 1966**, *"GOOD NEWS FOR MODERN MAN"* came out, (*TODAY'S ENGLISH VERSION*--a paraphrase) a perversion, using the DYNAMIC EQUIVALENCE method. The American Bible Society, for instance, in *GOOD NEWS FOR MODERN MAN* leaves out the word "blood" (*haima* is the Greek word) thirty-six of the 103 times it is used in the New Testament. Of the thirty-six times, sixteen of those times refer to the blood of Christ. They take out the blood of Christ and change it by the method of DYNAMIC EQUIVALENCE to "death," "sacrifice," or some other word. But *haima* in the Greek means "blood." There's no way to get around it. 1 Peter 1:18, 19 reads:

> *"Forasmuch as ye know that ye were not redeemed with corruptible things, as silver and gold, from your vain conversation received by tradition from your fathers; (v 19) But with the PRECIOUS BLOOD of Christ, as of a lamb without blemish and without spot."*

The TODAY'S ENGLISH VERSION says this was only a "**COSTLY SACRIFICE**," and they take "blood" right out and say it means "sacrifice." One of the popular Bible expositors of our day [JOHN

MACARTHUR] is doing the same thing, saying the blood just means death so we can just change it. He says that the BLOOD OF CHRIST is not essential. According to MacArthur, we are NOT saved by the BLOOD OF CHRIST and we are not cleansed by the BLOOD of Christ. [For further information on THE BLOOD OF CHRIST, and John MacArthur's HERESY, send for our **BROCHURE #5**. At this printing, there are over 150 items on this list.]

(12) **In 1975,** the WORLD COUNCIL OF CHURCHES at Nairobi adopted this same method. This is an apostate, Communist-led, Modernist-led, heretic-led Council of Churches that finances terrorists to kill, maim, and torture in Africa and other places. This WORLD COUNCIL OF CHURCHES adopted DYNAMIC EQUIVALENCE as the method of translation. They followed the Devil. **They followed Eugene Nida.** They followed the United Bible Society and the American Bible Society.

(13) **In 1978,** the NEW INTERNATIONAL VERSION came out and used this method. They pride themselves on using the diabolical method of DYNAMIC EQUIVALENCE--not a word-for-word equivalence, not verbal or formal equivalence, but DYNAMIC EQUIVA-LENCE.

(14) **In 1983,** *"BY THE WORD"* was published by the ASSOCIATION OF BAPTISTS FOR WORLD EVANGELISM [ABWE]. Perhaps some of your missionaries are out under that board. As of publication, their headquarters are close to us in Cherry Hill, New Jersey, but they are scheduled to move to Pennsylvania within a year. *"BY THE WORD"* is written by Lynn Silvernale. It's called *"THE PRIORITY AND PROCESS OF BIBLE TRANSLATION."* **She quotes Eugene Nida over and over.** He is an apostate who doesn't even believe that the Bible is inerrant and infallible. She wrote:

> *"I began to read everything I could about translation, and learned there are different types of translation. Various authors classified them differently but BEEKMAN'S classification in TRANSLATING THE WORD OF GOD made a lot of sense. He refers to two basic approaches of translation: literal and idiomatic. These give rise to four types of transla-tions: highly literal, modified literal, idiomatic and unduly free."* [Silvernale, op. cit., p. 13]

The problem with Silvernale is that she read the WRONG books on translation methods. Beekman and Callow are the ones who wrote the book, *TRANSLATING THE WORD OF GOD.* These men have set the pace for the DYNAMIC EQUIVALENCE translation of Scripture all over the world. Now Fundamental, Bible-believing missions are using the diabolical DYNAMIC EQUIVALENCE method to translate their Scriptures for their believers. It's a sad day in which we live. Lynn Silvernale and ABWE have used this method and favor the IDIOMATIC translation of Scripture, by which they mean DYNAMIC EQUIVA-LENCE, changing the Words of God. They think it's fine. They think it's all right. There's an interesting thing, however, that happened, and Silvernale mentions it on page thirty-three:

"*After a couple of years of translation experience,* [she's over in Bangladesh and has translate111

d the Bengali Bible] *the translator and I found we were experiencing a considerable degree of frustration because we were making all these adjustments [she calls them "adjustments," meaning changes in the Words of God, subtracting, adding and changing God's Words] yet there was always the nagging question in the back of our minds, are we taking too many liberties with the text?* [Their consciences smote them because of what they were doing.] *Is this really a faithful translation? The translator was especially concerned about the warning in Revelation 22:18 and 19!*" ['For I testify unto every man that heareth the words of the prophecy of this book, If any man shall add unto these things, God shall add unto him the plagues that are written in this book: (19) And if any man shall take away from the words of the book of this prophecy, God shall take away his part out of the book of life, and out of the holy city, and from the things which are written in this book.') [Silvernale, op. cit., pp. 33-34] The curse upon the DYNAMIC EQUIVALENCE approach is found right in Scripture. Silvernale continued:

"*This is when we realized we needed to have a well-defined set of guiding principles which would give us direction as to what specific types of adjust-ments* [That is, additions, subtractions and changes] *in Bengali are acceptable in a faithful translation.*" [To be perfectly clear about these quotations, my words are in brackets in this quotation]. *[Silvernale, op. cit., p. 34]*

How can you have faithful translation if you are adjusting it all the time? It's not faithful if it ADDS to the Words of God. It's not faithful if it SUBTRACTS from the Words of God. It's not faithful if it CHANGES the Words of God. Then she says,

> *"We worked out a list of thirty-five principles dealing with the types of adjustments mentioned in this paper, plus many more. These were then approved by our entire Field Council in order to have greater input and agreement in the widest possible forum." [Silvernale, loc. cit.]*

So they had all the ABWE missionaries on the field at Bangladesh rubber-stamping all these adjustments so their consciences would be clear. No longer would there be a nagging suspicion and doubt about whether they were faithful to the words of God. Listen, my friends: I don't care if a hundred thousand million people agree to **add, subtract,** or **change** the Words of God, it's still sin. It's not what we are to do to God's Words. It's wrong. She's trying to get consensus for sin.

      d. Summary of the History of DYNAMIC EQUIVA-LENCE. So in 1983, the Eugene Nida "virus" of DYNAMIC EQUIVA-LENCE (ADDING to, SUBTRACTING from, and CHANGING the Words of God) that started in the Garden of Eden with Satan, caught fire. It was in the apostate WORLD COUNCIL OF CHURCHES; now it is in the Fundamental, supposedly separated groups. As recently as several months ago, we saw articles produced by BIBLES INTERNATIONAL, a branch of BAPTIST MID-MISSIONS which is a Fundamental missionary agency in Ohio, which justified this DYNAMIC EQUIVALENCY. I've known one of the former Presidents for many years. In fact, he was on my ordination council at Berea, Ohio. We made known in our *BIBLE FOR TODAY NEWSREPORT* two reports questioning the DYNAMIC EQUIVALENCE that is used in BIBLES INTERNATIONAL. Several letters have been written to these people asking about changes. I got an order from BAPTIST MID-MISSIONS for both of these reports. I put it in my *NEWSREPORT* and said people should read them; so BAPTIST MID-MISSIONS sent for both of them. I hope they read them and change whatever is wrong in the DYNAMIC EQUIVALENCE approach. This is rampant. It is in two of our Baptist Fundamental missions. But it is just as diabolical, just as dangerous, and deadly, just as wrong in Fundamentalist, separatist agencies as it is in New Evangelical, modernist, or apostate agencies. What's the difference? **Truth is truth, error is error.** It's probably worse among those who ought to know better than to use the Devil's method of so-called "translation."

(1) With DYNAMIC EQUIVALENCE, Any Textual Base Will Do. Let's take a look at DYNAMIC EQUIVALENCE and the textual issue. We said the KING JAMES BIBLE uses the best and the most proper Hebrew text of the Old Testament, and the best and most proper Greek text of the New Testament. But, you know, if you take a DYNAMIC EQUIVALENCE approach to translation as a technique instead of verbal equivalence or formal equivalence--that is, the forms and the words being rendered from Hebrew or Greek into English as closely as possible--if you take the position that it really doesn't matter what the words are, what difference does it make which text you use? What difference does the Greek or Hebrew text make? You can change it any time you wish. If you can **add** to it any time you wish, **subtract** from it any time you wish, and **change** it any time you wish, who cares about the text you start with, whether it's the proper one or not? Who cares about the quality of the translators and their ability and credentials to translate properly from Hebrew or Greek into English? You don't need any degrees or education to **add, subtract** or **change** the Words of God like the Devil did in the Garden of Eden. If Satan could do it, anybody could do it. So, who cares about the proper text? Who cares about the proper translators if they use this DYNAMIC EQUIVALENCE technique of translation? They can change it at will.

That is the saddest thing in the whole picture of our modern versions and in the whole translation and version problem. They don't need the Masoretic text. They don't need the Syriac or Septuagint or Latin Vulgate. All of it is hypothesis and guesswork by men. Anything they want to come up with is right. So, we see that DYNAMIC EQUIV-ALENCE is more important even than the textual issue we have been discussing. **We should keep the KING JAMES BIBLE as our standard because of its excellency, and its correspondence with the Hebrew and Greek.** It does correspond because it REJECTS DYNAMIC EQUIVALENCE!

(2) A Four-Year Examination of Various Versions. For the last four years (and more) I've been examining and comparing the various versions used by Fundamentalists. The purpose was to see just how much they vary from the KING JAMES BIBLE and the Hebrew and

Greek text.

(a) **Analysis of the KJB-1611 Edition.** I took the 1611 Authorized Version the first year (the original KING JAMES BIBLE which has been reproduced by Nelson Publishers) and compared it with the current KING JAMES BIBLE to examine the changes. This study is twenty-five pages in length. [**B.F.T.** #1294] Though there are many spelling and punctuation changes, this report shows clearly only **421 changes** in sound (to the ear) compared to the present KING JAMES BIBLE, which is very slight indeed. Most of these changes are in minor details. The Introduction to this work is also available in brief, tract summary form. [**B.F.T.** #1495]

(b) **Analysis of the NEW KING JAMES VERSION.** I then took the NEW KING JAMES VERSION and compared it with the KING JAMES by listening to it on tape cassettes. We have the whole Bible on tapes, if you're interested in that; it's very helpful to have. [**B.F.T.** #777/1-43] After I found differences between the NEW KING JAMES and the KING JAMES, I checked the Hebrew text or Greek text and saw which was nearer to the original. The KING JAMES was the one closest to the Hebrew or Greek. So I have greater confidence than ever in the KING JAMES as being an excellent replica in the English language of that Hebrew or Greek. This study is spelled out in **ninety-five large pages** of computer printout. [**B.F.T.** #1442] The report specifies **over 2,000 examples** of DYNAMIC EQUIVALENCY (**additions, subtractions, and changes** to the Words of God). The Introduction is also available in summary tract form. [**B.F.T.** #1465] The specific comments on the Hebrew and Greek changes are available in nine, two-hour cassettes. [**B.F.T.** #1367/1-9]

(c) **Analysis of the NEW AMERICAN STANDARD VERSION.** The next year I took the NEW AMERICAN STANDARD VERSION and compared it with the KING JAMES and then the underlying Hebrew and Greek texts. Wherever there was a difference between the NEW AMERICAN STANDARD VERSION and KING JAMES BIBLE I checked it. **The closest rendering to the Hebrew and Greek text is the KING JAMES BIBLE. The NEW AMERICAN STANDARD is the one that is off in the places where they differ.** This study is spelled out in 187 pages of computer printout. [**B.F.T.** #1494-P] The report specifies **over 4,000 examples** of DYNAMIC EQUIVALENCY (**additions, subtractions, and changes** to the Words of God). The Introduction is also available in summary tract form. [**B.F.T.** #1518] The specific comments on the Hebrew and Greek changes are available in eleven, two-hour cassettes. [**B.F.T.** #1494/1-11]

    (d) **Analysis of the NEW INTERNATIONAL VERSION.** For another two years and eight months, I analyzed the NEW INTERNATIONAL VERSION in the same manner as the others. Listening to the KING JAMES BIBLE, seeing the differences, and comparing it with the Hebrew and Greek. This is available in computer printout form. [**B.F.T.** #1749-P] The NEW INTERNATIONAL VERSION is so filled with paraphrases, with DYNAMIC EQUIVALENCE, I couldn't put everything down. If I did, it would be many years before it would be finished. The report specifies **over 6,653** examples of DYNAMIC EQUIVALENCY (additions, subtractions, and changes to the Words of God). When I check the differences with the Hebrew and Greek, the KING JAMES BIBLE is the correct one every time. The specific comments on the Hebrew and Greek changes are available in sixteen, two-hour cassettes. There are over 4,600 examples given. [**B.F.T.** #1749/1-16] There is a pamphlet giving the preface of the larger study. It is entitled "*DEFECTS IN THE NEW INTERNATIONAL VERSION.*" [**B.F.T.** #2054]

    (3) **An Ordinary Person Doesn't Realize the DANGER of the New Versions.** An ordinary person, without comparing the versions with the original texts themselves, doesn't know which is right. All they know is, there's a difference. The NEW INTERNATIONAL VERSION or others say one thing, and the KING JAMES says another thing. If you don't know your Hebrew and you don't know your Greek, (and most people don't) you've got to have the words of God somewhere in the English language you DO know. Keep the KING JAMES as a standard. You'll find the Greek and Hebrew translated best of all right in that Book. If you don't understand some of the English words in the KING JAMES BIBLE, look them up in a dictionary, or you can get this little booklet published by the Trinitarian Bible Society. [**B.F.T.** #1060] It contains **618 words** which may be unfamiliar to you. The meanings are given in brief form. Every one of these words that you may not understand is in any good dictionary. "Habergeon," for instance, is a shield, or coat of mail. "Ouches" are pockets or pouches. The main thing is that they are **accurate** renderings of the Hebrew or Greek. As mentioned earlier in this book, a KING JAMES BIBLE has been prepared which has a brief definition of the words that may have changed their meanings since 1611. The BIBLE FOR TODAY has completed this project. It is called *The Defined King James Bible.* It is large print 12-point type and is available for a gift of **$40 + S&H** in genuine leather, in

either black or burgundy. Dr. S. H. Tow of Singapore has purchased 4,000 of these Bibles and is spreading them in various parts of the world. You may order your copy by phoning 1-800-JOHN 10:9. [For more details of the background, please refer back to page 2.]

(4) **The UNITED BIBLE SOCIETY to Publish Only DYNAMIC EQUIVALENCE Paraphrased Selections in the Future.** The principle of the United Bible Society is no longer to publish entire Bibles, that is, from Genesis through Revelation. Not only are they going to produce paraphrases and idiomatic translations, they will only publish portions of Bibles, NOT entire Bibles. In 1962, the UNITED BIBLE SOCIETY printed one Bible to every three and one-half selections or tracts; that was the proportion. In 1969, the UNITED BIBLE SOCIETY printed one Bible to eighteen and one-half selections (there are more selections and fewer Bibles). In 1974, the UNITED BIBLE SOCIETY printed one Bible to thirty-three selections. The Bibles are dwindling and now the rule is the only time they'll print whole Bibles is if special designated funds are given for that purpose. The Bible societies are always short of funds and the general funds will only be reproducing selections, which are tiny portions of Scripture. This is from *THE FUTURE OF THE BIBLE* which has been reprinted by the BIBLE FOR TODAY. [B.F.T. #1246] What is the future of the Bible? It has no future so far as the UNITED BIBLE SOCIETY is concerned!! That is why all the more we have to stick to our KING JAMES BIBLE and thank the Lord that we have it.

(5) **"DYNAMIC EQUIVALENCE" Defined Briefly.** What is DYNAMIC EQUIVALENCE? Here are a few definitions of the words that make up the concept of DYNAMIC EQUIVALENCE. "Dynamic" means:

> *"1b. Of or pertaining to dynamics; active; **opposed to static; Pertaining to change or process.**"*
> *[Webster's New Collegiate Dictionary, 1949, p. 257]*

In other words, **"dynamic" means "moving." Those who advocate DYNAMIC EQUIVALENCE want to move away from the exact Words of God.** That is the whole theory of Socialism and Communism: movement, change, dynamics. It's a change or process. I don't want to change the Words of God; I want to keep them the way they are. I don't want to alter them. I want to say, *"Thus saith the Lord."* **God gave us His Words and we ought to believe them and stick to them. We ought to keep them static.** We ought not to be changing them. I refer you once again to **APPENDIX A** which is a catalog of Bible verses that stress the importance of God's Words rather than merely thoughts, ideas, or concepts.

A related term is "dynamics." A partial definition of "dynamics" is:

> *"1. That branch of mechanics treating of MOTION of bodies (kinematics) and the action of forces in producing or CHANGING their motion (kinetics). 2. The MOVING MORAL, as well as physical, forces, or any kind, of the laws relating to them." [Webster, loc. cit.]*

The whole dynamic process is a process of change, a process of evolution, a process that was designed by Satan in the Garden of Eden. It is a moving force, a change, a flux, a flow--like a river. It's all right to sing, "Like a river glorious is God's perfect peace," but the image of rivers that flow, and change, and move, and are dynamic is not a picture of how God's Words should be put into our language. IT SHOULD BE SOMETHING FIXED, THAT WE CAN STAND ON. Our God is a Rock, a huge Rock mountain. Mountains don't move, flow, or fluctuate. Our Savior is a foundation on which we are to build our lives. *"Other foundation can no man lay than that is laid, which is Jesus Christ."* (1 Cor. 3:11)

Another word that must be defined is the word, **"equivalence."** It means:

> *"1. State of being equivalent, equality of worth, meaning, or force." [Webster's, op. cit., p. 279]*

The word, "equivalent" means:

> *"1. obs. equal in force or authority. 2. Alike in significance. 3. Equal in value, esp. for exchange. 4. Virtually or in effect identical; tantamount; as, his remark was equivalent to an insult." [Webster's, loc. cit.]*

In one sense "equivalent" is a good term, but in one of the senses listed above having to do with "virtually or in effect identical," there is too much latitude in my judgement. In that sense of the word, I don't want an equivalent, I want the actual Words of God. Why talk about any equivalence? **Do you want to know in English what God said in the Hebrew or Greek language?** I want to know exactly. I don't want just an equivalent. **I want the real thing. And that is what the KING JAMES BIBLE has given us: the real thing, the real Words of God, from Hebrew and Greek to English, based on the proper TEXT, with** superior **TRANSLATORS,** superior **TEAM TECHNIQUE,** and superior translating **TECHNIQUE.**

While we're taking up some definitions, we should also include the term **"idiom"** or **"idiomatic"** which is often used as a synonym for DYNAMIC EQUIVALENCY in translations and versions. "Idiom" as in "idiomatic translation" means:

"1. The language peculiar to a people (a tongue), or to a district, community, or class (a dialect). 2. The structural form peculiar to any language. 3. An expression in the usage of a language, that is peculiar to itself either in grammatical construction or in having a meaning which cannot be derived as a whole from the conjoined meanings of its elements (as, the more the merrier . . .)" [Webster's, op. cit., p. 411]

What we're interested in with a real translation is the language peculiar to Hebrew and Greek in which the Bible was originally given. While we want to make these original languages intelligible and understood in the language into which we are translating, this is never to be done at the expense of accurately rendering the Words of God. **"Idioms" that completely alter the Words of God are not acceptable as a translation. What the KING JAMES BIBLE translators gave us is a verbal and formal equivalence, not merely an idiomatic or dynamic equivalence.** There is a world of difference between these matters.

(6) **"TRANSLATION" Defined Briefly.** What is "translation"? The word comes from two Latin terms: *trans* and *latus*. *Trans* means "across." *Latus* is the past participle root which is short for *tal* or *tla* (*"tlatus"*) and means "to lift or carry." **The literal meaning of "translation" therefore is "to lift or carry across."** When speaking of translating of languages, the resultant meaning is to transfer or "carry over" (and I would take it BODILY) from one language to another." That is, Bible translation consists of picking up the words from the Hebrew and Greek, carrying these words over into English or any other language you might be translating into, and then dropping those words into that language without losing any parts, gaining any parts, or changing any parts. That is what the KING JAMES BIBLE has done in the English language. It has taken up the words bodily from the Hebrew or Greek and taken them over into English and set them down very gently, very accurately, and very specifically so we can understand them.

An example of what the KING JAMES BIBLE has done in

Hebrew is from Genesis 1:1: *"In the beginning God created the Heaven and the earth."* "In the beginning" (*baroshith*) "created" (*bara*) "God" (*Elohim*) "the heavens" (*eth hashamaim*) "and the earth" (*wa eth haerets*). An example from the Greek is John 1:1: The words are picked up from the Greek also and taken over into the English: "In the beginning" (*en archE*) "was the Word" (*En ho logos*) "and the Word" (*kai ho logos*) "was with God" (*En pros ton Theon*). **No other translation does the superior job that the KING JAMES translation does.** The others are using paraphrase whenever they wish and DYNAMIC EQUIVALENCE to a greater or lesser degree.

(7) **"PARAPHRASE" Defined Briefly.** What is paraphrase? If "translation" is *trans* and *latus*, "lifting up and carrying over from one language to another," what is paraphrase? The word paraphrase comes from the Greek *paraphrasis* which is *para* (along side, or near) and *phrasis* is "to speak" from *phrazein*. It means:

> *"To say the same thing in other words, . . . a re-statement of a text, passage or work, giving the meaning in another form; . . . To express, interpret or translate with latitude; to give the meaning of (a passage) in other language." [Webster's, op. cit., p. 610]*

Well, I don't want to "translate with latitude," or to use "other words," or to have anyone "interpret." But that is what we have in these other versions, like the NEW AMERICAN STANDARD which paraphrases over **4,000 times.** The NEW INTERNATIONAL VERSION is even worse. It paraphrases over **6,653 times.** Even the NEW KING JAMES VERSION, paraphrases over **2,000 times.** Paraphrase is interpretation rather than accurate translation.

(8) **Illustrations of Paraphrase in the Various Versions.** For a detailed study, look at the computer printouts we have on the NEW KING JAMES VERSION compared to the KING JAMES BIBLE and the underlying Hebrew and Greek texts. [B.F.T. #1442] It has ninety-five large pages and gives **over 2,000 examples** of DYNAMIC EQUIVALENCY. A similar printout is available for the NEW AMERICAN STANDARD VERSION. [B.F.T. #1494-P] It has 187 large pages and gives over **4,000 examples** of DYNAMIC EQUIVALENCY. A similar printout is also available for the NEW INTERNATIONAL VERSION. [B.F.T. #1749-P] It has 284 large pages and gives over **6,653 examples** of DYNAMIC EQUIVALENCY. This NIV is so wild. I don't know why Bible-believing Christians use it. It

certainly is filled with paraphrase.

A paraphrase makes no effort to carry over or translate the words of one language into the words of another language but rather to "re-state, interpret or translate with latitude." Since this is the object of a paraphrase there's no assurance of fidelity in carrying-over exactly what is there in one language--no more and no less--into the other language, no more and no less. Therefore, paraphrases take great liberty in doing any of these three things or all of them: ADDING words, phrases, ideas, thoughts or meanings; SUBTRACTING words, phrases, ideas, thoughts or meanings; or CHANGING words, phrases, ideas, thoughts or meanings. That is the essence of paraphrase; that is the essence of DYNAMIC EQUIVALENCE. So, it is commentary, it is interpretation, it is not translation.

(9)   A Detailed Definition Of "TRANSLATION." Here is a definition of what real translation is (which is fulfilled in our KING JAMES BIBLE in English). Dr. Francis Steele (who spoke to our Christian group at the University of Michigan when I was there in 1945-48 as a student) holds a Master of Arts and Ph.D. from the University of Pennsylvania, and taught there as Assistant Professor of Assyriology (that is the Assyrian language) from 1947-53. He is a linguist. He believed in the inerrancy of the Word of God. He wrote a little booklet called *"Translation or Paraphrase."* [B.F.T. #207] It is available from the BIBLE FOR TODAY. We carry this among the present inventory of over 2,300 items (with over 100 new items being added each year). At present, we carry over 900 titles which defend the superiority of the KING JAMES BIBLE, the inerrancy of Scripture, Bible preservation, and related themes. These titles are found at the back of this present book. Dr. Steele gave an excellent definition of what translation is. I've broken it down into a total of twenty-one elements:

> *"Therefore, allow me to substitute a definition learned by experience in translating Babylonian and Sumerian documents in which I valued highly the training received from one of America's outstanding scholars in the field of Assyriology. The discipline taught me the INVIOLABLE PRINCIPLES embodied in my concept of a LEGITIMATE TRANSLATION.*
>
> *"This is it: A translation should convey [1] as much of the original text [2] in as few words as possible [3] yet preserve the original atmosphere and emphasis. [4] The translator should strive for the nearest approximation in*

*words, [5] concepts, and [6] cadence.   [7] He should
scrupulously AVOID ADDING WORDS [8] or ideas not
demanded by the text* [this is exactly what they do in DY-
NAMIC EQUIVALENCE. They add words and ideas not
demanded by the text]. *[9] His job is not to expand [10] or to
explain, [11] but to translate [12] and preserve the spirit
and force of the original--[13] even, if need be, at the expense of modern colloquialisms--[14] so long as the resultant translation is intelligible. . . ." ["TRANSLATION OR
PARAPHRASE" Bible Memory Association, pp. 1-2]*

*"Certainly [14] many words and even passages in an
acceptable translation of the Bible will benefit from a more
extended treatment. [15] But SUCH TREATMENT BE-
LONGS IN A COMMENTARY, [16] NOT A TRANSLA-
TION. [17] We expect in a translation the closest approxi-
mation to the original text of the Word of God that linguist
and philological science can produce. [18] WE WANT TO
KNOW WHAT GOD SAID--[19] NOT WHAT DOCTOR
SO-AND-SO THINKS GOD MEANT BY WHAT HE SAID.
[20] There is a great difference between the two [21] and
we intrude into Holy Ground when we ignore the distinction."* [My words and numbers in brackets]. *["TRANSLATION
OR PARAPHRASE," op. cit., pp. 7-8]*

This sort of **superior, accurate** translation is exactly what the KING
JAMES translators have preserved for us in our KING JAMES BIBLE.

**(10) A Seven-fold Description of "DYNAMIC
EQUIVALENCE."** There are various adjectives I would like to use to
describe the DYNAMIC EQUIVALENCE approach that was used in the
Garden or Eden by Satan--SUBTRACTING from God's Words,
CHANGING His Words and ADDING to His Words. I have a list of
seventy-seven appropriate adjectives describing this HERESY (all beginning with "d"). I'll stress only seven of them, but, in case some of my
readers would like to know IN FULL what I think about this evil, I will
list them here. In my opinion, DYNAMIC EQUIVALENCY is

diabolical, defiant, **disobedient,** defective, destructive, disruptive, deforming, disturbing, defamatory, dwarfing, **deceptive,** dangerous, deadly, damaging, damnable, deadening, debilitating, defacing, defrauding, degenerating, degrading, **deifying of man,** deleting, delinquent, demolishing, demoting, depraved, depreciating, depriving, deserting, despicable, despoiling, double-minded, destitute, **determined,** detestable, deviant, devoid, diluting, diminishing, disabling, disadvantageous, disagreeable, disappointing, **disapproved,** disarming, disastrous, disbelieving, discarding, discomfiting, discordant, discouraging, discrediting, disdainful, disfiguring, disgusting, **dishonest,** dishonorable, disintegrating, disjointed, dislocating, dismantling, disowning, disparaging, displacing, disposing, disregarding, disrespectful, distasteful, distorted, distracting, distressing, divisive, **and, in short a death-blow to the Words of God in the Bible!**

Though I could comment on ALL of the above seventy-five adjectives concerning DYNAMIC EQUIVALENCY, the seven I wish to emphasize are in bold face in the paragraph above.

(a) DYNAMIC EQUIVALENCE Is DIABOLICAL. The first adjective is DIABOLICAL. There's nothing more Satanic than altering or changing the Words of God. That is why I'm so angry (in a Christian sense) with these men who have played fast and loose with the very Words of my God. No man on earth has the right or title to alter His words. That is how Adam and Eve got into trouble in the Garden of Eden in the first place and that is how we get in trouble when we think we know more than the Words of God. We say, "We are going to have it our way." But we don't have it our way when it comes to the Words of God. We have to keep the Words the way God gave them to us and then live them and practice them.

(b) DYNAMIC EQUIVALENCE Is DECEPTIVE. The second thing is, the DYNAMIC EQUIVALENCE method is DECEPTIVE. It's deceptive because it deceives people. People pick up one of these new versions and say,

"Isn't that wonderful! But it's different from the KING JAMES BIBLE. The KING JAMES must be wrong

*because it doesn't agree with the NEW AMERICAN
STANDARD or the NEW KING JAMES or the NEW
INTERNATIONAL, or others. The translators must
have been ignorant or misinformed."*
People think that because something is new that it means it is better. Isn't
a new car better than an old car? (Not necessarily, the way they make
them today.) But that is how many people think. A new house, a new
hat, a new dress, a new church building, isn't that better than the old ones?
Many times it's true, but **what's new is not necessarily true.** We have a
lot of new ideas.

Communists want the U.S.A. to disarm themselves. To do this
would be to throw away the wisdom of the Lord Jesus Christ. When the
U.S.A. disarms, a *"strong man"* is being disarmed so the Devil can come
and take over the "houses" of the world. This is insanity in our highest
echelon, as far as I'm concerned. That is the deceptiveness of this new
approach to translation. People are fooled. "Have you got the latest
thing?" But **the new is not necessarily the true.**

(c) **DYNAMIC EQUIVALENCE Is DETER-
MINED.** Then the third thing about this DYNAMIC EQUIVALENCE
approach is that it is DETERMINED. Publishers are determined to push
it, through the influence of Madison Avenue techniques, and all the hype
that advertising can do. They do this to help them make their millions and
millions of dollars. The Bible business is a huge multi-million dollar
business. I don't have the latest statistics and figures, but I'm talking
about **MILLIONS OF DOLLARS** in Bible publisher sales. Now, they're
not going to sell things if they have the same KING JAMES BIBLE all
the time, they have to get new merchandise.

The car salesmen aren't going to make sales if all they have is last
year's models. They have to get the new cars coming in. Who wants a
1990 model when you can get this year's model? So they change a few
things here and there. They have determined to out-sell the KING
JAMES BIBLE. The last year or so, they claimed to have done this when
they included all the various special editions for different groups of
people. The KING JAMES BIBLE, however, even though it's a 1611
product, has held its own throughout the years, and has led the sales in
Bibles through the years. Again, we invite you to consult the
chronological list of 135 complete English Bibles and 293 complete New
Testaments that have been printed in the 612 years of Bible history from
1380 through 1991. [p. 203] A Bible or a New Testament was produced
on the average of once every 1.4 years. During the 1900's, new ones have

come out once every .51 years, or once every six months! Bible publishers certainly have been making lots of money on printing English Bibles through the years, haven't they! I'm not against the profit motive. There is nothing wrong with free enterprise. But when you deal DECEPTIVELY and DIABOLICALLY and DETERMINEDLY to make the profit out the Words of God by CHANGING them and ADDING to and SUBTRACTING from them, that is making merchandise of the things of God, giving people a false hope and a false Bible that isn't true to God's Words.

(d) **DYNAMIC EQUIVALENCE Is DISHON-EST.** The fourth thing is that it is DISHONEST because it purports to be the Words of God and it isn't. They purport to give Christians the very Words of God and they don't. That is dishonesty. God's Words say, *"Thou shalt not bear false witness."* (Exodus 20:16a)

(e) **DYNAMIC EQUIVALENCE Is a DEIFY-ING of MAN.** The fifth thing is that DYNAMIC EQUIVALENCE is a DEIFYING of man. Why? Because it gives authority to man to alter the Words of God by using man's own brain, which is as small as a speck compared to God's omniscience. *"What is man, that Thou art mindful of him? . . . For thou hast made him a little lower than the angels . . ."* (Psalms 8:4-5, which is quoted in Hebrews 2:6-8). DYNAMIC EQUIVALENCE is a deification of man. That is saying: We write our own Bible. We make up our own ideas.

(f) **DYNAMIC EQUIVALENCE Is DISOBE-DIENT.** The sixth thing is that it is DISOBEDIENT because God said very clearly not to ADD to His Words, not to SUBTRACT from His Words, but to keep them as they are.

(g) **DYNAMIC EQUIVALENCE Is DISAP-PROVED BY GOD.** The seventh thing is that DYNAMIC EQUIVA-LENCE is DISAPPROVED by God. These DISOBEDIENT acts, these DIABOLICAL acts, DECEPTIVE, DISHONEST acts which DEIFY man are DISAPPROVED by God. God said in 2 Timothy 2:15:

"Study to show thyself APPROVED unto God, a workman that needeth not to be ashamed, rightly dividing the Word of Truth."

You don't have all the Words of Truth in these other versions. The only one that has all the Words of Truth is the KING JAMES BIBLE. God wants us to rightly divide these Words of Truth. We cannot do it if we try to divide something that has man's words all mixed up with God's Words.

      e. Biblical Passages Against DYNAMIC EQUIVA-
LENCE
            (1) Verses That Forbid "ADDING TO" the Words
of God.
●   **(a) Deuteronomy 4:2.**
"Ye shall NOT ADD unto the word which I command
you, neither shall ye diminish aught from it, that ye may
keep the commandments of the LORD your God which
I command you."
DYNAMIC EQUIVALENCE ADDS. It is therefore disobedient.
●   **(b) Deuteronomy 12:32.**
"What thing soever I command you, observe to do it:
thou shalt NOT ADD thereto, nor diminish from it."
God's Words forbid adding. DYNAMIC EQUIVALENCE permits it.
We have a conflict here, a disobedience here, a devilish, diabolical
situation.
●   **(c) Proverbs 30:6.**
"ADD THOU NOT unto his words, lest he reprove
thee, and thou be found a liar."
●   **(d) Revelation 22:18.**
"For I testify unto every man that heareth the words of
the prophecy of this book, If any man shall ADD unto
these things, God shall add unto him the plagues that
are written in this book."
We have a warning from Heaven against ADDING to God's Words, but
the new versions and the DYNAMIC EQUIVALENCE method add to
His Words repeatedly.
            (2) Verses That Forbid Any "TAKING AWAY" or
"SUBTRACTING" from The Words of God.
●   **(a) Deuteronomy 4:2.**
"Ye shall not add unto the word which I command you,
NEITHER shall ye DIMINISH AUGHT from it, that
ye may keep the commandments of the LORD your God
which I command you."
God says, "Don't take anything away," but the new versions do take away.
●   **(b) Deuteronomy 12:32.**
"What thing soever I command you, observe to do it:
thou shalt not add thereto, NOR DIMINISH from it."
That is the **SUBTRACTION**, yet Satan did add and subtract from God's
Words in the Garden of Eden.
●   **(c) Jeremiah 26:2.**

> *"Thus saith the LORD; Stand in the court of the LORD's house, and speak unto all the cities of Judah, which come to worship in the LORD's house, all the words that I command thee to speak unto them; **DIMINISH NOT A WORD.**"*

When Jeremiah the prophet was commissioned by the Lord to preach His Words He said, in effect, "Preach them all. Tell them all. Don't diminish or subtract a single word." Yet DYNAMIC EQUIVALENCE violates that all the time.

- **(3) Verses That Forbid Any "CHANGING" of the Words of God by Turning to the "RIGHT HAND" or the "LEFT HAND."** Now, when God says, "Don't go to the right hand or left hand," what is He saying? He's saying to go straight up the middle. When you're plowing a field, try to make the furrow straight. Don't go to the right or left or you'll have a problem. When you're mowing your lawn or using a snow plow, you'd better go straight instead of every which way.

- **(a) Deuteronomy 5:32-33.**

  > *"Ye shall observe to do therefore as the LORD your God hath commanded you: ye shall **NOT TURN ASIDE** to the **RIGHT** hand or to the **LEFT**. (v. 33) Ye shall walk in all the ways which the LORD your God hath commanded you, that ye may live, and that it may be well with you, and that ye may prolong your days in the land which ye shall possess."*

Why does God want us to walk in His way and not go to the right or left? When you go to the right or left, you're not following the path. Suppose there were booby-traps to the right or left and also a path free from bombs or incendiaries that might blow you up--you must walk the right path. I was a Navy Chaplain on active duty for five years. I served with the Marine Corps for two of those years. In combat conditions, some men are blown to bits by land mines. Sometimes demolition experts would go through the fields (in Vietnam, for example) and they would mark a path through the mine fields, so that land mines would not blow up any man. They would mark the paths to make a safe way to go. If that soldier or marine would say, "I'm not going to trust those markers, I'm going to take it on my own and go off any path I want, to the **RIGHT** or to the **LEFT**," he'd be blown to bits. God doesn't want us to be blown to bits. He wants us to follow His Words **just as they are** and NOT to go to the **RIGHT** or **LEFT** as these new versions have done repeatedly.

- **(b) Deuteronomy 17:18-20.**

*"And it shall be, when he sitteth upon the throne of his
kingdom, that he shall write him a copy of this law in a
book out of that which is before the priests the Levites:
(v. 19) And it shall be with him, and he shall read therein
all the days of his life: that he may learn to fear the
LORD his God, to keep all the words of this law and
these statutes, to do them: (v. 20) That his heart be not
lifted up above his brethren, and that he turn NOT aside
from the commandment to the RIGHT hand, or to the
LEFT: to the end that he may prolong his days in his
kingdom, he, and his children, in the midst of Israel."*

God wanted the kings to go right up the path. Wouldn't it be wonderful
if all the kings, not only of Israel, but all the leaders of this day would
write the Words of God in a special book and read it and follow
everything in that precious Book? Wouldn't that be great?

- **(c)   Deuteronomy 28:13-14.**

*"And the LORD shall make thee the head, and not the
tail; and thou shalt be above only, and thou shalt not be
beneath; if that thou hearken unto the commandments of
the LORD thy God, which I command thee this day, to
observe and to do them: (v. 14) And thou shalt NOT go
aside from any of the words which I command thee this
day to the RIGHT hand, or to the LEFT, to go after
other gods to serve them."*

- **(d)   Joshua 1:7-8.**

*"Only be thou strong and very courageous, that thou
mayest observe to do according to all the law, which
Moses my servant commanded thee: turn NOT from it to
the RIGHT hand or to the LEFT, that thou mayest
prosper whithersoever thou goest. (v. 8) This book of the
law shall not depart out of thy mouth; but thou shalt
meditate therein day and night, that thou mayest observe
to do according to all that is written therein: for then
thou shalt make thy way prosperous, and then thou shalt
have good success."*

- **(e)   2 Kings 22:2.**

This verse is speaking of King Josiah, only eight years old. Sometimes
a little child shall lead them. A little child sometimes has more sense than
some of the editors and publishers of these Bible translations and
versions. They know whether a thing is off or not.

*"And he did that which was right in the sight of the
LORD, and walked in all the way of David his father,
and turned NOT aside to the RIGHT hand or to the
LEFT."*

He was too young to know any different. And we ought to be that way
by using our KING JAMES BIBLE. We ought to stay right directly in
the path of God's Words.

(4) **Verses That Emphasize the Importance of God's
"WORDS" Rather Than Merely IDEAS, THOUGHTS, or CON-
CEPTS." WORDS are what God wants us to get into our heads and
hearts** and into our Bibles--not just ideas, concepts, or thoughts as the
DYNAMIC EQUIVALENCE people say. Their technique is to forget
about the words, just bringing the thought, the concept, or the idea over
into English. The words can be ADDED TO, SUBTRACTED or
CHANGED. But the KING JAMES translators believed that WORDS
were important, and that the WORDS of Hebrew were to be taken over
into WORDS of English as closely as possible. The KING JAMES
BIBLE translators believed that the Greek WORDS of the New
Testament were important WORDS and those very WORDS were to be
taken over into the English as closely and **accurately** as possible. That
is the confidence we can have in this Bible in English. This list here is
selective.   For a more extensive list, you are invited to consult
APPENDIX A in the back of the book.

- (a) **Isaiah 55:10.**

    *"For as the rain cometh down, and the snow from
    heaven, and returneth not thither, but watereth the
    earth, and maketh it bring forth and bud, that it may
    give seed to the sower, and bread to the eater: (v. 11)
    So shall My **WORD BE THAT GOETH FORTH OUT
    OF MY MOUTH**: it shall not return unto me void, but
    it shall accomplish that which I please, and it shall
    prosper in the thing whereto I sent it."*

God says it is His WORDS that will be blessed, not man's word. But
what if they take His WORDS out of the text, what if that is one of the
words they throw out? They won't be blessed. What if it is being added
to? Then it's not His Words. Only those Words *"that goeth out of His
mouth"* will *"not return unto Him void."* Only those Words *"that goeth
out of His mouth"* will *"accomplish that which He pleases, and . . .
prosper in the thing whereto He sent them."* This is an important point.

- (b) **Jeremiah 15:16.**

> *"Thy WORDS were found, and I did eat them; and thy*
> *WORD was unto me the joy and rejoicing of mine heart:*
> *for I am called by thy name, O LORD God of hosts."*

This is talking about God's Words, not man's words. God's WORDS cause rejoicing, that is why I'm glad I can find them in the KING JAMES BIBLE.

- **(c)   Jeremiah 23:36.**

> *"And the burden of the LORD shall ye mention no more:*
> *for every man's word shall be his burden; for ye have*
> *perverted the WORDS of the living God, of the LORD of*
> *hosts our God."*

These men had perverted the WORDS of the living God. And that is what I charge these translators with, those who use the DYNAMIC EQUIVALENCE approach and ADD to His WORDS and SUBTRACT from His WORDS and CHANGE His WORDS. They are BIBLE PER-VERTERS, perverting the WORDS of God.

- **(d)   Amos 8:11-12.**

> *"Behold, the days come, saith the LORD God, that I will*
> *send a famine in the land, not a famine of bread, nor a*
> *thirst for water, but of hearing the WORDS of the*
> *LORD: (v. 12) And they shall wander from sea to sea,*
> *and from the north even to the east, they shall run to and*
> *fro to seek the WORD of the LORD, and shall not find*
> *it."*

If you throw away the KING JAMES BIBLE, all you have left are the other versions and perversions. Where are you going to find the WORDS of God? "Hide and Seek" is a game we used to play as children. If we use these new versions, that is what we're going to have to play to find the WORDS of God. God's WORDS have become so scarce that there's a famine in the land, not of bread or water but of God's WORDS. (Amos 8:11) God says His WORDS are important. That is why we must have a Bible that preserves His WORDS like the KING JAMES BIBLE does.

- **(e)   Job 19:23-24.**

> *"Oh, that my WORDS were now written! oh that they*
> *were printed in a book! (v. 24) That they were graven*
> *with an iron pen and lead in the rock for ever!"*

Here is Job's desire--that his WORDS should be written, not concepts or ideas. We have His WORDS.

- **(f)   Psalm 12:6-7.**

> *"The WORDS of the LORD are pure WORDS: as silver*

tried in a furnace of earth, purified seven times. (v. 7)
Thou shalt keep **THEM**, *O LORD, thou shalt preserve*
THEM *from this generation for ever."*

The Lord's **WORDS** are pure, not just His thoughts or concepts, but His **WORDS**. It is His WORDS that must be preserved and they have been in our KING JAMES BIBLE in the English language.

- **(g)   Psalm 119:89.**
  "For ever, O LORD, thy **WORD** *is settled in heaven."*

- **(h)   Deuteronomy 8:3.**
  "And He humbled thee, and suffered thee to hunger, and fed thee with manna, which thou knewest not, neither did thy fathers know; that He might make thee know that man doth not live by bread only, but by **EVERY WORD** *that proceedeth out of the mouth of the LORD doth man live."*

EVERY WORD is important to God.

- **(I)   Matthew 4:4.**   During His temptation Jesus answered Satan:
  "But He answered and said, It is written, Man shall not live by bread alone, but by **EVERY WORD** *that proceedeth out of the mouth of God."*

So you can't throw away any of His WORDS. All are important.

- **(j)   Mark 8:38:.**
  "Whosoever therefore shall be ashamed of me and **MY WORDS** *[not just ideas, thoughts or concepts in general] in this adulterous and sinful generation; of him also shall the Son of Man be ashamed, when he cometh in the glory of his Father with his holy angels."*

- **(k)   Luke 9:26.**
  "For whosoever shall be ashamed of me and of **MY WORDS**, *of him shall the Son of Man be ashamed, when He shall come in His own glory, and in His Father's, and of the holy angels."*

- **(l)   Matthew 24:35.**
  "Heaven and earth shall pass away, but **MY WORDS** *shall not pass away."*

Mark 13:31; Luke 21:33 say the identical words.

- **(m)   Galatians 3:16.**
  "Now to Abraham and his seed were the promises made. He saith not, And to SEEDS, as of many; but as of one,

And to thy SEED, which is Christ."
The very PLURAL versus SINGULAR number of this noun is important
to prophetic Scripture!
     You know John 3:16. Some of you who may be lost may need
these WORDS which are very clear. We don't need translation or
DYNAMIC EQUIVALENCE to understand them:
     "For God [the greatest Lover]
     so loved [the greatest degree]
     the world [the greatest company of people]
     that He gave [the greatest gift]
     His only begotten Son [the greatest treasure of Heaven]
     that whosoever [the greatest company of people]
     believeth in Him [the greatest simplicity]
     should not perish [the greatest danger],
     but [the greatest difference]
     have [the greatest assurance]
     everlasting life [the greatest possession]."
What could be more clear than these words from the KING JAMES
BIBLE? These are the words of the Lord Jesus Christ. They are identical
to what is in the Greek, taken right over into the English.
     Now in Galatians 3:16 the Apostle Paul said we must guard even
the singulars and plurals of the Hebrew and Greek texts in bringing them
into the various languages so we don't get mixed up. This is "verbal" and
"formal" equivalence that was insisted upon by the Apostle Paul. Are we
authorized to use any other method? No!
     The NEW KING JAMES VERSION, the NEW AMERICAN
STANDARD VERSION, The NEW INTERNATIONAL VERSION,
The LIVING VERSION, TODAY'S ENGLISH VERSION, GOOD
NEWS FOR MODERN MAN (and many other versions listed in
APPENDIX B) do not always carry singulars and plurals over into the
English. But God's Words say we must pay heed to the very forms (*"not,
and to SEEDS, as of many; but as of one, And to thy SEED which is
Christ"*). You look into these new translations and try to make out head
or tail of the prophecies and look into the New Testament for fulfillment.
They have often mistranslated so many details of the prophecies with the
result that the Old Testament prophecy does not agree with the New
Testament fulfillment. They're completely changed.
     **f. Some Quotations Against DYNAMIC EQUIVA-
LENCE from "THE FUTURE OF THE BIBLE."** We want to
continue the subject of DYNAMIC EQUIVALENCE and how it is very

diabolical, deadly, determined, and deceptive. We want to illustrate some of these things.

(1) This Book Is Available from The BIBLE FOR TODAY. Let me explain DYNAMIC EQUIVALENCE again. Jakob Van Bruggen, from the Netherlands, wrote a book called *THE FUTURE OF THE BIBLE.* Nelson Publishers let it go out of print and refused to reinstate it because it wasn't selling fast enough and making them enough money. [**B.F.T. #1256**] The picture on the front of the book is a Bible and the sun. But is it a rising sun or a setting sun? It is a setting sun. It is the thesis of this man from the Netherlands that the Bible (as we know it) will have a very dim future. Now, we know that the Lord Jesus Christ has promised to come again and He will come again. The signs of His coming multiply. We know that the Rapture of the Church to snatch us out before the Tribulation period may occur at any moment.

(2) The Bible As We Know It in the KING JAMES BIBLE Has a Dim Future. We mentioned earlier that there are two reasons for the Bible having a dim future:

(1) One is that the entire Bible, from Genesis to Revelation, will never more be translated into other languages unless there are special funds designated for that purpose. There will be only little segments, tiny portions for this group or that, men, women, young people, doctors, etc.

(2) They will change that into Idiomatic or DYNAMIC EQUIVALENCE. This is a second reason why the Bible will have a dim future. They will change the words by means of DYNAMIC EQUIVALENCE. They will not translate faithfully the words of the original languages of Hebrew and Greek into the English. By their perverted system, they believe they can ADD words if they wish and they can SUBTRACT words. We are going to give you some illustrations of that. Does that mean the Hebrew and Greek are different for all different people? No, but they will have to change the Words of God from what the KING JAMES BIBLE has. **The KING JAMES BIBLE has taken the very words of the Hebrew and Greek and brought them over faithfully into English by way of verbal and formal equivalence.**

(3) Bible Translation Must Be Faithful to Text and Form Like the KING JAMES BIBLE Is. I want to quote again from Van Bruggen's book *THE FUTURE OF THE BIBLE* (which is out of print, but still available from us at BIBLE FOR TODAY.) On page 99:

"Since God has revealed His Word in a fixed and written form, the translator must be respectful of this form."

That is an interesting comment. The new look in translation, DYNAMIC EQUIVALENCE, does not pay heed to the FORMS of the Hebrew as they bring them into the English, or the FORMS of the Greek as they bring them into English. The forms can be changed. What do we mean by "forms?" The singular is a form. The plural is a form. This is the difference between the words "SEED" and "SEEDS" in Galatians 3:16. Paul makes the argument that God said in the Old Testament, *". . . not as of SEEDS, as of many; but of one. And to thy SEED, which is Christ."* Form was very important here. The forms of words are always important. So the KING JAMES translators have taken nouns (which are the names of persons, places, or things) and where possible have put nouns in the English instead of changing them into either pronouns or verbs, which are action words, or words indicating a state of being.

But in DYNAMIC EQUIVALENCE the editors often take verbs and change them into nouns, or they take the nouns and change them into verbs and change them all around. That is what they call "TRANSFORMATIONAL GRAMMAR" where you transform the grammatical forms and change them into some other form completely. To continue quoting from Van Bruggen:

> *"Readable translations may be made without this respect, but they ignore God's words, . . . 'to obey is better than sacrifice . . . '"* [When God says DON'T SUBTRACT, obey. When He says NOT TO ADD to His Words, obey. When He says NOT TO CHANGE His words, obey.] *"Obedience in Bible translating means a careful transmission of what God caused to be written." [Loc. cit.]*

Though that is a simple statement, it is the very essence of true Bible translation. The KING JAMES BIBLE has followed that admonition. The NEW AMERICAN STANDARD VERSION has not. The NEW KING JAMES has not. The NEW INTERNATIONAL VERSION has not. The LIVING VERSION has not. The NEW ENGLISH BIBLE has not. All these modern versions, to one degree or another have veered away from that methodology of which Van Bruggen writes:

> *"In order to be reliable, a translation must reflect faithfulness to the form, clarity, completeness, loyalty to the text, spirituality, authoritativeness, and ecclesiastical usage." [Loc. cit.]*

The KING JAMES BIBLE is the only English Bible on the scene and

in the foreseeable future that can fulfill that reliability. These other versions do not, cannot, and will not.

g. **Some Quotations Explaining the ERRORS of DYNAMIC EQUIVALENCE from "TRANSLATING THE WORD OF GOD."** I want to quote from this "bible" of Bible translations. This is what they use. It has gone out of print, but some are still available. Those who translate the Bible, like the Wycliffe Bible translators, etc., have and use Beekman and Callow's TRANSLATING THE WORD OF GOD. I want to illustrate the DYNAMIC EQUIVALENCE method by quoting from Chapter 3, the **"Implicit and Explicit Information."** **Implicit means something that is implied. Explicit means something clearly stated.** Let's start with that which is implicit, or implied. **The KING JAMES translators avoided DYNAMIC EQUIVALENCE.** They attested, agreed to, and followed the method of verbal or formal equivalence.

(1) The ERRORS of DYNAMIC EQUIVA-LENCE'S Rule of Handling "IMPLICIT" Information.

(a) 1 Thessalonians 4:14: For instance, as an example of man changing God's Words, using the implicit argument, take 1 Thessalonians 4:14:

> ". . . even so them also which sleep in Jesus will God bring with him."

These editors are using diabolical methods--and I say diabolical methods even though the editors may be saved. These methods are furthering Satan's business, the Devil's business, whoever uses them, even if they are Fundamentalists of some kind. No one has any right to use the Devil's methodology. That is my strong belief and I'll tell it to their faces. They have no business by their implicit argumentation to add, change, or subtract from God's Words. These paraphrasers say that implied in this verse, even though not stated, are the following words that can be added to that verse:

> ". . . even so them also which sleep in Jesus will God bring with him **WHEN HE DESCENDS FROM HEAVEN.**"

They say it is implied from the context. Now, is that the kind of Bible you want?

Most of these Bibles have no italic type (as the KING JAMES does) to show that something has been added, that it wasn't in the Hebrew, or Greek, but was added to make it easier to understand. But most of these newer versions **do not** have italic type for this purpose. The NEW

AMERICAN STANDARD does. The NIV doesn't. The NEW KING JAMES VERSION doesn't. The LIVING VERSION doesn't. You notice, by implicit justification, by DYNAMIC EQUIVALENCE, by saying the implication is there they can ADD those five words. It is a travesty. **The true translator is not to make up Scripture, or to interpret Scripture,** but that is what these editors have done.

           (b) 2 Timothy 1:7: Let me give you a second example of implicit DYNAMIC EQUIVALENCE. 2 Timothy 1:7 states:

> *"For God hath not given us the spirit of fear; but of power and of love, and of a sound mind."*

Now, that is what it says in the Greek language. That is what it says in the KING JAMES. By implicit addition to that text, they say these words can be implied by the context and you can go ahead and add them in your translation--which to me is not a translation but a perversion of Scripture. They add,

> *"For God hath not given us the spirit of fear; **BUT HE HAS GIVEN US THE SPIRIT** of power and of love, and of a sound mind."*

Now, for exegesis, for interpretation, for pastoral preaching, you may want to say that is what it means. But for translation that purports to be a translation of God's Words, **to add these words is absolutely diabolical.** It is adding to the Words of God.

           (c) Luke 4:29-30: Another example of this method is found in Luke 4:29-30. This is how the translators are told to translate their Scripture portions and selections, which they are now using, in all the languages involved. They say, "This is the way to do it." As a result, you can't trust a single Bible put out and published by the United Bible Society or the American Bible Society [except the KING JAMES BIBLE]. You cannot hold up that Bible and say it is the Words of God because of all these additions and changes. They have the wrong texts, questionable translators, wrong techniques because it is the DYNAMIC EQUIVALENCE technique, paraphrase technique, and the technique Satan used in the Garden. The verses read:

> *". . . (29) that they might cast him down headlong. (30) But He passing through the midst of them went his way."*

That is exactly what is said in the Greek language, a good translation, a clear translation. Now, here's what they say we can add to the Words of God by implication:

> *". . . (29) that they might cast him down headlong (30) But **THEY COULD NOT CAST HIM DOWN AND** He*

passing through the midst of them went his way. "
It is implication by context which, they say, is permissible in a translation.
It is NOT permissible for a translation that is reliable and accurate. It
may be permissible in a paraphrase.   It may be permissible in these
idiomatic translations.   Remember, the word, "translation" comes from
trans (which means across) and *latus* (to lift, carry, or bring).   It means
"to lift across" from one language to another exactly what is there and to
put it down in that other language, no more and no less.   For additional
examples, see *TRANSLATING THE WORD OF GOD*, By Beekman and
Callow, Chapter 3.
         (2)   The ERRORS of DYNAMIC EQUIVA-
LENCE'S Rule of Handling "EXPLICIT" Information.
         Let me give you a few examples of **how** the DYNAMIC
EQUIVALENCE followers handle some **explicit** information in their
suggested translations.   By the use of the **implicit technique**, the
translator can put in anything that he feels is implied in the immediate
context or the overall context.   **By the use of the explicit technique, the
translator, in effect, can be deified.** He can make himself God. He can
choose to eliminate what God has explicitly and definitely stated, word
for word, in the Hebrew or in the Greek.   This word, or that word, or
several words if he wants to, he need not bother to translate, or put into
the language.   Now that again is a diabolical scheme perpetrated by
Eugene Nida and his followers at the Wycliffe Bible Translators, the
American Bible Society, and the United Bible Society. This is what they
do. They believe that they themselves are like God, the Holy Spirit. To
me, they are blaspheming God's Holy Words--either in the **implicit** way
by adding what is implied, or in the **explicit** way by taking out what God
the Holy Spirit has put in His Holy Words.
         (a)   Luke 1:18. Luke 1:18 says:
         ". . . Whereby shall I know this? for I am an OLD man,
         and my wife WELL STRICKEN IN YEARS. "
What they say on that verse is this: Since you have two expressions for
age, "well stricken in years" and "old," you can wipe out and subtract one
or the other of these expressions concerning age. This is against the will
of God, and against the principles of God in translation. They say this
even though both of these expressions are explicitly in the Greek
language (and that is an excellent translation in the KING JAMES
BIBLE).   They say you can eliminate "old" or "well stricken in years."
You don't need them both. **In effect, they are saying that the Holy
Spirit of God is being redundant here.** It is near to blasphemy against
the Holy Spirit. In fact, they call it redundancy, being repetitious,

or not needed.

How can man arrogate to himself the prerogative of God? How can a translator say, "I don't have to translate that"? The Bible is not just simply another book. If they want to do that with their comic books or fiction books, that is one thing. They can leave out anything they want to leave out in such books. BUT, don't do it to God's Book! This is serious. This is diabolical. This is deadly. This is not being perpetrated only by some Modernists, apostates, unbelievers, or children of the devil. It is being perpetrated and promulgated by people who claim to be children of God. It is being done by Fundamentalists, separatists, evangelicals, Bible-believing, saved people. That is how serious it is! Adam and Eve were created innocent people before they sinned. But when they did what Satan told them to do, they agreed to diabolical methods. People who do such things to God's Words are as guilty before God of disobedience to His clear Words whether they be Adam and Eve, or Bible-believing Fundamentalists, atheists, or apostates.

If they do the Devil's work by using his methods, they help him. Even God's children can serve Satan. Did you know that? I don't say they can be demon-possessed, but they can serve Satan's goals and objects. That is a serious situation. The Lord Jesus turned to Peter and said, *"Get thee behind me, Satan."* (Matthew 16:23) He called Peter *"Satan."* Why? Because he contradicted the Lord Jesus Christ, altered and changed His Words. Jesus said He was going to Jerusalem and was going to be crucified for the sins of the world. He said He was going to die and the third day He would be raised from the dead. Peter opened his big mouth and said:

> *"Be it far from Thee, Lord: this shall not be unto Thee."*
> *(Matthew 16:22b)*

Then Jesus turned to him and said,

> *"Get thee behind me, Satan: thou art an offence unto*
> *me: for thou savorest not the things that be of God, but*
> *those that be of men."* *(Matthew 16:23b)*

We have believers translating these versions of the Bible here in the United States. Most of these are believers. **We also have believers on foreign fields translating the Scriptures, but most of them are doing it by using these diabolical methods that they believe are godly!**

(b) Luke 8:35-38: Another example of something explicitly in the Greek language which our KING JAMES BIBLE has translated accurately is Luke 8:35-38. Here, these believers in dynamic equivalence say that even though God put words right in the verse, these

DYNAMIC EQUIVALENT people say that some of God's Words can be dropped out.

> ". . . and found the man, **OUT OF WHOM THE DEVILS WERE DEPARTED**, sitting at the feet of Jesus. . . (36) They also which saw it told them by what means **HE THAT WAS POSSESSED OF THE DEVILS** was healed . . . (38) Now the **MAN OUT OF WHOM THE DEVILS WERE DEPARTED** besought him that he might be with him. . . . "

Here's what they say: Three times the verses indicate that the man had some devils. First, in v. 35, "OUT OF WHOM THE DEVILS WERE DEPARTED," second, in v. 36, "HE THAT WAS POSSESSED OF THE DEVILS," and third, v. 38, "THE MAN OUT OF WHOM THE DEVILS WERE DEPARTED." The DYNAMIC EQUIVALENCE followers say, by the explicit rule, even though God the Holy Spirit explicitly gave us these words in the Greek three times, these people say you can throw out two out of the three. Only one is needed.

That is what the authors of this book are suggesting to the translators all over the world. They imply it is redundancy and repetition. What they're saying is that the Holy Spirit of God shouldn't have put this in three times and we don't really need it. Why did God give it in the Greek language then if we didn't need it? Apparently, God the Holy Spirit wanted to impress on their minds that this was a man that Jesus healed by casting out the demons that had been in him. **"Repetition is the mother of learning."** But these diabolical men teach that people can toss God the Holy Spirit's and the Lord Jesus Christ's Words right out of the New Testament if they wish to do so.

If you ADD to the Words of God what you think is implicit in the words, that is disobedience. God said NOT TO ADD to His Words. The explicit argument says even though the words are in the Hebrew or Greek, if you think they are redundant or repetitious, you can leave them out. For additional examples, see *TRANSLATING THE WORD OF GOD*, By Beekman and Callow, Chapter 3.

h. Some Illustrations from the NEW VERSIONS of the Use of DYNAMIC EQUIVALENCE and Translation ERRORS.

(1) Computer Analyses of Various Versions. Let's take a look at these Bibles, the AMERICAN STANDARD VERSION, the NEW INTERNATIONAL VERSION, and the NEW KING JAMES VERSION. We believe they are inferior to the KING JAMES BIBLE for many reasons.

(a) The NEW KING JAMES VERSION. As mentioned above, the computer analysis of the NEW KING JAMES VERSION shows a total of **over 2,000 examples** of addition, subtraction, and change from the KING JAMES BIBLE, and from the Hebrew in the Old Testament or Greek in the New Testament. [B.F.T. #1442] It is ninety-five large pages. A summary of the preface of this study is found in a small pamphlet. [B.F.T. #1465] **I believe the NEW KING JAMES VERSION is probably the most dangerous of the new versions on the present market today** because it is the foot in the door and the camel's nose in the tent to lead eventually to even more DYNAMIC EQUIVALENCY. By using the word, "KING JAMES VERSION" in its title, it lowers people's guard. People think that it is very similar to the KING JAMES VERSION, using the same technique and so on.

This causes people to think, "Well, this is simply a NEW KING JAMES and there's nothing wrong in it." There are lots of things deceptive concerning it. We give thirteen examples where it adds words. It changes nouns to pronouns twenty-five times. It omits the subjunctive mood, etc. These are specific examples you can look at if you get this printout. **The diabolical nature of the NEW KING JAMES VERSION shows itself in their printing all the various readings of the Greek text in the footnotes. They print all sides and take their stand in favor of none of them. By so doing, they confuse the readers.** The editors have made no decision as to what God's Words really are. If that isn't confusing, you think about it. They claim to use the *Textus Receptus* as a basis for translation, but it's not as accurate as our KING JAMES BIBLE by any means.

Down at the bottom of the page, the editors indicated where the text they use differs from the so-called "Majority Text" (M) (of Hodges & Farstad which is a farce and a misnomer). If their text differs from the Nestle's and United Bible Society text, which is the *Nestle/Aland 26th Edition*, the Westcott and Hort apostate Greek text, differing from our *Received Text* in over 5,600 places (involving almost 10,000 Greek words) they put that reading in the footnotes. So what you have is a Christian trying to read his Bible and then, all of a sudden, there's a footnote that says something either should be added, should be subtracted, or should be changed to something else. Practically every page has changes in the New Testament Greek text suggested by these confusing footnotes. They take no stand whatever. At least the NEW AMERICAN STANDARD VERSION and the NEW INTERNATIONAL VERSION have honestly said they were NOT going to use the *Textus Receptus* but they were going to use the Westcott-and-Hort-type text and that is what it is. They have fewer footnotes about their text than the NKJV. But the NEW KING JAMES makes note of all the changes so that the new Christian, the young Christian, and all other Christians are supposed to be textual critics on their own, and make up their own mind about the proper Greek text.

On page 1235, in the back of the book, the editors make that very statement. They wrote:

*"It was the editors' conviction that the use of footnotes would encourage further inquiry by readers. They also recognized that it was **easier for the average reader TO DELETE** [subtract, or take away from] something he or she felt was not properly a part of the text **than TO INSERT a word or phrase** which had been left out by the revisers."*

So they say the editors have no opinion, no guess as to what the real text of the Words of God is. You take your pick and choose for yourself. To have a smorgasbord of textual variance down in the footnotes, as the NEW KING JAMES has, is a terrible travesty on the young Christian trying to find out what the Bible is. It certainly puts doubts in the mind whenever there's a difference. Which is right? Is it this reading or that one? No matter which you pick you have a question mark and a doubt; and the Devil is delighted!

(b) The NEW AMERICAN STANDARD VERSION. We have a printout on the NEW AMERICAN STANDARD VERSION comparing the Hebrew and Greek. [B.F.T. #1494-P] It has 187 large pages and has **over 4,000 examples** of DYNAMIC EQUIVALENCE. We also have a small pamphlet entitled: *"THE DEFECTS OF THE NEW AMERICAN STANDARD VERSION."* [B.F.T. #1518] It is the preface to this printout.

(c) The NEW INTERNATIONAL VERSION. As mentioned above, we also have a printout study on the NEW INTERNATIONAL VERSION comparing the Hebrew and Greek. [B.F.T. #1749-P] It has 284 large pages and has **over 6,653 examples** of DYNAMIC EQUIVALENCE. We also have a small pamphlet entitled: *"DEFECTS IN THE NEW INTERNATIONAL VERSION."* [B.F.T. #2054] It is the preface of the larger study. The NIV is a defective translation indeed. Yet it is used so many times by Fundamentalists and people who ought to be using the KING JAMES BIBLE. It should be pointed out in this part of the study that the NIV strong backers are the ones who believe they can replace the KING JAMES BIBLE and its popularity and substitute for it the NEW INTERNATIONAL VERSION. That is what they believe. They have millions and millions of dollars behind them. The NEW AMERICAN STANDARD VERSION is becoming outdated. It was born in 1960. As we go to press, it is now thirty-two years old. But the NIV has its own concordance, its own interlinear Hebrew Bible, and commentaries based upon it. The Dallas Theological Seminary, for instance, has a Commentary based on the NEW INTERNATIONAL VERSION. The Seminary has also published a two-volume abridgement of Dr. Chafer's eight-volume *SYSTEMATIC THEOLOGY which also uses the NIV*. It is a bandwagon phenomenon.

(2) **Various VERSES with ERRORS in the Various VERSIONS.** I am particularly following in the NIV the major changes that are made. For example: you know what a pronoun is--**I, he, she, we, you, they.** A pronoun is a word used instead of a noun. A noun is the name of a person, place or thing. The Hebrew has pronouns. The Greek has pronouns. English has pronouns. All three languages also have nouns. There is little reason for a translator who is faithful in his translating to change a pronoun and make it into a noun. That is interpretation. That is not translation. The same is true when they change a noun and make it into a pronoun. They may be right in interpretation, but that is not translation. It's commentary. It is changing the Words of God. Some of you may say, "Who cares whether they make a pronoun into a noun?" Well, I care. I'm using this example as something simple. I have been asked at times about changing the subjunctive into the indicative mood. People don't even know what a subjective mood is. Well, that may be a minor change in the NEW KING JAMES, let's say, or in the NIV, or the NEW AMERICAN STANDARD. But all three of these versions have virtually eliminated the subjunctive mood. They only have the indicative. Remember, Luke 16:10:

> *"He that is faithful in that which is LEAST is faithful also in MUCH; and he that is unjust in the LEAST is unjust also in MUCH."*

Now, let me just take a few examples:

(a) **Luke 22:61 and Other Verses:** The KING JAMES BIBLE in Luke 22:61 says (just as the Greek says), *". . . before the cock CROW . . ."* This is the subjunctive mood. Spanish, French, and English all have the subjunctive mood, as does the Greek. *"Before the cock CROW."* The NIV says, "before the rooster CROWS." "CROWS" is the indicative mood and "CROW" is the subjunctive mood. For instance, in the phrase in John 12:24 *"except a corn of wheat FALL into the ground," "FALL"* is in the subjunctive mood. The NIV translates that "FALLS." Probably most of us would understand it better if there is an "if" before it. For instance, Acts 4:35, *"if it BE of men"* is the subjunctive mood. The NIV changes it to "if it IS of men." *"Except God BE with him"* is changed to "unless God IS with him." "BE" is the subjunctive mood, and is still a part of the English language, yet all three of these versions omit them as if it were something outmoded. The subjunctive mood is not only used in the KING JAMES, but it is also standard English.

      (b) Mark 6:54 and Other Verses: Let's take a look at some of the changes from pronouns to nouns and nouns to pronouns. Take the KING JAMES VERSION, in Mark 6:54. It says: *". . . THEY knew him."* *"They"* is a pronoun and that is exactly what the Greek says, *". . . THEY knew him."* The **NEW** KING JAMES changes that to *". . . the PEOPLE recognized him."* Now, "recognize" is a synonym for *"knew,"* but they change *"THEY"* to "PEOPLE." The same is true in 1 Samuel 15:27, *"HE"* is changed to "SAUL." The Hebrew says *"HE"* but they change it to "SAUL."

      (c) Leviticus 8:15: What about changing nouns to pronouns: Leviticus 8:15, says: *"MOSES took the blood"* (KING JAMES and Hebrew).   The NEW KING JAMES VERSION in DYNAMIC EQUIVALENCY style changes that and says "HE took the blood" This is done over and over.

      (d) Acts 25:3 and Other Verses: In the NEW AMERICAN STANDARD: Acts 25:3 the pronoun *"HIM"* is changed to "PAUL. In John 10:38 *"HIM"* is changed into "THE FATHER." *"HIM"* is all that is in the Greek, but they change it. In Ezekiel 11:7, *"IT"* is changed to "THE CITY." In Zechariah 14:10 *"IT"* is changed into "JERUSALEM."

      (e) Numbers 5:18 and Other Verses: *"THE PRIEST"* in Numbers 5:17 is changed into "HE." Now, when God says *cohen* in the Hebrew, they change it into "HE." They alter the Words of God. Genesis 30:1 *"RACHEL"* is changed into "SHE." *"REHOBOAM"* changed into "HE." 2 Chronicles 13:7.

      (f) Job 3:11 and Other Verses: The pure paraphrases are rampant in these versions also; we have a whole section in the back regarding paraphrases. For instance, *"WOMB"* in Job 3:11 in the NEW KING JAMES is changed to "AT BIRTH." This is a paraphrase. In Mark 7:3 the Greek word is *"OFT"* or "OFTEN" but they paraphrase it, in the NEW KING JAMES, "IN A SPECIAL WAY." This has nothing to do with "OFTEN" which is frequency. "IN A SPECIAL WAY" is an entirely different idea, a paraphrase. **Don't let anyone say the NEW KING JAMES is an accurate, faithful, verbal equivalent. It is not. Examine some of these changes.** They change *"PASTORS"* to "RULERS," *"PALACE"* to "TEMPLES" etc.

(g) **Genesis 35:9:** The NEW INTERNATIONAL VERSION has the same policy of changing nouns to pronouns. In Genesis 35:9, the Hebrew and the KING JAMES BIBLE say *"HE came out"* and they change it to "JACOB returned." In the same verse the NIV says: "God appeared to HIM" and the KING JAMES and Hebrew say *"to JACOB."* Why don't they leave it the way the Holy Spirit wrote it?

We have **over 6,653** of these examples in the NEW INTERNATIONAL VERSION. **Did you know there is no longer either a *"vail"* or a *"veil"* that separates between the Holy Place and the Holy of Holies in the NIV?** That vail, which to us is so important, is reduced only to a "curtain." There are at least three Hebrew words for "curtain." But "vail" is a special Hebrew word.

Along this same line, the NIV has omitted some other doctrinal words. **Did you know there's no longer a "mercy seat" in the NIV? Did you know there's no longer the word "propitiation" in the NIV?** Here are some other words that appear in the KING JAMES BIBLE but are absent in the NIV:

WORDS IN KJB	TIMES IN KJB	TIMES IN NIV
advocate (N.T.)	1	0
chaste/chasten	3	0
concupiscence	3	0
sodomite/sodomites	3	0
carnal/carnally	14	0
impute/imputed/imputeth	13	0
fornicator(s)/fornication(s)	40	0
abide/abideth/abiding	114	0

For an analysis of thirty-three other doctrinal terms that have been significantly reduced by the NIV, though not yet eliminated, you can consult **B.F.T. #1923.**

(3) **Some Theological Changes.** Now let's take a few theological changes in the NEW AMERICAN STANDARD VERSION and the NEW INTERNATIONAL VERSION. For a more detailed

examination of the theological errors in the versions, please consult **CHAPTER V** which follows this chapter.

(a) **1 Timothy 3:16:** In 1 Timothy 3:16, this change is due to a **textual change** rather than a technique of translation. In the KING JAMES (and in the Greek) it says:

> *"And without controversy great is the mystery of godliness: GOD was manifest in the flesh, justified in the Spirit, seen of angels, preached unto the Gentiles, believed on in the world, received up into glory."*

In the NEW INTERNATIONAL VERSION they say,

> "Beyond question the mystery of godliness is great"

Then they say:

> "**HE** appeared in a body."

Where is the word "God"? Who is "HE?" To whom are they referring? They have taken the Greek word *"theos"* (God) and changed it into *"hos"* which is a relative pronoun which means "HE WHO" or "THE ONE WHO." **The miracle of the Incarnation of the Lord Jesus Christ is: GOD was manifest in the flesh.** "HE appeared in a body" doesn't say anything about the Incarnation. Every one of us has appeared in a body; we're all in a body. We're not "GOD" appearing in a body, manifest in a body. Theologically there's error in this NEW INTERNATIONAL VERSION.

What does it say in the NEW AMERICAN STANDARD VERSION? Again, this is a textual change, but also a deadly theological change.

> "Great is the mystery of godliness: **HE who** was revealed in the flesh . . . "

Not *"GOD"*--**GOD is gone from the NEW AMERICAN STANDARD VERSION and the NEW INTERNATIONAL VERSION here.**

(b) **Mark 16:15:** If you look at Mark 16:15, which is the Great Commission, in the NEW AMERICAN STANDARD VERSION Mark 16:15 comes in a section that has brackets around it and it says,

> *"Some of the oldest manuscripts omit verses 9 through 20."*

Casting doubt, they take out the Great Commission of Mark 16:15. That is doctrinal deviation and change.

What do they do in the NEW INTERNATIONAL VERSION? Again it comes in a section which has been separated from the first eight verses by a black line. As far as the New International translators are concerned, Mark ends at Mark 16:8. Then they print verses 9-20 and there is a footnote:

> *"The two most reliable early manuscripts do not have Mark 16:9-20."*

In other words, Mark 16:15 *("... Go ye into all the world, and preach the gospel to every creature")* doesn't even exist so far as their "most reliable" manuscripts are concerned.

          (c) Luke 2:33: Let's take an example in the Gospel of Luke, Luke 2:33:

> *"And **Joseph** and his mother marvelled at those things which were spoken of him."*

The NEW AMERICAN STANDARD VERSION says,

> "and **His FATHER** and mother."

Joseph is indicated as being Jesus' "FATHER." The Virgin Birth is denied by this rendering of the NEW AMERICAN STANDARD VERSION. Joseph wasn't Jesus' "FATHER"; the Holy Spirit was His FATHER. In the NEW INTERNATIONAL VERSION,

> "the child's **FATHER** and mother."

"**JOSEPH**" is in the Greek text. "**JOSEPH**" is **correct**.

          (d) Luke 24:51: Take the Ascension of the Lord Jesus Christ in Luke 24:51:

> *"And it came to pass, while he blessed them, he was part-ed from them and **CARRIED UP INTO HEAVEN.**"*

Now in the NEW AMERICAN STANDARD VERSION it has:

> "And it came about while he was blessing them he parted from them."

Is that what your Bible has? The phrase *"CARRIED UP INTO HEAVEN"* is missing. As far as the NEW AMERICAN STANDARD VERSION is concerned, the Ascension is gone here. Christ has not ascended into Heaven. They may have other verses that teach that He has, but not this one.

      Our computer studies of the NEW AMERICAN STANDARD VERSION, the NEW KING JAMES VERSION, and the NEW INTERNATIONAL VERSION point out that the DYNAMIC EQUIVALENCE changes, translation changes, and paraphrases are many. This gives you an idea of some of them. **You can trust with confidence the KING JAMES BIBLE in the English language** as the most accurate reflection of the original Hebrew and Greek text we have--and probably will have until the Lord returns in the Rapture of the Church. Read it! Study it! Memorize it! Understand it! Believe it! Practice it!

CHAPTER V

THE KING JAMES BIBLE IS GOD'S WORD KEPT INTACT IN ENGLISH BECAUSE OF ITS SUPERIOR THEOLOGY

A. BACKGROUND OF THIS SECTION.

1. Theology Was at First Omitted. I had talked about this subject of "The King James Bible's Superiority--God's Word Kept Intact In English" for about ten years under the THREE divisions of (1) TEXT, (2) TRANSLATORS, and (3) TECHNIQUE. Then, during a series of meetings in April and May of 1990, I saw so very definitely that our KING JAMES BIBLE had a fourth SUPERIORITY. It was "SUPERIOR IN ITS THEOLOGY!" Not only is it true that the KING JAMES BIBLE is superior in its THEOLOGY; but also the reverse is true, that is, all of the other versions of the Bible are INFERIOR IN THEIR THEOLOGY! It stands to reason that if the KJB is SUPERIOR to all other versions in its THEOLOGY, then all the other versions would have to be INFERIOR in that area. We found this to be the case.

2. How Theology Is Affected in Bible Versions. THEOLOGY is affected in the Bible versions in two possible ways: (1) Either the PARAPHRASE found in the versions causes doctrinal changes, or (2) The basic TEXT OF GREEK is in error. It is this latter area I would like to deal with in this section. Before beginning, here are NINE false statements by various writers about how DOCTRINE is affected either by the changes in the Westcott-and-Hort-type Greek New Testament text or in the English versions based upon it.

a. The False Statement of Dr. Philip Schaff about DOCTRINE Being Affected. Regarding "variant readings" in the Greek text, Dr. Schaff wrote:

> "Only about 400 affect the sense; and of these 400 only about 50 are of real significance for one reason or another, and **NOT ONE OF THESE 50 AFFECT AN ARTICLE OF FAITH** or a precept of duty which is not abundantly sustained by other and undoubted passages, or by the whole tenor of Scripture teaching." [In his Companion To The Greek Testament And English Version as quoted in Bible Translations by Evangelist R. L. Sumner, p. 8,

March, 1979].

As will be shown in the subsequent pages, this is a completely untrue and misleading statement. Many of these variant readings "affect" many "ARTICLES OF FAITH" whether or not they are "sustained by other and undoubted passages." **Schaff was an apostate in doctrine and practice**; yet he was the Chairman of the AMERICAN STANDARD VERSION of 1901.

b. The False Statement of Dr. Arthur T. Pierson about DOCTRINE Being Affected. Writing about this theme, Dr. Pierson wrote:

> *". . . it is remarkable how faithful **ALL THE STAN-DARD TRANSLATIONS ARE**, and most remarkable how, amid all the thousands of doubtful disputed renderings, even of the most perplexing passages, **NOT ONE** [doubtful disputed rendering] **AFFECTS A SINGLE VITAL DOCTRINE OF THE WORD OF GOD."** [In his Knowing The Scripture, the chapter on "Bible Versions And Translations" as quoted in Bible Translations by Evangelist R. L. Sumner, p. 21, 1979].*

As will be shown in the subsequent pages, this is a completely untrue and misleading statement. Many "doubtful disputed renderings" do "affect" many "VITAL DOCTRINES OF THE WORDS OF GOD." Dr. Pierson was one of the editors of the *Scofield Reference Bible.*

c. The False Statement Of Dr. Louis T. Talbot about DOCTRINE Being Affected. On this topic Dr. Talbot wrote:

> *"Yet, to repeat for emphasis, for all practical purposes, we still cling to the King James Version, using the **REVISED** [that is, the ENGLISH REVISED VERSION of 1881, or the AMERICAN STANDARD VERSION of 1901] as a kind of commentary for analytical study. And let me add that **NO FUNDA-MENTAL DOCTRINE HAS BEEN CHANGED IN THE LEAST BY THE LATER VERSION."** [As quoted in Bible Translations by Evangelist R. L. Sumner, p. 20, 1979]*

As will be shown in the subsequent pages, this is a completely untrue and misleading statement. Many "FUNDAMENTAL DOCTRINES HAVE BEEN CHANGED" by the "REVISED" versions, whether the ENGLISH

REVISED VERSION (ERV) of 1881, or the AMERICAN STANDARD VERSION (ASV) of 1901.

d. The False Statement of Dr. John R. Rice about DOCTRINE Being Affected. On this theme, Dr. Rice wrote:

> *"The **DIFFERENCES IN THE TRANSLATIONS ARE SO MINOR, SO INSIGNIFICANT, THAT WE CAN BE SURE NOT A SINGLE DOCTRINE, NOT A SINGLE STATEMENT OF FACT, NOT A SINGLE COMMAND OR EXHORTATION, HAS BEEN MISSED IN OUR TRANSLATIONS."** [As quoted in Bible Translations by Evangelist R. L. Sumner, p. 18, 1979]*

As will be shown in the subsequent pages, this is a completely untrue and misleading statement. The "DIFFERENCES IN THE TRANSLATIONS" are NOT "SO MINOR" or "SO INSIGNIFICANT" at all. Many "DOCTRINES," many "STATEMENTS OF FACT," and many "COMMANDS OR EXHORTATIONS" have been "MISSED" in many "TRANSLATIONS."

e. The False Statement of Dr. Robert L. Sumner about DOCTRINE Being Affected. On this subject, Dr. Sumner wrote:

> *"Faithful, textual criticism by honest Christian scholars has made it possible for us to be dead certain about the major portion of the Hebrew, Aramaic and Greek--especially the New Testament Greek--and **THE RARE PARTS ABOUT WHICH THERE IS STILL UNCERTAINTY DO NOT EFFECT [sic] IN ANY WAY ANY DOCTRINE."** [Bible Translations by Evangelist R. L. Sumner, p. 4, 1979]*

As will be shown in the subsequent pages, this is a completely untrue and misleading statement. The "PARTS" of the "NEW TESTAMENT GREEK" about which there is "STILL UNCERTAINTY" most certainly DO affect, in many "WAYS," many "DOCTRINES."

f. The False Statement of Dr. Robert L. Thomas about DOCTRINE Being Affected. On this area, Dr. Thomas wrote:

> *"**AND NO MAJOR DOCTRINE OF SCRIPTURE IS AFFECTED BY A VARIANT READING."** [From MASTERPIECE MAGAZINE, January/February, 1990, p. 17, "The King James Controversy" article by Dr. Robert L. Thomas, as quoted in MacArthur's*

Man Answered On EIGHTEEN ERRORS Concerning THE KING JAMES BIBLE by Rev. D. A. Waite, Th.D., Ph.D., p. 3, published by BIBLE FOR TODAY, 900 Park Avenue, Collingswood, NJ 08108]

As will be shown in the subsequent pages, this is a completely untrue and misleading statement. There are many "MAJOR DOCTRINES OF SCRIPTURE" that are "AFFECTED BY A VARIANT READING" in the Greek text. Dr. Thomas is a "Professor of New Testament Studies at The Master's Seminary" headed up by Dr. John MacArthur.

      g. The False Statement of Dr. H. S. Miller about DOCTRINE Being Affected. When telling about this topic, Dr. Miller wrote:

> *"These VARIATIONS include such matters as differences in spelling, transposition of letters, words, clauses, order of words, order of sentences, reduplication, etc. NO DOCTRINE IS AFFECTED, and very often not even the translation is affected." [From General Biblical Introduction as quoted by Dr. Ernest Pickering in "Questions And Answers About Bible Translations," pp. 7-8. Also quoted in "Refutation Of Dr. Ernest D. Pickering On Bible Translations," by Rev. D. A. Waite, Th.D., Ph.D., p. 33, 1991].*

As will be shown in the subsequent pages, this is a completely untrue and misleading statement. In the "VARIATIONS" in the original language texts, many "DOCTRINES ARE AFFECTED."

      h. The False Statement of Dr. Stanley Gundry about DOCTRINE Being Affected. On this same problem, Dr. Gundry wrote:

> *"ONLY A FEW OUTSTANDING PROBLEMS REMAIN, AND THESE DO NOT AFFECT DOCTRINE OR DIVINE COMMAND TO US." ["What Happened To Those King James Verses,?" Moody Monthly, 1990, p. 46, as quoted in "Questions And Answers About Bible Translations" by Dr. Ernest Pickering, p. 8. Also quoted in Refutation of Dr. Ernest D. Pickering On Bible Translations by Dr. D. A. Waite, op. cit., p. 34].*

As will be shown in the subsequent pages, this is a completely untrue and misleading statement. In the "FEW OUTSTANDING PROBLEMS" that "REMAIN," so far as the original language texts are concerned, there are many that "AFFECT DOCTRINE OR DIVINE COMMAND TO US."

I.   The False Statement of Dr. Ernest D. Pickering about DOCTRINE Being Affected.   With reference to this subject, Dr. Pickering wrote:

> *"IMPORTANT DIFFERENCES OF TEXTUAL READINGS ARE RELATIVELY FEW AND ALMOST NONE WOULD AFFECT ANY MAJOR CHRISTIAN DOCTRINE."   ["Questions and An-swers About Bible Translations," by Dr. Ernest D. Pickering, p. 3, as quoted in Refutation Of Dr. Ernest D. Pickering On Bible Translations by Dr. D. A. Waite, op. cit., p. 10].*

As will be shown in the subsequent pages, this is a completely untrue and misleading statement.   The "IMPORTANT DIFFERENCES OF TEXTUAL READINGS" are not "RELATIVELY FEW," but **many**; and **many** do "AFFECT" **many** "MAJOR CHRISTIAN DOCTRINES."

The bottom line of all these statements is that these writers declare that DOCTRINE or THEOLOGY is left UNTOUCHED by the various Greek and Hebrew texts and by the various English transla-tions/paraphrases of these texts. **This simply is false in the extreme!**

3.   Pastor Jack Moorman's Excellent Work on "DOC-TRINAL PASSAGES."   Our good friend, Pastor Jack Moorman, has written an excellent work entitled *Early Manuscripts and The Authorized Version--A Closer Look.*   It is **B.F.T. #1825** which is available from THE BIBLE FOR TODAY.   Brother Moorman takes up in some detail (with manuscript evidence) a total of **356 DOCTRINAL PASSAGES** that are affected by variations in Greek manuscript readings between the *Received Greek Text* that underlies the KING JAMES BIBLE, and the Revised Greek Text of Westcott and Hort, Nestle-Aland-26th, and others.   There are 5,604 places where these two texts differ.   This involves 9,970 Greek words.

In another of Pastor Moorman's books, *(Missing In Modern Bi-bles--Is The Full Story Being Told?)*, he has actually counted every word in every chapter of the New Testament Greek texts both of the *Received Text* and the Revised Text.   He found that, of the **140,521 Greek words** in the *Received Text,* a total of **2,886 words** which were OMITTED from the Revised Text of Nestle-Aland and Westcott and Hort. These 2,886 words would be the length, in English, of the entire books of 1 Peter and 2 Peter! [**B.F.T.** #1726] Obviously, with that many WORDS subtracted from the very WORDS OF GOD, you are going to have DOCTRINES and THEOLOGY affected. This is exactly what was found!

4. 158 Selected Doctrinal Passages Listed and Annotated. During my series of meetings in Michigan from April 17 through May 22, 1990, I looked at all 356 of Pastor Moorman's doctrinal passages, and selected 158 of them for specific illustration. On May 18, 1990, in the First Baptist Church of Harrison, Michigan, I spoke on the topic of *"EXTERNAL AND INTERNAL EVIDENCES AGAINST `B' AND `ALEPH.'"* These three messages are available on cassettes. In the discussion of the "INTERNAL EVIDENCES," I had four of the visiting pastors look up each of the verses mentioned. They were (1) Pastor Bob Steward, (2) Pastor Robert Barnett, (3) Pastor William VanKleeck, and (4) Pastor William McCallister. Each pastor had a different version of the New Testament. One had the *NEW INTERNATIONAL VERSION* (NIV). One had the *NEW AMERICAN STANDARD VERSION* (NASV). One had the *NEW KING JAMES VERSION WITH FOOTNOTES* (NKJV-FN). And one had *THE NEW BERKLEY VERSION* (NB). I used these FOUR English versions because they are the ones used mostly by Fundamentalists and/or New Evangelicals who have discarded the KING JAMES BIBLE. The same theological errors (and MORE) would be seen in other English versions such as the RSV, NRSV, LV, NEV, TEV, ASV, and many others. For a complete list of all the complete English Bibles and New Testaments that were ever printed, please consult **APPENDIX B** in the back of this book.

As I came to each verse where there was a variation in either "B" (Vatican) or "Aleph" (Sinai) manuscript, or in some other manuscript such as "D," I asked each of the four pastors to tell me whether or not their versions followed these false readings. It was on this basis that the following data were collected. The 158 doctrinal passages have been available heretofore under the title *Theological Errors In The Versions*. It was **B.F.T.** #1845, the same number as is presently available separately, but had only sixteen pages. This chapter of this book is also available in a separate study as of now. [**B.F.T.** #1845]

B. THEOLOGICAL ERRORS IN THE VERSIONS.

A few explanations are in order to interpret correctly the data that follow. First there will be a THEOLOGICAL DIVISION defined briefly. Then there will be a verse or passage of Scripture.

The word or words that are in italic type are either omitted entirely, or changed by some Greek manuscripts, usually "B" (Vatican) and/or "Aleph" (Sinai) or some other manuscript that is indicated. I have put a "-" sign where either "B" or "Aleph" (or other Greek manuscript) has omitted or altered the italicized words. "-B/ALEPH" would indicate that both "B" and "Aleph" have omitted or altered the words in question.

After the Greek textual information, there is information about the "English Versions." There is a -1 or -2 or -3 or -4 followed by the abbreviations for the versions that follow "B" and/or "Aleph" with a "-" before them such as -NIV (for the NEW INTERNA-TIONAL VERSION); -NASV (for the NEW AMERICAN STANDARD VERSION); -NKJV-FN (for the NEW KING JAMES VERSION FOOTNOTES); or -NB (for the NEW BERKLEY VERSION).

There will then be a brief explanation of what sort of THEOLOGICAL ERROR this represents both in the versions represented and in the Greek manuscripts indicated. It is not our purpose here to defend the Greek *Textus Receptus* readings as opposed to the Revised texts of "B" and/or "Aleph" and their allies. This has been done in the various books by Dean John William Burgon, Dr. Frederick Scrivener, Rev. Frederick Nolan, Rev. S. C. Malan, Rev. G. W. Samson, Rev. H. C. Hoskier, and more recently, our good friend and excellent researcher, Pastor Jack Moorman. All of these books have been published or reprinted by THE BIBLE FOR TODAY, and are available for those who wish to dig deeper into textual matters. **[See back of book]**

1. THEOLOGY PROPER (The Doctrine of the Godhead).

•   **a. The Denial of the Trinity.**

"For there are three that bear record *in heaven, the Father, the Word, and the Holy Ghost: and these three are one.*" (1 John 5:7) *"And there are three that bear witness in earth,* the spirit, and the water, and the blood: and these three agree in one." (1 John 5:8)

Greek Texts: -B/ALEPH;
English Versions: (-4) -NIV, -NASV, -NKJV-FN, -NB

The *italicized* portion is ELIMINATED in the Greek texts and English versions specified above. It is one of the clearest references to the Trinity in the Bible. **This is certainly a matter of doctrine and theology.** At this point, these Greek texts and these English versions are **theologically deficient,** whereas the *Textus Receptus* and the KING JAMES BIBLE are **theologically superior.**

2.   ECCLESIOLOGY (The Doctrine Of the Church).
●   **a.   The Denial of Christ's Hatred of Nicolaitanism.**
"So hast thou also them that hold the doctrine of the Nicolaitans, *which thing I hate.*" (Revelation 2:15)
Greek Texts: -Aleph, (There is no B in Revelation)
English Versions: (-4) -NIV, -NASV, -NKJV-FN, -NB

The *italicized* portion is ELIMINATED in the Greek text and English versions specified above. The fact that the Lord Jesus Christ "HATES" this practice is theologically important. The "Nicolaitans" were "conquerors of the people" and held to a form of church government such as the Roman Catholic system where the clergy make the decisions leaving the congregations with little or no authority. **This is certainly a matter of doctrine and theology.** At this point, this Greek text and these English versions are **theologically deficient,** whereas the *Textus Receptus* and the KING JAMES BIBLE are **theologically superior.**

3.   ANGELOLOGY (The Doctrine of Angels).
●   **a.   The Denial That Angels Strengthened Christ.**
"And there appeared an angel unto him from heaven, strengthening Him." (Luke 22:43)
Greek Texts: -B/ALEPH;
English Versions: (-1) -NKJV-FN

The *italicized* portion is ELIMINATED in the Greek texts and English version specified above. The ENTIRE VERSE has been purged from the texts indicated. This shows the strengthening, heavenly angel assisting the Lord Jesus Christ. **This is certainly a matter of doctrine and theology.** At this point, these Greek texts and this English version are **theologically deficient,** whereas the *Textus Receptus* and the KING JAMES BIBLE are **theologically superior.**

4.   SATANOLOGY (The Doctrine of Satan).

-      **a. The Denial That Satan Was Commanded by Christ.**
"And Jesus answered *and said unto him, Get thee behind Me, Satan*: for it is written, Thou shalt worship the Lord thy God, and Him only shalt thou serve." (Luke 4:8)
       Greek Texts: -B/ALEPH;
English Versions: (-4) -NIV, -NASV, -NKJV-FN, -NB

The *italicized* portion is ELIMINATED in the Greek texts and English versions specified above. It shows clearly the power of the Lord Jesus Christ to order and command Satan to do His bidding. **This is certainly a matter of doctrine and theology.** At this point, these Greek texts and these English versions are **theologically deficient**, whereas the *Textus Receptus* and the KING JAMES BIBLE are **theologically superior.**

     5. BIBLIOLOGY (The Doctrine of The Bible).
-      **a. The Denial of Large Twelve-Verse Sections.**
        (1) The Denial of Mark 16:9-20.

"Now when {Jesus} was risen early the first {day} of the week, He appeared first to Mary Magdalene, out of whom He had cast seven devils. Mark 16:9
{And} she went and told them that had been with Him, as they mourned and wept. Mark 16:10
And they, when they had heard that He was alive, and had been seen of her, believed not. Mark 16:11
After that He appeared in another form unto two of them, as they walked, and went into the country. Mark 16:12
And they went and told {it} unto the residue: neither believed they them. Mark 16:13
Afterward He appeared unto the eleven as they sat at meat, and upbraided them with their unbelief and hardness of heart, because they believed not them which had seen Him after He was risen. Mark 16:14
And He said unto them, Go ye into all the world, and preach the gospel to every creature. Mark 16:15
He that believeth and is baptized shall be saved; but he that believeth not shall be damned. Mark 16:16
And these signs shall follow them that believe; In My name shall they cast out devils; they shall speak with new tongues; Mark 16:17
They shall take up serpents; and if they drink any deadly thing, it shall not hurt them; they shall lay hands on the

sick, and they shall recover. Mark 16:18
So then after the Lord had spoken unto them, He was
received up into heaven, and sat on the right hand of
God. Mark 16:19
And they went forth, and preached every where, the Lord
working with {them}, and confirming the word with signs
following. Amen." Mark 16:20

Greek Texts: -B/ALEPH;

English Versions: (-3) -[NIV], -[NASV], -NKJV-FN

The *italicized* portion is ELIMINATED in the Greek texts and English versions specified above. The NIV and the NASV **bracket** or make lines to separated these verses from the rest of their text with questionable footnotes, explaining that they do not believe the twelve verses are genuine. There are MANY DOCTRINES mentioned in these verses, all of which are doubted in this place. **This is certainly a matter of doctrine and theology.** At this point, these Greek texts and these English versions are **theologically deficient**, whereas the *Textus Receptus* and the KING JAMES BIBLE are **theologically superior.**

-         **(2)   The Denial of John 7:53--8:11.**
  "And every man went unto his own house. John 7:53
  Jesus went unto the mount of Olives. John 8:1
  And early in the morning he came again into the temple,
  and all the people came unto him; and he sat down, and
  taught them. John 8:2
  And the scribes and Pharisees brought unto him a
  woman taken in adultery; and when they had set her in
  the midst, John 8:3
  They say unto him, Master, this woman was taken in
  adultery, in the very act. John 8:4
  Now Moses in the law commanded us, that such should
  be stoned: but what sayest thou? John 8:5
  This they said, tempting him, that they might have to
  accuse him. But Jesus stooped down, and with {his}
  finger wrote on the ground, {as though he heard them
  not}. John 8:6
  So when they continued asking him, he lifted up himself,
  and said unto them, He that is without sin among you, let
  him first cast a stone at her. John 8:7
  And again he stooped down, and wrote on the ground.
  John 8:8

And they which heard {it}, being convicted by {their
own} conscience, went out one by one, beginning at the
eldest, {even} unto the last: and Jesus was left alone, and
the woman standing in the midst. John 8:9
When Jesus had lifted up himself, and saw none but the
woman, he said unto her, Woman, where are those thine
accusers? hath no man condemned thee? John 8:10
She said, No man, Lord. And Jesus said unto her, Neither
do I condemn thee: go, and sin no more." John 8:11

Greek Texts: -B/ALEPH;
English Versions: (-3) -[NIV], -[NASV], -NKJV-FN

The *italicized* portion is ELIMINATED in the Greek texts and English
versions specified above. The NIV, the NASV, and the NKJV-FN either
bracket these twelve verses or set them apart in some way from the text.
Their footnotes question or doubt outright their authenticity. There are
MANY DOCTRINES mentioned in these verses, all of which are doubted
in this place. **This is certainly a matter of doctrine and theology.** At
this point, these Greek texts and these English versions are **theologically
deficient,** whereas the *Textus Receptus* and the KING JAMES BIBLE are
theologically superior.

* **b. The Denial of the Historicity and Prophet Role of
Daniel.**

"But when ye shall see the abomination of desolation,
spoken of by Daniel the prophet, standing where it ought
not, (let him that readeth understand,) then let them that
be in Judaea flee to the mountains:" (Mark 13:14)

Greek Texts: -B/ALEPH;
English Versions: (-4) -NIV, -NASV, -NKJV-FN, -NB

The *italicized* portion is ELIMINATED in the Greek texts and English
versions specified above. **The REMOVAL of the underlined words
denies that Daniel was the author of the book of Daniel.** It also denies
that Daniel was a "prophet," lending credence to the heresy of the
modernist/liberal/apostates who claim that Daniel is merely post-written
history rather than pre-written prophecy. **This certainly is a matter of
doctrine and theology.** At this point, these Greek texts and these English
versions are **theologically deficient,** whereas the *Textus Receptus* and the
KING JAMES BIBLE are **theologically superior.**

* **c. The Denial of Peter's Authorship of 2 Peter and of His
Apostleship.**

"That ye may be mindful of the words which were

spoken before by the holy prophets, and of the commandment of *us* the apostles of the Lord and Saviour:"
(2 Peter 3:2)

Greek Texts: -B/ALEPH;
English Versions: (-4) -NIV, -NASV, -NKJV-FN, -NB

The *italicized* portion is ELIMINATED in the Greek texts and English versions specified above. In the place of the word, "US" is the word "THEIR" in these Greek and English texts. This does two things: (1) It takes away or doubts Peter's authorship of the book of 2 Peter; and (2) It takes away or doubts that Peter was an "apostle." If Peter were writing this (and we are certain that he was), and if he were an apostle (and we are certain that he was), he would have written "US THE APOSTLES." If, on the other hand Peter were NOT writing this, and if the author were NOT an apostle, he would have written, as in the false Greek texts of "B" and "Aleph," "THEIR APOSTLES." **This certainly is a matter of doctrine and theology.** At this point, these Greek texts and these English versions are **theologically deficient**, whereas the *Textus Receptus* and the KING JAMES BIBLE are **theologically superior**.

● **d. The Denial of the Value of Bible Words.**

(1) The Denial That "Every Word" of The Bible Is Important.

"And Jesus answered him, saying, It is written, That man shall not live by bread alone, *but by every word of God.* (Luke 4:4)

Greek Texts: -B/ALEPH;
English Versions: (-3) -NIV, -NASV, -NKJV-FN

The *italicized* portion is ELIMINATED in the Greek texts and English versions specified above. The Lord Jesus Christ is exalting "**EVERY WORD OF GOD**" to the Devil. The omission of these words changes the whole teaching of the verse. **This certainly is a matter of doctrine and theology.** At this point, these Greek texts and these English versions are **theologically deficient**, whereas the *Textus Receptus* and the KING JAMES BIBLE are **theologically superior**.

● **(2) The Denial That God's Words Alone Are "TRUTH."**

"Sanctify them through *Thy* truth: Thy Word is truth." John 17:17

Greek Texts: -B
English Versions: (-3) -NIV, -NASV, -NB

The *italicized* portion is ELIMINATED in the Greek text and English

versions specified above. The Lord prayed to the Father concerning that which "sanctifies." It is not merely "THE TRUTH" that can "sanctify," but only "THY TRUTH"! It is God's truth. **This certainly is a matter of doctrine and theology.** At this point, this Greek text and these English versions are **theologically deficient**, whereas the *Textus Receptus* and the KING JAMES BIBLE are **theologically superior.**

- **e. The Denial of the Fulfillment of Prophecy.**
    (1) The Denial That Matthew 27:34 Should Be the Fulfillment of the Prophecy in Psalm 69:21. Matthew 27:34 says:
    "They gave Him *vinegar* to drink mingled with gall: and when He had tasted {thereof}, He would not drink."
    (Matthew 27:34)

Greek Texts: -B/ALEPH
English Versions: (-4) -NIV, -NASV, -NKJV-FN (+TEXT), -NB
The *italicized* portion is ELIMINATED in the Greek texts and English versions specified above. Since Psalm 69:21 prophesies that the Lord would taste **"vinegar"** instead of **"wine,"** the Bible would be inaccurate and in error if this change were to stand. The NKJV not only puts **"wine"** in the footnotes, but even departs from the *Textus Receptus* by putting it in the text itself. **This certainly is a matter of doctrine and theology.** At this point, these Greek texts and these English versions are **theologically deficient,** whereas the *Textus Receptus* and the KING JAMES BIBLE are **theologically superior.**

Psalm 69:21 reads clearly:
"They gave me also gall for my meat; and in my thirst they gave me **vinegar** to drink." (Psalms 69:21)
To use a reference available to everyone, we'll refer to a few references from Strong's Concordance for the Greek and Hebrew words for "vinegar" and "wine." **The Greek word for "vinegar" is:**
"3690. oxos {oz-os}; from 3691; vinegar, i.e. sour wine: -vinegar." [Strong's Hebrew word for **"vinegar"** is:] *"2558. chomets {kho'-mets}; from 2556; vinegar: -vinegar."*
Neither the Old Testament nor the New Testament says anything about "wine," yet the above Greek texts and English versions change "vinegar" to "wine" (Greek "oinos") which completely removes the fulfillment of prophecy in Psalm 69:21. **Strong's Hebrew word for "wine" is:**
"3196. yayin {yah'-yin}; from an unused root meaning to effervesce; wine (as fermented); by

implication, intoxication: -banqueting, wine, wine[-bibber."

It is an entirely different word from "vinegar" in both Hebrew and Greek. Another Hebrew word is:

"8492. tiyrowsh {tee-roshe'}; or tiyrosh {tee-roshe'}; from 3423 in the sense of expulsion; must or fresh grape-juice (as just squeezed out); by implication (rarely) fermented wine: -(new, sweet) wine."

● **(2) The Denial That Matthew 27:35 Should Be the Fulfillment of the Prophecy in Psalm 22:18.** Matthew 27:35 says:

"And they crucified Him, and parted His garments, casting lots: *that it might be fulfilled which was spoken by the prophet, They parted my garments among them, and upon my vesture did they cast lots.*" (Matthew 27:35)

Greek Texts: -B/ALEPH
English Versions: (-3) -NIV, -NASV, -NB

The *italicized* portion is ELIMINATED in the Greek texts and English versions specified above. Since Psalm 22:18 prophesies that Christ's garments would be parted, the elimination of this fulfilled prophecy makes the Bible incapable of fulfillment. **This certainly is a matter of doctrine and theology.** At this point, these Greek texts and these English versions are **theologically deficient**, whereas the *Textus Receptus* and the KING JAMES BIBLE are **theologically superior**.

Psalm 22:18 reads clearly:

"They part my garments among them, and cast lots upon my vesture." (Psalms 22:18)

● **(3) The Denial That Mark 1:2 Should Be the Fulfillment of the Prophecy in Malachi 3:1.** Mark 1:2 says:

"As it is written *in the prophets*, Behold, I send my messenger before Thy face, which shall prepare Thy way before Thee." (Mark 1:2)

Greek Texts: -B/ALEPH
English Versions: (-4) -NIV, -NASV, -NKJV-FN, -NB

The *italicized* portion is ELIMINATED in the Greek texts and English versions specified above. Instead of **"IN THE PROPHETS,"** the B/ALEPH texts and the English versions have **"IN THE PROPHET ISAIAH."** Though Mark 1:3 does refer to Isaiah 40:3, this verse 2 is found in Malachi 3:1 and NOT Isaiah! The way it stands in these false texts, it makes the Bible out as false and in error. This certainly is a matter of doctrine and theology. At this point, these Greek texts and these English versions are **theologically deficient**, whereas the *Textus Receptus* and the KING JAMES BIBLE are **theologically superior.**

Malachi 3:1 reads clearly:

"**Behold, I will send my messenger, and he shall prepare the way before me**: and the Lord, whom ye seek, shall suddenly come to his temple, even the messenger of the covenant, whom ye delight in: behold, he shall come, saith the Lord of hosts." (Malachi 3:1)

- **(4) The Denial That Mark 15:28 Should Be the Fulfillment of the Prophecy in Isaiah 53:12.** Mark 15:28 reads:

"And the scripture was fulfilled, which saith, And He was numbered with the transgressors." (Mark 15:28)

Greek Texts: -B/ALEPH

English Versions: (-3) -NIV, -[NASV], -NKJV-FN

The *italicized* portion is ELIMINATED in the Greek texts and English versions specified above. By the omission of this entire verse, there is again a failure of the Old Testament prophesy in Isaiah 53:12 to find a fulfillment in the New Testament. **This certainly is a matter of doctrine and theology.** At this point, these Greek texts and these English versions are **theologically deficient**, whereas the *Textus Receptus* and the KING JAMES BIBLE are **theologically superior.**

Isaiah 53:12 reads clearly:

"Therefore will I divide Him {a portion} with the great, and He shall divide the spoil with the strong; because He hath poured out his soul unto death: and **He was numbered with the transgressors**; and He bare the sin of many, and made intercession for the transgressors." (Isaiah 53:12)

- **6. ESCHATOLOGY (The Doctrine of Last Things or Prophecy.**

    a. The Denial of the Return of Christ.

"Watch therefore, for ye know neither the day nor the hour *wherein the Son of man cometh*." (Matthew 25:13)

Greek Texts: -B/ALEPH

English Versions: (-3) -NIV, -NASV, -NKJV-FN

The *italicized* portion is ELIMINATED in the Greek texts and English versions specified above. With these words gone, the clear reference to the return of Christ is gone from the verse. This is a serious omission!

This is certainly a matter of doctrine and theology. At this point, these Greek texts and these English versions are **theologically deficient,** whereas the *Textus Receptus* and the KING JAMES BIBLE are **theologically superior.**

- **b.   The Denial of the Bodily Resurrection of People.**
  "In the resurrection *therefore, when they shall rise,* whose wife shall she be of them? for the seven had her to wife." (Mark 12:23)

Greek Texts: -B/ALEPH

English Versions: (-1) -NIV [NASV changed in latest edition]

The *italicized* portion is ELIMINATED in the Greek texts and English versions specified above. These words clarify the sort of "resurrection" that is referred to. It is one where people will "rise" in a literal and bodily sense. **Strong defines the word for "rise" here:**

  "450. anistemi {an-is'-tay-mee}; from 303 and 2476; to stand up (literal or figurative, transitive or intransitive): -arise, lift up, raise up (again), rise (again), stand up(-right)."

This is certainly a matter of doctrine and theology. At this point, these Greek texts and these English versions are **theologically deficient,** whereas the *Textus Receptus* and the KING JAMES BIBLE are **theologically superior.**

- **c.   The Denial of Future Judgement.**
    (1)   The Denial of Degrees in Future Judgement.
    "And whosoever shall not receive you, nor hear you, when ye depart thence, shake off the dust under your feet for a testimony against them. *Verily I say unto you, It shall be more tolerable for Sodom and Gomorrha in the day of judgment, than for that city.*" (Mark 6:11)

Greek Texts: -B/ALEPH

English Versions: (-3) -NIV, -NASV, -NKJV-FN

The *italicized* portion is ELIMINATED in the Greek texts and English versions specified above. These words have always been used by sound Bible teachers to indicate that there will be "DEGREES" of punishment in hell, based on the light received by the unbelievers in their lifetime. **This is certainly a matter of doctrine and theology.** At this point, these Greek texts and these English versions are **theologically deficient,** whereas the *Textus Receptus* and the KING JAMES BIBLE are **theologically superior.**

- **(2)   The Denial of the Recipients of Future Judge-**

ment.

"For which things' sake the wrath of God cometh *on the*
children of disobedience:" (Colossians 3:6)
Greek Texts: -B
English Versions: (-2) -NIV, -NASV
The *italicized* portion is ELIMINATED in the Greek text and English
versions specified above.   These words indicate clearly the exact
recipients of God's wrath and judgement.   It also indicates that God
considers some to be **"children of disobedience." This is certainly a
matter of doctrine and theology.** At this point, the Greek text and these
English versions are **theologically deficient**, whereas the *Textus Receptus*
and the KING JAMES BIBLE are **theologically superior.**
- (3)   **The Denial That the Earth Will Be Burned Up.**
"But the day of the Lord will come as a thief in the night;
in the which the heavens shall pass away with a great
noise, and the elements shall melt with fervent heat, the
earth also and the works that are therein shall be *burned*
up." (2 Peter 3:10)
Greek Texts: -B/ALEPH
English Versions: (-2) -NIV, -NKJV-FN
The *italicized* portion is ALTERED in the Greek texts and English
versions specified above.   Instead of the words **"burned up,"** the words
"laid bare" are used in the references above.   There is a decided
difference between **"burned up"** and **"laid bare."**   The word for
"burned up" is:
*"2618. katakaio {kat-ak-ah'-ee-o}; from 2596 and
2545; to burn down (to the ground), i.e. consume
wholly: -burn (up, utterly)."*
The word for **"laid bare"** is an entirely different concept and word
picture. **This is certainly a matter of doctrine and theology.** At this
point, these Greek texts and these English versions are **theologically
deficient**, whereas the *Textus Receptus* and the KING JAMES BIBLE are
theologically superior.
- (4)   **The Denial That Christ Will Be a Judge.**
"But why dost thou judge thy brother? or why dost thou
set at nought thy brother? for we shall all stand before
the judgment seat *of Christ.*" (Romans 14:10)
Greek Texts: -B/ALEPH
English Versions: (-4) -NIV, -NASV, -NKJV-FN, -NB
The *italicized* portion is ALTERED in the Greek texts and English

versions specified above. Instead of the words **"judgement seat of Christ,"** the words **"judgement seat of God"** or **"God's judgement"** are used. Since the context concerns "brethren," it must be the **"judgement seat of Christ."** **"God's judgement"** might refer to the judgement of **"the great white throne"** which is for the unsaved people. **This is certainly a matter of doctrine and theology.** At this point, these Greek texts and these English versions are **theologically deficient**, whereas the *Textus Receptus* and the KING JAMES BIBLE are **theologically superior.**

- **d.   The Denial of Hell.**
        (1)   The Denial of the Reality of Perishing in Hell.
        "That whosoever believeth in Him *should not perish*, but
        have eternal life." (John 3:15)
            Greek Texts: -B/ALEPH
        English Versions: (-3) -NIV, -NASV, -NKJV-FN

The *italicized* portion is ELIMINATED in the Greek texts and English versions specified above. By the removal of **"should not perish,"** the very reality of hell has been taken away from the verse. **This is certainly a matter of doctrine and theology.** At this point, these Greek texts and these English versions are **theologically deficient**, whereas the *Textus Receptus* and the KING JAMES BIBLE are **theologically superior**.

- **(2)   The Denial of Literal Fire in Hell.**
        *"Where their worm dieth not, and the fire is not
        quenched."* (Mark 9:44) *"Where their worm dieth not,
        and the fire is not quenched."* (Mark 9:46)
            Greek Texts: -B/ALEPH
        English Versions: (-3) -NIV, -NKJV-FN, -[NASV]

The *italicized* portion is ELIMINATED in the Greek texts and English versions specified above. In this case, **both** of these verses are omitted in their entirety.   Both verses teach clearly that hell is a place of unquenchable, literal fire. **This is certainly a matter of doctrine and theology.** At this point, these Greek texts and these English versions are **theologically deficient**, whereas the *Textus Receptus* and the KING JAMES BIBLE are **theologically superior.**

- **(3)   The Denial of the Everlasting Nature of Hell.**
        (a)   Mark 3:29.
        "But he that shall blaspheme against the Holy Ghost hath
        never forgiveness, but is in danger of eternal
        damnation:" (Mark 3:29)
            Greek Texts: -B/ALEPH

English Versions: (-3) -NIV, -NASV, -NB

The *italicized* portion is ALTERED in the Greek texts and English versions specified above. They have "sin" in place of "damnation." The two terms are quite different. Strong's defines "damnation" as:

> "2920. *krisis {kree'-sis}; decision (subjectively or objectively, for or against); by extension, a tribunal; by implication, justice (especially, divine law): - accusation, condemnation, damnation, judgment.*"

In this verse, and others, it is "eternal." **This is certainly a matter of doctrine and theology.** At this point, these Greek texts and these English versions are **theologically deficient,** whereas the *Textus Receptus* and the KING JAMES BIBLE are **theologically superior.**

- **(b) 2 Peter 2:17:**

  "These are wells without water, clouds that are carried with a tempest; to whom the mist of darkness is reserved *for ever*." (2 Peter 2:17)

  Greek Texts: -B/ALEPH

  English Versions: (-4) -NIV, -NASV, -NKJV-FN, -NB

The *italicized* portion is ELIMINATED in the Greek texts and English versions specified above. To eliminate the words, **"for ever,"** is to eliminate also the eternality of eternal judgement in hell. **This is certainly a matter of doctrine and theology.** At this point, these Greek texts and these English versions are **theologically deficient,** whereas the *Textus Receptus* and the KING JAMES BIBLE are **theologically superior.**

- **e. The Denial of a Literal Heaven.** There are five verses that we will examine briefly.

  (1) Luke 11:2.

  "And he said unto them, When ye pray, say, Our Father *Which art in heaven*, Hallowed be Thy name. Thy kingdom come. *Thy will be done, as in heaven*, so in earth." (Luke 11:2)

  Greek Texts: -B/ALEPH

  English Versions: (-4) -NIV, -NASV, -NKJV-FN, -NB

The *italicized* portion is ELIMINATED in the Greek texts and English versions specified above. To take away the word **"heaven"** in two separate places in this verse certainly reveals the theological perversion of the above texts and versions. **This is certainly a matter of doctrine and theology.** At this point, these Greek texts and these English versions are **theologically deficient,** whereas the *Textus Receptus* and the

KING JAMES BIBLE are **theologically superior.**

●   **(2)   Luke 22:43-44.**

"And there appeared an angel unto Him from heaven, strengthening Him." (Luke 22:43).   "And being in an agony He prayed more earnestly: and His sweat was as it were great drops of blood falling down to the ground." (Luke 22:44).

Greek Texts: -B/ALEPH
English Versions: (-0) -[NIV], -[NKJV-FN]

The *italicized* portion is ELIMINATED for **both** of these verses in the Greek texts and is mentioned in the footnotes of the two English versions specified above.   They have not yet removed the verses in these two versions, but what will the NEXT edition bring forth?   Taking away the entire verses as the two Greek texts have done lessens the belief in both heaven and angels (as well as the other details in these verses).   **This is certainly a matter of doctrine and theology.**   At this point, these Greek texts and these English versions are **theologically deficient,** whereas the *Textus Receptus* and the KING JAMES BIBLE are **theologically superior.**

●   **(3)   Hebrews 10:34.**

"For ye had compassion of me in my bonds, and took joyfully the spoiling of your goods, knowing in yourselves that ye have *in heaven* a better and an enduring substance." (Hebrews 10:34).

Greek Texts: -ALEPH (No B here)
English Versions: (-4): -NIV, -NASV, -NKJV-FN, -NB

The *italicized* portion is ELIMINATED in the Greek text and English versions specified above.   To take away the words **"in heaven"** takes away the reality of that **place.   This is certainly a matter of doctrine and theology.**   At this point, this Greek text and these English versions are **theologically deficient,** whereas the *Textus Receptus* and the KING JAMES BIBLE are **theologically superior.**

●   **(4)   1 John 5:7-8.**

"For there are three that bear record *in heaven, the Father, the Word, and the Holy Ghost: and these three are one.*" (1 John 5:7) "*And there are three that bear witness in earth,* the spirit, and the water, and the blood: and these three agree in one." (1 John 5:8)

Greek Texts: -B/ALEPH
English Versions: (-4) -NIV, -NASV, -NKJV-FN, -NB

The *italicized* portion is ELIMINATED in the Greek texts and English versions specified above. It consists of twenty-four English words in parts of two verses. Again the removal of the words, **"in heaven"** denies this place. **This is certainly a matter of doctrine and theology.** At this point, these Greek texts and these English versions are **theologically deficient**, whereas the *Textus Receptus* and the KING JAMES BIBLE are **theologically superior.**

- **(5) Revelation 16:17.**
  "And the seventh angel poured out his vial into the air;
  and there came a great voice out of the temple *of heaven*,
  from the throne, saying, It is done." (Revelation 16:17)
  Greek Texts: -ALEPH (No B in Revelation)
  English Versions: (-3) -NIV, -NASV, -NB

The *italicized* portion is ELIMINATED in the Greek text and English versions specified above. By removing the words, **"of heaven,"** you take away the location of the "temple." **This is certainly a matter of doctrine and theology.** At this point, this Greek text and these English versions are **theologically deficient**, whereas the *Textus Receptus* and the KING JAMES BIBLE are **theologically superior.**

- **7. SOTERIOLOGY (The Doctrine of Salvation).**
  a. The Denial That Salvation Is Limited Only to the Saved.
  "And the nations *of them which are saved* shall walk in
  the light of it: and the kings of the earth do bring their
  glory and honour into it." (Revelation 21:24)
  Greek Texts: -ALEPH (No B in Revelation)
  English Versions: (-4) -NIV, -NASV, -NKJV-FN, -NB

The *italicized* portion is ELIMINATED in the Greek text and English versions specified above. By removing the words, **"of them which are saved,"** it teaches that ALL NATIONS will walk in the light of it, rather than only those who are "saved." **This is certainly a matter of doctrine and theology.** At this point, this Greek text and these English versions are **theologically deficient**, whereas the *Textus Receptus* and the KING JAMES BIBLE are **theologically superior.**

- **b. The Denial That Salvation Is by Faith Rather Than by "Growth."**
  "As newborn babes, desire the sincere milk of the word,
  that ye may *grow thereby*:" (1 Peter 2:2)
  Greek Texts: -B/ALEPH

English Versions: (-4) -NIV, -NASV, -NKJV-FN, -NB
The *italicized* portion is CHANGED in the Greek texts and English
versions specified above. They change the words, "grow thereby" to
something like "grow into salvation." This clearly teaches salvation by
GROWTH which is false. **This is certainly a matter of doctrine and
theology.** At this point, these Greek texts and these English versions are
theologically deficient, whereas the *Textus Receptus* and the KING
JAMES BIBLE are **theologically superior.**

- **c. The Denial That Confession of Sins Should Be Made
to God Rather Than Man.**
    "Confess {your} *faults* one to another, and pray one for
    another, that ye may be healed. The effectual fervent
    prayer of a righteous man availeth much." (James 5:16)
    Greek Texts: -B/ALEPH
    English Versions: (-4) -NIV, -NASV, -NKJV-FN, -NB
The *italicized* portion is CHANGED in the Greek texts and English
versions specified above. They change the word, **"faults"** to **"sins."**
Confession of "sins" is to GOD, and not to men. "Faults" should be
"confessed" to one another when appropriate. **This is certainly a matter
of doctrine and theology.** At this point, these Greek texts and these
English versions are **theologically deficient,** whereas the *Textus Receptus*
and the KING JAMES BIBLE are **theologically superior.**

- **d. The Denial of the Biblical Meaning of Eternal Life.**
    "Laying up in store for themselves a good foundation
    against the time to come, that they may lay hold on
    eternal life." (1 Timothy 6:19)
    Greek Texts: -ALEPH (No B here)
    English Versions: (-4) -NIV, -NASV, -NKJV-FN, -NB
The *italicized* portion is CHANGED in the Greek text and English
versions specified above. They change the words, **"eternal life"** to "life
that is," thus casting doubt on the reality of **"eternal life." This is
certainly a matter of doctrine and theology.** At this point, this Greek
text and these English versions are **theologically deficient,** whereas the
Textus Receptus and the KING JAMES BIBLE are **theologically
superior.**

- **e. The Denial of Instantaneous Peace with God.**
    "Therefore being justified by faith, *we have* peace with
    God through our Lord Jesus Christ:" (Romans 5:1)
    Greek Texts: -B/ALEPH
    English Versions: (-2) -NKJV-FN, -NB

The *italicized* portion is CHANGED in the Greek texts and English versions specified above. Instead of the rendering, *"we have peace with God"* they have "let us have peace with God." This is an exhortation to have "peace" instead of a clear affirmation that we right now, if we're saved, "have peace with God." **This is certainly a matter of doctrine and theology.** At this point, these Greek texts and these English versions are **theologically deficient,** whereas the *Textus Receptus* and the KING JAMES BIBLE are **theologically superior.**

- **f. The Denial of the Miracle of Darkness at Calvary.**
"And the sun *was darkened,* and the veil of the temple was rent in the midst." (Luke 23:45)
Greek Texts: -B/ALEPH
English Versions: (-4) -NIV, -NASV, -NKJV-FN, -NB
The *italicized* portion is CHANGED in the Greek texts and English versions specified above. Instead of the rendering, **"was darkened,"** they have **"was eclipsed."** The *Textus Receptus* Greek word means that a miracle of God occurred in the **"darkening."** The other rendering states that there was an **"eclipse"** of the sun, which, at the time in question, would have been absolutely impossible, hence a grave scientific error! **This is certainly a matter of doctrine and theology.** At this point, these Greek texts and these English versions are **theologically deficient,** whereas the *Textus Receptus* and the KING JAMES BIBLE are **theologically superior.**

- **g. The Denial of Christ's Substitutionary, Vicarious Atonement.**
    (1)   1 Corinthians 5:7.
"Purge out therefore the old leaven, that ye may be a new lump, as ye are unleavened. For even Christ our passover is sacrificed *for us:*" (1 Corinthians 5:7)
Greek Texts: -B/ALEPH
English Versions: (-4) -NIV, -NASV, -NKJV-FN, -NB
The *italicized* portion is ELIMINATED in the Greek texts and English versions specified above. They leave off **"for us"** which teaches Christ's substitutionary, vicarious atonement. **This is certainly a matter of doctrine and theology.** At this point, these Greek texts and these English versions are **theologically deficient,** whereas the *Textus Receptus* and the KING JAMES BIBLE are **theologically superior.**

- **(2)   1 Peter 4:1.**
"Forasmuch then as Christ hath suffered *for us* in the flesh, arm yourselves likewise with the same mind: for

He that hath suffered in the flesh hath ceased from sin;"
(1 Peter 4:1)

Greek Texts: -B

English Versions: (-4): -NIV, -NASV, -NKJV-FN, -NB

The *italicized* portion is ELIMINATED in the Greek text and English versions specified above. As in the previous reference, they leave off **"for us"** which teaches Christ's substitutionary, vicarious atonement. **This is certainly a matter of doctrine and theology.** At this point, this Greek text and these English versions are **theologically deficient,** whereas the *Textus Receptus* and the KING JAMES BIBLE are **theologically superior.**

● **h. The Denial of Redemption by Divinely Provided Blood.**

      (1) Acts 20:28.

      "Take heed therefore unto yourselves, and to all the flock, over the which the Holy Ghost hath made you overseers, to feed the church *of God*, which He hath purchased with His own blood." (Acts 20:28)

Greek Texts: -"Many Manuscripts" (B/ALEPH Follow TR)

English Versions: (-1) -NKJV-FN

The *italicized* portion is CHANGED in the Greek texts and English version specified above. They change **"church of God"** to **"church of the Lord"** which removes the reference to the fact that Christ's Blood was "of God" as to Divine source. **This is certainly a matter of doctrine and theology.** At this point, these Greek texts and this English version are **theologically deficient,** whereas the *Textus Receptus* and the KING JAMES BIBLE are **theologically superior.**

●   **(2) Colossians 1:14.**

      "In whom we have redemption *through His blood*, {even} the forgiveness of sins:" (Colossians 1:14)

Greek Texts: -B/ALEPH

English Versions: (-3) -NIV, -NASV, -NKJV-FN

The *italicized* portion is ELIMINATED in the Greek texts and English versions specified above. The omission of **"through His Blood"** removes the Source of God's redemption and gives aid and comfort to the host of liberals/modernists/apostates (and even some genuine Bible believing, professing Christians) who have despised that Blood down through the centuries. **This is certainly a matter of doctrine and theology.** At this point, these Greek texts and these English versions are **theologically deficient,** whereas the *Textus Receptus* and the KING JAMES BIBLE are

theologically superior.
- ### (3)   1 John 1:7.
  "But if we walk in the light, as He is in the light, we have fellowship one with another, and the blood of Jesus *Christ* His Son cleanseth us from all sin." (1 John 1:7)
  ### Greek Texts: -B/ALEPH
  ### English Versions: (-3) -NIV, -NASV, -NB
The *italicized* portion is ELIMINATED in the Greek texts and English versions specified above. Since Christian Science and liberals make a distinction (as in early church times) between the human "Jesus" and the Divine "Christ," the cleansing "Blood" might be considered as merely human blood rather than having its source in God Himself. It's the "**Blood of Jesus Christ**" not merely the "**blood of Jesus.**" that "cleanseth us from all sin"! **This is certainly a matter of doctrine and theology.** At this point, these Greek texts and these English versions are **theologically deficient**, whereas the *Textus Receptus* and the KING JAMES BIBLE are **theologically superior.**
- ### I.   The Denial of Salvation and Redemption Only in Christ.
  ### (1)   Mark 9:42.
  "And whosoever shall offend one of {these} little ones that believe *in Me*, it is better for him that a millstone were hanged about his neck, and he were cast into the sea." (Mark 9:42)
  ### Greek Texts: -ALEPH
  ### English Versions: (-1) -NASV
The *italicized* portion is ELIMINATED in the Greek text and English version specified above. It's not enough merely to "**believe,**" but it must be to "**believe in me.**" He is the only way of salvation! **This is certainly a matter of doctrine and theology.** At this point, this Greek text and this English version are **theologically deficient**, whereas the *Textus Receptus* and the KING JAMES BIBLE are **theologically superior.**
- ### (2)   John 6:47.
  "Verily, verily, I say unto you, He that believeth *on Me* hath everlasting life." (John 6:47)
  ### Greek Texts: -B/ALEPH
  ### English Versions: (-3) -NIV, -NASV, -NKJV-FN
The *italicized* portion is ELIMINATED in the Greek texts and English versions specified above. This is, perhaps, one of the CLEAREST theological errors in these three versions. To make salvation only a

matter of "**believing**" rather than solely, as Christ said in this verse, "**believing on Me**," is truly "**ANOTHER GOSPEL**"! If you were trying to lead someone to Christ with the NIV or NASV, using this verse, they could "believe" in anything and still have "everlasting life"--whether in Santa Claus, in the Easter Bunny, in the Tooth Fairy, in Rudolph the Red-nosed Reindeer, or in any of the false world religions! This is **SERIOUS THEOLOGICAL PERVERSION!** **This is certainly a matter of doctrine and theology.** At this point, these Greek texts and these English versions are **theologically deficient**, whereas the *Textus Receptus* and the KING JAMES BIBLE are **theologically superior**.

-         **(3)   Romans 1:16.**

   "For I am not ashamed of the gospel *of Christ*: for it is the power of God unto salvation to every one that believeth; to the Jew first, and also to the Greek." (Romans 1:16)

   Greek Texts: -B/ALEPH

   English Versions: (-4) -NIV, -NASV, -NKJV-FN, -NB

The *italicized* portion is ELIMINATED in the Greek texts and English versions specified above. It was not merely the "**gospel**" that Paul was unashamed of, but it was the "**gospel of Christ**"! There were (and are) many false "gospels." **This is certainly a matter of doctrine and theology.** At this point, these Greek texts and these English versions are **theologically deficient**, whereas the *Textus Receptus* and the KING JAMES BIBLE are **theologically superior**.

-         **(4)   Galatians 3:17.**

   "And this I say, {that} the covenant, that was confirmed before of God *in Christ*, the law, which was four hundred and thirty years after, cannot disannul, that it should make the promise of none effect." (Galatians 3:17)

   Greek Texts: -B/ALEPH

   English Versions: (-4) -NIV, -NASV, -NKJV-FN, -NB

The *italicized* portion is ELIMINATED in the Greek texts and English versions specified above. The words, "**in Christ**," show the exclusiveness of Christ in the confirmation of the promises of God the Father. Without these words, Christ is demeaned and demoted. **This is certainly a matter of doctrine and theology.** At this point, these Greek texts and these English versions are **theologically deficient**, whereas the *Textus Receptus* and the KING JAMES BIBLE are **theologically superior**.

-         **(5)   Galatians 4:7.**

"Wherefore thou art no more a servant, but a son; and if
a son, then an heir of God *through Christ*." (Galatians
4:7)

Greek Texts: -B/ALEPH

English Versions: (-4) -NIV, -NASV, -NKJV-FN, -NB

The *italicized* portion is ELIMINATED in the Greek texts and English
versions specified above. Only **"through Christ"** can anyone become an
"heir of God." These words are vital. **This is certainly a matter of
doctrine and theology.** At this point, these Greek texts and these English
versions are **theologically deficient**, whereas the *Textus Receptus* and the
KING JAMES BIBLE are **theologically superior.**

- **(6)   Galatians 6:15.**

"For *in Christ Jesus* neither circumcision availeth any
thing, nor uncircumcision, but a new creature." (Galatians 6:15)

Greek Texts: -B

English Versions: (-3) -NIV, -NASV, -NB

The *italicized* portion is ELIMINATED in the Greek text and English
versions specified above. The only way you can be a **"new creature"** is
if you are **"in Christ Jesus."** Again, these words are vital. **This is
certainly a matter of doctrine and theology.** At this point, this Greek
text and these English versions are **theologically deficient**, whereas the
Textus Receptus and the KING JAMES BIBLE are **theologically
superior.**

- **(7)   Hebrews 1:3.**

"Who being the brightness of {His} glory, and the ex-
press image of His person, and upholding all things by
the word of His power, when He had *by Himself* purged
our sins, sat down on the right hand of the Majesty on
high;" (Hebrews 1:3)

Greek Texts: -B/ALEPH

English Versions: (-4) -NIV, -NASV, -NKJV-FN, -NB

The *italicized* portion is ELIMINATED in the Greek texts and English
versions specified above. The Lord Jesus Christ "purged our sins" all **"by
Himself."** We could not help Him in this undertaking. **This is certainly
a matter of doctrine and theology.** At this point, these Greek texts and
these English versions are **theologically deficient**, whereas the *Textus
Receptus* and the KING JAMES BIBLE are **theologically superior.**

- **(8)   1 Peter 2:24.**

"Who His own self bare our sins in His own body on the

tree, that we, being dead to sins, should live unto righteousness: by *Whose* stripes ye were healed." (1 Peter 2:24)

Greek Texts: -B/ALEPH
English Versions: (-0)

The *italicized* portion is ELIMINATED in the Greek texts specified above. Though none of the English Versions above have yet adopted this change, their Greek text reads: "**by stripes ye were healed.**" In other words, beatings can save you rather than simply trusting in the Savior Who suffered in our place. Since both B and ALEPH have this, future editions of the English versions might likely carry it also. **This is certainly a matter of doctrine and theology.** At this point, these Greek texts are **theologically deficient**, whereas the *Textus Receptus* and the KING JAMES BIBLE are **theologically superior.**

- **8. CHRISTOLOGY (the Doctrine of Christ).**
  a. The Denial of the Omnipresence of Christ.
  "And no man hath ascended up to heaven, but He that came down from heaven, {even} the Son of man *Which is in heaven.*" (John 3:13)

Greek Texts: -B/ALEPH
English Versions: (-3) -NIV, -NASV, -NKJV-FN

The *italicized* portion is ELIMINATED in the Greek texts and English versions specified above. With the removal of the words, "**Which is in heaven,**" the omnipresence of Christ is erased. **This is certainly a matter of doctrine and theology.** At this point, these Greek texts and these English versions are **theologically deficient**, whereas the *Textus Receptus* and the KING JAMES BIBLE are **theologically superior.**

- **b. The Denial of Parts of Christ's Communion Supper.**
  (1) The Denial That Christ's Body Was "Broken."
  "And when He had given thanks, He brake {it}, and said, *Take, eat*: this is My body, which is *broken* for you: this do in remembrance of Me." (1 Corinthians 11:24)

Greek Texts: -B/ALEPH
English Versions: (-3): -NIV, -NASV, -NKJV-FN

The *italicized* portion is ELIMINATED in the Greek texts and English versions specified above. The word, "**broken**" does not imply broken bones which would be against the prophecy. It indicates the lacerations of Christ's skin by the thorns, nails, and spear. Removing "**Take, eat**" might be used against the Roman Catholic Church practice of withholding the wine from their people in their Mass. **This is certainly a matter of doctrine and theology.** At this point, these Greek texts and these English versions are **theologically deficient**, whereas the *Textus Receptus* and the KING JAMES BIBLE are **theologically superior.**

-        **(2) The Denial of a Proper Understanding of the Word "Unworthily."**

> "For he that eateth and drinketh *unworthily*, eateth and drinketh damnation to himself, not discerning the Lord's body." (1 Corinthians 11:29)

Greek Texts: -B/ALEPH

English Versions: (-3) -NIV, -NASV, -NKJV-FN

The *italicized* portion is ELIMINATED in the Greek texts and English versions specified above. The removal of the word, "**unworthily,**" does not make sense. It would teach that if a Christian partakes of the Lord's Table, he automatically "**eateth and drinketh damnation to himself.**" Rather, it is drinking "**unworthily**" that brings this result. **This is certainly a matter of doctrine and theology.** At this point, these Greek texts and these English versions are **theologically deficient**, whereas the *Textus Receptus* and the KING JAMES BIBLE are **theologically superior.**

-        **c.   The Denial That "God" Was Manifest in The Flesh.**
          (1)   1 Timothy 3:16.

> "And without controversy great is the mystery of god-liness: *God* was manifest in the flesh, justified in the Spirit, seen of angels, preached unto the Gentiles, believed on in the world, received up into glory." (1 Timothy 3:16)

Greek Texts: -ALEPH (No B in 1 Timothy)

English Versions: (-4) -NIV, -NASV, -NKJV-FN, -NB

The *italicized* portion is CHANGED in the Greek text and English versions specified above. The word, "**God**" is changed to "**He**," thus removing the clearest teaching in all the Bible that Jesus Christ was "**God**" Himself. It is the difference between "**theos**" (which is well attested) and "**hos**" (which, as a relative pronoun does not even make syntactical sense). **This is certainly a matter of doctrine and theology.** At this point, this Greek text and these English versions are **theologically deficient**, whereas the *Textus Receptus* and the KING JAMES BIBLE are **theologically superior.**

-        **(2)   1 John 4:3.**

> "And every spirit that confesseth not that Jesus *Christ is*

come in the flesh is not of God: and this is that {spirit} of
antichrist, whereof ye have heard that it should come;
and even now already is it in the world." (1 John 4:3)
Greek Texts: -B (No ALEPH here)
English Versions: (-2) -NASV, -NKJV-FN
The *italicized* portion is ELIMINATED in the Greek text and English
versions specified above. Leaving out "**Christ is come in the flesh**" is a
denial of His incarnation. **This is certainly a matter of doctrine and
theology.** At this point, this Greek text and these English versions are
theologically deficient, whereas the *Textus Receptus* and the KING
JAMES BIBLE are **theologically superior.**

- **d. The Denial of the Veracity and Truthfulness of Christ.**
  "Go ye up unto this feast: I go not up *yet* unto this feast;
  for my time is not yet full come." (John 7:8)
  Greek Texts: -ALEPH
  English Versions: (-2) -NASV, -NKJV-FN
The *italicized* portion is ELIMINATED in the Greek text and English
versions specified above. Since the Lord Jesus Christ DID go up to the
"feast" later on, for Him to have said "**I go not up unto this feast**" would
have been a lying falsehood. The word, "**yet,**" is essential to Christ's
veracity and truthfulness. **This is certainly a matter of doctrine and
theology.** At this point, this Greek text and these English versions are
theologically deficient, whereas the *Textus Receptus* and the KING
JAMES BIBLE are **theologically superior.**

- **e. The Denial of the Sinlessness of Christ.**
  "And when the days of *her* purification according to the
  law of Moses were accomplished, they brought him to
  Jerusalem, to present {him} to the Lord;" (Luke 2:22)
  Greek Texts: -B/ALEPH
  English Versions: (-3) -NIV, -NASV, -NB
The *italicized* portion is CHANGED in the Greek texts and English
versions specified above. The word, "**her,**" is changed to "**their,**" thus
making the Lord Jesus Christ One Who needed "purification," and
therefore was a sinner! This is unthinkable! One of these perversions was
used in 1991, in my home church in the Christmas program they were
using, making Christ a sinner thereby! It also demeaned the Lord Jesus
in its rendering of Micah 5:2. **I hope you will check in advance your
own church's CHRISTMAS and EASTER programs. Unless they use
the KING JAMES BIBLE, they will be in serious doctrinal trouble!
This is certainly a matter of doctrine and theology.** At this point, these

Greek texts and these English versions are **theologically deficient**, whereas the *Textus Receptus* and the KING JAMES BIBLE are **theologically superior.**

● **f. The Denial of the Importance of the "Doctrine" of Christ.**

> "Whosoever transgresseth, and abideth not in the doctrine *of Christ*, hath not God. He that abideth in the doctrine of Christ, he hath both the Father and the Son." (2 John 1:9)

Greek Texts: -B/ALEPH
English Versions: (-1) -NIV

The *italicized* portion is ELIMINATED in the Greek texts and English version specified above. It is failure to abide in the doctrine **"of Christ"** rather than in just **doctrine in general.** Christ makes the difference! Having "doctrine of Christ" later in the verse does not excuse its absence earlier. BOTH places should have "of Christ." **This is certainly a matter of doctrine and theology.** At this point, the Greek texts and the English version are **theologically deficient**, whereas the *Textus Receptus* and the KING JAMES BIBLE are **theologically superior.**

● **g. The Denial of the Bodily Ascension of Christ.**

> "And it came to pass, while he blessed them, he was parted from them, and *carried up into heaven*." (Luke 24:51)

Greek Texts: -ALEPH
English Versions: (-1) -NASV

The *italicized* portion is ELIMINATED in the Greek text and English version specified above. The removal of the words, **"carried up into heaven"** takes away the bodily ascension of the Lord Jesus Christ into heaven. Though only one version omits it, who knows what further years will bring? **This is certainly a matter of doctrine and theology.** At this point, the Greek text and the English version are **theologically deficient**, whereas the *Textus Receptus* and the KING JAMES BIBLE are **theologically superior.**

● **h. The Denial of the Forgiveness by Christ of His Enemies.**

> "*Then said Jesus, Father, forgive them; for they know not what they do.* And they parted his raiment, and cast lots." (Luke 23:34)

Greek Texts: -B/ALEPH
English Versions: (-1) -NKJV-FN

The *italicized* portion is ELIMINATED in the Greek texts and English version specified above. This **entire sentence** is doubted by mentioning it in the footnotes of NKJV and also those of the NIV. Since B and ALEPH both remove it, what of the future editions in the texts? **This is certainly a matter of doctrine and theology.** At this point, the Greek texts and the English version are **theologically deficient,** whereas the *Textus Receptus* and the KING JAMES BIBLE are **theologically superior.**

- **I. The Denial of the Mission of Christ.**
  (1) Matthew 18:11.
  "For the Son of man is come to save that which was lost." (Matthew 18:11)
  Greek Texts: -B/ALEPH
  English Versions: (-3) -NIV, [-NASV], -NKJV-FN

The *italicized* portion is ELIMINATED in the Greek texts and English versions specified above. The **entire verse** has been removed by NIV and the NASV brackets it, showing great doubt upon it. Here is a clear statement of the mission of Christ. **This is certainly a matter of doctrine and theology.** At this point, these Greek texts and these English versions are **theologically deficient,** whereas the *Textus Receptus* and the KING JAMES BIBLE are **theologically superior.**

- **(2) Luke 9:56.**
  "For the Son of man is not come to destroy men's lives, but to save {them}. And they went to another village."(Luke 9:56)
  Greek Texts: -B/ALEPH
  English Versions: (-3) -NIV, -NASV, -NKJV-FN

The *italicized* portion is ELIMINATED in the Greek texts and English versions specified above. **This entire sentence has been removed.** Again, this is a sound statement of the **mission** of our Saviour into this world. **This is certainly a matter of doctrine and theology.** At this point, these Greek texts and these English versions are **theologically deficient,** whereas the *Textus Receptus* and the KING JAMES BIBLE are **theologically superior.**

- **j. The Denial of the Virgin Birth of Christ.**
  (1) Matthew 1:25.
  "And knew her not till she had brought forth her *First-born* Son: and he called His name JESUS." (Matthew 1:25)
  Greek Texts: -B/ALEPH

English Versions: (-3) -NIV, -NASV, -NKJV-FN

The *italicized* portion is ELIMINATED in the Greek texts and English versions specified above. By the omission of the word, **"firstborn,"** two things are done: (1) It is only "a son" rather than her "firstborn" Son. Mary might have had previous children and hence it would not have been a virgin birth. (2) If it is only "a son" rather than her "firstborn" Son, nothing is implied as to other children. "Firstborn" Son, however, implies that there may have been other sons as was the case, thus denying the Roman Catholic error of Mary's perpetual virginity. **This is certainly a matter of doctrine and theology.** At this point, these Greek texts and these English versions are **theologically deficient,** whereas the *Textus Receptus* and the KING JAMES BIBLE are **theologically superior.**

- **(2)   Luke 2:33.**

  "And *Joseph* and his mother marvelled at those things which were spoken of him." (Luke 2:33)

  Greek Texts: -B/ALEPH

  English Versions: (-4) -NIV, -NASV, -NKJV-FN, -NB

The *italicized* portion is CHANGED in the Greek texts and English versions specified above. After eliminating **"Joseph,"** they substitute the words, **"the child's father,"** thus possibly calling Joseph, Christ's literal "father," thereby denying His virgin birth. **This is certainly a matter of doctrine and theology.** At this point, these Greek texts and these English versions are **theologically deficient,** whereas the *Textus Receptus* and the KING JAMES BIBLE are **theologically superior.**

- **k.   The Denial of the Bodily Resurrection of Christ.**

  (1)   Luke 24:6.

  "*He is not here, but is risen*: remember how he spake unto you when he was yet in Galilee," (Luke 24:6)

  Greek Texts: -D

  English Versions: (-1) -NASV-FN

The *italicized* portion is ELIMINATED in the Greek text and English version specified above. The NASV questions the accuracy of the portion by its footnote reference. This is a clear reference to the bodily resurrection of the Lord Jesus Christ. **This is certainly a matter of doctrine and theology.** At this point, the Greek text and the English version are **theologically deficient,** whereas the *Textus Receptus* and the KING JAMES BIBLE are **theologically superior.**

- **(2)   Luke 24:12.**

  "*Then arose Peter, and ran unto the sepulchre; and stooping down, he beheld the linen clothes laid by*

themselves, and departed, wondering in himself at that
which was come to pass." (Luke 24:12)
Greek Texts: -D
English Versions: (-1) -[NASV-FN]
The *italicized* portion is ELIMINATED in the Greek text and English version specified above. The NASV questions the accuracy of this **entire verse** by putting it in brackets and by its footnote reference. Here is another clear verse on the miraculous bodily resurrection of the Lord Jesus Christ. **This is certainly a matter of doctrine and theology.** At this point, the Greek text and the English version are **theologically deficient**, whereas the *Textus Receptus* and the KING JAMES BIBLE are **theologically superior.**

- **(3)   Luke 24:40.**
  "And when he had thus spoken, he shewed them {his}
  hands and {his} feet." (Luke 24:40)
  Greek Texts: -D
  English Versions: (-2) -NASV-FN, -NKJV-FN

The *italicized* portion is ELIMINATED in the Greek text and English versions specified above. The **entire verse** is dropped out in the text of the NASV and only inserted in its footnotes, putting doubt on its authenticity. This is another solid proof of Christ's bodily resurrection. **This is certainly a matter of doctrine and theology.** At this point, the Greek text and the English versions are **theologically deficient**, whereas the *Textus Receptus* and the KING JAMES BIBLE are **theologically superior.**

- **(4)   Acts 2:30.**
  "Therefore being a prophet, and knowing that God had sworn with an oath to him, that of the fruit of his loins, *according to the flesh, He would raise up Christ* to sit on his throne;" (Acts 2:30)
  Greek Texts: -B/ALEPH
  English Versions: (-3) -NIV, -NASV, -NKJV-FN

The *italicized* portion is ELIMINATED in the Greek texts and English versions specified above. By taking out the words, **"according to the FLESH, He would raise up Christ,"** there is a denial of the bodily resurrection of the Lord Jesus Christ. **This is certainly a matter of doctrine and theology.** At this point, these Greek texts and these English versions are **theologically deficient**, whereas the *Textus Receptus* and the KING JAMES BIBLE are **theologically superior.**

- **(5)   1 Corinthians 15:54.**
  "So when *this corruptible shall have put on incorruption,*

and this mortal shall have put on immortality, then shall
be brought to pass the saying that is written, Death is
swallowed up in victory." (1 Corinthians 15:54)

Greek Texts: -ALEPH

English Versions: (-0)

The *italicized* portion is ELIMINATED in the Greek text specified above.
The words, **"this corruptible shall have put on incorruption,"** speak of
a **bodily resurrection.** Though none of these versions have YET
discarded the phrase, it reveals the doctrinal corruption of ALEPH. **This
is certainly a matter of doctrine and theology.** At this point, the Greek
text is **theologically deficient,** whereas the *Textus Receptus* and the KING
JAMES BIBLE are **theologically superior.**

- **I. The Denial of The Eternality (Past or Future) of
Christ the Eternal Son of God.**

    (1) John 1:18.

    "No man hath seen God at any time; the Only Begotten
    Son, Which is in the bosom of the Father, He hath
    declared {Him}." (John 1:18)

    Greek Texts: -B/ALEPH

    English Versions: (-3) -NIV, -NASV, -NKJV-FN

The *italicized* portion is CHANGED in the Greek texts and English
versions specified above. They take away the word, **"Son,"** and change
it to **"God."** This is pure HERESY! It is not possible to have an **"Only
Begotten God."** This is an example of the Gnostic error that teaches
Christ was only one of the many **"gods"** that were mere **"emanations."**
You MUST have an **"Only Begotten Son"** to be doctrinally correct. **This
is certainly a matter of doctrine and theology.** At this point, these
Greek texts and these English versions are **theologically deficient,** whereas the *Textus Receptus* and the KING JAMES BIBLE are **theologically
superior.**

- **(2) John 5:30.**

    "I can of Mine Own Self do nothing: as I hear, I judge:
    and My judgment is just; because I seek not Mine Own
    will, but the will of the *Father* Which hath sent Me."
    (John 5:30)

    Greek Texts: -B/ALEPH

    English Versions: (-3) -NIV, -NASV, -NB

The *italicized* portion is CHANGED in the Greek texts and English
versions specified above. They remove the word, **"Father,"** and change
it to **"him."** The Lord Jesus knew that God the **"Father"** sent Him. It was

not some indefinite "him." **This is certainly a matter of doctrine and theology.** At this point, these Greek texts and these English versions are **theologically deficient**, whereas the *Textus Receptus* and the KING JAMES BIBLE are **theologically superior.**

- **(3) Revelation 1:8.**
  "I am Alpha and Omega, *the Beginning and the Ending,* saith the Lord, Which is, and Which was, and Which is to come, the Almighty." (Revelation 1:8)
  Greek Texts: -ALEPH (No B in Revelation)
  English Versions: (-4) -NIV, -NASV, -NKJV-FN, -NB

The *italicized* portion is ELIMINATED in the Greek text and English versions specified above. When they took away the title for the Lord Jesus Christ, **"the Beginning and the Ending,"** they cast doubt on the eternal past of the eternal Son of God. **This is certainly a matter of doctrine and theology.** At this point, these Greek texts and these English versions are **theologically deficient**, whereas the *Textus Receptus* and the KING JAMES BIBLE are **theologically superior.**

- **(4) Revelation 1:11.**
  "Saying, *I am Alpha and Omega, the First and the Last*: and, What thou seest, write in a book, and send {it} unto the seven churches which are in Asia; unto Ephesus, and unto Smyrna, and unto Pergamos, and unto Thyatira, and unto Sardis, and unto Philadelphia, and unto Laodicea." (Revelation 1:11)
  Greek Texts: -ALEPH (No B in Revelation)
  English Versions: (-4) -NIV, -NASV, -NKJV-FN, -NB

The *italicized* portion is ELIMINATED in the Greek text and English versions specified above. To remove the words, **"I am Alpha and Omega, the First and the Last,"** which are Divine titles for the Lord Jesus Christ, is to take away His eternity past and future. **This is certainly a matter of doctrine and theology.** At this point, this Greek text and these English versions are **theologically deficient**, whereas the *Textus Receptus* and the KING JAMES BIBLE are **theologically superior.**

- **(5) Revelation 5:14.**
  "And the four beasts said, Amen. And the four {and} twenty elders fell down and worshiped *Him that liveth for ever and ever*." (Revelation 5:14)
  Greek Texts: -ALEPH (No B in Revelation)
  English Versions: (-4) -NIV, -NASV, -NKJV-FN, -NB

The *italicized* portion is ELIMINATED in the Greek text and English

versions specified above. Without the words, "**Him that liveth for ever and ever,**" there is a denial of Christ's eternity future. **This is certainly a matter of doctrine and theology.** At this point, this Greek text and these English versions are **theologically deficient,** whereas the *Textus Receptus* and the KING JAMES BIBLE are **theologically superior.**

- **(6)   Revelation 11:17.**

"Saying, We give Thee thanks, O Lord God Almighty, Which art, and wast, *and art to come*; because Thou hast taken to Thee Thy great power, and hast reigned." (Revelation 11:17)

Greek Texts: -ALEPH (No B in Revelation)
English Versions: (-4) -NIV, -NASV, -NKJV-FN, -NB

The *italicized* portion is ELIMINATED in the Greek text and English versions specified above. The absence of the words, "**and art to come,**" takes away the eternal future of Christ. **This is certainly a matter of doctrine and theology.** At this point, this Greek text and these English versions are **theologically deficient,** whereas the *Textus Receptus* and the KING JAMES BIBLE are **theologically superior.**

- **(7)   Revelation 16:5.**

"And I heard the angel of the waters say, Thou art righteous, O Lord, which art, and wast, *and shalt be*, because thou hast judged thus." (Revelation 16:5)

Greek Texts: -ALEPH (No B in Revelation)
English Versions: (-3) -NIV, -NASV, -NB

The *italicized* portion is ELIMINATED in the Greek text and English versions specified above. Again, the removal of "**and shalt be,**" puts in doubt the eternal future of the Lord Jesus Christ. **This is certainly a matter of doctrine and theology.** At this point, this Greek text and these English versions are **theologically deficient,** whereas the *Textus Receptus* and the KING JAMES BIBLE are **theologically superior.**

- **m. The Denial of the Divine Power and Omnipotence of Christ.**

(1)   The Denial of Christ's Power in General.
(a)   Matthew 21:44.

"*And whosoever shall fall on this stone shall be broken: but on whomsoever it shall fall, it will grind him to powder.*" (Matthew 21:44)

Greek Texts: -D
English Versions: (-1) [-NIV-FN]

The *italicized* portion is ELIMINATED in the Greek text and English

version specified above. Though the NIV has this verse in the text, it casts great doubt on it by its questionable footnote. The verse is a clear testimony to the power of the Lord Jesus Christ. **This is certainly a matter of doctrine and theology.** At this point, this Greek text and this English version are **theologically deficient,** whereas the *Textus Receptus* and the KING JAMES BIBLE are **theologically superior.**

-            **(b)   John 8:59.**

> Then took they up stones to cast at Him: but Jesus hid Himself, and went out of the temple, *going through the midst of them, and so passed by.*" (John 8:59)

Greek Texts: -B/ALEPH
English Versions: (-4) -NIV, -NASV, -NKJV-FN, -NB

The *italicized* portion is ELIMINATED in the Greek texts and English versions specified above. The words, **"going through the midst of them, and so passed by,"** show clearly the mighty power of the Lord Jesus Christ to pass through a crowd that sought His life. The absence of these words erases this miracle. **This is certainly a matter of doctrine and theology.** At this point, these Greek texts and these English versions are **theologically deficient,** whereas the *Textus Receptus* and the KING JAMES BIBLE are **theologically superior.**

-            **(c)   Philippians 4:13.**

> "I can do all things through *Christ* Which strengtheneth me." (Philippians 4:13)

Greek Texts: -B/ALEPH
English Versions: (-4) -NIV, -NASV, -NKJV-FN, -NB

The *italicized* portion is ELIMINATED in the Greek texts and English versions specified above. They CHANGE the word, **"Christ,"** to **"him who,"** thus making **indefinite** who or what **"strengtheneth me."** Is it "Christ," or could it be such things as the Force, evolution, atheism, humanism, modernism, or something else?! **This is certainly a matter of doctrine and theology.** At this point, these Greek texts and these English versions are **theologically deficient,** whereas the *Textus Receptus* and the KING JAMES BIBLE are **theologically superior.**

-            **(2)   The Denial of Christ's Power to Raise the Dead.**

> "Knowing that He which raised up the Lord Jesus shall raise up us also *by* Jesus, and shall present {us} with you." (2 Corinthians 4:14)

Greek Texts: -B/ALEPH
English Versions: (-4) -NIV, -NASV, -NKJV-FN, -NB

The *italicized* portion is CHANGED in the Greek texts and English

versions specified above. They remove the word, "**by**," and change it to
"**with**." To be "raised up" BY the Lord Jesus as the Agent of resurrection,
is quite different from merely being "raised up" WITH Him! **This is
certainly a matter of doctrine and theology.** At this point, the Greek
texts and English versions are **theologically deficient**, whereas the *Textus
Receptus* and the KING JAMES BIBLE are **theologically superior**.

- **(3) The Denial of Christ's Power to Create All
Things.**

> "And to make all {men} see what {is} the fellowship of
> the mystery, which from the beginning of the world hath
> been hid in God, who created all things *by Jesus Christ*:"
> (Ephesians 3:9)

Greek Texts: -B/ALEPH
English Versions: (-4) -NIV, -NASV, -NKJV-FN, -NB

The *italicized* portion is ELIMINATED in the Greek texts and English
versions specified above. In removing the words, "**by Jesus Christ**," they
take away His part in the creation of "all things." **This is certainly a
matter of doctrine and theology.** At this point, the Greek texts and
English versions are **theologically deficient**, whereas the *Textus Receptus*
and the KING JAMES BIBLE are **theologically superior**.

- **n.   The Denial of the Deity of Christ.**
    **(1)   The Denial of Christ's Deity by Removing the
Word "Lord."**
        (a)   Matthew 13:51.

> "Jesus saith unto them, Have ye understood all these
> things? They say unto Him, Yea, *Lord*." (Matthew
> 13:51)

Greek Texts: -B/ALEPH
English Versions: (-4) -NIV, -NASV, -NKJV-FN, -NB

The *italicized* portion is ELIMINATED in the Greek texts and English
versions specified above. The word, "**Lord**," refers to the Lord Jesus
Christ. It is a title of deity.   By removing it, HIS DEITY IS QUES-
TIONED, undermined and denied.   **This is certainly a matter of
doctrine and theology.**   At this point, the Greek texts and English
versions are **theologically deficient**, whereas the *Textus Receptus* and the
KING JAMES BIBLE are **theologically superior**.

- **(b)   Mark 9:24.**

> "And straightway the father of the child cried out, and
> said with tears, *Lord*, I believe; help Thou mine
> unbelief." (Mark 9:24)

Greek Texts: -B/ALEPH
English Versions: (-3) -NIV, -NASV, -NB

The *italicized* portion is ELIMINATED in the Greek texts and English versions specified above. The word, "**Lord**," refers to the Lord Jesus Christ. It is a title of deity. By removing it, HIS DEITY IS QUESTIONED, undermined and denied. **This is certainly a matter of doctrine and theology.** At this point, the Greek texts and English versions are **theologically deficient**, whereas the *Textus Receptus* and the KING JAMES BIBLE are **theologically superior.**

- (c) **Luke 9:57.**

  "And it came to pass, that, as they went in the way, a certain {man} said unto him, *Lord*, I will follow Thee whithersoever Thou goest." (Luke 9:57)

  Greek Texts: -B/ALEPH
  English Versions: (-3) -NIV, -NASV, -NB

The *italicized* portion is ELIMINATED in the Greek texts and English versions specified above. The word, "**Lord**," refers to the Lord Jesus Christ. It is a title of deity. By removing it, HIS DEITY IS QUESTIONED, undermined and denied. **This is certainly a matter of doctrine and theology.** At this point, the Greek texts and English versions are **theologically deficient**, whereas the *Textus Receptus* and the KING JAMES BIBLE are **theologically superior.**

- (d) **Luke 22:31.**

  "*And the Lord said*, Simon, Simon, behold, Satan hath desired {to have} you, that he may sift {you} as wheat:" (Luke 22:31)

  Greek Texts: -B
  English Versions: (-4) -NIV, -NASV, -NKJV-FN, -NB

The *italicized* portion is ELIMINATED in the Greek text and English versions specified above. The word, "**Lord**," refers to the Lord Jesus Christ. It is a title of deity. By removing it, HIS DEITY IS QUESTIONED, undermined and denied. **This is certainly a matter of doctrine and theology.** At this point, the Greek text and English versions are **theologically deficient**, whereas the *Textus Receptus* and the KING JAMES BIBLE are **theologically superior.**

- (e) **Luke 23:42.**

  "And he said unto Jesus, *Lord*, remember me when thou comest into Thy kingdom." (Luke 23:42)

  Greek Texts: -B/ALEPH
  English Versions: (-4) -NIV, -NASV, -NKJV-FN, -NB

The *italicized* portion is ELIMINATED in the Greek texts and English versions specified above. The word, "**Lord**," refers to the Lord Jesus Christ. It is a title of deity. By removing it, HIS DEITY IS QUES-TIONED, undermined and denied. **This is certainly a matter of doctrine and theology.** At this point, the Greek texts and English versions are **theologically deficient**, whereas the *Textus Receptus* and the KING JAMES BIBLE are **theologically superior**.

- **(f)   Romans 6:11.**
"Likewise reckon ye also yourselves to be dead indeed unto sin, but alive unto God through Jesus Christ *our Lord*." (Romans 6:11)
Greek Texts: -B
English Versions: (-3) -NIV, -NASV, -NB
The *italicized* portion is ELIMINATED in the Greek text and English versions specified above. The word, "**Lord**," refers to the Lord Jesus Christ. It is a title of deity. By removing it, HIS DEITY IS QUES-TIONED, undermined and denied. **This is certainly a matter of doctrine and theology.** At this point, the Greek text and English versions are **theologically deficient**, whereas the *Textus Receptus* and the KING JAMES BIBLE are **theologically superior**.

- **(g)   1 Corinthians 15:47.**
"The first man {is} of the earth, earthy: the second man {is} *the Lord* from heaven." (1 Corinthians 15:47)
Greek Texts: -B/ALEPH
English Versions: (-4) -NIV, -NASV, -NKJV-FN, -NB
The *italicized* portion is ELIMINATED in the Greek texts and English versions specified above. The word, "**Lord**," refers to the Lord Jesus Christ. It is a title of deity. By removing it, HIS DEITY IS QUES-TIONED, undermined and denied. In this verse, the word, "**man**," is put in place of "**Lord**," making Christ merely a "**man from heaven.**" **This is certainly a matter of doctrine and theology.** At this point, the Greek texts and English versions are **theologically deficient**, whereas the *Textus Receptus* and the KING JAMES BIBLE are **theologically superior**.

- **(h)   2 Corinthians 4:10.**
"Always bearing about in the body the dying of *the Lord* Jesus, that the life also of Jesus might be made manifest in our body." (2 Corinthians 4:10)
Greek Texts: -B/ALEPH
English Versions: (-3) -NIV, -NASV, -NB
The *italicized* portion is ELIMINATED in the Greek texts and English

versions specified above. The word, "**Lord**," refers to the Lord Jesus Christ. It is a title of deity. By removing it, HIS DEITY IS QUES- TIONED, undermined and denied. **This is certainly a matter of doctrine and theology.** At this point, the Greek texts and English versions are **theologically deficient**, whereas the *Textus Receptus* and the KING JAMES BIBLE are **theologically superior.**

- **(I) Galatians 6:17.**
  "From henceforth let no man trouble me: for I bear in my body the marks of *the Lord* Jesus." (Galatians 6:17)
  Greek Texts: -B (No ALEPH here)
  English Versions: (-3) -NIV, -NASV, -NB

The *italicized* portion is ELIMINATED in the Greek text and English versions specified above. The word, "**Lord**," refers to the Lord Jesus Christ. It is a title of deity. By removing it, HIS DEITY IS QUES- TIONED, undermined and denied. **This is certainly a matter of doctrine and theology.** At this point, the Greek text and English versions are **theologically deficient**, whereas the *Textus Receptus* and the KING JAMES BIBLE are **theologically superior.**

- **(j) 1 Timothy 1:1.**
  "Paul, an apostle of Jesus Christ by the commandment of God our Saviour, and *Lord* Jesus Christ, {which is} our hope;" (1 Timothy 1:1)
  Greek Texts: -D (No B here)
  English Versions: (-3) -NIV, -NASV, -NB

The *italicized* portion is ELIMINATED in the Greek text and English versions specified above. The word, "**Lord**," refers to the Lord Jesus Christ. It is a title of deity. By removing it, HIS DEITY IS QUES- TIONED, undermined and denied. **This is certainly a matter of doctrine and theology.** At this point, the Greek text and English versions are **theologically deficient**, whereas the *Textus Receptus* and the KING JAMES BIBLE are **theologically superior.**

- **(k) 1 Timothy 5:21.**
  "I charge {thee} before God, and the *Lord* Jesus Christ, and the elect angels, that thou observe these things without preferring one before another, doing nothing by partiality." (1 Timothy 5:21)
  Greek Texts: -ALEPH (No B here)
  English Versions: (-3) -NIV, -NASV, -NB

The *italicized* portion is ELIMINATED in the Greek text and English versions specified above. The word, "**Lord**," refers to the Lord Jesus

Christ. It is a title of deity. By removing it, HIS DEITY IS QUES-
TIONED, undermined and denied. **This is certainly a matter of
doctrine and theology.** At this point, the Greek text and English versions
are **theologically deficient,** whereas the *Textus Receptus* and the KING
JAMES BIBLE are **theologically superior.**

- **(l)   2 Timothy 4:1.**
  "I charge {thee} therefore before God, and *the Lord*
  Jesus Christ, who shall judge the quick and the dead at
  his appearing and his kingdom;" (2 Timothy 4:1)
  Greek Texts: -ALEPH (No B here)
  English Versions: (-3) -NIV, -NASV, -NB

The *italicized* portion is ELIMINATED in the Greek text and English
versions specified above. The word, "**Lord,**" refers to the Lord Jesus
Christ. It is a title of deity. By removing it, HIS DEITY IS QUES-
TIONED, undermined and denied. **This is certainly a matter of
doctrine and theology.** At this point, the Greek text and English versions
are **theologically deficient,** whereas the *Textus Receptus* and the KING
JAMES BIBLE are **theologically superior.**

- **(m)   Titus 1:4.**
  "To Titus, {mine} own son after the common faith:
  Grace, mercy, {and} peace, from God the Father and the
  Lord Jesus Christ our Saviour." (Titus 1:4)
  Greek Texts: -ALEPH (No B here)
  English Versions: (-4) -NIV, -NASV, -NKJV-FN, -NB

The *italicized* portion is ELIMINATED in the Greek text and English
versions specified above. The word, "**Lord,**" refers to the Lord Jesus
Christ. It is a title of deity. By removing it, HIS DEITY IS QUES-
TIONED, undermined and denied. **This is certainly a matter of
doctrine and theology.** At this point, the Greek text and English versions
are **theologically deficient,** whereas the *Textus Receptus* and the KING
JAMES BIBLE are **theologically superior.**

- **(n)   2 John 1:3.**
  "Grace be with you, mercy, {and} peace, from God the
  Father, and from *the Lord* Jesus Christ, the Son of the
  Father, in truth and love." (2 John 1:3)
  Greek Texts: -B
  English Versions: (-3) -NIV, -NASV, -NB

The *italicized* portion is ELIMINATED in the Greek text and English
versions specified above. The word, "**Lord,**" refers to the Lord Jesus
Christ. It is a title of deity. By removing it, HIS DEITY IS QUES-

TIONED, undermined and denied. **This is certainly a matter of doctrine and theology.** At this point, the Greek text and English versions are **theologically deficient,** whereas the *Textus Receptus* and the KING JAMES BIBLE are **theologically superior.**
- **(2) The Denial of Christ's Deity by Removing the Worship of Him.**
    (a) Luke 24:52.
  "And they *worshiped him,* and returned to Jerusalem with great joy: Luke 24:52
    Greek Texts: -D
   English Versions: (-1) -NASV,
The *italicized* portion is ELIMINATED in the Greek text and English version specified above. The removal of **"worshiped Him"** takes away His need to be deity. **This is certainly a matter of doctrine and theology.** At this point, the Greek text and English version are **theologically deficient,** whereas the *Textus Receptus* and the KING JAMES BIBLE are **theologically superior.**
-    **(b) John 9:38.**
  "And he said, Lord, I believe. And he worshiped Him." (John 9:38)
    Greek Texts: -ALEPH
    English Versions: (-0)
The *italicized* portion is ELIMINATED in the Greek text specified above. The entire verse, including the words, **"he worshiped Him,"** is removed from ALEPH. Even though the versions above have not yet followed, what of the future? **This is certainly a matter of doctrine and theology.** At this point, the Greek text is **theologically deficient,** whereas the *Textus Receptus* and the KING JAMES BIBLE are **theologically superior.**
-    **(3) The Denial of Christ's Deity by Removing His Title As the "Son of God."**
    (a) Mark 1:1.
  "The beginning of the gospel of Jesus Christ, *the Son of God;"* (Mark 1:1)
    Greek Texts: -ALEPH
   English Versions: (-1) -[NASV-FN]
The *italicized* portion is ELIMINATED in the Greek text and English version footnote specified above. Removal of **"the Son of God"** reflects on the deity of Christ. **This is certainly a matter of doctrine and theology.** At this point, the Greek text and English version footnote are

theologically deficient, whereas the *Textus Receptus* and the KING
JAMES BIBLE are theologically superior.
- **(b)   John 6:69.**
  "And we believe and are sure that Thou art that *Christ,*
  the Son of the living God." (John 6:69)
  Greek Texts: -B/ALEPH
  English Versions: (-4) -NIV, -NASV, -NKJV-FN, -NB
The *italicized* portion is CHANGED in the Greek texts and English
versions specified above. The words, **"Christ, the Son of the living
God,"** are replaced by **"the holy one of God,"** a weaker expression. **This
is certainly a matter of doctrine and theology.** At this point, the Greek
texts and English versions are **theologically deficient,** whereas the *Textus
Receptus* and the KING JAMES BIBLE are **theologically superior.**
- **(c)   John 9:35.**
  "Jesus heard that they had cast him out; and when He
  had found him, He said unto him, Dost thou believe on
  the Son of *God?*" (John 9:35)
  Greek Texts: -B/ALEPH
  English Versions: (-4) -NIV, -NASV, -NKJV-FN, -NB
The *italicized* portion is CHANGED in the Greek texts and English
versions specified above. The word, **"God,"** is reduced to **"man"** thus
questioning the deity of Christ. **This is certainly a matter of doctrine
and theology.** At this point, the Greek texts and English versions are
theologically deficient, whereas the *Textus Receptus* and the KING
JAMES BIBLE are **theologically superior.**
- **(d)   Acts 8:37.**
  "*And Philip said, If thou believest with all thine heart,*
  thou mayest. And he answered and said, I believe that
  Jesus Christ is the Son of God." (Acts 8:37)
  Greek Texts: -B/ALEPH
  English Versions: (-3) -NIV, -NASV, -NKJV-FN
The *italicized* portion is ELIMINATED in the Greek texts and English
versions specified above. The entire verse is removed, taking away **"the
Son of God,"** and many other important truths. **This is certainly a
matter of doctrine and theology.** At this point, the Greek texts and
English versions are **theologically deficient,** whereas the *Textus Receptus*
and the KING JAMES BIBLE are **theologically superior.**
- **(4)   The Denial of Christ's Deity by Changing "My"
Father to "The" Father.**
  - **(a)   John 8:28.**

"Then said Jesus unto them, When ye have lifted up the Son of man, then shall ye know that I am {He}, and {that} I do nothing of Myself; but as *My* Father hath taught Me, I speak these things." (John 8:28)

Greek Texts: -B/ALEPH

English Versions: (-3) -NIV, -NASV, -NB

The *italicized* portion is CHANGED in the Greek texts and English versions specified above. In the expression, **"My Father,"** the word, **"My,"** is removed in favor of merely **"the,"** thus robbing Christ of His close relationship and intimacy with His Father. **This is certainly a matter of doctrine and theology.** At this point, the Greek texts and English versions are **theologically deficient,** whereas the *Textus Receptus* and the KING JAMES BIBLE are **theologically superior.**

- **(b) John 8:38.**

  "I speak that which I have seen with *My* Father: and ye do that which ye have seen with your father." (John 8:38)

  Greek Texts: -B

  English Versions: (-2) -NIV, -NB

The *italicized* portion is CHANGED in the Greek text and English versions specified above. In the expression, **"My Father,"** the word, **"My,"** is removed in favor of merely **"the,"** thus robbing Christ of His close relationship and intimacy with His Father. **This is certainly a matter of doctrine and theology.** At this point, the Greek text and English versions are **theologically deficient,** whereas the *Textus Receptus* and the KING JAMES BIBLE are **theologically superior.**

- **(c) John 10:32.**

  "Jesus answered them, Many good works have I shewed you from *My* Father; for which of those works do ye stone Me?" (John 10:32)

  Greek Texts: -B/ALEPH

  English Versions: (-3) -NIV, -NASV, -NB

The *italicized* portion is CHANGED in the Greek texts and English versions specified above. In the expression, **"My Father,"** the word, **"My,"** is removed in favor of merely **"the,"** thus robbing Christ of His close relationship and intimacy with His Father. **This is certainly a matter of doctrine and theology.** At this point, the Greek texts and English versions are **theologically deficient,** whereas the *Textus Receptus* and the KING JAMES BIBLE are **theologically superior.**

- **(d) John 14:28.**

"Ye have heard how I said unto you, I go away, and come {again} unto you. If ye loved Me, ye would rejoice, because I said, I go unto the Father: for *My* Father is greater than I." (John 14:28)

Greek Texts: -B/ALEPH

English Versions: (-3) -NIV, -NASV, -NB

The *italicized* portion is CHANGED in the Greek texts and English versions specified above. In the expression, "**My Father**," the word, "**My**," is removed in favor of merely "**the**," thus robbing Christ of His close relationship and intimacy with His Father. **This is certainly a matter of doctrine and theology.** At this point, the Greek texts and English versions are **theologically deficient**, whereas the *Textus Receptus* and the KING JAMES BIBLE are **theologically superior**.

- **(e) John 16:10.**

"Of righteousness, because I go to *My* Father, and ye see Me no more;" (John 16:10)

Greek Texts: -B/ALEPH

English Versions: (-3) -NIV, -NASV, -NB

The *italicized* portion is CHANGED in the Greek texts and English versions specified above. In the expression, "**My Father**," the word, "**My**," is removed in favor of merely "**the**," thus robbing Christ of His close relationship and intimacy with His Father. **This is certainly a matter of doctrine and theology.** At this point, the Greek texts and English versions are **theologically deficient**, whereas the *Textus Receptus* and the KING JAMES BIBLE are **theologically superior**.

- **(5) The Denial of Christ's Deity by Removing the "Father" from a Connection with the "Lord Jesus Christ."**

(a) Ephesians 3:14.

"For this cause I bow my knees unto the Father *of our Lord Jesus Christ*," (Ephesians 3:14)

Greek Texts: -B/ALEPH

English Versions: (-4) -NIV, -NASV, -NKJV-FN, -NB

The *italicized* portion is ELIMINATED in the Greek texts and English versions specified above. They remove the words, "**of our Lord Jesus Christ**," from any connection with His "Father." **This is certainly a matter of doctrine and theology.** At this point, the Greek texts and English versions are **theologically deficient**, whereas the *Textus Receptus* and the KING JAMES BIBLE are **theologically superior**.

- **(b) Colossians 1:2.**

"To the saints and faithful brethren in Christ which are at
Colosse: Grace {be} unto you, and peace, from God our
Father *and the Lord Jesus Christ.*" (Colossians 1:2)
Greek Texts: -B
English Versions: (-3) -NIV, -NASV, -NKJV-FN
The *italicized* portion is ELIMINATED in the Greek text and English
versions specified above. They remove the words, **"and the Lord Jesus
Christ,"** from any connection with His "Father." **This is certainly a
matter of doctrine and theology.** At this point, the Greek text and
English versions are **theologically deficient,** whereas the *Textus Receptus*
and the KING JAMES BIBLE are **theologically superior.**
●   **(6) The Denial of Christ's Deity by Removing
"Lord" from "Jesus" or "Jesus Christ."**
                    (a)   Acts 9:29.
"And he spake boldly in the name of the Lord *Jesus,* and
disputed against the Grecians: but they went about to
slay him." (Acts 9:29)
Greek Texts: -B/ALEPH
English Versions: (-3) -NIV, -NASV, -NB
The *italicized* portion is ELIMINATED in the Greek texts and English
versions specified above.   **"Jesus"** is removed from **"Lord,"** thus
REMOVING HIS DEITY. **This is certainly a matter of doctrine and
theology.** At this point, the Greek texts and English versions are **theolog-
ically deficient,** whereas the *Textus Receptus* and the KING JAMES
BIBLE are **theologically superior.**
●   **(b)   1 Corinthians 5:5.**
"To deliver such an one unto Satan for the destruction of
the flesh, that the spirit may be saved in the day of the
Lord *Jesus.*" (1 Corinthians 5:5)
Greek Texts: -B
English Versions: (-3) -NIV, -NASV, -NKJV-FN
The *italicized* portion is ELIMINATED in the Greek text and English
versions specified above.   **"Jesus"** is again removed from **"Lord,"** thus
REMOVING HIS DEITY. **This is certainly a matter of doctrine and
theology.** At this point, the Greek text and English versions are **theolog-
ically deficient,** whereas the *Textus Receptus* and the KING JAMES
BIBLE are **theologically superior.**
●   **(c)   1 Corinthians 16:22.**
"If any man love not the Lord *Jesus Christ,* let him be
Anathema Maranatha." (1 Corinthians 16:22)

Greek Texts: -B/ALEPH
English Versions: (-3) -NIV, -NASV, -NB
The *italicized* portion is ELIMINATED in the Greek texts and English versions specified above. "**Jesus Christ**" is removed from "**Lord**," thus REMOVING HIS DEITY. **This is certainly a matter of doctrine and theology.** At this point, the Greek texts and English versions are **theologically deficient**, whereas the *Textus Receptus* and the KING JAMES BIBLE are **theologically superior.**

- (7) **The Denial of Christ's Deity by Removing "Son" or "Son of God" from "Jesus."**
  - (a)   **Acts 3:26.**
    "Unto you first God, having raised up his Son *Jesus,* sent him to bless you, in turning away every one of you from his iniquities." (Acts 3:26)

Greek Texts: -B/ALEPH
English Versions: (-3) -NIV, -NASV, -NB
The *italicized* portion is ELIMINATED in the Greek texts and English versions specified above. "**Jesus**" is separated from "**Son**," or, as in some versions, the word "**Son**" is lowered to merely "**servant.**" **This is certainly a matter of doctrine and theology.** At this point, the Greek texts and English versions are **theologically deficient**, whereas the *Textus Receptus* and the KING JAMES BIBLE are **theologically superior.**

- (b)   **Matthew 8:29.**
    "And, behold, they cried out, saying, What have we to do with thee, *Jesus,* thou Son of God? art Thou come hither to torment us before the time?" (Matthew 8:29)

Greek Texts: -B/ALEPH
English Versions: (-3) -NIV, -NASV, -NB
The *italicized* portion is ELIMINATED in the Greek texts and English versions specified above. "**Jesus**" is removed from "**the Son of God**," thus removing this Name for deity from Him. **This is certainly a matter of doctrine and theology.** At this point, the Greek texts and English versions are **theologically deficient**, whereas the *Textus Receptus* and the KING JAMES BIBLE are **theologically superior.**

- (8) **The Denial of Christ's Deity by Removing "Jesus" from "Christ."**

One of the heresies of the early church which flourished *especially in the land of* Egypt where manuscripts "B" (Vatican) and "Aleph" (Sinai) originated, was the heresy of "ADOPTIONISM." **This heresy taught that there was a distinction between the human "Jesus"** and Divine "Christ." This same heresy was carried down through the centuries and appears in Liberalism/Modernism/Apostasy as well as in so-called "Christian Science." In the following verses, we will just indicate the verses in question, the changes or eliminations, the Greek texts and English versions involved without further comment.

The *italicized* portion is ELIMINATED in the Greek texts and English versions specified. **This is certainly a matter of doctrine and theology.** At this point, the Greek texts and English versions are **theologically deficient**, whereas the *Textus Receptus* and the KING JAMES BIBLE are **theologically superior.**

- **(a) Romans 15:8.**

  "Now I say that *Jesus* Christ was a minister of the circumcision for the truth of God, to confirm the promises {made} unto the fathers:" (Romans 15:8)

  Greek Texts: -B/ALEPH

  English Versions: (-3) -NIV, -NASV, -NB

- **(b) 1 Corinthians 9:1.**

  "Am I not an apostle? am I not free? have I not seen Jesus *Christ* our Lord? are not ye my work in the Lord?" (1 Corinthians 9:1)

  Greek Texts: -B/ALEPH

  English Versions: (-3) -NIV, -NASV, -NB

- **(c) 2 Corinthians 5:18.**

  "And all things {are} of God, who hath reconciled us to himself by *Jesus* Christ, and hath given to us the ministry of reconciliation;" (2 Corinthians 5:18)

  Greek Texts: -B/ALEPH

  English Versions: (-3) -NIV, -NASV, -NB

- **(d) Colossians 1:28.**

  "Whom we preach, warning every man, and teaching every man in all wisdom; that we may present every man perfect in Christ *Jesus*:" (Colossians 1:28)

  Greek Texts: -B/ALEPH

  English Versions: (-3) -NIV, -NASV, -NB

- **(e) Hebrews 3:1.**

  "Wherefore, holy brethren, partakers of the heavenly calling, consider the Apostle and High Priest of our profession, *Christ* Jesus;" (Hebrews 3:1)

  Greek Texts: -B/ALEPH

  English Versions: (-3) -NIV, -NASV, -NB

- **(f)   1 Peter 5:10.**

"But the God of all grace, Who hath called us unto his eternal glory by Christ *Jesus*, after that ye have suffered a while, make you perfect, stablish, strengthen, settle {you}." (1 Peter 5:10)

Greek Texts: -B/ALEPH
English Versions: (-3) -NIV, -NASV, -NB

- **(g)   1 Peter 5:14.**

"Greet ye one another with a kiss of charity. Peace {be} with you all that are in Christ *Jesus*. Amen." (1 Peter 5:14)

Greek Texts: -B
English Versions: (-3) -NIV, -NASV, -NB

- **(h)   Revelation 1:9.**

"I John, who also am your brother, and companion in tribulation, and in the kingdom and patience of Jesus *Christ*, was in the isle that is called Patmos, for the word of God, and for the testimony of Jesus *Christ*." (Revelation 1:9)

Greek Texts: -ALEPH (No B in Revelation)
English Versions: (-4) -NIV, -NASV, -NKJV-FN, -NB

- **(I)   Revelation 12:17.**

"And the dragon was wroth with the woman, and went to make war with the remnant of her seed, which keep the commandments of God, and have the testimony of Jesus *Christ*." (Revelation 12:17)

Greek Texts: -ALEPH (No B in Revelation)
English Versions: (-4) -NIV, -NASV, -NKJV-FN, -NB

- **(9)   The Denial of Christ's Deity by Removing "Christ" from "Son of God" and "Saviour."**

    (a)   Luke 4:41.

"And devils also came out of many, crying out, and saying, Thou art *Christ* the Son of God. And He rebuking {them} suffered them not to speak: for they knew that He was Christ." (Luke 4:41)

Greek Texts: -B/ALEPH
English Versions: (-4) -NIV, -NASV, NKJV-FN, -NB

- **(b)   John 4:42.**

"And said unto the woman, Now we believe, not because of thy saying: for we have heard {him} ourselves, and know that this is indeed *the Christ*, the Saviour of the world." (John 4:42)

Greek Texts: -B/ALEPH

English Versions: (-4) -NIV, -NASV, NKJV-FN, -NB

- **(10) The Denial of Christ's Deity by Removing "Christ" from "Lord Jesus."**

(a)   Acts 15:11.

"But we believe that through the grace of the Lord Jesus *Christ* we shall be saved, even as they." (Acts 15:11)

Greek Texts: -B/ALEPH

English Versions: (-4) -NIV, -NASV, NKJV-FN, -NB

- **(b)   Acts 16:31.**

"And they said, Believe on the Lord Jesus *Christ*, and thou shalt be saved, and thy house." (Acts 16:31)

Greek Texts: -B/ALEPH

English Versions: (-3) -NIV, -NASV, -NB

- **(c)   Acts 20:21.**

"Testifying both to the Jews, and also to the Greeks, repentance toward God, and faith toward our Lord Jesus *Christ*." (Acts 20:21)

Greek Texts: -B

English Versions: (-2) -NIV, -NB

- **(d)   1 Corinthians 5:4.**

"In the name of our Lord Jesus *Christ*, when ye are gathered together, and my spirit, with the power of our Lord Jesus *Christ*," (1 Corinthians 5:4)

Greek Texts: -B/ALEPH

English Versions: (-3) -NIV, -NASV, -NB

- **(e)   1 Corinthians 16:23.**

"The grace of our Lord Jesus *Christ* {be} with you." (1 Corinthians 16:23)

Greek Texts: -B/ALEPH

English Versions: (-3) -NIV, -NASV, -NB

- **(f)   2 Corinthians 11:31.**

"The God and Father of our Lord Jesus *Christ*, which is blessed for evermore, knoweth that I lie not." (2 Corinthians 11:31)

Greek Texts: -B/ALEPH

English Versions: (-3) -NIV, -NASV, -NB

- **(g)   1 Thessalonians 3:11.**

"Now God himself and our Father, and our Lord Jesus *Christ*, direct our way unto you." (1 Thessalonians 3:11)

Greek Texts: -B/ALEPH

English Versions: (-3) -NIV, -NASV, -NB

- **(h)   1 Thessalonians 3:13.**

"To the end he may stablish your hearts unblameable in holiness before God, even our Father, at the coming of our Lord Jesus *Christ* with all his saints." (1 Thessalonians 3:13)

Greek Texts: -B/ALEPH

English Versions: (-3) -NIV, -NASV, -NB

- **(I)   2 Thessalonians 1:8.**

"In flaming fire taking vengeance on them that know not God, and that obey not the gospel of our Lord Jesus *Christ*:" (2 Thessalonians 1:8)

Greek Texts: -B

English Versions: (-3) -NIV, -NASV, -NB

- **(j)   2 Thessalonians 1:12.**

"That the name of our Lord Jesus *Christ* may be glorified in you, and ye in him, according to the grace of our God and the Lord Jesus Christ." (2 Thessalonians 1:12)

Greek Texts: -B/ALEPH

English Versions: (-3) -NIV, -NASV, -NB

- **(k)   Revelation 22:21.**

"The grace of our Lord Jesus *Christ* {be} with you all. Amen." (Revelation 22:21)

Greek Texts: -ALEPH (No B in Revelation)

English Versions: (-2) -NIV, -NASV

This is the end of these doctrinal passages. Much more could be said for each, but this should be helpful in the refutation of those who say that there are no doctrines involved in any variant Greek reading of the New Testament.

We're building Bible CONFIDENCE--
CONFIDENCE in the KING JAMES BIBLE,
because the KING JAMES BIBLE
is the BIBLE FOR TODAY!

APPENDIX A

THE IMPORTANCE OF GOD'S "WORDS"

One of the reasons for the "**THEOLOGICAL ERRORS IN THE VERSIONS**" is their lack of diligence in regarding the very "**WORDS**" of the Living God! If the modern versions and perversions had kept all the Hebrew and Greek "**WORDS**" that form the underlying basis for the KING JAMES BIBLE, and if they had actually TRANS-LATED these words correctly as did the KING JAMES BIBLE, instead of PARAPHRASING them, there would have been very few, if any, "THEOLOGICAL ERRORS" to talk and write about!

The BATTLE for God's Words in our day is a BATTLE about "**WORDS.**" In order to win that BATTLE, as the KING JAMES BIBLE has done, two things must be true: (1) you must have the exact "**WORDS**" in Hebrew and Greek to begin with, and (2) you must have a proper translating technique which respects these exact "**WORDS**" in English. Dynamic equivalence and paraphrase will not do.

Below are some of the verses from both the Old and New Testaments which show the great importance of "**WORDS**," whether of God, of His Prophets, or of other men. God is interested in preserving His "**WORDS**" rather than merely His "IDEAS" or "CONCEPTS." It ill behooves the modern paraphrasers who pervert these very "**WORDS**" by **ADDING** to them, **SUBTRACTING** from them, or **CHANGING** them as they have done in the English Revised Version (ERV of 1881), American Standard Version (ASV of 1901), New American Standard Version (NASV of 1960), New International Version (NIV of 1969), and even the New King James Version (NKJV of 1979), as well as the many other versions listed in **APPENDIX B.**

There are a total of **140,521 Greek words** in the Received Greek New Testament. The *Received Text* differs from the Revised Text of Westcott and Hort in **5,604 places** which involve a total of **9,970 Greek words.** This is **7%** of the Greek words in the New Testament. It is a total of **15.4 Greek words per page.** If totaled up in consecutive pages of the Greek New Testament, these variations would amount to a total of **45.9 pages** in the Greek New Testament. So you can see, this battleground is a battle of **WORDS.** Dr. Jack Moorman has tabulated a total of **2,886 WORDS** which have been completely eliminated from the *Received Text* that underlies the KING JAMES NEW TESTAMENT. This serious breach of trust was put into print by the Revised Text of the

Nestle-Aland Edition which follows The "B/ALEPH" (VATICAN/SINAI manuscripts). The modern versions have adopted, by and large, this false Greek text with its omission of these **2,886 words**. This has led to the many theological errors in these versions.

No attempt has been made to comment on the verses below. The lessons of each are self evident. You can see how important to God His **WORDS** are by searching some of the many verses on this theme. These verses give support to the approach used by the KING JAMES BIBLE translators in their verbal and formal equivalence technique. On the contrary, the same verses condemn severely the DYNAMIC EQUIVALENCE approach adopted by the modern versions.

VARIOUS VERSES THAT DEAL WITH "WORDS"

Exodus 4:28: "And **MOSES TOLD AARON ALL THE WORDS OF THE LORD** who had sent him, and all the signs which he had commanded him." (KJB)

Exodus 19:6: "And ye shall be unto me a kingdom of priests, and an holy nation. **THESE ARE THE WORDS WHICH THOU SHALT SPEAK** unto the children of Israel." (KJB)

Exodus 19:7: "And Moses came and called for the elders of the people, and **LAID BEFORE THEIR FACES ALL THESE WORDS WHICH THE LORD COMMANDED HIM**". (KJB)

Exodus 20:1: "And **GOD SPAKE ALL THESE WORDS**, saying," (KJB)

Exodus 24:3: "And **MOSES CAME AND TOLD THE PEOPLE ALL THE WORDS OF THE LORD**, and all the judgments: and all the people answered with one voice, and said, **ALL THE WORDS WHICH THE LORD HATH SAID** will we do." (KJB)

Exodus 24:4: "And **MOSES WROTE ALL THE WORDS OF THE LORD,** and rose up early in the morning, and builded an altar under the hill, and twelve pillars, according to the twelve tribes of Israel." (KJB)

Exodus 24:8: "And Moses took the blood, and sprinkled it on the people, and said, Behold the blood of the **COVENANT, WHICH THE LORD HATH MADE WITH YOU CONCERNING ALL THESE WORDS**." (KJB)

Exodus 34:1: "And the LORD said unto Moses, Hew thee two tables of stone like unto the first: and **I WILL WRITE UPON THESE TABLES THE WORDS** that were in the first tables, which thou brakest." (KJB)

Exodus 34:27: "And **THE LORD SAID UNTO MOSES, WRITE THOU THESE WORDS**: for after the tenor of **THESE WORDS** I have made a covenant with thee and with Israel." (KJB)

Exodus 34:28: "And he was there with the LORD forty days and forty nights; he did neither eat bread, nor drink water. And **HE WROTE UPON THE TABLES THE WORDS OF THE COVENANT**, the ten commandments." (KJB)

Exodus 35:1: "And Moses gathered all the congregation of the children of Israel together, and said unto them, **THESE ARE THE WORDS WHICH THE LORD HATH COMMANDED**, that ye should do them." (KJB)

Num 11:24: "And **MOSES WENT OUT, AND TOLD THE PEOPLE THE WORDS OF THE LORD**, and gathered the seventy men of the elders of the people, and set them round about the tabernacle." (KJB)

Deut 1:1: "**THESE BE THE WORDS WHICH MOSES SPAKE UNTO ALL ISRAEL** on this side Jordan in the wilderness, in the plain over against the Red sea, between Paran, and Tophel, and Laban, and Hazeroth, and Dizahab." (KJB)

Deut 4:10: "Specially the day that thou stoodest before the LORD thy God in Horeb, when **THE LORD** said unto me, Gather me the people together, and **I WILL MAKE THEM HEAR MY WORDS**, that they may learn to fear me all the days that they shall live upon the earth, and that they may teach their children." (KJB)

Deut 4:12: "And **THE LORD SPAKE** unto you out of the midst of the fire: **YE HEARD THE VOICE OF THE WORDS**, but saw no similitude; only ye heard a voice." (KJB)

Deut 4:36: "Out of heaven he made thee to hear his voice, that he might instruct thee: and upon earth he shewed thee his great fire; and **THOU HEARDEST HIS WORDS** out of the midst of the fire." (KJB)

Deut 5:22: "**THESE WORDS THE LORD SPAKE** unto all your assembly in the mount out of the midst of the fire, of the cloud, and of the thick darkness, with a great voice: and he added no more. And he wrote them in two tables of stone, and delivered them unto me." (KJB)

Deut 6:6: "And **THESE WORDS**, which I command thee this day, **SHALL BE IN THINE HEART**:" (KJB)

Deut 9:10: "And the LORD delivered unto me two tables of stone written with the finger of God; and on them was **WRITTEN ACCORDING TO ALL THE WORDS, WHICH THE LORD SPAKE** with you in the mount out of the midst of the fire in the day of the assembly." (KJB)

Deut 10:2: "And **I WILL WRITE ON THE TABLES THE WORDS** that were in the first tables which thou brakest, and thou shalt put them in the ark." (KJB)

Deut 11:18: "Therefore shall ye **LAY UP THESE MY WORDS IN YOUR HEART** and in your soul, and bind them for a sign upon your hand, that they may be as frontlets between your eyes." (KJB)

Deut 12:28: "**OBSERVE AND HEAR ALL THESE WORDS WHICH I COMMAND THEE**, that it may go well with thee, and with thy children after thee for ever, when thou doest that which is good and right in the sight of the LORD thy God." (KJB)

Deut 17:19: "And it shall be with him, and he shall read therein all the days of his life: that he may learn to fear the LORD his God, **TO KEEP ALL THE WORDS OF THIS LAW** and these statutes, to do them:" (KJB)

Deut 18:18: "I will raise them up a Prophet from among their brethren, like unto thee, and **WILL PUT MY WORDS IN HIS MOUTH**; and he shall speak unto them all that I shall command him." (KJB)

Deut 18:19: "And it shall come to pass, that **WHOSOEVER WILL NOT HEARKEN UNTO MY WORDS** which he shall speak in my name, I will require it of him." (KJB)

Deut 27:3: "And thou shalt **WRITE UPON THEM ALL THE WORDS OF THIS LAW**, when thou art passed over, that thou mayest go in unto the land which the LORD thy God giveth thee, a land that floweth with milk and honey; as the LORD God of thy fathers hath promised thee." (KJB)

Deut 27:8: "And thou shalt **WRITE UPON THE STONES ALL THE WORDS OF THIS LAW** very plainly. (KJB)

Deut 27:26 **CURSED BE HE THAT CONFIRMETH NOT ALL THE WORDS OF THIS LAW** to do them. And all the people shall say, Amen." (KJB)

Deut 28:14: "And **THOU SHALT NOT GO ASIDE FROM ANY OF THE WORDS WHICH I COMMAND THEE** this day, to the right hand, or to the left, to go after other gods to serve them." (KJB)

Deut 28:58: "If thou wilt not observe to **DO ALL THE WORDS OF THIS LAW** that are written in this book, that thou mayest fear this glorious and fearful name, THE LORD THY GOD;" (KJB)

Deut 29:1: "**THESE ARE THE WORDS OF THE COVE-NANT**, which the LORD commanded Moses to make with the children of Israel in the land of Moab, beside the covenant which he made with them in Horeb." (KJB)

Deut 29:9: "**KEEP THEREFORE THE <u>WORDS</u> OF THIS COVENANT, and do them, that ye may prosper in all that ye do.**" (KJB)

Deut 29:29: "The secret things belong unto the LORD our God: but **THOSE THINGS WHICH ARE REVEALED BELONG TO US AND TO OUR CHILDREN FOR EVER, THAT WE MAY DO ALL THE <u>WORDS</u> OF THIS LAW.**" (KJB)

Deut 31:12: "Gather the people together, men, and women, and children, and thy stranger that is within thy gates, that they may hear, and that they may learn, and fear the LORD your God, and observe to **DO ALL THE <u>WORDS</u> OF THIS LAW**:" (KJB)

Deut 31:24: "And it came to pass, when **MOSES HAD MADE AN END OF WRITING THE <u>WORDS</u> OF THIS LAW IN A BOOK,** until they were finished," (KJB)

Deut 32:46: "And he said unto them, **SET YOUR HEARTS UNTO ALL THE <u>WORDS</u> WHICH I TESTIFY AMONG YOU** this day, which ye shall command your children to observe to **DO, ALL THE <u>WORDS</u> OF THIS LAW.**" (KJB)

Joshua 3:9: "And Joshua said unto the children of Israel, Come hither, and **HEAR THE <u>WORDS</u> OF THE LORD YOUR GOD.**" (KJB)

Joshua 8:34: "And afterward **HE READ ALL THE <u>WORDS</u> OF THE LAW,** the blessings and cursings, according to all that is written in the book of the law." (KJB)

1 Sam 3:19: "And Samuel grew, and the LORD was with him, and **DID LET NONE OF HIS [that is, God's] <u>WORDS</u> FALL TO THE GROUND.**" (KJB)

1 Sam 15:1: "Samuel also said unto Saul, The LORD sent me to anoint thee to be king over his people, over Israel: now therefore **HEARKEN THOU UNTO THE VOICE OF THE <u>WORDS</u> OF THE LORD.**" (KJB)

2 King 22:13: "Go ye, inquire of the LORD for me, and for the people, and for all Judah, **CONCERNING THE <u>WORDS</u> OF THIS BOOK THAT IS FOUND**: for great is the wrath of the LORD that is kindled against us, because **OUR FATHERS HAVE NOT HEARKENED UNTO THE <u>WORDS</u> OF THIS BOOK,** to do according unto all that which is written concerning us." (KJB)

2 King 23:2: "And the king went up into the house of the LORD, and all the men of Judah and all the inhabitants of Jerusalem with him,

and the priests, and the prophets, and all the people, both small and great: and **HE READ IN THEIR EARS ALL THE <u>WORDS</u> OF THE BOOK OF THE COVENANT** which was found in the house of the LORD." (KJB)

2 King 23:3: "And the king stood by a pillar, and made a covenant before the LORD, to walk after the LORD, and to keep his commandments and his testimonies and his statutes with all their heart and all their soul, **TO PERFORM THE <u>WORDS</u> OF THIS COVENANT** that were written in this book. And all the people stood to the covenant." (KJB)

2 Chr 11:4: "Thus saith the LORD, Ye shall not go up, nor fight against your brethren: return every man to his house: for this thing is done of me. And **THEY OBEYED THE <u>WORDS</u> OF THE LORD**, and returned from going against Jeroboam." (KJB)

2 Chr 34:21: "Go, inquire of the LORD for me, and for them that are left in Israel and in Judah, **CONCERNING THE <u>WORDS</u> OF THE BOOK THAT IS FOUND**: for great is the wrath of the LORD that is poured out upon us, because our fathers have not kept the word of the LORD, to do after all that is written in this book." (KJB)

2 Chr 34:30: "And the king went up into the house of the LORD, and all the men of Judah, and the inhabitants of Jerusalem, and the priests, and the Levites, and all the people, great and small: and **HE READ IN THEIR EARS ALL THE <u>WORDS</u> OF THE BOOK OF THE COVENANT** that was found in the house of the LORD." (KJB)

2 Chr 34:31: "And **THE KING** stood in his place, and **MADE A COVENANT** before the LORD, to walk after the LORD, and to keep his commandments, and his testimonies, and his statutes, with all his heart, and with all his soul, **TO PERFORM THE <u>WORDS</u> OF THE COVENANT** which are written in this book." (KJB)

Ezra 7:11: "Now this is the copy of the letter that the king Artaxerxes gave unto **EZRA THE PRIEST, THE SCRIBE, EVEN A SCRIBE OF THE <u>WORDS</u> OF THE COMMANDMENTS OF THE LORD**, and of his statutes to Israel." (KJB)

Ezra 9:4. "Then were **ASSEMBLED UNTO ME EVERY ONE THAT TREMBLED AT THE <u>WORDS</u> OF THE GOD OF ISRAEL**, because of the transgression of those that had been carried away; and I sat astonied until the evening sacrifice." (KJB)

Neh 8:9: "And Nehemiah, which is the Tirshatha, and Ezra the priest the scribe, and the Levites that taught the people, said unto all the people, This day is holy unto the LORD your God; mourn not, nor weep.

For all **THE PEOPLE WEPT, WHEN THEY HEARD THE <u>WORDS</u> OF THE LAW.**" (KJB)

Neh 8:13: "And on the second day **WERE GATHERED** together the chief of the fathers of all the people, the priests, and the Levites, **UNTO EZRA THE SCRIBE, EVEN TO UNDERSTAND THE <u>WORDS</u> OF THE LAW.**" (KJB)

Job 6:10: "Then should I yet have comfort; yea, I would harden myself in sorrow: let him not spare; for **I HAVE NOT CONCEALED THE <u>WORDS</u> OF THE HOLY ONE.**" (KJB)

Job 19:23: "**OH THAT MY <u>WORDS</u> WERE NOW WRIT-TEN! OH THAT THEY WERE PRINTED IN A BOOK!**" (KJB)

Job 22:22: "Receive, I pray thee, the law from his mouth, and **LAY UP HIS <u>WORDS</u> IN THINE HEART.**" (KJB)

Job 23:12: "Neither have I gone back from the commandment of his lips; **I HAVE ESTEEMED THE <u>WORDS</u> OF HIS MOUTH MORE THAN MY NECESSARY FOOD.**" (KJB)

Ps 12:6: "**THE <u>WORDS</u> OF THE LORD ARE PURE WORDS**: as silver tried in a furnace of earth, purified seven times." (KJB)

Ps 107:11: "Because **THEY REBELLED AGAINST THE <u>WORDS</u> OF GOD**, and contemned the counsel of the most High:" (KJB)

Ps 119:57: "Thou art my portion, **O LORD: I HAVE SAID THAT I WOULD KEEP THY <u>WORDS</u>.**" (KJB)

Ps 119:103: "**HOW SWEET ARE THY <u>WORDS</u> UNTO MY TASTE!** yea, sweeter than honey to my mouth!" (KJB)

Ps 119:130: "**THE ENTRANCE OF THY <u>WORDS</u> GIVETH LIGHT**; it giveth understanding unto the simple." (KJB)

Ps 119:139: "My zeal hath consumed me, because **MINE ENEMIES HAVE FORGOTTEN THY <u>WORDS</u>.**" (KJB)

Prov 30:6: "**ADD THOU NOT UNTO HIS <u>WORDS</u>, LEST HE REPROVE THEE, AND THOU BE FOUND A LIAR.**" (KJB)

Isaiah 51:16: "And **I HAVE PUT MY <u>WORDS</u> IN THY MOUTH**, and I have covered thee in the shadow of mine hand, that I may plant the heavens, and lay the foundations of the earth, and say unto Zion, Thou art my people." (KJB)

Jer 1:9: "Then the LORD put forth his hand, and touched my mouth. And **THE LORD SAID UNTO ME, BEHOLD, I HAVE PUT MY <u>WORDS</u> IN THY MOUTH.**" (KJB)

Jer 6:19: "Hear, O earth: behold, I will bring evil upon this people, even the fruit of their thoughts, because **THEY HAVE NOT**

HEARKENED UNTO MY <u>WORDS</u>, nor to my law, but rejected it." (KJB)

Jer 7:8: "Behold, **YE TRUST IN LYING <u>WORDS</u>**, that cannot profit." (KJB)

Jer 7:27: "Therefore **THOU SHALT SPEAK ALL THESE <u>WORDS</u> UNTO THEM**; but they will not hearken to thee: thou shalt also call unto them; but they will not answer thee." (KJB)

Jer 11:3: "And say thou unto them, Thus saith the LORD God of Israel; **CURSED BE THE MAN THAT OBEYETH NOT THE <u>WORDS</u> OF THIS COVENANT**," (KJB)

Jer 11:6: "Then the LORD said unto me, **PROCLAIM ALL THESE <u>WORDS</u> IN THE CITIES** of Judah, and in the streets of Jerusalem, saying, **HEAR YE THE <u>WORDS</u> OF THIS COVENANT**, and do them." (KJB)

Jer 11:8: "Yet they obeyed not, nor inclined their ear, but walked every one in the imagination of their evil heart: therefore **I WILL BRING UPON THEM ALL THE <u>WORDS</u> OF THIS COVENANT**, which I commanded them to do; but they did them not." (KJB)

Jer 13:10: "**THIS EVIL PEOPLE, WHICH REFUSE TO HEAR MY <u>WORDS</u>**, which walk in the imagination of their heart, and walk after other gods, to serve them, and to worship them, shall even be as this girdle, which is good for nothing." (KJB)

Jer 15:16: "**THY <u>WORDS</u> WERE FOUND, AND I DID EAT THEM**; and thy word was unto me the joy and rejoicing of mine heart: for I am called by thy name, O LORD God of hosts." (KJB)

Jer 16:10: "And it shall come to pass, when **THOU SHALT SHEW THIS PEOPLE ALL THESE <u>WORDS</u>**, and they shall say unto thee, Wherefore hath the LORD pronounced all this great evil against us? or what is our iniquity? or what is our sin that we have committed against the LORD our God?" (KJB)

Jer 19:2: "And go forth unto the valley of the son of Hinnom, which is by the entry of the east gate, and **PROCLAIM THERE THE <u>WORDS</u> THAT I SHALL TELL THEE**," (KJB)

Jer 23:22: "But if they had stood in my counsel, and had **CAUSED MY PEOPLE TO HEAR MY <u>WORDS</u>**, then they should have turned them from their evil way, and from the evil of their doings." (KJB)

Jer 23:30: "Therefore, behold, **I AM AGAINST THE PROPHETS, SAITH THE LORD, THAT STEAL MY <u>WORDS</u> EVERY ONE FROM HIS NEIGHBOUR**." (KJB)

Jer 23:36: "And the burden of the LORD shall ye mention no more: for every man's word shall be his burden; for **YE HAVE PERVERTED THE WORDS OF THE LIVING GOD, OF THE LORD OF HOSTS OUR GOD.**" (KJB)

Jer 26:2: "Thus saith the LORD; Stand in the court of the LORD's house, and **SPEAK** unto all the cities of Judah, which come to worship in the LORD's house, **ALL THE WORDS THAT I COMMAND THEE TO SPEAK UNTO THEM; DIMINISH NOT A WORD:**" (KJB)

Jer 26:15. "But know ye for certain, that if ye put me to death, ye shall surely bring innocent blood upon yourselves, and upon this city, and upon the inhabitants thereof: for of a truth **THE LORD HATH SENT ME UNTO YOU TO SPEAK ALL THESE WORDS IN YOUR EARS.**" (KJB)

Jer 29:19: "Because **THEY HAVE NOT HEARKENED TO MY WORDS, SAITH THE LORD,** which I sent unto them by my servants the prophets, rising up early and sending them; but ye would not hear, saith the LORD." (KJB)

Jer 29:23: "Because they have committed villany in Israel, and have committed adultery with their neighbours' wives, and have **SPOKEN LYING WORDS IN MY NAME, WHICH I HAVE NOT COMMANDED THEM;** even I know, and am a witness, saith the LORD." (KJB)

Jer 30:2: "Thus speaketh the LORD God of Israel, saying, **WRITE THEE ALL THE WORDS THAT I HAVE SPOKEN UNTO THEE IN A BOOK.**" (KJB)

Jer 34:18: "And I will give the men that have transgressed my covenant, which **HAVE NOT PERFORMED THE WORDS OF THE COVENANT** which they had made before me, when they cut the calf in twain, and passed between the parts thereof," (KJB)

Jer 35:13: "Thus saith the LORD of hosts, the God of Israel; Go and tell the men of Judah and the inhabitants of Jerusalem, **WILL YE NOT RECEIVE INSTRUCTION TO HEARKEN TO MY WORDS? SAITH THE LORD.**" (KJB)

Jer 36:2: "**TAKE THEE A ROLL OF A BOOK, AND WRITE THEREIN ALL THE WORDS THAT I HAVE SPOKEN UNTO THEE** against Israel, and against Judah, and against all the nations, from the day I spake unto thee, from the days of Josiah, even unto this day." (KJB)

Jer 36:4: "Then Jeremiah called Baruch the son of Neriah: and **BARUCH WROTE FROM THE MOUTH OF JEREMIAH ALL**

THE WORDS OF THE LORD, WHICH HE HAD SPOKEN UNTO HIM, upon a roll of a book." (KJB)

Jer 36:6: "Therefore go thou, and READ IN THE ROLL, which thou hast written from my mouth, THE WORDS OF THE LORD in the ears of the people in the LORD's house upon the fasting day: and also thou shalt read them in the ears of all Judah that come out of their cities." (KJB)

Jer 36:8: "And Baruch the son of Neriah did according to all that Jeremiah the prophet commanded him, READING IN THE BOOK THE WORDS OF THE LORD IN THE LORD'S HOUSE." (KJB)

Jer 36:11: "When Michaiah the son of Gemariah, the son of Shaphan, had HEARD OUT OF THE BOOK ALL THE WORDS OF THE LORD," (KJB)

Jer 36:18: "Then Baruch answered them, HE PRONOUNCED ALL THESE WORDS UNTO ME WITH HIS MOUTH, AND I WROTE THEM WITH INK IN THE BOOK." (KJB)

Jer 36:27: "Then the word of the LORD came to Jeremiah, after that THE KING HAD BURNED THE ROLL, AND THE WORDS WHICH BARUCH WROTE at the mouth of Jeremiah, saying," (KJB)

Jer 36:28: "Take thee again another roll, and WRITE IN IT ALL THE FORMER WORDS THAT WERE IN THE FIRST ROLL, which Jehoiakim the king of Judah hath burned." (KJB)

Jer 45:1: "The word that Jeremiah the prophet spake unto Baruch the son of Neriah, when HE HAD WRITTEN THESE WORDS IN A BOOK AT THE MOUTH OF JEREMIAH, in the fourth year of Jehoiakim the son of Josiah king of Judah, saying," (KJB)

Ezek 2:7: "And THOU SHALT SPEAK MY WORDS UNTO THEM, WHETHER THEY WILL HEAR, OR WHETHER THEY WILL FORBEAR: for they are most rebellious." (KJB)

Ezek 3:4: "And he said unto me, Son of man, go, get thee unto the house of Israel, and SPEAK WITH MY WORDS UNTO THEM." (KJB)

Ezek 3:10: "Moreover he said unto me, Son of man, ALL MY WORDS THAT I SHALL SPEAK UNTO THEE RECEIVE IN THINE HEART, AND HEAR WITH THINE EARS." (KJB)

Ezek 33:32: "And, lo, thou art unto them as a very lovely song of one that hath a pleasant voice, and can play well on an instrument: for THEY HEAR THY WORDS, BUT THEY DO THEM NOT." (KJB)

Amos 8:11: "Behold, the days come, saith the Lord GOD, that I WILL SEND A FAMINE IN THE LAND, not a famine of bread, nor a thirst for water, but **OF HEARING THE WORDS OF THE LORD:"** (KJB)

Zech 7:7: **"SHOULD YE NOT HEAR THE WORDS WHICH THE LORD HATH CRIED BY THE FORMER PROPHETS,** when Jerusalem was inhabited and in prosperity, and the cities thereof round about her, when men inhabited the south and the plain?" (KJB)

Zech 7:12: "Yea, they made their hearts as an adamant stone, **LEST THEY SHOULD HEAR THE LAW, AND THE WORDS WHICH THE LORD OF HOSTS HATH SENT IN HIS SPIRIT BY THE FORMER PROPHETS:** therefore came a great wrath from the LORD of hosts." (KJB)

Matt 24:35: "Heaven and earth shall pass away, but **MY WORDS SHALL NOT PASS AWAY."** (KJB)

Mark 8:38: **"WHOSOEVER THEREFORE SHALL BE ASHAMED OF ME AND OF MY WORDS** in this adulterous and sinful generation; **OF HIM ALSO SHALL THE SON OF MAN BE ASHAMED,** when he cometh in the glory of his Father with the holy angels." (KJB)

Mark 13:31: "Heaven and earth shall pass away: but **MY WORDS SHALL NOT PASS AWAY."** (KJB)

Luke 9:26: "For **WHOSOEVER SHALL BE ASHAMED OF ME AND OF MY WORDS, OF HIM SHALL THE SON OF MAN BE ASHAMED,** when he shall come in his own glory, and in his Father's, and of the holy angels." (KJB)

Luke 21:33: "Heaven and earth shall pass away: but **MY WORDS SHALL NOT PASS AWAY."** (KJB)

Luke 24:8: "And **THEY REMEMBERED HIS WORDS,"** (KJB)

Luke 24:44: "And he said unto them, **THESE ARE THE WORDS WHICH I SPAKE UNTO YOU, WHILE I WAS YET WITH YOU,** that all things must be fulfilled, which were written in the law of Moses, and in the prophets, and in the psalms, concerning me." (KJB)

John 3:34: "For **HE WHOM GOD HATH SENT SPEAKETH THE WORDS OF GOD:** for God giveth not the Spirit by measure unto him." (KJB)

John 6:63: "It is the spirit that quickeneth; the flesh profiteth nothing: **THE WORDS THAT I SPEAK UNTO YOU, THEY ARE SPIRIT, AND THEY ARE Life."** (KJB)

John 6:68: "Then Simon Peter answered him, Lord, to whom shall we go? **THOU HAST THE <u>WORDS</u> OF ETERNAL LIFE.**" (KJB)

John 8:47: "**HE THAT IS OF GOD HEARETH GOD'S <u>WORDS</u>**: ye therefore hear them not, because ye are not of God. (KJB)

John 12:48: "**HE THAT REJECTETH ME, AND RECEIVETH NOT MY <u>WORDS</u>, HATH ONE THAT JUDGETH HIM; THE WORD THAT I HAVE SPOKEN**, the same shall judge him in the last day." (KJB)

John 14:10: "Believest thou not that I am in the Father, and the Father in me? **THE <u>WORDS</u> THAT I SPEAK UNTO YOU I SPEAK NOT OF MYSELF; BUT THE FATHER THAT DWELLETH IN ME**, he doeth the works." (KJB)

John 14:23: "Jesus answered and said unto him, **IF A MAN LOVE ME, HE WILL KEEP MY <u>WORDS</u>**: and my Father will love him, and we will come unto him, and make our abode with him." (KJB)

John 15:7: "**IF YE ABIDE IN ME, AND MY <u>WORDS</u> ABIDE IN YOU**, ye shall ask what ye will, and it shall be done unto you." (KJB)

John 17:8: "For **I HAVE GIVEN UNTO THEM THE <u>WORDS</u> WHICH THOU GAVEST ME**; and they have received them, and have known surely that I came out from thee, and they have believed that thou didst send me." (KJB)

Acts 15:15: "And **TO THIS AGREE THE <u>WORDS</u> OF THE PROPHETS**; as it is written," (KJB)

1 Cor 2:4: "And **MY SPEECH AND MY PREACHING WAS NOT WITH ENTICING <u>WORDS</u> OF MAN'S WISDOM**, but in demonstration of the Spirit and of power:" (KJB)

1 Cor 2:13: "**WHICH THINGS ALSO WE SPEAK, NOT IN THE <u>WORDS</u> WHICH MAN'S WISDOM TEACHETH, BUT WHICH THE HOLY GHOST TEACHETH**; comparing spiritual things with spiritual." (KJB)

Eph 5:6: "**LET NO MAN DECEIVE YOU WITH VAIN <u>WORDS</u>**: for because of these things cometh the wrath of God upon the children of disobedience." (KJB)

Col 2:4: "And **THIS I SAY, LEST ANY MAN SHOULD BEGUILE YOU WITH ENTICING <u>WORDS</u>**." (KJB)

1 Thes 4:18: "Wherefore **COMFORT ONE ANOTHER WITH THESE <u>WORDS</u>**." (KJB)

1 Tim 4:6: "If thou put the brethren in remembrance of these things, **THOU SHALT BE A GOOD MINISTER OF JESUS CHRIST, NOURISHED UP IN THE <u>WORDS</u> OF FAITH AND OF GOOD DOCTRINE**, whereunto thou hast attained." (KJB)

1 Tim 6:3: "**IF ANY MAN TEACH OTHERWISE, AND CONSENT NOT TO WHOLESOME WORDS, EVEN THE WORDS OF OUR LORD JESUS CHRIST**, and to the doctrine which is according to godliness;" (KJB)

2 Tim 1:13: "**HOLD FAST THE FORM OF SOUND WORDS**, which thou hast heard of me, in faith and love which is in Christ Jesus." (KJB)

2 Pet 2:3: "And through covetousness shall they **WITH FEIGNED WORDS** make merchandise of you: whose judgment now of a long time lingereth not, and their damnation slumbereth not. (KJB)

2 Pet 3:2: "That ye may **BE MINDFUL OF THE WORDS WHICH WERE SPOKEN BEFORE BY THE HOLY PROPHETS**, and of the commandment of us the apostles of the Lord and Saviour:" (KJB)

Jude 1:17: "But, beloved, **REMEMBER YE THE WORDS WHICH WERE SPOKEN BEFORE OF THE APOSTLES OF OUR LORD JESUS CHRIST;**" (KJB)

Rev 1:3: "**BLESSED IS HE THAT READETH, AND THEY THAT HEAR THE WORDS OF THIS PROPHECY**, and keep those things which are written therein: for the time is at hand." (KJB)

Rev 22:18: "For **I TESTIFY UNTO EVERY MAN THAT HEARETH THE WORDS OF THE PROPHECY OF THIS BOOK**, If any man shall add unto these things, God shall add unto him the plagues that are written in this book:" (KJB)

Rev 22:19: "And **IF ANY MAN SHALL TAKE AWAY FROM THE WORDS OF THE BOOK OF THIS PROPHECY, GOD SHALL TAKE AWAY HIS PART OUT OF THE BOOK OF LIFE**, and out of the holy city, and from the things which are written in this book." (KJB)

APPENDIX B

A CHRONOLOGICAL LIST OF COMPLETE ENGLISH BIBLES AND NEW TESTAMENTS PRINTED DURING THE LAST 612 YEARS, FROM 1380 TO 1991

I. INTRODUCTORY REMARKS

A. The Abundance of Complete English Bibles and New Testaments. As a part of this discussion about the *FOURFOLD SUPERIORITY OF THE KING JAMES BIBLE*, we believe it will be helpful for the readers to see for themselves the many complete English Bibles and New Testaments that have been available through the years. From 1388 through 1991 (604 years), there have been a total of 135 complete English Bibles printed. In addition to these complete Bibles, from 1380 through 1991 (612 years), there have been printed a total of 293 complete English New Testaments.

B. The Source of the Study. As the basis for this CHRONO-LOGICAL LIST, we have relied on the 1991, volume entitled *CATA-LOGUE OF ENGLISH BIBLE TRANSLATIONS--A Classified Bibliography of Versions and Editions Including Books, Parts, and Old and New Testament Apocrypha and Apocryphal Books* by William J. Chamberlin. It is published by the Greenwood Press, located in New York City, and Westport, Connecticut. Our readers are urged to contact the publisher, and to purchase a copy of this invaluable work for themselves. There are many details on each English Bible and New Testament listed here. The complete Bibles are from Chamberlin's pages 1-52. The complete New Testaments are from Chamberlin's pages 527-593. To our knowledge, it is the most exhaustive book of its kind in print.

C. The Method of Presentation. We will take up the following order: (1) A Chronological List of Complete English Bibles, (2) A Chronological List of Complete English New Testaments, (3) An Analysis of The Frequency of Publication of English Bibles and New Testaments, and (4) Some Conclusions About the Need for Publication of **NEW** Complete Bibles or **NEW** Complete New Testaments.

II. A CHRONOLOGICAL LIST
OF COMPLETE ENGLISH BIBLES (604 YEARS, 1388--1991)

The list will be as brief as possible, giving only the date (if known), the author or editor (if known), and usually a short title.

1. **UNDATED**, Timothy Priestly, The New Evangelical Family Bible Paraphrased.
2. **1388**, John Wycliffe, *The Holy Bible.*
3. **1388**, John Purvey, *The Holy Bible.*
4. **1390**, Nicholas de Hereford, *The Holy Bible.*
5. **1535**, Myles Coverdale, *Biblia.*
6. **1537**, Thomas Matthews, *The Byble.*
7. **1537**, James Nycolson, *Biblia, The Bible.*
8. **1539**, The Great Bible (Cranmer's Bible), *The Byble In Englyshe.*
9. **1539**, Richard Taverner, *The Most Sacred Bible.*
10. **1549**, Anonymous, *The Byble.*
11. **1549**, Anonymous, *The Byble* (a second Bible by the same name and date).
12. **1553**, Richard Jugge, *The Whole Bible.*
13. **1560**, Geneva Version, *The Bible And Holy Scriptvres.*
14. **1568**, Bishops' Bible, *The Holie Bible.*
15. **1599**, Geneva-Tomson-Junius Bible, *The Bible.*
16. **1609**, Douay-Rheims Version, *The New And Old Testaments.*
17. **1611**, Authorised Version, *The Holy Bible.*
    Special Editions Of The Authorised Version came out as follows:
    1613, 1616, 1617, 1618, 1629, 1630, 1633, 1634, 1637, 1638, 1640, 1642, 1653, 1659, 1675, 1679, 1833, 1896, 1904.
    Curious Editions Of The Authorised Version came out as follows:
    (1) **1611**, *Great "He" Bible*, (Ruth 3:15, "and he went into the city.")
    (2) **1611**, *Great "She" Bible*, (Ruth 3:15), "and she went into the city.")
    (3) **1611**, *"Judas" Bible*, (Mat. 26:36, "Judas" for "Jesus.")
    (4) **1631**, *"Wicked" Bible*, (Ex. 20:14, omits the "not.")

(5) **1638**, *"Forgotten Sins" Bible*, (Luke 7:47).

(6) **1641**, *"More Sea" Bible*, (Rev. 21:1, "There was more sea.")

(7) **1653**, *"Unrighteous" or Field's Bible*, (1 Cor. 6:9, "unrighteous shall inherit.")

(8) **1702**, *"Printers" Bible*, (Ps. 119:161, "Printers have persecuted.")

(9) **1711**, *"Profit" Bible*, (Isa. 57:12, "shall profit" instead of "shall not profit.")

(10) **1716**, *"Sin On" Bible*, (John 5:14, "sin on more" for "sin no more.")

(11) **1717**, *"Vinegar" Bible*, (Luke 20, "parable of the Vinegar" instead of "Vineyard."

(12) **1746**, *"Sting" Bible*, (Mark 7:37, "sting of his tongue" not "string."

(13) **1792**, *"Denial" Bible*, (Lk. 22:34, Philip denies Jesus instead of Peter.

(14) **1801**, *"Murderers" Bible*, (Jude 1:16, "murderers" used instead of "murmurers."

(15) **1802**, *"Discharge" Bible*, (1 Tim. 5:21, "I discharge" instead of "I charge."

(16) **1804**, *"Lions" Bible*, (1 Kings 7:19, "out of thy lions" instead of "loins."

(17) **1805**, *"To-Remain" Bible*, (Gal. 4:29, "to remain" inserted instead of a comma.

(18) **1806**, *"Standing Fishes" Bible*, (Ezek. 47:10, "the fishes shall stand" instead of "fishers."

(19) **1807**, *"Ears to ear" Bible*, (Mat. 13:43, "ears to ear" instead of "to hear."

(20) **1810**, "*Wife-Hater" Bible*, (Lk. 14:26, "hate not . . . and his own wife" instead of "life.")

(21) **1823**, *"Camels" Bible*, (Gen. 24:61, "Rebekah arose, and her camels" instead of "damsels."

(22) **1829**, *"Large Family" Bible*, (Isa. 66:9, "not cease to bring to birth" instead of "not cause to bring forth."

(23) **undated**, *"Fool" Bible*, Psalm 14:1, "The fool hath said in his heart there is a God" instead of "there is no God."

18. **1629**, Anonymous, *The Holy Bible*.

19. **1638**, Anonymous, The Holy Bible.
20. **1657**, Theodore Haak, *The Dutch Annotations Upon The Whole Bible.*
21. **1709**, Edward Wells, *An Help For The More Easy And Clear Understanding Of The Bible.*
22. **1715**, Anonymous, *Bible With Annotations.*
23. **1718**, Edward Wells, *The Common Translation Corrected.*
24. **1724**, B. Harris, The Holy Bible . . . Done Into Verse.
25. **1749**, Richard Challoner, *The Holy Bible.*
26. **1762**, Anonymous, *The Holy Bible.*
27. **1764**, Anthony Purver, *A New And Literal Translation.*
28. **1766**, Anonymous, *The Universal Bible.*
29. **1769**, Benjamin Blayney, *The Holy Bible.*
30. **1773**, Henry Southwell, *The Universal Family Bible.*
31. **1778**, John Fellows, *The Bible In Verse.*
32. **1785**, Clement Cruttwell, Editor, *The Holy Bible.*
33. **1786**, Anonymous, *The Holy Bible.*
34. **1791**, H. Fitzpatrick, *Douay-Rhemish Bible . . . Newly Revised.*
35. **1791**, Rev. Bernard MacMahon, *The Holy Bible.*
36. **1794**, Joseph Butler, *The Christian's New . . . Universal Family Bible.*
37. **1799**, Anonymous, *A Revised Translation and Interpretation of The Sacred Scriptures.*
38. **1800**, John Kendall, *The Holy Scriptures.*
39. **1802**, John Reeves, *The Holy Bible.*
40. **1808**, Charles Thomson, The Holy Bible.
41. **1811**, George Leo Haydock, *The Holy Bible.*
42. **1811**, Thomas Haydock, *The Holy Bible.*
43. **1817**, Benjamin Boothroyd, *A New Family Bible.*
44. **1818**, John Bellamy, *The Holy Bible.*
45. **1822**, Rev. Dr. Hamil, *The Holy Bible.*
46. **1825**, Israel Alger, *The Pronouncing Bible.*
47. **1825**, Daniel Murray, *The Holy Bible.*
48. **1833**, Noah Webster, *The Holy Bible.*
49. **1834**, George Townsend, *The Holy Bible.*
50. **1838**, Dr. Denvir, *Holy Bible.*
51. **1841**, J. T. Conquest, *The Holy Bible.*
52. **1842**, Anonymous, *The Holy Bible.*
53. **1844**, Rev. T. J. Hussey, *The Holy Bible.*
54. **1847**, Charles Roger, *A Collation of the Sacred Scriptures.*

55. **1848**, American Bible Society, *The Holy Bible*.
56. **1848**, James Nourse, *The Holy Bible*.
57. **1849**, Francis Patrick Kenrick, *The Holy Bible*.
58. **1850**, Alexander John Ellis, *The Holy Bible*.
59. **1850**, Josiah Forshall and Sir Fredrick Madden, *editors, The Holy Bible*.
60. **1852**, J. R. Bayley, Editor, *The Holy Bible*.
61. **1860**, Leicester Ambrose Sawyer, *The Holy Bible*.
62. **1863**, Robert Young, *The Holy Bible*.
63. **1864**, Lange's Commentaries, *The Scriptures*.
64. **1867**, Joseph Smith, Jr., *Holy Scriptures*.
65. **1869**, Otis Clapp, *The Word of the Lord*.
66. **1870**, Anonymous, *The Holy Bible*.
67. **1870**, Thomas Newberry, *The Englishman's Bible*.
68. **1871**, Frederick Charles Cook, *The Speaker's Commentary*.
69. **1876**, T. K. Cheyne and others, *The Holy Bible*.
70. **1876**, Julia Evelina Smith, *The Holy Bible*.
71. **1877**, Revised English Bible, *Revised English Bible*.
72. **1881**, English Revised Version, *The Holy Bible*.
73. **1881**, Samuel Sharpe, *The Holy Bible*.
74. **1884**, F. Oakeley and T. G. Law, *The Holy Bible*.
75. **1885**, William Alexander, *The Holy Bible*.
76. **1890**, Isaac Pitman, *The Holy Bible*.
77. **1895**, International Critical Commentary, *International Critical Commentary*.
78. **1895**, Richard Green Moulton, *The Modern Reader's Bible*.
79. **1897**, Joseph Bryant Rotherham, *The Emphasised Bible*.
80. **1898**, American Revised Version, *The Holy Bible*.
81. **1899**, Frank Schell Ballantine, *The Modern American Bible*.
82. **1899**, Murphy Bible, *Holy Bible*.
83. **1901**, American Standard Version, *The Holy Bible*.
84. **1901**, Ferrar Fenton, The Bible In Modern English.
85. **1902**, Frank Schell Ballentine, The American Bible.
86. **1903**, Anonymous, *The Holy Bible*.
87. **1903**, F. H. Scrivener, *The English Bible*.
88. **1904**, Isaac Pitman, *The Holy Bible*.
89. **1911**, Anonymous, *The 1911 Tercentenary Commemoration Bible*.
90. **1913**, American Baptist Publication Society, The Holy Bible.
91. **1913**, Westminster Version, *The Westminster Version Of The Bible*.

92. **1926**, Master Library, *The Master Library By Walter Scott.*
93. **1926**, James Moffatt, *The Holy Bible.*
94. **1929**, Charles Maclean, *A Homiletical And Exegetical Version Of The Bible.*
95. **1931**, Edgar J. Goodspeed and J. M. Powis Smith, *The Bible, An American Translation.*
96. **1933**, Charles K. Ogden, *The Bible In Basic English.*
97. **1935**, James Moffatt, A New Translation Of The Bible.
98. **1939**, John Nelson Darby, *The `Holy Scriptures.'*
99. **1948**, Anonymous, *The Holy Bible.*
100. **1949**, Anonymous, *The Bible In Basic English.*
101. **1950**, Watchtower Bible & Tract Society, *The New World Translation Of The Holy Scriptures.*
102. **1952**, Revised Standard Version, *The Holy Bible.*
103. **1956**, Anonymous, *The Holy Bible.*
104. **1957**, George M. Lamsa, *The Holy Bible From Ancient Eastern Manuscripts.*
105. **1959**, Berkeley Version, The Holy Bible, The Berkeley Version In Modern English.
106. **1960**, New American Standard Bible, *The New American Standard Bible.*
107. **1961**, New English Bible, *The New English Bible.*
108. **1962**, Anonymous, *Modern King James Version.*
109. **1962**, Kenneth N. Taylor, *The Living Bible Paraphrased.*
110. **1963**, A. B. Traina, *The Holy Name Bible.*
111. **1964**, Anchor Bible, *Anchor Bible.*
112. **1965**, Amplified Bible, *Amplified Bible.*
113. **1966**, Jerusalem Bible, *The Jerusalem Bible.*
114. **1967**, New Scofield Reference Bible, *The New Scofield Reference Bible.*
115. **1969**, Anonymous, *The Bible Reader, and Interfaith Interpretation.*
116. **1969**, New International Version, *New International Version.*
117. **1970**, Anonymous, *The Restoration of Original Sacred Name Bible.*
118. **1970**, New American Bible, *The New American Bible.*
119. **1971**, Anonymous, *King James II Version Of The Bible.*
120. **1972**, Steven T. Byington, *The Bible In Living English.*
121. **1973**, Common Bible, *The Holy Bible: Revised Standard Version.*
122. **1976**, Anonymous, *Holy Bible, Today's English Version.*
123. **1976**, William F. Beck, *The Holy Bible In The Language Of*

Today, An American Translation.
124. **1976**, Jay Green, General Editor And Translator, *The Interlinear Hebrew/Greek English Bible.*
125. **1977**, Anonymous, *The Psalms, A New Translation for Worship.*
126. **1979**, New King James Bible, *The New King James Bible.*
127. **1981**, Anonymous, *The Sacred Scriptures, Bethel Edition.*
128. **1982**, Word Biblical Commentary, *Word Biblical Commentary.*
129. **1983**, Open Bible, *Holy Bible.*
130. **1987**, Anonymous, *The Holy Bible: English Version For The Deaf.*
131. **1988**, Anonymous, *Christian Community Bible Translation.*
132. **1989**, Revised English Bible, *The Revised English Bible With The Apocrypha.*
133. **1990**, Anonymous, *The Holy Bible, Simplified Living Bible.*
134. **1990**, New Revised Standard Version, *Holy Bible.*
135. **1991**, Anonymous, *The Bible For Today's Family* (N.T.--O.T. due in 1996).

To these 135 "COMPLETE BIBLES," could be added ninety-nine "ABRIDGED BIBLES" which are listed in Chamberlin's compendium on pages 52-70.

III. A CHRONOLOGICAL LIST OF
COMPLETE ENGLISH NEW TESTAMENTS
(612 YEARS, 1380--1991)

The list will be as brief as possible, giving only the date (if known), the author or editor (if known), and usually a short title.

1. **UNDATED**, Anonymous, *Classic Interlinear Translations, The Greek English New Testament.*
2. **UNDATED**, Philip W. Comfort and Robert K. Brown, *The New Greek-English Interlinear New Testament.*
3. **UNDATED**, Cook, *New Testament, Plain Translation By A Student.*
4. **UNDATED**, Robert Gordon, *New Testament.*
5. **UNDATED**, Samuel P. Linn, editor, *The New Testament.*
6. **UNDATED**, Luther A. Weigle, editor, *The New Testament Octapla.*
7. **1380**, John Wycliffe, *The New Testament.*
8. **1525**, William Tyndale, *The New Testament.* At Worms.
9. **1525**, William Tyndale, *The New Testament.* At Cologne.
10. **1534**, George Joye, *The New Testament.*

11. **1534**, William Tyndale, *The Newe Testament.* At Antwerp.
12. **1535**, George Joye, *The New Testament In Tyndale's Version.*
13. **1535**, William Tyndale, *The Newe Testament Yet Once Agayne. Corrected By Willyam Tindale.*
14. **1538**, Myles Coverdale, *The New Testament.*
15. **1538**, Myles Coverdale, *The New Testament Both In Latine And Englyshe.*
16. **1538**, Johan Hollybushe, *The Newe Testament Both In Latine And Englyshe.*
17. **1538**, Thomas Matthew, *The Newe Testament.*
18. **1539**, Richard Taverner, *The Nevv Testament in Englysshe.*
19. **1540**, R. Grafton and E. Whitchurch, *New Testament.*
20. **1548**, William Tyndale, *The Newe Testament.*
21. **1549**, Anonymous, *The First Tome Or Volume Of The Paraphrase Of Erasmus vpon the Newe Testamente.*
22. **1549**, Myles Coverdale, *The Newe Testament.*
23. **1552**, Richard Jugge, *The Newe Testament.*
24. **1557**, William Whittingham, *The Nevve Testament.*
25. **1576**, Laurence Tomson, *The New Testament.*
26. **1589**, William Fulke, *The Text of the New Testament.*
27. **1599**, Anonymous, *New Testament, English and 11 Other Languages.*
28. **1602**, Geneva-Tomson-Junius New Testament, *The New Testament.*
29. **1653**, Henry Hammond, *A Paraphrase, and Annotations Upon All the Books of the New Testament.*
30. **1685**, Richard Baxter, *A Paraphrase on the New Testament.*
31. **1701**, William Lloyd, *The Holy Bible.*
32. **1703**, Daniel Whitby, *Paraphrase And Commentary On The New Testament.*
33. **1719**, Cornelius Nary, *The New Testament.*
34. **1729**, Anonymous, *The New Testament In Greek and English.*
35. **1730**, Anonymous, *Annotations On The New Testament.*
36. **1730**, William Webster, *The New Testament.*
37. **1731**, John Lewis, *The New Testament.*
38. **1736**, John Lindsey, *A Critical And Practical Commentary On The New Testament.*
39. **1738**, Anonymous, *The New Testament.*
40. **1739**, Philip Doddridge, *The New Testament With Paraphrase And Notes.*
41. **1739**, John Guyse, *An Exposition Of The New Testament, In The*

Form Of A Paraphrase.
42. **1745**, William Whiston, *Mr. Whiston's Primitive New Testament.*
43. **1755**, John Wesley, *Explanatory Notes On The New Testament By John Wesley.*
44. **1764**, Richard Wynne, *The New Testament.*
45. **1765**, Anonymous, *A New Translation Of The New Testament.*
46. **1765**, Samuel Clarke and Thomas Pyle, *New Testament.*
47. **1768**, Edward Harwood, *A Liberal Translation of the New Testament; Being An Attempt To Translate The Sacred Writings With The Same Freedom, Spirit, and Elegance, With Which Other English Translations From The Greek Classics Have Lately Been Executed.*
48. **1770**, John Worsley, *The New Testament.*
49. **1774**, James Ashton, *The New Testament.*
50. **1783**, John Barclay, *The Experience And Example Of The Lord Jesus Christ.*
51. **1783**, Carpenter, *New Testament.*
52. **1783**, Rev. Bernard MacMahon, *The New Testament.*
53. **1790**, William Gilpin, *An Exposition Of The New Testament.*
54. **1791**, Gilbert Wakefield, *A Translation Of The New Testament.*
55. **1792**, Anonymous, *The New Testament.*
56. **1795**, Thomas Haweis, *A Translation Of The New Testament.*
57. **1796**, William Newcome, *The New Covenant.*
58. **1796**, Nathaniel Scarlett, *A Translation Of The New Testament.*
59. **1807**, S. Palmer, *The New Testament.*
60. **1808**, Anonymous, *The New Testament.*
61. **1810**, Henry Harvey Baber, *New Testament.*
62. **1812**, Anonymous, *A Modern, Correct, and Close Translation Of The New Testament.*
63. **1812**, Anonymous, *The New Testament.*
64. **1813**, Rev. John McDonald, *The New Testament.*
65. **1815**, Anonymous, *The New Testament.*
66. **1816**, William Thompson, *The New Testament.*
67. **1818**, Rev. M. Horrabin, *The New Testament.*
68. **1822**, Israel Alger, *The New Testament.*
69. **1823**, Abner Kneeland, *The New Testament.*
70. **1824**, Anonymous, *The New Testament.*
71. **1824**, Elizabeth Jones, *The New Testament; Syriac, Arabic and English Interlineary.*
72. **1825**, George Townsend, *The New Testament, Arranged In*

Chronological & Historical Order.

73. **1826**, Alexander Campbell, *The Sacred Writings Of The Apostles And Evangelists.*
74. **1827**, J. A. Cummings, *New Testament.*
75. **1827**, James Nourse, *The New Testament.*
76. **1828**, Anonymous, *The New Testament.*
77. **1828**, Alexander Greaves, *Gospel of God's Anointed.*
78. **1831**, John Bird Summer, *A Practical Exposition of the New Testament.*
79. **1833**, Rodolophus Dickinson, *A New And Corrected Version of the New Testament.*
80. **1833**, William Lyon MacKenzie, *The Productions of the Evangelists and Apostles.*
81. **1834**, Anonymous, *The New Testament.*
82. **1835**, J. M. Caldecott, *The Holy Writings of the First Christians.*
83. **1836**, Granville Penn, *The Book of the New Covenant.*
84. **1837**, Edward Cardwell, *The New Testament In Greek And English.*
85. **1837**, J. P. Dabney, *The New Testament.*
86. **1838**, George Croft Cell, *Explanatory Notes On The New Testament.*
87. **1840**, Anonymous, *The New Testament.*
88. **1840**, Samuel Sharpe, *The New Testament.*
89. **1841**, English Hexapla, *English Hexapla.*
90. **1842**, Herman Heinfetter, *The New Testament.*
91. **1843**, Sir John Clarke, *The New Testament.*
92. **1843**, J. W. Etheridge, *The New Testament.*
93. **1845**, George Campbell and J. MacKnight, *The New Testament.*
94. **1847**, Anonymous, *The Holy Bible.*
95. **1848**, A. Komstok, *The New Testament.*
96. **1848**, Jonathan Morgan, *The New Testament.*
97. **1849**, Anonymous, *The Good News Of Our Lord Jesus Christ.*
98. **1850**, Anonymous, *The New Testament.*
99. **1850**, Spencer H. Cone and William R. Wyckoff, editors, *The Commonly Received Version of the New Testament . . . With Several Hundred Emendations.*
100. **1850**, James McMahon, *The New Testament.*
101. **1851**, Clement Moody, *The New Testament Expounded.*
102. **1851**, James Murdock, *The New Testament.*
103. **1852**, John Taylor, *The Emphatic New Testament.*
104. **1855**, Anonymous, *The New Testament.*

105. **1857**, Jotham Albrecht Bengel, *English Translation Of The New Testament*.
106. **1857**, J. A. Giles, *The New Testament*.
107. **1858**, Leicester Ambrose Sawyer, *The New Testament*.
108. **1861**, Anonymous, *The New Testament*.
109. **1861**, William Kelly, *New Testament*.
110. **1862**, American Bible Union, *The New Testament*.
111. **1862**, Rev. B. Highton, *A Revised Translation of the New Testament*.
112. **1863**, Henry Alford, *The New Testament For English Readers*.
113. **1864**, Henry Tompkins Anderson, *The New Testament*.
114. **1864**, Anonymous, *The New Testament . . . In Phonetic Spelling*.
115. **1864**, Benjamin Wilson, *The Emphatic Diaglott*.
116. **1865**, Thomas Sheldon Green, *The Twofold New Testament*.
117. **1868**, Joseph Bryant Rotherham, *The New Testament*.
118. **1869**, Rev. Robert Ainslie, *The New Testament*.
119. **1869**, Henry Alford, *The New Testament*.
120. **1869**, George R. Noyes, *The New Testament*.
121. **1870**, Anonymous, *A Critical English New Testament*.
122. **1870**, John Bowes, *The New Testament*.
123. **1871**, Edward Arber, editor, *William Tyndale, New Testament*.
124. **1871**, John Nelson Darby, *The New Testament*.
125. **1875**, Samuel Davidson, *The New Testament*.
126. **1877**, Anonymous, *The Englishman's Greek New Testament*.
127. **1877**, W. L. Blackley and James Hawes, editors, *The Critical English Testament*.
128. **1877**, John August Richter, *The New Testament*.
129. **1881**, American Revised Version, *The New Testament*.
130. **1881**, R. L. Clarke and others, editors, *The Variorum Edition of the New Testament*.
131. **1881**, English Revised Version, *The New Testament*.
132. **1881**, Isaac H. Hall, *The Revised New Testament*.
133. **1881**, Constantine Tischendorf, *The Sinai And Comparative New Testament*.
134. **1881**, Samuel Williams, *The New Testament*.
135. **1882**, Daniel Curry, *The New Testament*.
136. **1883**, John Wesley Hanson, *The New Covenant*.
137. **1883**, Cortes Jackson, *The New Testament*.
138. **1885**, American Baptist Publication Society, *The New Testament*.
139. **1885**, W. D. Dillard, *The New Testament*.

140. **1886**, Isaac Pitman, *The New Testament.*
141. **1891**, Leicester Ambrose Sawyer, *The New Testament.*
142. **1892**, Anonymous, *The New Testament.*
143. **1895**, Ferrar Fenton, *The New Testament.*
144. **1896**, W. Stevens, *The New Testament, Authorised Version, Written In Orthic Shorthand.*
145. **1896**, H. Vaughan, *The New Testament.*
146. **1897**, George Ricker Berry, *The Interlinear Literal Translation of the Greek New Testament.*
147. **1897**, Horace E. Morrow, *The New Testament Emphasized.*
148. **1898**, Anonymous, *The Twentieth Century New Testament.*
149. **1898**, G. W. Horner, *The Coptic Version of the New Testament.*
150. **1901**, American Standard Version, *The New Covenant.*
151. **1901**, James Moffatt, *The Historical New Testament.*
152. **1901**, Murdoch Nisbet, *The New Testament In Scots.*
153. **1901**, William Wye Smith, *The New Testament In Braid Scots.*
154. **1902**, Anonymous, *The "Revised English" New Testament.*
155. **1902**, James Cooper and A. J. MacLean, *The Testament of our Lord.*
156. **1902**, W. B. Godbey, *Translation of the New Testament.*
157. **1903**, Richard Francis Weymouth, *The Modern Speech New Testament.*
158. **1904**, Samuel Lloyd and George Washington Moon, editors, *The Authorized . . . In "Revised English."*
159. **1904**, Adolphus S. Worrell, *The New Testament.*
160. **1906**, Anonymous, *The New Testament.*
161. **1906**, Thomas M. Lindsey, *The New Testament.*
162. **1907**, Robert Young, *The Book of the New Covenant.*
163. **1909**, Anonymous, *The Bible In Modern English.*
164. **1909**, Anonymous, *Evolutionary Edition of the New Testament, Translated By An Evolutionist.*
165. **1909**, Ernest Hampdon-Cook, *New Testament.*
166. **1909**, S. Townsend Weaver, *The University New Testament.*
167. **1911**, G. W. Horner, *The Coptic Version of the New Testament.*
168. **1913**, Sir Edward George Clarke, *The New Testament.*
169. **1913**, W. L. Courtney, *The Literary Man's New Testament.*
170. **1913**, James Moffatt, *The New Testament.*
171. **1914**, Edward Ernest Cunnington, *The New Covenant.*
172. **1914**, Ivan Panin, *The New Testament From The Greek Text As Established By Bible Numerics.*

173. **1915**, Leighton Pullan, *Oxford Church Bible Commentary.*
174. **1915**, S. Townsend Weaver, *The Greatest Book Ever Written.*
175. **1917**, Johannes Rudolph Lauritzen, *The New Testament.*
176. **1917**, James Moffatt, *The New Testament.*
177. **1918**, Henry Tompkins Anderson, *The New Testament.*
178. **1921**, Anonymous, *A Plain Translation of the New Testament.*
179. **1922**, Frank Schell Ballantine, *A Plainer Bible For Plain People In Plain America.*
180. **1923**, William G. Ballantine, *The Riverside New Testament.*
181. **1923**, Edgar J. Goodspeed, *The New Testament.*
182. **1924**, H. T. Andrews, *The New Testament In Modern Speech.*
183. **1924**, Anonymous, *The New Covenant.*
184. **1924**, S. W. Green, *New Testament.*
185. **1924**, Helen Barrett Montgomery, *Centenary Translation of the New Testament.*
186. **1924**, Several Well-Known New Testament Scholars, *New Testament.*
187. **1925**, Arthur E. Overbury, *The People's New Covenant.*
188. **1926**, Concordant Version, *Concordant Version.*
189. **1927**, Isaac Pitman, *The New Testament.*
190. **1928**, A. Hamilton, *The Student's Greek Testament.*
191. **1929**, George N. LeFevre, *The Christian's Bible.*
192. **1929**, William Wallace Martin, *The New Testament.*
193. **1929**, James Alexander Robertson, *New Testament.*
194. **1929**, George W. Wolff, *The New Testament In Blank Verse.*
195. **1931**, R. C. H. Lenski, *A New Commentary on the New Testament.*
196. **1932**, Frank Schell Ballantine, *Our God And Godhealth, Our Healer.*
197. **1934**, Montague Rhodes James and Delia Lyttelton, *The Aldine Bible.*
198. **1934**, G. Woosung Wade, *The Documents of the New Testament.*
199. **1935**, James A. Carey, *New Testament.*
200. **1937**, Fr. Charles Jerome Callan, editor, *The New Testament.*
201. **1937**, Johannes Greber, *The New Testament.*
202. **1937**, Francis Aloysius Spencer, *The New Testament.*
203. **1937**, Charles B. Williams, *The New Testament.*
204. **1938**, Anonymous, *The Book of Books.*
205. **1938**, Edgar Lewis Clementson, *The New Testament.*
206. **1938**, N. Hardy Willis, editor, *The Newe Testament.*
207. **1939**, Zed Hopeful Copp, *The Book of Life.*

208. **1940**, George M. Lamsa, *The New Testament.*
209. **1941**, Anonymous, *The New Testament In Basic English.*
210. **1941**, Anonymous, *The New Testament.*
211. **1943**, Ervin Edward Stringfellow, *The New Testament.*
212. **1944**, Anonymous, *The Beginnings Of The Way.*
213. **1944**, Anonymous, *The New Testament.*
214. **1945**, Berkeley Version, *Berkeley Version Of The New Testament.*
215. **1946**, Revised Standard Version, *The New Covenant.*
216. **1947**, J. P. Arendzen, *New Testament.*
217. **1947**, J. B. Phillips, *The New Testament In Modern English.*
218. **1947**, George Swann, *New Testament.*
219. **1948**, Thomas Francis Ford and Ralph Ewart Ford, *The New Testament.*
220. **1949**, Albert George Alexander, *Interpretation Of The Entire New Testament.*
221. **1950**, Anonymous, *The New Testament.*
222. **1951**, Anonymous, *The New Testament.*
223. **1951**, Olaf Morgan Norlie, *The New Testament.*
224. **1952**, Charles Kingsley Williams, *The New Testament.*
225. **1953**, William Barclay, *The Daily Study Bible.*
226. **1953**, George Albert Moore, *The New Testament.*
227. **1954**, Morton C. Bradley, Jr., *The New Testament In Cadenced Form.*
228. **1954**, James A. Kleist and Joseph L. Lilly, *The New Testament.*
229. **1955**, F. G. Parker, *The Clarified New Testament.*
230. **1955**, Hugh J. Schonfield, *The Authentic New Testament.*
231. **1956**, Kenneth S. Wuest, *Wuest's Expanded Translation of the Greek New Testament.*
232. **1957**, Adam and Charles Black, *Black's New Testament Commentaries.*
233. **1958**, Amplified New Testament, *Amplified New Testament.*
234. **1958**, British and Foreign Bible Society, *A Diaglot New Testament For Use Of Translators.*
235. **1958**, Harper's New Testament Commentaries, *Harper's New Testament Commentaries.*
236. **1958**, Ashley S. Johnson, *The Self-Interpreting New Testament.*
237. **1958**, Alfred Marshall, *The Interlinear Greek-English New Testament.*
238. **1958**, James L. Tomanek, *The New Testament.*
239. **1958**, Translation For Translators, *The New Testament: A*

Translation For Translators.
240. **1959**, John W. Fraser, *Calvin's New Testament Commentaries.*
241. **1959**, New International Commentary on the N.T., *New International Commentary On The N.T.*
242. **1960**, Vincent T. Roth, *A Critical Emphatic Paraphrase Of The New Testament.*
243. **1961**, John J. Heenan and others, *The New Testament.*
244. **1961**, New English Bible, *The New English Bible.*
245. **1961**, Metropolitan Fan S. Noli, *The New Testament.*
246. **1961**, Olaf Morgan Norlie, *Simplified New Testament In Plain English.*
247. **1962**, Dr. Dymond, *New Testament.*
248. **1962**, Emil G. Kraeling, *Clarified New Testament.*
249. **1962**, Richmond Lattimore, *The New Testament.*
250. **1963**, William F. Beck, *The New Testament In the Language Of Today.*
251. **1963**, New American Standard Version, *New Testament.*
252. **1966**, Anonymous, *Today's English Version of the New Testament.*
253. **1966**, Anonymous, *The Living Scriptures.*
254. **1966**, Jerusalem Bible, *The New Testament.*
255. **1966**, C. S. Lovett, *The Personal New Testament.*
256. **1967**, Edward J. Craddock, *The Christ Emphasis New Testament.*
257. **1967**, Don J. Klingensmith, *The New Testament.*
258. **1967**, Kenneth Taylor, *The Living New Testament.*
259. **1968**, Anonymous, *The New Testament of Our Master.*
260. **1968**, William Barclay, *The New Testament.*
261. **1969**, Annie Crassman, *Good News For The World.*
262. **1969**, Gleason H. Ledyard, *The New Life New Testament.*
263. **1969**, Watchtower Bible and Tract Society, *The Kingdom Interlinear Translation of the Greek Scriptures.*
264. **1970**, Anonymous, *King James II Version of the New Testament.*
265. **1970**, Anonymous, *New Testament.*
266. **1972**, Anonymous, *King James Version New Testament--Twentieth Century Edition.*
267. **1973**, Don J. Klingensmith, *Today's English New Testament.*
268. **1973**, Chester Estes, *The Better Version of the New Testament.*
269. **1973**, New International Version, *The New Testament.*
270. **1973**, Translator's N.T., *The Translator's New Testament.*
271. **1975**, Christianity Today, *The Greek-English New Testament.*
272. **1976**, Randolph O. Yeager, *The Renaissance New Testament.*

273. **1977**, Jay E. Adams, *The Christian Counselor's New Testament.*
274. **1978**, Anonymous, *The Simple English Bible.*
275. **1978**, Anonymous, *The New Testament: English Version for the Deaf.*
276. **1978**, Anonymous, *International Children's Version.*
277. **1979**, John L. Abbott, *New Testament: Judgment Hour Version.*
278. **1979**, Jay E. Adams, *The New Testament In Everyday English.*
279. **1980**, Roy Greenhill, *The Distilled Bible.*
280. **1981**, Anonymous, *The Compact Bible.*
281. **1981**, Anonymous, *May Your Name Be Inscribed in the Book Of Life.*
282. **1983**, William Laughton Lorimer, *The New Testament In Scots.*
283. **1984**, Julian G. Anderson, *A New Accurate Translation.*
284. **1984**, New Century Version, *The Word.*
285. **1985**, Hugh J. Schonfield, *The Original New Testament.*
286. **1985**, Lee Witness, John C. Ingalis, and others, *The Recovery Version.*
287. **1986**, Lowell Hagan and Jack Westerhof, *Theirs Is The Kingdom New Testament.*
288. **1987**, Anonymous, *The New American Bible.*
289. **1988**, Phillip B. Giessler, *God's Word To The Nations.*
290. **1989**, Hugo McCord, *New Testament.*
291. **1989**, Heinz W. Cassirer, *God's New Covenant.*
292. **1989**, John Wesley Sawyer, *The Newe Testament.*
293. **1989**, David H. Stern, *Jewish New Testament.*

To these 293 "COMPLETE NEW TESTAMENTS," could be added twenty-three "ABRIDGED NEW TESTAMENTS" which are listed in Chamberlin's compendium on pages 594-597.

IV. AN ANALYSIS OF THE FREQUENCY OF PUBLICATION OF COMPLETE ENGLISH BIBLES AND NEW TESTAMENTS

A. Frequency of Publication of Complete English Bibles. From the chronological listing of the complete English Bibles, the following chart summarizes, by centuries, the number of complete Bibles published. It also includes the number of years between new Bibles. The records include the 604 years from 1388 through 1991.

YEARS	NEW BIBLES	YRS. BETWEEN BIBLES
Undated	1	----------
1300's	3	33.3 years
1400's	0	100 years
1500's	11	9 years
1600's	5	20 years
1700's	17	5.8 years
1800's	45	2.2 years
1900's	53	1.9 years
1300's--1900's	135	4.4 years

It should be noted that from the publication of the REVISED STANDARD VERSION in 1952 to 1991 (forty years), there were thirty-four new complete Bibles, or only 1.1 years between new Bibles. From this, it would appear that the frequency of complete Bible publication was increasing decidedly in the last half of the twentieth century.

B. **Frequency of Publication of Complete English New Testaments.** From the chronological listing of the complete New Testaments, the following chart summarizes, by centuries, the number of complete New Testaments published. It also includes the number of years between new New Testaments. The records include the 612 years from 1380 through 1991.

YEARS	NEW N.T.'s	YRS. BETWEEN N.T.'s
Undated	6	----------
1300's	1	99 years
1400's	0	100 years
1500's	20	5 years
1600's	3	33.3 years
1700's	29	3.4 years
1800's	90	1.1 years
1900's	144	.69 years
1300's--1900's	293	2.1 years

It should be noted that from the publication of the REVISED STANDARD VERSION in 1952 to 1991 (forty years), there were seventy new complete New Testaments, or only .57 years between new New Testaments. From this, it would appear that the frequency of complete New Testament publication was increasing appreciably in the last half of the twentieth century.

C. Frequency of Publication of Complete English Bibles and New Testaments Combined. If we were to combine both of the above tables, showing both the complete English Bibles as well as New Testaments, the table would look like this for the 612 years from 1380 through 1991:

YEARS	BIBLES/N.T.'s	YRS. BETWEEN
Undated	1+6 = 7	---------
1300's	3+1 = 4	25 years
1400's	0+0 = 0	100 years
1500's	11+20 = 31	3.2 years
1600's	5+3 = 8	12.5 years
1700's	17+29 = 46	2.1 years
1800's	45+90 = 135	.74 years
1900's	53+144 = 197	.51 years
1300's--1900's	135+293 = 428	1.4 years

V. SOME CONCLUSIONS ABOUT THE NEED FOR PUBLICATION OF *NEW* COMPLETE BIBLES OR *NEW* COMPLETE NEW TESTAMENTS.

From this chronological survey of new complete English Bibles and New Testaments during the 612 years from 1380 through 1991, it is certainly evident that there has been no lack of these resources. Since there have been 135 complete new Bibles and 293 complete new New Testaments, or a total of 428 Bibles or New Testaments combined throughout these 612 years, it must be concluded that there has been a super abundance of these documents for the English speaking world!

We are of the considered opinion that we do NOT need another new complete Bible or New Testament. The only thing that might be helpful to us--and THE BIBLE FOR TODAY has prepared it--is *The Defined King James Bible*. It is in large print 12-point type for tired eyes. It is 7½ by 10" in size. It is genuine leather (not bonded leather) and comes in either black or burgundy. It is **BFT #3000L** and is available for a gift of **$40 + S&H**. To get your copy, you can **phone 1-800-JOHN 10:9.** The text is the OLD KING JAMES BIBLE printed word for word **without any changes in the text.** We have merely added a **brief but accurate definition** of words which might be uncommon, might have changed their meanings, or might be difficult for some to understand. Some reject the KING JAMES BIBLE because they say they cannot understand the words that have changed their meanings since 1611. In reality, there are only 500 or 600 of these words in the entire Bible. Since each of these words has a brief meaning given in the footnotes, the use of such a study Bible removes that excuse completely.

In addition to the large Bible, we also have a medium sized *Defined King James Bible* which is 6" by 8" in size. It is 10-point type, very easy reading, and comes in genuine leather, either black or burgundy, with accurate definitions of uncommon words in the footnotes. It is **BFT #3000M.** It is for a gift of **$35 + S&H.** You can order your copy by calling toll free **1-800-JOHN 10:9.** **[For more background details on this Bible, please turn back to page 2.]**

Rather than to have any NEW Bible or New Testament, we need to understand, live by, and practice the truth that is found in what we consider to be the best and finest translation of the Bible in the English language--the KING JAMES BIBLE.

APPENDIX C

QUESTIONS AND ANSWERS ON THE SUBJECT OF
"DEFENDING THE KING JAMES BIBLE--
GOD'S WORDS KEPT INTACT IN ENGLISH"

1. WHAT GREEK TEXTS WERE USED BEFORE PRINTED
TEXTS?

Q. You said that Beza's text came out in 1598. What did
they use before that?
A. They used the manuscripts they had copied. The
manuscripts were handwritten, not in printed form, being copies of
copies, beginning with the original Greek New Testament writings. The
first printed form of the *Received Text* was that of Erasmus in 1516.
In the preface to the Trinitarian Bible Society's Greek New Testament
there is a history of the text. It mentions there that Desiderius Erasmus
printed the text in 1516. Erasmus was a Roman Catholic. A lot of people
who follow Westcott and Hort like to say, "Well, Erasmus was a Roman
Catholic and he was no good; therefore, we shouldn't follow his text."
They say he was a Humanist and therefore bad. Well, he was a
Humanist, but not like the Humanists of Secular Humanism today. He
believed the Bible. He believed it was God's Word. He wanted people
to read it in the Greek text in which it was originally written, not just in
the Latin Vulgate that most people had. In his day, Erasmus was the
greatest Greek scholar on the European continent. He was the one
everyone looked to, and under whom they wanted to study. A number of
people studied Greek under Erasmus. He was the one who gave the
Greek pronunciation we still use today.
In 1516, Erasmus' Greek New Testament came out in the first
edition. He had many other editions. Martin Luther used one of
Erasmus' editions for his German translation. The *Complutensian
Polyglot* was edited by Cardinal Ximenes and was published in Acala,
Spain. It was called a "polyglot" because it contained a number of
languages in addition to the Greek. That was printed in 1514, but wasn't
circulated until 1522. Actually the first Greek New Testament to be
printed was the *Complutensian Polyglot.* Erasmus' edition came out in
1516. Once the printing press got into use, the changes were not as great,

because the editions would be type-set. Before that, they just had to use handwritten manuscripts.

2. DID THE CHURCHES HAVE COMPLETE NEW TESTA-MENTS?

Q. Did the early churches have the New Testament in its entirety or only parts? Did all the different churches have their own complete manuscript?

A. Not at all times; but they did, presumably, as time went on. Some of these manuscripts that are preserved for us are partial. Some are more complete. B and Aleph were quite complete except B, the Vatican manuscript that Westcott and Hort practically worshiped, was defective in certain parts. Dr. Frederick H. A. Scrivener, in his *PLAIN IN-TRODUCTION TO NEW TESTAMENT TEXTUAL CRITICISM--4th EDITION* made this observation about Vatican manuscript "B":

> *"The New Testament is complete down to Hebrews ix. 14 katha: the rest of the Epistle to the Hebrews (the Catholic Epistles had followed the Acts, see p. 74), and the Apocalypse, being written in the later hand alluded to above." [Scrivener, op. cit., Volume I, p. 106;* This is available as **B.F.T. #1285**. It is 920 pages in two volumes.]

Some of the manuscripts were fairly complete, but not many. It would indicate that some in the early church did have rather complete Bibles. I am sure they all would have liked a complete New Testament, but they would have been very expensive.

In 325 A.D., the Council of Nicea determined which canonical books should be followed and which were spurious and not to be followed. I'm sure in order to make that decision they would have to have a *complete* Greek New Testament in their hands. I'm sure there were some Christians who couldn't afford handwritten manuscripts for all the books. They had certain portions, maybe one Gospel. By and large, the entire New Testament was copied.

3. DO ANY SCHOOLS USE THE *TEXTUS RECEPTUS* RATHER THAN WESTCOTT & HORT?

Q. Are there any colleges or seminaries that teach from the

Textus Receptus, or do they all use the Westcott and Hort text?
        A.   There are some schools that use the *Received Text.* I know
Dr. Robert Gray's school in Jacksonville, Florida uses the KING JAMES
BIBLE and the *Received Text.* There's a man in Massilon, Ohio, Dr.
Bruce Cummons, who is strong on the *Received Text.* He also has a
school. Another school that you might look into is the Heritage Baptist
University in the Indianapolis, Indiana, area. The president is Dr. Russell
Dennis. He works with Dr. Clinton Branine. Then there are other schools
that are ambivalent. They preach only from the KING JAMES BIBLE,
but in their Greek departments they teach the Westcott and Hort text. Bob
Jones University does this.
        It's interesting. We've had a reversal in some of the colleges that
used to use the *Received Text* and have gone back into the Westcott-and-
Hort-type of text. I speak of Maranatha Baptist Bible College in
Watertown, Wisconsin. I spoke there three or four times when Dr.
Cedarholm was president. He was a believer in the Received Text. He
asked me to come and tell the students about the superiority of this text,
so I did. Then the school got another president and he has made a
complete turn-around. The Dean Burgon Society Chapter of students has
been disbanded because the president opposed it. They no longer use the
Received Text in school, but use the Westcott and Hort text instead. It was
a wonderful, refreshing atmosphere to start with; yet, within a matter of
a few short years, it went back to the old line. The Theological Seminary
connected with the TABERNACLE BAPTIST BIBLE COLLEGE (717
N. Whitehorse Landing Road) in Virginia Beach, Virginia, with Dr.
Rodney Bell as Pastor, and Dr. Thomas Strouse as Professor of Greek,
stands for the *Textus Receptus* and the KING JAMES BIBLE. Another
school that uses the *Received Text* and the KING JAMES BIBLE is Dr.
Ronald Comfort's school in North Carolina, where Dr. James Qurollo is
presently the head of the Greek department.
        There are very few schools that will come out strongly and use
the *Received Text.* I think there is need for seminaries and colleges and
others that will stand strongly on this issue because pastors, I'm sure, are
confused. They think they aren't confused; but when you only know part
of the equation, you aren't aware of any confusion. There's nothing to
confuse you. Your mind is made up because that is all you know. I
wasn't confused at Dallas Theological Seminary when I was using the
Westcott and Hort text. I didn't know there was any other. I was starting
to learn Greek. I was trying to learn the language. I didn't have time then
to weigh the evidence. I was going to school, working my way through,

supporting my family, studying hard, and later, going to two graduate schools at once. The professors didn't even give us the other side of the evidence. They didn't say there was another side.

In fact, Sandra DeVos, one of my students when I was Professor of Speech and Greek at Shelton College, in Cape May, New Jersey, asked me a question one day. She said, "Did you ever hear of Dean John William Burgon?" I said, "No, I'm sorry, I never heard of him." She said, "I've been reading a book in the library by Burgon." It was *REVISION REVISED.* It is a 591-page book which the BIBLE FOR TODAY has reprinted. It is a careful and accurate criticism of the ENGLISH REVISED VERSION of 1881, and the Westcott and Hort Greek text that underlies it. It is an excellent piece of research. [**B.F.T. #611.**] She said, "He believes that the *Received Text* that underlies the KING JAMES BIBLE is the best text to use." I said, "That is interesting." I began from that point to think about it. I hadn't known such a person or case existed until a student told me about it. My future mother-in-law had given me the book *God Wrote Only One Bible,* but I had not read it as yet. We must get good materials into the hands of people and urge them to read them!

4. WHAT SEMINARY WOULD YOU CHOOSE TODAY?

Q. If you had to choose a seminary to go to today, which would it be?

A. Your pastor is from the Baptist Bible Seminary in the Boston area. I have been told that it takes a good position on both the *Received Text* and the KING JAMES BIBLE as well as its sister school, BIBLE BAPTIST COLLEGE in Springfield, Missouri. Though there had been some difference on this at one time, I was told the position there has solidified. In their catalog, they have a statement to the effect that the KING JAMES BIBLE is "God's Words kept intact." To answer your direct question, where would I recommend? Though it's a small school, I would check into the Heritage Baptist University in the Indianapolis, Indiana, where Dr. Dennis is the president. They are a Baptist College that offers a number of degrees and they also stand for the KING JAMES BIBLE and the *Received Text.*

Philadelphia College of Bible is pushing the NIV strongly. The school is responsible for the wedding (a strange union indeed) of the Scofield notes and the NEW INTERNATIONAL VERSION that has been published. Dr. Scofield, in his Preface, says:

> *"XI. After mature reflection it was determined TO USE THE AUTHORIZED VERSION. None of the many Revisions have commended themselves to the people at large. The REVISED VERSION, which has now been before the public for twenty-seven years, gives no indication of becoming in any general sense the people's Bible of the English-speaking world. . . ." [The Scofield Reference Bible (1917 edition), pp. iii-iv].*

He **refused** to use the AMERICAN STANDARD VERSION of 1901, the ENGLISH REVISED VERSION of 1881, or the AMERICAN REVISED VERSION of 1898, all of which followed the perverted Westcott and Hort, *Nestle/Aland* text. Consult **APPENDIX B** for the various Bibles that could have been used. I wonder what he would think about putting his notes into the NEW INTERNATIONAL VERSION and changing them. Every time there is a change in the text, they put a note saying, "We follow the Syriac (or Septuagint, etc.)." **It's a disgrace.** The president of Philadelphia College of Bible was on that Oxford University Press Revision Committee of the NEW INTERNATIONAL VERSION. PCB has boosted this edition widely, which is unfortunate indeed.

Now, as for my own seminary, Dallas Theological Seminary, I wouldn't send anybody there. Dallas Theological Seminary is not Baptist, does not take any theological position on baptism, and so on. It is still "dispensational"--I am also. The school is rapidly changing its original dispensational position taught by its Founder, and my Professor from 1948-52, Dr. Lewis Sperry Chafer. They no longer require their graduates to accept the entire Doctrinal Statement of the Seminary as we had to do. They have merely a brief few things they must believe. In my opinion, it is New Evangelical in the extreme. It still sends its graduates right back into the United Methodist Church and its apostasy, the United Presbyterian Church and its apostasy, the American Baptist Convention churches and their apostasy--anywhere and to any group. They did it when I was going there in 1948-53 and they are doing it today. So I couldn't send anybody there. In an ad carried by *Moody Monthly* in September, 1992, Dallas Theological Seminary boasted as follows:

> *"DID YOU KNOW . . .? Dallas graduates preach the Bible in over 50 different denominations! . . ."*

Among the fifty denominations represented, there were pictures of churches with the names as follows:

> *"Independent   Churches,   Evangelical   Free,*

Presbyterian, Baptist, Methodist, Lutheran, and Brethren."
Dallas is a large school now. It's getting bigger and bigger. They are even training women there, although I don't know what they're training them to do. I don't know if they are going to switch eventually and come out in favor of women preachers. They say now they don't believe in women preachers, but what are the women going to do when they have been trained at Dallas? If they belong to a church that has women preachers, they'll go preach. Dallas can say they don't believe in women preachers, but they are training women in some of the same disciplines as the men.

Dallas recently fired one professor, and two teachers resigned. The issue was **sign-gifts** such as **miracles** and **tongues.** I've just been reading snatches and hearing on the telephone. Apparently some of the teachers didn't take a position on the Charismatic Movement as they should have. Dr. Charles Ryrie also left his very influential position at Dallas Seminary after some marital problems.

5.   WHAT DO YOU THINK OF THE "RYRIE STUDY BIBLE"?

Q. Do you have an opinion on the Ryrie Study Bible's notes?
A. Dr. Ryrie has written some very good books and materials such as *DISPENSATIONALISM TODAY* and other books. This book favors the dispensational approach and is **against** hyper-dispensationalism which is the belief of some of the cults and other groups. As for his Study Bible, he has that in the NASV, the KJB, and the NIV. Of course, **that shows he doesn't have a preference, which is unfortunate.** Anyone who permits himself to be used for any of these, obviously has no preference. So that is the first thing I would say.

Secondly, even in the KING JAMES BIBLE edition of the Ryrie Study Bible, I was horrified to look up Mark 16:9-20 (the last 12 verses of Mark) and see the footnote in that place. That was enough for me! He may have some excellent notes in the rest of the Bible. He's a good scholar and a student of the Scriptures. There's nothing wrong with his background. He's been the Dean of the Graduate School for many years. He has a Ph.D. from somewhere in Great Britain and a Th.D. from Dallas Seminary in 1949. He's a good speaker and I'm sure he has many helpful things in his notes. But because of his view on the text, and the way it's written, I would not recommend his notes. Here is his note on Mark 16:9-20:

*"These verses do not appear in **THE TWO MOST
TRUSTWORTHY MANUSCRIPTS** of the New
Testament. Although they are a part of many other
manuscripts and versions, **THEY ARE NOT PART
OF THE GENUINE TEXT OF MARK.** The abrupt
ending at verse 8 is probably because the original
closing verses were lost. **THE DOUBTFUL GENU-
INENESS OF VERSES 9-20 MAKES IT UNWISE
TO BUILD A DOCTRINE OR BASE AN EXPE-
RIENCE ON THEM."***

Now, he says, in that remark, all kinds of things. It isn't simple. *THE
LAST 12 VERSES OF MARK* by Burgon (350 pages), has the facts,
evidence, and proof. **It shows these verses are genuine.** [This is
available as **B.F.T. #1139.**] Now, either Dr. Ryrie, who is a scholar and
a student, has never read Burgon's book, or doesn't know about it (as I
didn't know about it for years), or he has read it and denies it. It has not
been in print for years. He has made some serious errors on the texts in
this footnote. If he had said the verses do not appear in the two OLDEST
manuscripts, that would have been an honest statement. They are **not** in B and
Aleph, **but in practically every other Greek manuscript of the Gospel
of Mark, the verses do appear without question of any kind!**

By the way, the notes of the Old Scofield Bible, which I use, are
strongly favorable to the Westcott and Hort text. The footnotes and
marginal references reflect this. I want you to recognize that. **Notice
how Scofield reads on Mark 16:9-20:**

*"The passage from verse 9 to the end is not found
in THE TWO MOST ANCIENT MANUSCRIPTS,
THE SINAITIC AND THE VATICAN. . . "*

That is Aleph and B. **That is a true statement, not an opinion, not a
question.** He goes on to say:

*"Others have it with partial omissions and variations
but it is quoted by IRENAEUS and HIPPOLYTUS in
the second and third century." [The Scofield
Reference Bible, (1917 edition), p. 1069 under Mark
16:9.]*

So **Scofield does include some evidence in favor of the last twelve
verses of Mark.** By the way, Irenaeus was about 150 A. D.; these other
two manuscripts, Vatican and Sinai, were 350 or 375 A. D., two hundred
years after Irenaeus. If, indeed, the last twelve verses of Mark were not
genuine in 350 A. D., where did Irenaeus get them when he quoted and

cited them? Where did the other Church Fathers get them? That is the burden of Burgon's message as he goes through Church Father after Church Father quoting portions of the last twelve verses of Mark written before B and Aleph (the Vatican and Sinai manuscripts) ever saw the light of day. Why did the Church Fathers quote them? They were in the original text! What I'm saying is, Scofield's footnote is an **honest** footnote even though I wish it were not there. I wish he would have accepted those verses without doubt.

But Ryrie says the verses are **not** found in the "TWO MOST TRUSTWORTHY MANUSCRIPTS." The NEW INTERNATIONAL VERSION footnote says:

> "The **TWO MOST RELIABLE EARLY MANU-SCRIPTS** do not have Mark 16:9-20."

Now, if you look up Mark 16:9-20 in the NEW AMERICAN STAN-DARD VERSION, the footnote says:

> "Some of THE OLDEST manuscripts omit from verse 9 through 20."

The note does NOT call them the "**MOST TRUSTWORTHY**" manuscripts, or the "**MOST RELIABLE**" manuscripts. Scofield says, "**MOST ANCIENT**." That doesn't necessarily imply "BEST" or "WORST," just "**MOST ANCIENT**." Scofield's note is even better because he states, "the **TWO MOST ANCIENT**." In the NEW AMERICAN STANDARD it says "some of the oldest" and you don't know how many. You might think there were a hundred of them that don't have the verses. Scofield says "TWO" and names them: Sinai and Vatican. In Ryrie's footnote it says

> "two of the MOST TRUSTWORTHY . . . the doubt-ful genuineness . . . "

That causes doubt that the verses are God's Words and implies they should be thrown out.

Some say it is better that these verses are not considered to be part of God's Words because some Pentecostals and Charismatics use them to defend "snake handling" and other doubtful practices. **But listen, the answer is that these gifts of laying on of hands, casting out demons, etc., were Apostolic gifts given to those Apostles until the canon was closed in about 90 A. D.** The Apostles had those gifts, but they did not pass them to their successors. The conclusion is that Dr. Ryrie may be all right in many areas, but in this area of the text he is wrong, and that is why I cannot recommend using his notes with the KING JAMES BIBLE.

6. WHAT DO YOU THINK ABOUT THE NEW SCOFIELD BIBLE?

Q. How about the *New Scofield Bible*?

A. My wife bought a *New Scofield.* I have never bought one myself. She had been reading it. First, there are serious questions on the *New Scofield* because they do not believe in the accuracy of the Bible's chronology. I do. I believe the Bible is accurate in chronology as well as everything else. In Genesis 5 and 10 you have the lists of the patriarchs, and you can add up those years and come up with a Biblical chronology. This Biblical chronology is given in Usher's Chronology, which in the Old Scofield starts with B. C. 4004. That is a legitimate Biblical chronological date.

I have written a study on that based upon Dr. Charles Fred Lincoln's notes which he taught us when I was a student at the **OLD** Dallas Theological Seminary. [**B.F.T.** #9] He taught us a course on "Covenants and Dispensations." He quoted Berosis, and Martin Anstey *The Romance of Bible Chronology.* Dr. Lincoln taught us that the Masoretic text of Genesis 5 and 10 is accurate and the Septuagint text is not. The first question is: Can you use the genealogies in Genesis 5 and 10? Can they be used as chronological data? We say yes. The second question is: Which text do you use, the Septuagint text or the Masoretic Hebrew text? Well, we take the Masoretic Hebrew text. The Septuagint text, instead of 4004 B. C. lists about 2000 more years--you get about 6004 B. C. The Septuagint adds extra years. The years are not the same.

I have written a summary of Dr. Charles Fred Lincoln's notes on that. For instance, in Genesis 5:1, we read:

> *"This is the book of the generations of Adam. In the day that God created man, in the likeness of God made he him. . . (v 3)* ***And Adam lived an hundred and thirty years, and begat a son in his own likeness, after his*** *image; and called his name Seth: (v 4)* ***And the days of Adam after he had begotten Seth were eight hundred years:*** *and he begat sons and daughters: (v 5)* ***And all the days that Adam lived were nine hundred and thirty years:*** *and he died."*

Now, if that can't be used for chronological purposes, why did God put it in the Book? It's airtight. It's not the same as the genealogies in Matthew which just hits a few generations in general. Here it is actual years, and son after father, etc.

The *New Scofield Bible* notes don't believe the Bible is accurate as far as chronology is concerned. The secular world dates the time of David at about "1000 B. C." (or whatever date they assign). It is at about this point that the New Scofield begins their chronology in the margin. They listen to the world. It's interesting to note that there's been a change between the 1917 Scofield Edition, which I have, and the 1909 original Scofield. Did you know that? Someone gave me a copy. In that 1909 edition there are no chronology notes either. The 1917 edition has the dates and the *NEW SCOFIELD BIBLE* drops them out again.

Secondly, on the NEW SCOFIELD: **Some of their notes are changed dispensationally,** questioning certain things. I don't have the details, but in our brochure #1 and catalog you will find a small booklet we carry that does tell something about it.

Another thing about it: In the actual text, they claim it's the KING JAMES BIBLE and then in the margins they say, "We changed this word here but the KJB says so-and-so." The impression you get is that in every instance where they made a change in the text, the KJB is in the margin to show what it used to be. We had a man in the Dean Burgon Executive Committee one summer who spoke on the *New Scofield Bible*, its shortcomings, etc. He estimated 50% of the instances (I think that was the percent) are **NOT** indicated in the margin, just changed without any indication. To me, that is **deceitful.** If they say it is the KING JAMES, fine. If they show where they made the changes, fine. That is, at least, aboveboard, although I'd rather have the KING JAMES as it is. But when they say it is the KING JAMES and perhaps 50% of the changes were not indicated in the margin, that is not honest.

Some year I want to analyze the *NEW SCOFIELD Bible* because many have asked that question, and I would like to nail it down and say, "These are the changes. Here's a computer printout. This is the Hebrew and Greek, etc." Until that time I really can't be specific, but I do have these doubts and questions. The footnotes are changed for the worse, I believe. As a matter of fact, they say it is based on the same text, but there is a change in the Greek text.

It's one thing to change the KING JAMES English text, but in 2 Thessalonians they change even the Greek text. 2 Thessalonians 2:2,

". . . *neither by spirit, nor by word, nor by letter as from us, as that the day of Christ is at hand.*"

The *Received Text* says "*the day of Christ.*" The Westcott and Hort text says, "day of the **Lord.**" The *New Scofield* changes "*the day of Christ*" into "the day of the **Lord.**" All these other changes they claim makes the text more understandable. For instance, "shall not prevent" changed to "shall not precede" in I Thessalonians 4:15. In the case of 2 Thessalonians 2:2, how is "day of **Christ**" clarified by changing it to "day of the **Lord**?" **How do you know how many other places are changed?**

7. WHAT TEXT DOES THE *"OPEN BIBLE"* USE?

Q. What text does The *Open Bible* use?
A. At one time, I started to use the *Open Bible* when I compared the Authorized 1611 KING JAMES BIBLE to today's KING JAMES. Suddenly, I came to some words that were spelled differently, so I couldn't make a true comparison. I had to have a standard. For instance, the spelling of "vail." It could be "vail" or "veil." I couldn't tell if it was a change from the original KING JAMES or not. I'm not sure what text they use.

A new Bible has been reprinted. It is NOAH WEBSTER'S VERSION. I haven't analyzed that either. It has been printed by Baker Book House. Webster is the one who compiled the dictionary. He was an excellent man who knew many languages and he worked on the KING JAMES BIBLE. When it came time to clarify certain words, he changed them in his edition of the Bible. It looks fairly good. It is basically the KING JAMES BIBLE except in certain areas where he attempted to clarify some points. It is purported to be the KING JAMES BIBLE.

I have recently been given a NEW KING JAMES VERSION which is called the "OPEN BIBLE" edition. So Nelson publishers really don't mind **which version** of the Bible they call their "OPEN BIBLE."

8. WHAT STUDY HELPS COULD YOU USE WITH THE KING JAMES BIBLE?

Q. What would you suggest as a help to use with the KING JAMES BIBLE--one source or two you would use in everyday study?
A. Strong's Concordance is good. It is keyed to Greek and Hebrew words, and in the back you have the Greek and Hebrew words given in alphabetical order, including the meaning of each word. You would also be helped by a good Bible dictionary. You don't really need much in addition to this in the beginning of your Bible study.

9. IS IT DIFFICULT TO GET THE REAL MEANING IN ENGLISH?

Q. Isn't it difficult to get the real meaning in the English language?

A. The English language is a wide and expansive language with technical terms and detailed words from Latin, Greek and all languages. We have a way of saying it in English that many languages do not have. We have a vast number of adjectives, nouns, verbs, etc. that they don't even have in other languages. I would think the English language would be a good one to be able to say exactly what you mean and precisely what is in the Hebrew and Greek.

10. IS IT DIFFICULT TO RENDER THE HEBREW EXACTLY INTO ENGLISH?

Q. Is it difficult to make the Hebrew exact into English?

A. No, it is easy. But these men who translated the NEW AMERICAN STANDARD VERSION and especially the NEW INTERNATIONAL VERSION (probably the greatest transgressor-- except for the LIVING VERSION which is far-out) have purposely avoided bringing it over exactly. They don't want that. It's not a question that it is difficult and therefore they cannot succeed. They succeed in the goal they have set for themselves.

Let me show you in the NEW INTERNATIONAL VERSION of 1969, a word on what their goal was (page viii of the Preface):

> "The first concern of the translators has been the accuracy of the translation and its fidelity to the THOUGHT of the Biblical writers."

Now, what's wrong with that? Is that what we're interested in, only the THOUGHT? You see, we're interested in the WORDS. We believe in plenary, VERBAL inspiration of Scripture. "Plenary" is "full," (that is, from Genesis to Revelation). "Verbal" means the very words are "God-breathed." If you're only interested in fidelity to the THOUGHT, then you don't care about the WORDS. You can throw this one away, or that one away. And they do. It just grieves me when I look at the NIV.

I listened every morning at 5:45 a.m. to the KING JAMES BIBLE on the cassettes while reading in the NIV to compare the two. How they rend it, twist it, add to it, and move it around! I have finished it finally. I found over **6,653 examples** of DYNAMIC EQUIVALENCY without even half trying. There are many, many more. The NIV editors **could** have translated the Bible literally, with verbal and formal equivalence, but **they wanted to stay with the THOUGHT, not the WORDS.** To continue reading from the NIV Preface:

> *"They have weighed the significance of the lexical and grammatical details of the Hebrew, Aramaic and Greek texts.* At the same time they have striven for MORE THAN a WORD-FOR-**WORD** translation."* [They don't want **WORD-FOR-WORD** translation] *"Because **THOUGHT** patterns and syntax differ from language to language, faithful communication of the **MEANING** of the writers of the Bible **DEMANDS FREQUENT MODIFICATION IN SENTENCE STRUCTURE** and constant regard for the contextual meanings of words."* [NEW INTERNATIONAL VERSION, 1978 edition, p. viii.]

So they have to change the sentence structure, and they do. If it's a question, they often turn it into a statement. If it's a statement, they turn it into a question. Many of the things are backwards. So when you read this, you can see the purpose of it is not to make it exact. They think that is a wrong way to make it. It's not a question of being too difficult.

Let me start from the Hebrew copy. It says *bera-shith.* *b* is "in" and *rashith* is "the head, or beginning." So, Genesis 1:1 says, *"In the beginning God created the heaven and the earth."* The KING JAMES translators wrote, *"In the beginning . . . "* That is a good start, simple, clear, easy. The next word, *bara* "created" *elohim* "God" (the Hebrew has the words in different order) *eth* (the sign of the accusative, or direct object) *ha shamaim* "the heavens" *wa eth* "and" plus the accusative sign again *ha erets* "the earth." This is exactly the way it is. You don't have to change it around.

You will find that the NIV and the others have probably kept this verse just as it is. I'll tell you something about the NIV as well as some of the others. The favorite and the familiar verses they keep pretty well intact in order to sell their Bibles. You turn to Psalm 23 in any of these Bibles they will be very much like the KING JAMES translation because they don't want to take you too far away from what you're used to. They know people look at John 3:16, Psalm 23, Genesis 1:1. The NEW AMERICAN STANDARD has the same rendering of Genesis 1:1. But that doesn't mean that is the way they handle things throughout their translations. They purposely do it.

11. WHAT ABOUT HEBREW WORDS WITH SEVERAL ENGLISH MEANINGS?

Q. What about words in the Hebrew that have the meaning of several different words in the English?

A. There are some words in the Greek and in the Hebrew that have several different nuances, styles, or types of meanings. The job of the translator (as the KING JAMES BIBLE translators have done) is to pick one of those meanings that fits, one of the proper meanings of that word. It is not to change it to some other word that has nothing to do with it. For instance, there is a Hebrew word *beth* which means "house." *Bethel* means "house of God." There's another word in the Hebrew language for temple, *hacol*. Now, *hacol* is "temple" and *beth* is "house." In the NIV, over and over again they say so-and-so built a "temple" when the word is "house." **They don't translate what is there. They change it.**

With the other versions that I analyzed, I didn't have to make so many marks, and I could get through my eighty-five verses a day and finish the Bible in a year. Every time I saw a change I put a red mark and a number. I got clear over to Mark 11 before I found 1,800 serious problems in the NEW AMERICAN STANDARD VERSION. In the NIV, I had already reached over 1,800 serious problems by 2 Samuel. Yet, this is the version that some Fundamentalists of the GENERAL ASSOCIATION OF REGULAR BAPTIST CHURCHES (GARBC) are pushing more than any version we have. Dr. Ernest Pickering was one of the ones pushing it the hardest. He went over to Toledo, as Pastor of the Immanuel Baptist Church, for a few years. I have been told by **reliable witnesses** that one of the things he did was say to his deacons, in effect, "I'm not preaching from the KING JAMES BIBLE any more. I'm going to use the NEW INTERNATIONAL VERSION." They said all right, and they got copies of the NIV and discount NIVs for the people in the pews, and loaded down that large GARBC church with NIVs. Now, I'm an Ohio boy. I was born in Ohio. It is a **sad thing** when an Ohio church, a GARBC church, is packed with the NEW INTERNATIONAL VERSION. **It is a heartache to me.**

I went to Dallas Seminary with Dr. Pickering the entire four years. He was in every required class I sat in--Hebrew, Greek, Theology, and all the others. We were both in the class of 1952. How he can push the NIV, which is so inferior when it comes to the Words of God, is beyond me. Throughout the Old Testament the expression is used, "my own flesh and bones." The word "bone" in Hebrew is *etsem* and "flesh" is *basar*. The NIV renders that expression "flesh and blood." Now, the word "blood" is *dam*, not *etsem*. Blood is blood and bones are bones, and never the two shall meet. But the NIV translators don't care. They're giving the **THOUGHT**. They say, "Those stupid Hebrews, they say `flesh and bones.' Don't they know any better? Don't they know it should be `flesh and blood'"? So we're going to translate it "flesh and blood." They write their own ticket. They have a blank check and anything they want to do, they do it.

The people in the pews, reading the NIV and comparing it to the KING JAMES BIBLE say, "Those silly KING JAMES people, didn't they know any better? Look at this better translation in the NIV." I've heard tell just recently from a dear lady who came to me and said, "My pastor loves the KING JAMES BIBLE, but occasionally he will quote from the NEW INTERNATIONAL VERSION." Now, here's the thing: Whenever someone says, "The KING JAMES BIBLE says this, but the NIV makes it a little plainer," you don't know whether it really is plainer or just a fairy tale, because the NIV translators don't stick to the **WORDS** of God. **What the NIV says is not necessarily what the Hebrew or Greek says.**

If people want to find out what the Greek or Hebrew says, they can look it up in the Greek or Hebrew Bible, or go to the Strong's Concordance and look at the number in the back and see what the **original word** is and look that up in a Greek or Hebrew lexicon. **You can't trust these versions** because their purpose is not a **WORD-FOR-WORD** translation, but only the **THOUGHT**.

12. WHY WAS "WINE" USED FOR "GRAPE JUICE" IN THE KING JAMES BIBLE?

Q. Why did they translate "wine" for what was grape juice? Didn't they have a word for grape juice then? I know that confuses many people today.

A. The word "wine" is a good English word. If you take the "w" and make it into a "v" it becomes "vine" as in "vineyard." That is all wine is, fruit of the vineyard. The Hebrew word is *yayin* and the Greek word is *oinos*. They both mean "fruit of the vine." We have to interpret the meaning of *yayin* and *oinos* in English. The best book on the subject of wine in the Bible is *Wines in the Bible* by William Patton, which we carry (**B.F.T. #514**), and would recommend it to anyone. What they say in that book is that the Hebrews knew how to keep wines that would not ferment.

If you want to have fermented wine, or hard liquor, the words "strong drink" are usually used. Unless it's specifically given by the context, *yayin* in the Hebrew, and *oinos,* in the Greek, always means "unfermented fruit of the vine." Look in a good English dictionary and you will see that "wine" doesn't necessarily always mean an alcoholic beverage, but may merely mean the fruit of the grape.

   We have a great many more words that the Hebrews didn't have. We have thousands of entries in the *Third International Webster's Dictionary.* The Hebrew vocabulary is not that extensive. There are fewer words in the Hebrew lexicon than the English. It may be the same for the Greek language. I have Liddell and Scott's classical Greek lexicon which has a sizeable number of terms, more than the Hebrew language has. **Hebrew is a simple,** agricultural or shepherd-type language, nothing complex. **Greek,** now, **is very complex,** very specific. and analytical. That is why God chose to give His New Testament in that language so He could be specific on doctrine, and theology, and the fine-hewn doctrines that we have in the New Testament. Hebrew doesn't have all the distinctions in terms that we have. I wouldn't fault the word "wine" necessarily. It is "fruit of the vine." You know the word "Volkswagen," the German "w" is pronounced "v." So the word "wine" is "of the vine." A lot of people accused the Lord of being a drunkard and a wine-bibber, though. But this book *Bible Wines and the Laws of Fermentation*, teaches very clearly that there are things you have to do to make wine ferment. There are ways of keeping it from fermenting, also. It's all there in detail.

13. WHEN DID YOU FEEL LED TO GET INTO THIS "TRANSLATION" MINISTRY?

   Q. How long ago did you feel led to get into this type of ministry on the translations?
   A. This isn't my only ministry. It is a portion of it. We carry at present over 900 titles (and we add many additional titles each year) in The BIBLE FOR TODAY concerning textual matters, KING JAMES superiority, Bible Preservation, inspiration, etc. That is about a fourth of our total of over 2,300 titles. We are strong on this topic and have strong beliefs on it. I wrote *The Case For The KING JAMES BIBLE* (that was the first study I made on the theme) in June, 1971. So it's been twenty-one years as of now that I have been active on this.
   The "why" of it is because "necessity is laid upon me." There are very few people doing this job, defending the KING JAMES BIBLE, the

greatest Bible ever penned in the English language. **We feel that we don't want to lose the battle by default.** I believe a lot of errors have been made. I was brought up on the Westcott and Hort text and, until I began to read for myself, I didn't know there was another side. We have had, ever since 1965, a ministry that we call THE BIBLE FOR TODAY.

We have a pamphlet that gives my background and the background of BIBLE FOR TODAY. **[B.F.T. #168]** We started out as a ministry of our local church, at that time Faith Baptist Church in Newton, Massachusetts, where I was pastor. We had a radio broadcast and called it THE BIBLE FOR TODAY. The purpose was to take the Word of God, the Bible (which in 1965, was only the KING JAMES BIBLE) and apply it to the issues of today--abortion, Bibles in the school, Communism, salvation, or whatever. We have as our emblem a sword (the sword of the Spirit) on a shield (the shield of faith) on the open Bible, the Word of God with the darkness on the left side, the light on the right. The Word of God is that which divides between darkness and light. So, when we began, that was the type of ministry. Our *BIBLE FOR TODAY NEWSREPORT* began in 1971.

We still have many issues. In 1960, there arose the NEW AMERICAN STANDARD VERSION. The question was: Is that the Bible? Is that THE BIBLE for **today?** We looked at it, studied it, and decided it **wasn't** THE BIBLE for today. Then there came another one, the NEW INTERNATIONAL VERSION in 1969, nine years later. Then the question was: Is **that** THE BIBLE for today? Of course there have been a lot of others, GOOD NEWS FOR MODERN MAN, the LIVING VERSION, etc. For a complete history of English Bibles, refer to APPENDIX B. Then in 1979, another so-called Bible, the NEW KING JAMES VERSION. Is that THE BIBLE for today? So we are in a sea of "Bibles" and the task is to get some evidence and some facts. So I felt it was important.

Now, behind your question, although you didn't ask, is: "Why is it important to bring to the people a firm confidence in what the Bible is?" It is important because of all the THEOLOGICAL ISSUES there are in the church today. **Bibliology is the most important issue, that is, the study or doctrine of the Bible.** You can believe all you want about the Bible, you can talk about its revelation, authority, inspiration, inerrancy, infallibility, but where the rubber meets the road is: **Where is our Bible TODAY?** If you don't have it in your hand, how are you going to have any confidence that anything you say is going to hit the heart of the sinner and cause him to see Jesus Christ as Savior? How can you know confidently unless you have confidence in the Book you have in your hands that God says this, and this, and that.

To me, the greatest assault the Devil has made in the 20th century, is the assault on the Word of God. That assault started in the Garden of Eden--"Hath God said?" It was carried on in the temptation of Jesus Christ in Matthew 4, where Satan quotes Scripture, mixes up Scripture, and the Lord answers with Scripture, *"It is written . . . it is written."* That was the greatest Satanic attack!

A side issue of that is the confusion on the part of Christian believers. Young people, lost people, and unbelieving people throw up their hands and say, "I don't know what the Bible is; therefore I don't have to believe any of it. If I can't be sure of it, if there are so many of them around, I won't believe any of them." **What we need is CONFIDENCE in the Word of God.** That is why I'm trying to build CONFIDENCE in every one of you holding in your hands the KING JAMES BIBLE. Our slogan that we use on every one of our radio programs currently is:

"We're   building   Bible   CONFIDENCE, CONFIDENCE in the KING JAMES BIBLE, because the KING JAMES BIBLE is the Bible for TODAY!"

Don't throw it in the ash can. It's not outmoded or wrong. **There never has been a translation like it, and probably never will be one like it in the future.** The reason for this is that the foundational texts of Hebrew and Greek that the KING JAMES translators believed to be God's Words, preserved up until that time, will never again be used by any translator anywhere in the world from now on.

Now, that is a broad statement, but I think I can prove it. Who believes that these **TEXTS** should be the foundation for any translation? Very few people believe that any more. The people in the hierarchy-- the colleges, seminaries, and publishing houses that are making the money on it--don't believe it at all. This other text, sponsored by apostates, modernists, and Roman Catholic cardinals is the book they say is the New Testament in the Greek. Also, they'll **never** have **TRANSLATORS** again like the KING JAMES translators. These modern ones are pygmies and dwarfs, compared to the giants who gave us the KING JAMES translation. And the **TECHNIQUE,** verbal and formal equivalence, are considered passe, believe me. But the KING JAMES people did translate this way. Today, DYNAMIC EQUIVALENCE is believed to be the way to do it. **This is paraphrase**--adding this, taking away that, changing the other. **So we'll never have another Bible like the KING JAMES.** That is why I'm trying to create CONFIDENCE in it.

I have a radio broadcast, which I began on WVVW in St. Mary's, West Virginia, a little station, of 1000 watts (but the cheapest I've ever heard tell of, $13.50 for half an hour a week). I took it because I saw it was open and the first question I asked the man when I sent a letter to him was, "Do we have liberty to speak our mind on the air?" He said, "Yes, go ahead, but be responsible." I'm always responsible in what I say, factual. So I opened it up for the issue of Bible translation. As of this writing, we now have both a thirty-minute weekly program and a five-minute daily program. One or the other, or both, of these programs are now heard on fifteen radio stations, with a possibility soon of having them on satellite to be heard in England, Europe, Canada, and South America. We are getting good responses from these broadcasts as people are phoning and writing for our materials. The theme of both broadcasts is, "IN DEFENSE OF TRADITIONAL BIBLE TEXTS."

I'm dealing with a hot issue, a controversial issue. But I didn't do it only for the people listening in West Virginia, Ohio, Pennsylvania, Alabama, North Carolina, Florida, Kentucky, South Carolina, Wyoming, and Maryland. I did it for myself as well, because it forces me to spend an hour per week of broadcast time recording by tape on this issue. I take those tapes and offer them to our BIBLE FOR TODAY readers (over 2300 of them at present, some in this country, some in other parts of the world--people who are on our mailing list and get our *BIBLE FOR TODAY NEWSREPORT*). I offer these tapes, and people can hear what I've said on this subject, and I never would have said it if I didn't have to make the deadline for radio. It's a bad excuse, but that is the truth. Nobody would make me sit down for four hours a month and record these things that we have discussed here. I talk about them in various meetings, but I have so many other things to do. **In time to come, my grandchildren can listen to these tapes if they want to.** The tapes lay it out as straight as I know how to lay it out.

14. COULD THE HOLY SPIRIT USE A NON-KING JAMES BIBLE?

Q. If a person who never read the Bible, didn't know the Gospel, picked up the NIV, or the LIVING VERSION, and read John 3:16--couldn't the Holy Spirit use that?

A. Yes, the Holy Spirit of God is able to do that with a portion which is His Words. It may not be as much of a portion as you would get if you read the KING JAMES BIBLE (depending on which verse you were talking about). But, He would be limited, restricted in His ability to use the maximum value of any given verse based upon the accuracy or inaccuracy of the translation. It's like the needle in the haystack. The LIVING VERSION has a lot more hay around the needle. The hay represents the words of men. Very few Words of God, most of it hay. The NEW INTERNATIONAL VERSION may have less hay than the LIVING VERSION--but you don't know which is which and how to find it.

All Scripture is given by inspiration. Now "*all Scripture*": *pasa* (all) *graphE* (Scripture) and the next word in Greek is *theopneustos* (God-breathed). All Scripture is God-breathed and profitable. **It follows that that which is not God-breathed is not profitable. It's only that which God has breathed out that is His Words in Hebrew or Greek, and faithfully translated into English as it is in the KING JAMES BIBLE.** So how much is unprofitable in these other versions? That is the problem that we have. It's like a person who has a very bad diet, and you ask the question, "Will that diet, bad as it is, sustain life?" Well, you can eke out a low existence on some foods (and many of our young people are doing just that with their junk food). It will sustain life, but if you want to go "first class" there are dietary rules God has given us so we can really feel like a million dollars. Shaklee Food Supplements, for example, have helped me. Shaklee is expensive, but it is a food supplement God has used to help this ex-cancer patient to get back into a healthy sphere of life, able to work again.

What I'm saying is, God's Words are the milk that causes us to grow. 1 Peter 2:2 says:

> "*As newborn babes, desire the sincere milk of the word,*
> *that ye may grow thereby.*"

Now, which is the milk? Which is the **sincere** milk? Let's go first class.

15. SHOULDN'T THE WORDS OF GOD BE MORE DIFFICULT THAN OTHER BOOKS?

Q. The other versions read like any other book, but the KING JAMES seems like the Words of God. It seems proper that the Words of God should be more difficult.

A. Some people say they like a particular version because they say it's more readable. Now, readability is one thing, but does the readability conform to what's in the original Greek and Hebrew language? You can have a lot of readability. Comics, magazines, and newspapers have a lot of "readability," but if it doesn't match up with what God has said, it's of no profit. **In the KING JAMES BIBLE, the words match what God has said.** You may say it's difficult to read, but study it out. It's hard in the Hebrew and Greek and, perhaps, even in the English of the KING JAMES BIBLE. But to change it around just to make it simple, or interpreting it, instead of translating it, is wrong. You've got lots of interpretation, but we don't want that in a translation. We want exactly what God said in the Hebrew or Greek brought over into English.

16. SHOULD WE STUDY THE BIBLE, OR ONLY READ IT?

Q. Should we read God's Words, or study them?
A. In 1 Timothy 4:15 it says to:
*"Meditate upon these things; give thyself wholly to
them; that thy profiting may appear to all."*
And the command to meditate "day and night" on God's Word is used many times. Certainly READING is a beginning to any STUDY we might do in God's Word. Without READING, we cannot STUDY, even though the two are somewhat different concepts.

17. WERE THE KING JAMES TRANSLATORS GODLY MEN, OR ONLY INTELLECTUALS?

Q. Were the KING JAMES translators known as godly men back then, or were they thought of as just intellectuals?
A. You can refer to **CHAPTER III** in the book for some of the beliefs of the KING JAMES BIBLE translators. This statement to the readers reveals the spiritual depth of these men. The bulk of them were godly men, either Puritan-Anglicans, living holy, puritanical lives, or Regular-Anglicans. I think approximately eight to ten of the fifty-seven or so who lived to see the translation finished were Puritans. I can't say the Anglicans were as close to the Lord as were the Puritans, but basically they were godly men. These men had a high regard for the Words of God, and counted it as the very WORDS of God Himself that they were translating.

I have a regular pamphlet called *Translators to the Reader* [B.F.T. #1121, part of which is quoted in CHAPTER III **of this book**] which shows these men had a respect for the Words of God, the Spirit of God, and had a desire to please the Lord. They weren't just intellectuals of the day. They had a lot of learning and qualifications, but with that learning they also had the piety, holy lives, and a desire to please the Lord.

18. WHAT IS THE DIFFERENCE BETWEEN THE 1611 AND THE PRESENT KING JAMES BIBLE?

Q. What are the differences between the 1611 KING JAMES and the ones we have today?

A. In the NEW KING JAMES VERSION (I will say that for them) they have the history of the KING JAMES BIBLE in the back. On page 1229 of my edition, the editors wrote:

*"Over the years from 1611 to 1616, **words and phrases** in the KING JAMES BIBLE were changed, and **printing errors** were corrected."* [So that is the first change.] *"In 1629 the first edition of the Authorized Version, printed by the presses of Cambridge University, underwent a thorough and systematic revision of the text, the italics and the marginal references. Dr. Samuel Ward and Dean Bois,* [he is the one who read the Hebrew Bible when he was five] *two of the 1611 translators, participated in that revision. A still further revision, more thorough than the first, was carried out in the Cambridge edition of 1638. This carefully supervised revision covered 'from the beginning of the volume to the end.'. . . [page 1230] The first Bible to contain dates of biblical events in the margin was a three-volume edition in 1701. . . . In 1762 Dr. Thomas Paris, a Fellow of Trinity College, Cambridge issued a major revision of the KING JAMES BIBLE; and seven years later the Oxford Revision, the work of Dr. Benjamin Blayney was released. . . Marginal notes were increased to almost 65,000, half of which were cross-references."*

Basically, those are the revisions up to 1769. The question is, how great were those revisions? How much was the wording changed? That is why I compared the present day OLD SCOFIELD KING JAMES VERSION and read the original 1611, and looked not just at the spelling changes. Some say there are 40,000 to 50,000 changes, and if you listened to them you would think we don't have anything like the original today. That would be a tremendous number of changes in my judgment. More confusion. They want an excuse to give us a "**new**" KING JAMES VERSION. That is why they give the history of the changes, to make us think this is JUST ONE MORE CHANGE. If there are 40,000 to 50,000 changes, they are related, by and large, to spelling differences, NOT to changes in the meanings or sounds of words.

For instance, take John 9, the account of the man born blind. Now, the word "blind" in verse 1 is spelled "blinde." It's a change. But is "blind" any different from "blinde"? If that is a change you're talking about, it doesn't affect the ear. Now, in the second verse, "sin" is spelled "sinne." That is a change. Then the word "born" is spelled "borne." But the sound is the same. What I did, was to count only the changes that could be HEARD. And from Genesis to Revelation, did I get 30,000? No. Did I get 20,000? No. 1,000? No. I got **421 CHANGES** to the ear, that could be heard, out of the **791,328 words**. Just **421**. That is actually one change out of 1,880 words. As for those 421 CHANGES to the ear--most of them were minor, just changes in spelling.

There were **ONLY 136 SUBSTANTIAL CHANGES** that were different words. The others were only **285 MINOR CHANGES OF FORM ONLY**. Of these **285 MINOR CHANGES**, there are **214 VERY MINOR CHANGES** such as "towards" for "toward"; "burnt" for "burned"; "amongst" for "among"; "lift" for "lifted"; and "you" for "ye." These kinds of changes represent **214 out of the 285 MINOR CHANGES OF FORM ONLY**. Now you're talking about **ONLY 136 REAL CHANGES** out of 791,328 words. Many people imply that the KING JAMES BIBLE is completely changed from what they had in 1611, that there are THOUSANDS of differences. You tell them about the **MERE 136 CHANGES OF SUBSTANCE** plus **285 MINOR CHANGES OF FORM ONLY**. Argue them down. You might like to send for our **B.F.T. #1294** entitled: "*THE KING JAMES VERSION OF 1611 COMPARED TO THE KING JAMES VERSION OF 1917 OLD SCOFIELD BIBLE.*" It is a computer print-out which lists every single instance of the **421 CHANGES** from Genesis to Revelation and also grouped alphabetically according to the change itself.

19. WHAT ABOUT THE "NUMERICAL" BIBLE?

Q.   A mathematician did a study of the Bible in the original languages where the letters represented number values and proved

that it was God's Words. They added up to certain numbers and it proved that God had put His stamp on His Words. I agree that He didn't intend for it to be changed, and even though He used men over many generations, the same mathematical formula ran all the way from Genesis to Revelation, and nothing could be added to the Bible without sticking out like a sore thumb. I think this is another proof to what you say that God never intended His Words to change. Anything else literally wouldn't add up.

A. **Certainly we have the Divine preservation of the Bible.** There have been various disputes about whether the numbers add up and so on, but anything that God does will be preserved and kept. I know that Ivan Panin sought to do that for the New Testament. He has a New Testament called *The New Testament From The Greek Text And Established By Bible Numerics*. It is New Testament #172 in our **APPENDIX B**. It came out in 1914. Panin's New Testament compared to these 162 key verses listed here in *THE CASE FOR THE KING JAMES BIBLE* (**B.F.T.** #83) has 138 out of the 162 verses omitted (either in part or in whole)--at least for the New Testament although he claims it stacks up numerically. He goes with the Westcott and Hort Greek text 85% of the time. (I don't know whether the questioner was referring to this book, or not). **So, I would have questions about that particular New Testament.**

20. IS THE REGULAR KING JAMES BIBLE FOR SALE NOW?

Q. Do you have the KING JAMES BIBLES for sale?
A. Yes, we can order them. We have a very inexpensive copy of the regular KING JAMES BIBLE which is put out by the Trinitarian Bible Society, in small print. We can order the 1611 KING JAMES, or order the regular KING JAMES in other sizes and bindings.

21. IS THE KING JAMES BIBLE WITHOUT TRANSLATION ERRORS OR "INSPIRED"?

Q. Do you believe the KING JAMES BIBLE to be without translation errors or "inspired"?
A. Yes, I would say regarding translation errors that I haven't found any either in the Old Testament Hebrew or in the New Testament Greek. I don't like to use the word "inerrant" of any English (or other language) translation of the Bible because the word "inerrant" is implied

from the Greek Word, *theopneustos* (2 Timothy 3:16) which means literally, "**GOD-BREATHED**." God Himself did NOT "**BREATHE OUT**" English, or German, or French, or Spanish, or Latin, or Italian. He DID "**BREATHE OUT**" Hebrew/Aramaic, and Greek. Therefore, **ONLY THE HEBREW/ARAMAIC AND GREEK CAN BE RIGHTLY TERMED "GOD-BREATHED" OR "INERRANT," not ANY translation!!** It is my **personal** belief and faith that the HEBREW/ARAMAIC and GREEK TEXTS that underlie the KING JAMES BIBLE have been PRESERVED by God Himself so that these texts can properly be called "INERRANT" as well as being the very "INSPIRED and INFALLIBLE WORDS OF GOD"!! **I think that INERRANCY has to do with God's words in the Hebrew/Aramaic and Greek.**

We can't always take over completely 100% what He has there. I think that the KING JAMES translators, when they took the Hebrew or Aramaic, putting it into English, and the Greek, putting it into English, that they matched up one of the Hebrew meanings, or one of the Greek meanings, as they translated into the English language. There are many other choices in English they could have used, but what they did pick was within the rules of both the Hebrew and Greek grammar and English grammar. **Therefore, I have not found any translation errors in the KING JAMES BIBLE, but I do not use "inspired" for it.**

22. IS "IT" IN ROMANS 8:16 A TRANSLATION ERROR?

Q. In Romans 8:16 in the NEW KING JAMES the pronoun for the Holy Spirit is translated as "he" but in the KING JAMES it is translated "it." Which is the correct translation?

A. Strictly speaking, the exact and literal translation is what the KING JAMES translation has, *"itself."* You see, the Holy Spirit in Greek is *to pneuma*, a neuter noun. A neuter noun has pronouns which are also neuter. You have this In Romans 8:16. For instance, it says *touto* (*itself*). The pronoun agrees in gender with the noun. **So, *"Spirit itself"* is what is actually in the Greek language.** Now, I don't fault anyone saying that it refers to the Holy Spirit as he expounds or preaches on this passage. The **Person** of the Holy Spirit is "He," but **the form of the Greek noun is a neuter gender.** That would not be considered a translation error because that is exactly what it says.

23. IS "EASTER" IN ACTS 12:4 A TRANSLATION ERROR?

Q. In Acts 12:4 the KING JAMES says "Easter," but the NEW KING JAMES renders it as "Passover." That is quite a difference; which one is proper? From what I understand, Easter is a pagan holiday that didn't come about until later on.

A. The rendering there is from the Greek text *to pascha* which is "Passover" but that particular Passover was at the same time as the Easter festival. The KJB followed Tyndale and many other translations in rendering this *"EASTER"* in Acts 12:4.

I would recommend two of our publications on this subject. **B.F.T.** #1673 by Pastor Raymond Blanton, and **B.F.T.** #1737 by Pastor Jack Moorman. This passover was apparently a travesty on what should have been done at that season and the pagan feast ISHTAR, which is a very pagan feast, was a proper picture for what they were doing. Now, I take issue with you that Easter is something new. ISHTAR was a pagan festival which went way back in the Old Testament times to the Phoenician and various pagan cultures. Ashteroth is the origin of the term Easter--a feminine Baal. Baal was the male and Ashteroth the female. That is one translation some have asked about, and I would say certainly that "passover" would not be a wrong rendering; yet since they were carrying on as they were, "Easter" would be a good rendering also because it was at the same time. As you know, our pagan feast of Easter and our festival of Easter, with the egg-rolling and other things, is extremely pagan. There is no question about it. It occurs on or about the time of the Jewish Passover. For more details, consult the above-mentioned articles that take this issue up in detail. If you notice the context of Acts 12:4, you'll notice in verse 3 that "then were the days of UNLEAVENED BREAD." If you remember, the date of "UNLEAVENED BREAD" as specified in Leviticus 23:6, was the "fifteenth day" of the first month. In Leviticus 23:5, the date for the "PASSOVER" was the "fourteenth day" of the first month. In Acts 12:4, we read the words: "intending after Easter (or Passover) to bring him forth to the people." If it was already the "DAYS OF UNLEAVENED BREAD" or the 15th of the month, how could the 14th of the month come AFTER the 15th? This would be the case if this were the normal "Passover."

24. WHAT ABOUT LUKE 1:18?

Q. In Luke 1:18 you were talking about Zacharias and his wife being old and stricken in years; could it be that the Lord wanted to be sure that THIS wife was meant since it was the custom of that time to have more than one wife?

A. No. I don't believe this is the reason for it. I believe the Lord is speaking of Zacharias' wife in two different ways--both *"old"* and *"stricken in age."* I believe he had only one wife. They were both old, and this was a child of their old age. God knew what He wanted to say and neither of the words should be omitted.

25. WHAT ABOUT THE FOOTNOTES IN THE NEW KING JAMES VERSION?

Q. You said the footnotes in the NEW KING JAMES were confusing but weren't they just the original Greek?

A. No, the footnotes represent the Nestle/United Bible Society text ["NU"] and not the Greek of the *Received Text.* The Nestle/United Bible Society text ["NU"] is the one the liberals believe, and many Fundamentalists believe, is the best Greek text--the *Nestle/Aland 26th Edition.* The Nestle & United Bible Society have united on this one edition. It differs from the *Textus Receptus* that underlies our KING JAMES BIBLE over **5,600 times**, involving **9,970 Greek words**. The footnotes are confusing because to the young believer, or even an older believer, it causes doubt as to what is the Words of God. For instance, in the communion service, when your pastor is trying to read from 1 Corinthians 11:24, *". . . this is my body which is BROKEN for you."* The SCOFIELD VERSION in the margin casts doubt upon the word *"broken."* They want to take it out. I'm against the Scofield note in that particular instance. The word *"broken"* is in the Greek language, in the Textus Receptus--there is no doubt about it. The NEW KING JAMES VERSION has the same doubt about that particular place and has a foot-note. "The Nestle/United Bible Society omits `broken.'" Here you have a new believer (or older believer) reading his NEW KING JAMES VERSION, and there's doubt cast on the authenticity of the words of God during the communion service. In addition to the "NU" footnotes which represent the Westcott-and-Hort-type of text, there is the letter "M" which refers, when used, to the so-called "majority text" of Hodges and Farstad which departs from the *Textus Receptus.* **B.F.T. #1617** is a 160-page analysis which thoroughly disputes the truthfulness of this so-called "majority text." It is by Dr. Jack A. Moorman. You may also get a short refutation of this so-called "majority text" by writing for **B.F.T. #1448** by yours truly. It is entitled, *DEFECTS IN THE SO-CALLED 'MAJORITY GREEK TEXT.'* There is another booklet that is helpful in all of this question. It is a small, yet valuable pamphlet condensing Dr. Moorman's longer book by yours truly. It is entitled, *"WHY REJECT THE SO-CALLED 'MAJORITY' TEXT."* It is **B.F.T. #1727**.

26. WHY ARE THERE SO MANY OTHER VERSIONS OTHER THAN THE KING JAMES BIBLE?

Q. Why do they have these other versions? Why didn't they stick to the KING JAMES BIBLE?
A. The translation business is a business. **The translation of the Bible, I believe, should be in the hands of the local churches.** Churches are the ones who should produce the Words of God. They did produce it in KING JAMES' day. It was the Puritans and the Anglicans, the Church of England, that got together and with the authority of KING JAMES--yet **it was the churches, not the publishing house,** that got this Bible together. **It's the publishing houses that decide to publish a new version, NEW AMERICAN STANDARD, NEW INTERNATIONAL, or NEW KING JAMES.** They also select the ones to be on the committees. **They** see in the translation of these Bibles a chance for millions upon millions of dollars in profits for their publishing houses. This is what sells. How do you account for many of the **135 complete English Bibles** and the **293 complete English New Testaments** (a total of **428** altogether) that have flooded the English-speaking world during the 612 years of 1380 through 1991? Consult **APPENDIX B** for the names and dates of all of these. This is at a rate of one new complete Bible or complete New Testament in English (not counting the partial and other Bibles and New Testaments that have come off the presses) **every 1.4 years**. And during the 1900's, it has averaged **one every .51 years** or, in other words, **one new one every six months**. I maintain (though there may be other reasons an individual has produced one) that the main motivation on the part of the publishers in producing many of these 428 English Bibles and New Testaments during the last 612 years is to make money. With very few, I believe, there were other reasons. **I'm not against the profit motive in general, but when it comes as the main reason for printing Bibles, I would raise a question.** Do you know of very many Bible publishers who are printing Bibles and/or New Testaments in English or in other languages without charge to the recipients? There are some, but very, very few indeed.

What is the motivation of the people who buy them? You didn't ask that, but let me answer it anyway. **My** motivation in buying all these new versions is to analyze them and see what they say and how they differ in their text. I want to know who their translators are, their qualities, their abilities, their linguistic training, and their theology.

The publishers of the NEW AMERICAN STANDARD VERSION refused to tell who their translators were. They wrote me back when I asked them and said, "I'm sorry, we're not going to give that out." They wouldn't say who the translators were of the NEW AMERICAN STANDARD VERSION. In fact, in this analysis of the NEW AMERI-CAN STANDARD VERSION I quoted the letter from the president verbatim, right here in my document. They say, in effect, "We believe all the glory should be to the Lord." [Much later, they have reversed themselves and released the names for those who write for them.] Well, that is true, but all the errors and the mixups ought to be blamed on the translators. Don't blame the Lord for them. So, my motivation for getting these versions is to analyze them.

Other people may get them because it makes the reading a little easier, but maybe they don't read their Bibles anyhow. Listen, we should read our Bible from Genesis to Revelation every single year. Eighty-five verses per day will take you through in a year. We have a *"YEARLY BIBLE READING SCHEDULE"* [**B.F.T. #179**] that will help you get through the Scriptures in a year. I've been reading my Bible ever since I've been saved (in 1944) and I read it once a year minimum, sometimes more. I enjoy the Bible. I've read it in the KING JAMES BIBLE every time except to check some other translation.

At the present time, I'm going through these new versions, but I don't have to change horses in the middle of the stream when I have a faithful, reliable translation of the Words of God in English as the KING JAMES is. If you don't know some of the meanings of the words, you can look them up in a dictionary, or get the Trinitarian Bible Society Word List of 618 words that may be outmoded or might not be familiar to you. [**B.F.T. #1060**] It's a whole lot easier to read the KING JAMES BIBLE and search out the **VERY FEW WORDS** you need to look up in a dictionary, than it is to weed out all the **additions, omissions,** and **changes** of God's Words found in these other Bibles, and then compare every word with the original Hebrew and Greek to be sure the translation is ACCU-RATE!

I don't know what motivates people to buy the new versions. Maybe they want to put them on their shelf or table, or be more intellectually stimulated. It's a very difficult thing to have one reading in the KING JAMES BIBLE. and another in the NEW INTERNATIONAL VERSION, and another in some other version, and try to have Scripture reading in a church. What people do on their own in their study is up to them; but I believe the motivation on the part of the publishers is financial. When a VERSION stops making money they stop publishing it. If you don't believe me, here's a little exercise you can take. Consult the 428 complete English Bibles and New Testaments in our **APPENDIX B**. Then go to your local library. Ask for the reference section. Find the reference series entitled *BOOKS IN PRINT*. Look up each of these 428 titles and find out how many of them are still in print as of now. You'll find, as our B.F.T. secretary did when she looked, that there are very, very few that are still in print. But the KING JAMES BIBLE is still "ALIVE AND WELL ON PLANET EARTH"! Have you ever stopped to question why this is so? Because this incomparable Bible has had the blessings of God upon it through the years, and still has to this very day! That is why they've stopped publishing *THE FUTURE OF THE BIBLE* by Jakob Van Bruggen and *THE IDENTITY OF THE NEW TESTAMENT TEXT* by Wilbur Pickering. [I don't agree with everything in these books, but there is much that is profitable in them.] Nelson has stopped publishing these two books (as they told me when I phoned them) because nobody wants to buy them, or maybe they don't want people to get them because they undermine all the DYNAMIC EQUIVALENCY approaches of other Bibles that Nelson also publishes. These books were not selling, so they stopped publishing them. I called them up and asked if they would consider republishing them but they said they wouldn't. [The BIBLE FOR TODAY has re-printed these. *THE FUTURE OF THE BIBLE* is **B.F.T. #1256**. *THE IDENTITY OF THE NEW TESTAMENT TEXT* is **B.F.T. #556**.] I was successful in getting *THE MEN BEHIND THE KING JAMES VERSION* reprinted, though. This was published by Baker Publishers.

27. WHAT ABOUT DR. MCGEE'S KING JAMES BIBLE EDITION?

Q. What do you think of Dr. J. Vernon McGee's KING JAMES BIBLE in which he gives different definitions in the margin?
    A. Dr. McGee was one of our special Bible lecturers at Dallas Theological Seminary when I went there as a student from 1948-53. If he has put out a KING JAMES BIBLE and put definitions in the margin I think that is great.
    Anyone who wants to use the KING JAMES BIBLE and wants to clarify in the margin the meaning of this or that word, that is fine. It

will save you the trouble of looking it up. I haven't seen that particular edition, but I take it that it is a valuable one. If that is all it does, I can see nothing wrong with it. I hope our readers will write or call and ask us about our *Defined King James Bible* (Phone us at **1-800-JOHN 10:9**). It is in genuine leather either black or burgundy (7.5" by 10" 12-point large print). There are no changes in the KING JAMES BIBLE'S text, but this edition has brief definitions of any words which might have changed their meanings. We have compared every word of our edition to make certain that it follows closely the **CAMBRIDGE** edition rather than the **OXFORD** edition of the KING JAMES BIBLE. There are slight errors in the **OXFORD** edition which do not conform either to the Hebrew and Greek or to the original AUTHORIZED VERSION OF 1611. This has proved to be a very useful edition. The BIBLE FOR TODAY carries this *Defined King James Bible* for a gift of **$40 + S&H**. For further details on this very fine Bible, please call us toll free at **1-800-JOHN 10:9**. Ask us about the medium sized *Defined King James Bible*. It is 10-point type and is still very easy to read. It measures 6" by 8" in size. It comes in beautiful genuine leather, either black or burgundy. It is for a gift of **$35 + S&H**. **[For background details, please turn back to page 2.]**

28. COULD "REVERSE TRANSLATION" SHOW THE ACCURACY OR INACCURACY OF A VERSION?

Q. Maybe some of the confusion would be cleared up by doing a reverse translation from the English text of the NEW AMERICAN STANDARD, NEW INTERNATIONAL VERSION, etc. back into the Hebrew and Greek and see what comes out.

A. That is exactly what I've been maintaining. The KING JAMES BIBLE will be the one that will come out ahead every time on the basis of my experiences in reading and comparing these versions with the Hebrew and Greek. Take the KING JAMES English and translate into Hebrew and Greek and it will come out as close as any language could.

29. WHAT ABOUT "CORN" VERSUS "GRAIN"?

Q. In Matthew 12:1, the New KING JAMES speaks of "grain fields" and "grain" and the KING JAMES speaks about "corn." I know this isn't a doctrinal matter, but in the Greek it does mean "grain."

A. The word is *sporima* "fields which are sown, fields of grain, cornfields." I know that throughout the Old and New Testaments the NEW KING JAMES VERSION, the NEW AMERICAN STANDARD VERSION, and NEW INTERNATIONAL VERSION for some reason or another hate "corn." They just throw away "corn" and make it "grain." I'm no farmer or agricultural expert, but the debate is on which kind of grain was referred to. To me, it may have very well been corn; so far as I can see, "corn" is a very valid translation of the word *sporima*. [The next few follow-up questions on "corn" versus "grain" clarify this point in greater detail.]

30. CAN VINE'S BOOK BE TRUSTED?

Q. Can we trust Vine's Greek translation on this? His book says that in Matthew 12:1, "corn" should be "an ear of grain."
A. Well, it might be "an ear of corn" as well. *Vine's Expository Dictionary of New Testament Words* is a tool, but it is neither a concordance of Greek terms (in which all the uses of the word *sporima* would be listed) nor a Greek lexicon, a Greek dictionary which gives the various meanings. He may think it is "grain," but that is just a part of the meaning of the Greek term. Liddell and Scott's, for example, is in two volumes, and that classical Greek lexicon probably has as much as a page or maybe more on that one Greek term.
> [In checking Liddell & Scott under "sporimos" I find, among the meanings, "solid corn-fields" and "corn-fields" and "seed-corn."]

"Grain" may be one valid meaning in the list, but "corn" is another valid meaning. The KING JAMES translators knew both the Greek language and the English language better than Vine or the modern "scholars." We don't have to apologize for them, or hang our heads at any so-called inaccurate renderings from either the Hebrew or the Greek languages. I can't say that Vine is the last word on that Greek term. You can use it for what it is worth. It is for the English-speaking reader. It's not for the Greek student.

31. HOW DO YOU KNOW WHICH GREEK MEANING IS RIGHT?

Q. People say, "The Greek word means this," and Dr. So-And-So will get up and say, "The Greek word means that." Who's right? When I'm studying for my Greek words, I can't use Vine. I

have to go to the lexicon to get the proper tense, the moods, the declension it's in. Vine doesn't do that for you. How do you know who's right?

A. I would certainly not use Vine to refute the translation of the KING JAMES BIBLE in favor of the NEW KING JAMES VERSION. I would use a lexicon, like Liddell and Scott's, or Moulton and Geden's, or Thayer's Greek Lexicon, or Arndt and Gingrich's which is one of the newer ones. There's a *THEOLOGICAL DICTIONARY OF THE NEW TESTAMENT* (By G. Kittel) which I also have. It is a ten volume set. This set has about eleven pages on the word group from which *sporima* comes, that is, the word *sperma*. That is where I would suggest that you go if you really want to see what the various Greek word meanings are. To find out what the various English word meanings are, I would suggest that you also check the *OXFORD ENGLISH DICTIONARY--UN-ABRIDGED* to see what the word meant historically in 1611 when the KING JAMES BIBLE was translated.

32. DOES "CORN" DIFFER TODAY FROM FORMER TIMES?

Q. The corn we have today is not the corn they had in that day. Today's has a lot more kernels on it. It has always been feed grain.

A. The second answer to that question about *sporima* is that whenever you analyze the KING JAMES BIBLE of 1611, consult an excellent English dictionary also to see meanings of words as used in 1611. For that word "corn," for example, I would suggest you might consult the *Oxford English Dictionary*. I have a micro-print set, which you have to use a magnifying glass to read. It gives every English word as it occurred in 1000 A. D., 1600 A. D., right on down. It would give you the meaning of "corn" in 1611. I've found this principle true in many instances: **don't look only at the Greek word, look also at the English word for its meaning at that particular time.**

33. WHY DOESN'T THE KING JAMES BIBLE CAPITALIZE PRONOUNS REFERRING TO DEITY?

Q. When referring to Jesus, it is not very often that the KING JAMES BIBLE capitalizes the "H" in the pronoun, "HIM." It seems like a lack of respect.

A. That is a **stylistic practice** that they determined to use when they first translated. They didn't have a rule, I guess, at that time, that references to Deity should be capitalized. Today when we write about God the Father, or the Lord Jesus, or the Holy Spirit we capitalize the pronouns. In 1611, it did not indicate a lack of respect, or a negation of the Deity of Christ. In the KING JAMES BIBLE the policy was never to use capital letters for pronouns referring to Deity. No disrespect at all is meant. But in these other Bibles, having this rule and NOT capitalizing pronouns referring to Deity are blaspheming His Name.

34. WHAT ABOUT "THEE" AND "THOU"?

Q. What about "thee" and "thou?"
A. That is another thing. As best I recall, one or two versions say they will refer to Deity and use "Thee" or "Thou," but in referring to humanity they will use "you." In those instances, many times, referring to Jesus they use "you" instead of "Thou" or "Thee." That would be blasphemy against the Lord and disrespect. The KING JAMES BIBLE, in their use of the pronouns, *thee, thy, thyself, thou, thine, ye, you, your, and yourselves,* have rendered **accuracy** a great service. All the pronouns beginning with the letter "T" are singular. All the pronouns beginning with the letter "Y" are plural. In this way, the English reader can pick up his KING JAMES BIBLE, and, unlike any of the other modern versions, he can tell immediately whether the second person pronoun is singular or plural. For example, look at John 3:7:

*Marvel not that I said unto **thee**, Ye must be born again.*
John 3:7

If you look at the modern versions, they have the personal pronoun, "you," for both the *"thee"* and the *"ye,"* thus confusing the meaning. The Lord is using the SINGULAR (*"thee"*) and then the PLURAL (*"ye"*) in the same sentence, and in the same verse, one word right after the other. There are many other instances where the modern versions obscure the true meaning of the English "you." Is it singular or plural? With your KING JAMES BIBLE in hand, you are **NEVER** left in doubt. And you don't need to know Greek or Hebrew to find out the answer!

35. WHAT DOES "PROPHECY" MEAN IN REVELATION 22:19?

Q. In Revelation 22:19, does "this prophecy" refer to just the book of Revelation, or does it refer to the whole Bible?
A. It's entirely possible that it refers to the book of Revelation.

But, since the book of Revelation, as far as we know, was the last book of the Bible to be written, it would also include anyone adding anything else to the Bible of any kind. For instance, if you have a book that has twelve chapters and in the twelfth chapter you say, "anyone that adds anything to this chapter (meaning the 12th)" would have a certain curse placed upon him, it would also mean anyone adding to the whole book also. The last chapter would also imply the others. It may also mean just this prophecy of Revelation, but adding anything after Revelation was closed would be adding to the Word of God.

36. DO FALSE VERSIONS CONTRIBUTE TO FALSE DOCTRINES?

Q. Do you think that these new versions lead to groups of people getting off track on the various points of doctrine--tongues, healings, etc.?
A. I absolutely do believe they have a part in this. I specifically mention *The LIVING VERSION* as a version that has been responsible for the increase in the Charismatic Movement, when it comes to their various translations of the tongues chapters, 1 Corinthians 14, etc. They are very free and seem to justify the speaking in tongues and the whole Charismatic Movement. It's so loose and has so many of man's words around God's words, you don't know which are which. Whether these other versions have assisted or not, I don't know. But I know in attending the "Jesus 76" rally (which I attended and recorded in the cow pastures of Pennsylvania) I saw more copies of *THE LIVING VERSION* than another other version. I saw the boys bare chested, the girls in halters, swimsuits, and scantily clad. I saw kissing, necking, hugging, and lots of strange behavior on the part of young people. But throughout all that, *THE LIVING VERSION* was used on the platform by these tongues-speakers, Charismatics, Bob Mumford, and all his crowd. They were pushing *THE LIVING VERSION* as the best translation possible. One of the finest books refuting the LIVING VERSION is our book, *THE PARAPHRASED PERVERSION*. [B.F.T. #127]. It's an excellent analysis.

"Behold, the days come,
saith the Lord GOD,
that I WILL SEND A FAMINE IN THE LAND,
not a famine of bread,
nor a thirst for water,
but OF HEARING THE <u>WORDS</u> OF THE LORD."
(Amos 8:11)

INDEX OF SUBJECTS

INDEX OF SCRIPTURE REFERENCES

New Testament
Scripture References

NOTE: On the following pages are over 1,000 titles defending the King James Bible and its underlying Hebrew, Aramaic, and Greek Words. For a complete list, you may do one or several of the following:

1 You can phone our Bible For Today at **856-854-4452**
2. You can go to our Web at **www.BibleForToday.org**.
3. You can go to **www.DeanBurgonSociety.org**
4. You can request **Brochure #1**

TITLES DEFENDING THE KING JAMES BIBLE

BFT Brochure #1
Order From:
The Bible for Today, 900 Park Avenue, Collingswood, NJ 08108
Phone: 609-854-4452; FAX: 609-854-2464: Orders: 1-800-JOHN 10:9
Please Add the Greater of $4.00 or 15% for Postage & Handling
6/1/98 Edition—Credit Cards Welcomed

The Bible--Text/Translation/Inspiration/Inerrancy

Item ##	P/C	Gift	Title	Author
			1. The Apocrypha--Why It Should Not Be Accepted	
1110	C	$4.00	Why Apocrypha Should Be Rejected From Our Bibles	Waite, Dr. D. A.
			2. The Chronology of the Bible	
2662	28	$3.00	Bible Events--Defense of the Dates of Various Bible Events	von Rohr, Rev. Oscar E.
2818	36	$3.50	Bible Genealogies in Chart Form from the AV 1611	KJB translators
0009	31	$3.00	Biblical Chronology-Why It Should Be Accepted	Waite, Dr. D. A.
2427	288	$29.00	Chronology of the Old Testament--A Return to the Basics	Jones, Dr. Floyd
0044	12	$1.50	Discovering the Calendar of Creation	Lowe, Rev. Wm.
			4. The Dean Burgon Society (For Traditional Texts)	
			a. Dean Burgon Society Tracts	
0958	16	3/$1.50	DBS Tracts--Articles Of Faith, Operation & Organization	DBS Exec. Com.
1738	40	$1.50	DBS Tracts--Awana Churches, Keep Using The "Old" KJB	Waite, Dr. D. A./Barnett
1389	8	4/$1.50	DBS Tracts--Bible Preservation (Exec.Com.Statement)	DBS Exec.Com.
1448	16	3/$1.50	DBS Tracts--Defects In So-Called "Majority Text"	Waite, Dr. D. A.
1518	38	2/$1.50	DBS Tracts--Defects In The "New American Standard"	Waite, Dr. D. A.
1465	28	2/$1.50	DBS Tracts--Defects In The "New KJV" (Cf. #1442)	Waite, Dr. D. A.
2054	38	2/$1.50	DBS Tracts--Defects In The "NIV" (Cf. #1749)	Waite, Dr. D. A.
1562	38	2/$1.50	DBS Tracts--How We Got Our Bible	Waite, Dr. D. A.
1495	12	3/$1.50	DBS Tracts--KJB 1611 Compared To The Present KJB	Waite, Dr. D. A.
1727	12	3/$1.50	DBS Tracts--Why Reject The So-Called "Majority Text"	Waite, Dr. D. A.
			b. Dean Burgon Society Meetings	
0758/1-7	C	$19.00	Dean Burgon Society '79 Meetings (Watertown, Wisconsin)	Waite, Dr. D. A. et al.
1402/1-5	C	$15.00	Dean Burgon Society '86 Meetings (Michigan)	Waite, Dr. D. A., et al.
1402V/1-5	C	$30.00	Dean Burgon Society '86 Meetings (Michigan)	Waite, Dr. D. A., et al.
1403/1-3	C	$9.00	Dean Burgon Society '86 Meetings (Women's Meeting, Mic	Waite, Yvonne S. +
1517/1-6	C	$18.00	Dean Burgon Society '87 Meetings (Pennsylvania)	Waite, Dr. D. A., et al.
1517VC1-2	C	$25.00	Dean Burgon Society '87 Meetings (Pennsylvania)	DBS Exec.Com.
16371-5	C	$15.00	Dean Burgon Society '88 Meetings (Louisville)	Waite, Dr. D. A., et al.
1637VC1	C	$15.00	Dean Burgon Society '88 Meetings (Louisville)	Waite, Dr. D. A., et al.
1637VC1&	C	$25.00	Dean Burgon Society '88 Meetings (Louisville)	Waite, Dr. D. A., et al.
1637VC2	C	$15.00	Dean Burgon Society '88 Meetings (Louisville)	Waite, Dr. D. A., et al.
1739/1-6	C	$18.00	Dean Burgon Society '89 Meetings (Illinois)	Waite, Dr. D. A., et al.
1739VC1-2	C	$25.00	Dean Burgon Society '89 Meetings (Illinois)	Waite, Dr. D. A., et al.
1850/1-6	C	$18.00	Dean Burgon Society '90 Meetings (Maine)	Waite, Dr. D. A., et al.
1850VC1-2	C	$25.00	Dean Burgon Society '90 Meetings (Maine)	Waite, Dr. D. A., et al.
2002/1-6	C	$18.00	Dean Burgon Society '91 Meetings (Illinois)	Waite, Dr. D. A., et al.

Item ##	P/C	Gift	Title	Author
02VC1-2	C	$25.00	Dean Burgon Society '91 Meetings (Illinois)	Waite, Dr. D. A., et al.
2022	161	$16.00	Dean Burgon Society '91 Meetings (Printed Messages)	DBS Men,9
2002/6	C	$4.00	Dean Burgon Society '91 Women's Meeting (Illinois)	Waite, Yvonne S. +
2242	251	$25.00	Dean Burgon Society '92 Meetings (Printed Messages)	DBS Men,13
482/1-6	C	$18.00	Dean Burgon Society '92 Meetings (Toronto, Canada)	Waite, Dr. D. A., et al.
82VC1-2	C	$25.00	Dean Burgon Society '92 Meetings (Toronto, Canada)	Waite, Dr. D. A., et al.
369/1-6	C	$18.00	Dean Burgon Society '93 Meetings (Greenwood, Indiana)	Various Speakers
69VC1-2	C	$25.00	Dean Burgon Society '93 Meetings (Greenwood, Indiana)	Various Speakers
2422	212	$21.00	Dean Burgon Society '93 Meetings (Printed Messages)	Various Speakers
90VC1-2	C	$25.00	Dean Burgon Society '94 Meetings (Hagerstown, MD)	Various Speakers
490\1-8	C	$24.00	Dean Burgon Society '94 Meetings (Hagerstown, MD)	Various DBS Women
490-P	304	$30.00	Dean Burgon Society '94 Meetings (Printed Messages)	Various Speakers
490VC2	C	$15.00	Dean Burgon Society '94 Women's Meeting (Hagerstown,	Various DBS Women
2565-P	247	$25.00	Dean Burgon Society '95 Meetings (Printed Messages)	DBS speakers
565/1-6	C	$18.00	Dean Burgon Society '95 Meetings (Toronto, Canada)	DBS speakers
65VC1-2	VC	$25.00	Dean Burgon Society '95 Meetings (Toronto, Canada)	DBS speakers
675/1-7	C	$21.00	Dean Burgon Society '96 Meetings (Franklin, Massachusetts	Various Speakers
75VC1-2	C	$25.00	Dean Burgon Society '96 Meetings (Franklin, Massachusetts	Various Speakers
675-P	327	$32.00	Dean Burgon Society '96 Meetings (Printed Messages)	Various Speakers
769-P	243	$24.00	Dean Burgon Society '97 Meetings (Printed Messages)	Waite, Dr. D. A. + 17
769/1-8	C	$24.00	Dean Burgon Society '97 Meetings (Tennessee)	Waite, Dr. D. A. + 17
69VC1-3	C	$35.00	Dean Burgon Society '97 Meetings (Tennessee)	Waite, Dr. D. A. + 17
88VCR	VC	$15.00	Dr. Tow of Singapore Defends the KJB/Mrs. Tow's Testimo	Tow, Dr. & Tow, Mrs.
688TP	TP	$4.00	Dr. Tow of Singapore Defends the KJB/Mrs. Tow's Testimo	Tow, Dr. & Tow, Mrs.
			c. Books by Dean John Burgon	
1160	316	$15.00	Causes Of Corruption Of The Traditional Text (hardback)	Burgon, Dean John W.
1220	567	$25.00	Inspiration & Interpretation (copy format)	Burgon, Dean John W.
1139	400	$15.00	Last 12 Verses Of Mark (perfect bound)	Burgon, Dean John W.
0611	640	$25.00	Revision Revised, The (hardback)	Burgon, Dean John W.
1159	350	$16.00	Traditional Text Of The Holy Gospels Vindicated (hardbac	Burgon, Dean John W.
			d. DBS Miscellaneous	
850/5	C	$4.00	10 Reasons For The DBS Name & 1 Walk By Faith With K	Waite, Dr. D. A./Stewar
0956	5	$1.50	Analysis Of 'Chicago Statement On Biblical Inerrancy'	Waite, Dr. D. A.
0955	7	$1.50	Answer To 'Textus Receptus: Is It Fund. To Our Faith'	Waite, Dr. D. A.
0954	13	$2.00	Answer To 'What Is The Inspired Word Of God?'	Waite, Dr. D. A.
2002/4	C	$4.00	Answer To Price Attack + 1 John 5:7-8 Defense +	Barnett +
2002/3	C	$4.00	Atonement & Preservation/Spanish TR/Doctrinal Heart #2	VanKleeck +
739/5	C	$4.00	Baptist 17th Century Heritage & Why Reject "Majority Te	Barnett/Waite
637/3	C	$4.00	Believing God's English Bible & Student's Defense	Barnett,Al.
1803	7	2/$1.50	Beware Of The 'Revised' Gary Hudson--Traitor To KJB	Barnett, Dr. Robert
182/2	C	$4.00	Critical Text & W/H's Tie With Greek Philosophy	Gibson/S'tler
490/7	C	$4.00	Dean Burgon's Vindication of Mark 16:9-20	Waite, Dr. D. A.
2591	36	$3.00	Dean J. W. Burgon's CONFIDENCE in the KJB	Waite, Dr. D. A.
083/1-2	C	$7.00	Dean John William Burgon--Highlights Of His Life	Waite, Dr. D. A.
637/5	C	$4.00	Doctrinal Defects In New Versions (14) + In Writing	Waite, Dr. D. A./Fedena
182/4	C	$4.00	Doers Of The Word & God's Infallible Word	D.Hol/Barnett
88VCR	C	$15.00	Dr. Tow of Singaore Defends the KJB + Mrs. Tow's Testim	Tow, Dr. & Mrs. S. H.

Item ##	P/C	Gift	Title	Author
2688	C	$4.00	Dr. Tow of Singapore Defends the KJB + Mrs. Tow's Testi	Tow, Dr. & Mrs. S. H.
1637/2	C	$4.00	Dr.Fuller's Help To KJB & Future Defense Of KJB	Hollowood, Dr. M. J.
2182/6	C	$4.00	Dr.Logsdon's Change From NASV & Devotional Talks	Waite, Yvonne/Hollow
2490/4	C	$4.00	Erasmus/T.R. & Computers & Testimonies	Hollowood/DiVietro
1850/2	C	$4.00	Heresies Of Westcott/Hort & Testimonies On KJB	Sightler/Al.
2002/2	C	$4.00	History Of Westcott/Ht.Heresy + KJB Verse + NKJB Defect	Sightler +
1850/6-P	7	2/$1.50	How "Ye" And "Thee" Help Me—A Worksheet	Waite, Yvonne S.
1850/6	C	$4.00	How "Ye" And "Thee" Help Me—Pesky Thee's & Thou's	Waite, Yvonne S.
2002/1	C	$4.00	Inspiration/Every Word Of God/Doctrinal Heart #1	Hollowood,D.+
2002/5	C	$4.00	KJB Errors (18) Of MacArthur's Man + Bible Basics	Waite, Dr. D. A., et al.
BFTD/68-7	C	$9.00	Last 12 Verses of Mark Defended--Burgon's Book(#1-3)	Waite, Dr. D. A.
1820	7	2/$1.50	Life's Fabric--Testimonial To Dr.David Otis Fuller	Hollowood, Dr. M. J.
2182/1	C	$4.00	Living Bible's Author/Correcting The Uncorrectable	LaMore/Steward
1088	C	$4.00	Meet Dean Burgon & Burgon Evaluated Nelson's Majority	Waite, Dr. D. A.
1739/6	C	$4.00	New KJV--A Danger To Our Children & Devotions	Waite, Yvonne S.+GH
1739/3	C	$4.00	No Hebrew Or Greek--Who Do I Believe? & Problem Passa	Hendricks + Sr
1637/1	C	$4.00	Perversion Establishment, The, & Removing Landmarks	Golden/Steward
0828/1-4	C	$12.00	Purposes & Program Of Dean Burgon Society (4 cass.)	Waite, Dr. D. A.
1739/4	C	$4.00	Questions & Answers & The Bible And I & Testimonies	Randolph/Etc.
0763/1-8	C	$22.00	Questions And Answers On Burgon's Views Of Textual Crit	Waite, Dr. D. A.
2490/1	C	$4.00	Robinson Majority Text & Thy Word is Truth	Champeon/Barnett
2490/5	C	$4.00	Softening Words & KJB for Colleges & Q. & A.	LaMore,Dr./Dennis,D
1847	30	$3.00	Ten Reasons Why The D.B.S. Deserves Its Name	Waite, Dr. D. A.
1850/4	C	$4.00	Textual Criticism And Preaching & Q & A On KJB	Gibson/Et.Al.
1850/4-P	11	$1.50	Textual Criticism, Its Impact On Faithful Preaching	Gibson, Pastor Denis
1739/2	C	$4.00	Textual Problem Causes	Hollowood, Dr. M. J.
1850/3	C	$4.00	The Doctrine Of Inspiration & Q & A On The KJB	Hollowood/Al.
2490/6	C	$4.00	Trifling with God's Words & The Word Once Given	Gibson/Hendricks
1637/5	C	$4.00	We Have It In Writing & New Versions Doct. Defects	Fedena/Waite
1637/4	C	$4.00	Which Bible? & Where & How + Questions & Answers	Hollowood, Dr. M. J.
1850/1	C	$4.00	Why Churches Should Support DBS & Hills' On The KJB	Champeon/Barn.
1739/1	C	$4.00	Why I Believe As I Do & Betrayal Of The Word Of God	Steward +DH
2141	C	$4.00	Why The Dean Burgon Society & The Bible For Today	Waite, Dr. D. A.

8. False Views of the Bible

Item ##	P/C	Gift	Title	Author
0246	53	$5.00	Dooyeweerdian Concept of the Word of God, The	Morey, Robert
0961	C	$4.00	Response To Ruckus Of Ruckmanism In Local Church	Waite, Dr. D. A.

9. Greek Studies of the Bible

Item ##	P/C	Gift	Title	Author
0471-G	269	$18.00	Beginner's Greek Grammar Of The New Testament	Davis, Dr. William H
2707	53	$5.50	Did Jesus and the Apostles Quote the Septuagint (LXX)?	DiVietro, Dr. Kirk
1055/1-4	C	$12.00	English & Greek Reading Verse by Verse-Gosp.of John	Waite, Dr. D. A.
0060	53	$5.00	Granville Sharp's Rule--Proving Deity of Christ	Durham, Dr. Richar
0186	811	$25.00	Interlinear Greek/English New Testament	Berry, George
0455	946	$80.00	Interlinear Hebrew/Greek/English Bible in One Volume	Jay Green, EDT
0998/1-40	C	######	N.T. Greek Course-8 Sem. Hrs. (40-2hr.Cass;Grammar)(A)	Waite, Dr. D. A.
1260/1-37	C	######	N.T.Greek Course-8 Sem.Hrs. (40-2hr. Cass.;Grammar)(B)	Waite, Dr. D. A.
0141	19	$2.00	Salvation By Grace Through Faith (Eph. 2:1-10)	Waite, Dr. D. A.
1064/1-30	C	$80.00	Second Year Greek--Translation of John & Exegesis-30 cass	Waite, Dr. D. A.

Item ##	P/C	Gift	Title	Author
0159	93	$9.00	Successful Church–Exegesis of Titus, The	Waite, Dr. D. A.
2708	48	$5.00	Where the King James Bible Leaves Beza 1598 Greek Text	DiVietro, Dr. Kirk D.
			11. History of the Bible	
1757	347	$17.00	Authorized Edition (1611)–History Of & Changes In	Scrivener, Dr. Frederick
0015	17	$1.50	Brief History of The English Bible	Devos, Sandra
1562	34	2/$1.50	DBS Tract–How We Got Our Bible–Preservation	Waite, Dr. D. A.
2578	467	$40.00	For the Love of the Bible–Catalog of Bible Defenders	Cloud, Rev. David W.
1247	22	$2.00	How We Got Our Bible–Outline Lectures	Waite, Dr. D. A.
1034	22	$2.50	William Tyndale–His Life,Bible Trans. & Legacy	Waite, Daniel Stephen
1033	C	$4.00	William Tyndale–Protestant Reformer	Paisley, Dr. Ian R. K..
			12. Bible Inspiration, Preservation & Inerrancy	
			a. Bible Inerrancy & Infallibility	
0956	5	$1.50	Analysis Of 'Chicago Statement On Biblical Inerrancy'	Waite, Dr. D. A.
1041	C	$4.00	Authority Of Bible & Precious Blood Of Christ	Payton, Pastor C. Power
0410	218	$10.00	Battle For The Bible (Inerrancy Defended)	Lindsell, Dr. Harold
1149/01	C	$4.00	Bible Foundations;Revelation,Inspiration,Inerrancy, Preser	Waite, Dr. D. A.
0744	384	$19.00	Bible In The Balance, The	Lindsell, Dr. Harold
2329	15	$1.50	Biblical Inerrancy–Its Definition & Importance–ACCC Co	Keep, Pastor Jack
0246	53	$5.00	Dooyeweerdian Concept of the Word of God, The	Morey, Robert
1352	1	5/$1.50	Eight Propositions Favoring The KJB N.T. and T.R.	Lutheran,Ill.
0849	6	$1.50	God's Inerrant Word	Fitch, Rev. P.
1165	C	$4.00	How Far Inerrancy?	Waite, Dr. D. A.
1228/1-2	C	$7.00	How We Got Our Bible (4 Days With H.S.Seniors)	Waite, Dr. D. A.
1220	567	$25.00	Inspiration & Interpretation	Burgon, Dean John W.
2182/3	C	$4.00	Inspiration & KJB's Rythms For Easy Memorization	Hollowood/Champeon
2451	31	$3.00	Myths About the KJB–Myth 4 Inspiration Perfect Preserva	Cloud, Rev. David
1255/1	C	$4.00	Revelation,,Inspiration,Preserv.,Translation & Super.KJB	Waite, Dr. D. A.
0152	18	$2.00	Science Upholds Inerrency of Scripture	Von Rohr,Jr.,Rev.O.E.
2702	211	$21.00	*Sola Scriptura*– A New Call to Biblical Authority	Watson, Dr. J. D.
2703	20	$2.00	The King James Version Debate: A Plea for Authority	Watson, Dr. J. D.
2511	486	$35.00	Way of Life Encyclopedia of the Bible & Christianity	Cloud, Rev. David
1358	109	$6.00	What You Should Know About Inerrancy	Ryrie, Dr. Charles
0925/1-5	C	$14.00	Wonderful Word Of God-5 cassettes, 9 hours	Waite, Dr. D. A.
1411	C	$4.00	Written Word & Living Word–Separation 1st & 2ndary	Ketcham, Dr. Robert T.
			b. Bible Inspiration	
0954	13	$2.00	Answer To 'What Is The Inspired Word Of God?'	Waite, Dr. D. A.
0810	C	$4.00	Back To School Special & Our Textbook	Waite, Dr. D. A.
2089	4	3/$1.50	Bible Writings Were Inspired, Not The Writers	Various
0877	14	$1.50	Divine Inspiration Of The Holy Scriptures,The	TBS Staff
0725	77	$3.50	God's Inspired Preserved Bible	Rockwood, Dr. Perry F.
0676/1-3	C	$9.00	God's Word–Important, Written, Inspired, Infallible	Waite, Dr. D. A.
1228/1-2	C	$7.00	How We Got Our Bible (4 Days With High School Seniors)	Waite, Dr. D. A.
1220	567	$25.00	Inspiration & Interpretation	Burgon, Dean John W.
1848/13	C	$4.00	Inspiration & Our 17th Century Baptist Heritage	Steward/Barn.
2047	6	2/$1.50	Inspiration Of The Hebrew Letters And Vowel-Points	Bishop,G.S.
1232	C	$4.00	Inspiration Of Word Of God/Preservation Of the Word Of	Reno,Rev.J.P.
BFT/46	C	$4.00	Inspiration–Gromacki Answered–#1 (Radio #181-184)	Waite, Dr. D. A.

Item ##	P/C	Gift	Title	Author
BFT/47	C	$4.00	Inspiration--Gromacki Answered--#2 (Radio #185-188)	Waite, Dr. D. A.
BFT/48	C	$4.00	Inspiration--Gromacki Answered--#3 (Radio #189-192)	Waite, Dr. D. A.
BFT/49	C	$4.00	Inspiration--Gromacki Answered--#4 (Radio #193-196)	Waite, Dr. D. A.
2002/1	C	$4.00	Inspiration/Every Word Of God/Doctrinal Heart #1	Hollowood,D.+
2237TP	C	$4.00	Meaning Of Biblical Inspiration	Waite, Dr. D. A.
0961	C	$4.00	Response To Ruckus Of Ruckmanism In Local Church	Waite, Dr. D. A.
1255/1	C	$4.00	Revelation,,Inspiration,Preserv.,Translation & Super.KJB	Waite, Dr. D. A.
2702	211	$21.00	*Sola Scriptura*-- A New Call to Biblical Authority	Watson, Dr. J. D.
1850/3	C	$4.00	The Doctrine Of Inspiration & Q & A On The KJB	Hollowood/Al.
2338	2	5/$1.50	The Eternal Sonship of Christ--Refutes MacArthur	Houghton, Dr. Myron
2703	20	$2.00	The King James Version Debate: A Plea for Authority	Watson, Dr. J. D.
			c. Bible Preservation	
2002/3	C	$4.00	Atonement & Preservation/Spanish TR/Doctrinal Heart #2	VanKleeck +
2094	C	$4.00	Bible Perservation Is Taught In Scripture	Waite, Dr. D. A.
1942VC1-2	C	$25.00	Bible Preservation & KJB Superiority + An Evangelist	Waite, Dr. D. A./Tully
1942/1-2	C	$7.00	Bible Preservation And The KJB's Superiority	Waite, Dr. D. A.
1266	C	$4.00	Bible Preservation Defended-17th Century Puritan John O	Letis,Ted
1941	5	2/$1.50	Bible Preservation Is Taught In Scripture!	Waite, Dr. D. A.
1103	C	$4.00	Bible Preservation Of Words--Not Just 'Message'	Waite, Dr. D. A.
1989/1-2	C	$7.00	Bible Preservation, 40 Doctrinal Errors In Versions	Waite, Dr. D. A.
1960	10	$1.50	Bible Preservation--A Forgotten Fundamental	Graham,Dr.M.A.
2753	12	2/$1.50	Bible Preservation--Bible Practicality	Waite, Mr. Daniel S.
1497	3	4/$1.50	Bible Preservation--Direct Proof God Has Promised!	ANONYMOUS
1480	32	$3.00	Bible Preservation--We Have It In Writing!	Fedena, Pastor Paul
1025	60	$6.00	Bible--Our Book--Study Guide	Pangburn,Dr.F.
1174/02	C	$4.00	Bible--Preserved For Our Grandchildren	Waite, Dr. D. A.
1389	8	4/$1.50	DBS Tracts--Bible Preservation (Exec.Com.Statement)	DBS Exec.Com.
1402/1-5	C	$15.00	Dean Burgon Society '86 Meetings (Michigan)	Waite, Dr. D. A., et al.
1402VC1-3	C	$35.00	Dean Burgon Society '86 Meetings (Michigan)	Waite, Dr. D. A., et al.
1850/1-6	C	$18.00	Dean Burgon Society '90 Meetings (Maine)	Waite, Dr. D. A., et al.
1850VC1-2	C	$25.00	Dean Burgon Society '90 Meetings (Maine)	Waite, Dr. D. A., et al.
2245	20	$1.50	Defending God's True Words Until Christ Returns	Proper,Gordon
2286/1-7	C	$21.00	Defending The King James Bible--Bible Institute Course	Waite, Dr. D. A.
2286VC1-3	C	$36.00	Defending The King James Bible--Bible Institute Course	Waite, Dr. D. A.
1594-P	340	$12.00	Defending The King James Bible--Four Superiorities	Waite, Dr. D. A.
1352	1	5/$1.50	Eight Propositions Favoring The KJB N.T. and T.R.	Lutheran,Ill.
1388	9	$1.50	Enduring Word Of God--Its Providential Preservation	Scott-Pearson, Rev.
1087	C	$4.00	Every Word Of God & KJB Superiority	Waite, Dr. D. A.
2221	1	0/$1.5	Every Word--Importance Of The Bible's Words	Blanton, Rev. R.
1195	35	$3.50	Fresh Look At The King James Bible	Yarnell,Dr.R.
0588	C	$4.00	God Perserved The Bible	Waite, Dr. D. A.
1094	8	3/$1.50	How Shall Child Of God Know Which Is Word Of God?	Madden,D.K.
1228/1-2	C	$7.00	How We Got Our Bible (4 Days With H.S.Seniors)	Waite, Dr. D. A.
1220	567	$25.00	Inspiration & Interpretation	Burgon, Dean John W
1232	C	$4.00	Inspiration Of Word Of God/Preserv. Of Word Of God	Reno,Rev.J.P.
1153	C	$4.00	Jeremiah--God's Protection Of His Word & Servant	Waite, Dr. D. A.
2108/1	C	$4.00	KJB Superiority--Bible Preservation/O.T. & N.T. Text	Waite, Dr. D. A.

Item ##	P/C	Gift	Title	Author
BFT/31	C	$4.00	KJB's Superiority #1–Preservation (Radio #121-124)	Waite, Dr. D. A.
1526-P	12	$1.50	KJB–Why It's God's Word Kept Intact (Outline)	Waite, Dr. D. A.
1526TP	C	$4.00	KJB–Why We Believe It's God's Word Kept Intact	Waite, Dr. D. A.
2451	31	$3.00	Myths About the KJB–Myth 4 Inspiration Perfect Preserva	Cloud, Rev. David
1848/16	C	$4.00	Practical Ideas On Bible Preservation	VanKleeck, Rev. Wm.
2772	53	$5.50	Preservation of God's Words–Answer to Dan Wallace	DiVietro, Dr. K. D.
1418/1-3	C	$9.00	Preservation Of The Written & Living Word	Waite, Dr. D. A./Doom
1622	4	3/$1.50	Promise Of Bible Preservation, The	Blanton, Rev. R.
1255/1	C	$4.00	Revelation,Inspiration,Preserv.,Translation & Super.KJB T	Waite, Dr. D. A.
2702	211	$21.00	*Sola Scriptura*– A New Call to Biblical Authority	Watson, Dr. J. D.
2703	20	$2.00	The King James Version Debate: A Plea for Authority	Watson, Dr. J. D.
2186	14	$1.50	The Preserved Word (1 Peter 1:23-25)	DeWitt, Dr. Edward E.
1942/3	C	$4.00	Threefold Superiority Of The KJB–A Plea To Pastors	Waite, Dr. D. A.
1152	C	$4.00	Verbal Preservation Of The Bible	Rasmussen, Dr. Roland
1551VCR	C	$15.00	Why I Believe The KJB Is 'God's Word Kept Intact'	Waite, Dr. D. A.
			13. The King James Bible, Masoretic Text,	
			Textus Receptus & "Majority" Text	
			a. Dean John William Burgon (By or About)	
2696	225	$11.00	A Scientific Investigation of the Old Testament	Wilson, Dr. Robert Dick
0804	55	$5.50	Burgon's Prerequisites For Revision Of T.R. & KJB N.T.	Waite, Dr. D. A.
1160	316	$14.00	Causes Of Corruption Of The Traditional Text (hardback)	Burgon, Dean John W.
0758/1-7	C	$19.00	Dean Burgon Society '79 Meetings (Wisconsin)	Waite, Dr. D. A. et al.
1619	801	$40.00	Dean John Burgon's Biography	Goulburn,Dr.E.
2428	35	$3.50	Early Church Fathers' Witness to Antiquity of Traditional	Burgon, Dean John W.
1220	567	$25.00	Inspiration & Interpretation	Burgon, Dean John W.
1600/2-3	C	$7.00	King James Version–God's Word Kept Intact + Q & A	Waite, Dr. D. A.
BFTD/68-7	C	$9.00	Last 12 Verses of Mark Defended–Burgon's Book(#1-3)	Waite, Dr. D. A.
1139	350	$15.00	Last 12 Verses Of Mark–BFT reprint	Burgon, Dean John W.
1088	C	$4.00	Meet Dean Burgon & Burgon's Evaluation of Majority Text	Waite, Dr. D. A.
BFT/04	C	$4.00	Methods Of Burgon Vs. Westcott/Hort (Radio #13-16)	Waite, Dr. D. A.
1753	C	$4.00	Ministry of The Bible For Today–On Family Radio	Waite, Dr. D. A.
0828/1-4	C	$12.00	Purposes & Program Of Dean Burgon Society (4 cass.)	Waite, Dr. D. A.
0611	640	$25.00	Revision Revised, The (New HARDBACK Book!)	Burgon, Dean John W.
1250/1-19	C	$60.00	Seminar On Bible Texts & Translations	Waite, Dr. D. A.
1159	350	$15.00	Traditional Text Of The Holy Gospels Vindicated (hardbac	Burgon, Dean John W.
BFT/22	C	$4.00	When/How Burgon Revise TR/KJB?–#1 (Radio #85-88)	Waite, Dr. D. A.
BFT/23	C	$4.00	When/How Burgon Revise TR/KJB?–#2 (Radio #89-92)	Waite, Dr. D. A.
BFT/24	C	$4.00	When/How Burgon Revise TR/KJB?–#3 (Radio #93-96)	Waite, Dr. D. A.
BFT/25	C	$4.00	When/How Burgon Revise TR/KJB?–#4 (Radio #97-100)	Waite, Dr. D. A.
BFT/26	C	$4.00	When/How Burgon Revise TR/KJB?–#5 (Radio #101-104)	Waite, Dr. D. A.
BFT/27	C	$4.00	When/How Burgon Revise TR/KJB?–#6 (Radio #105-108)	Waite, Dr. D. A.
BFT/28	C	$4.00	When/How Burgon Revise TR/KJB?–#7 (Radio #109-112)	Waite, Dr. D. A.
BFT/29	C	$4.00	When/How Burgon Revise TR/KJB?–#8 (Radio #113-116)	Waite, Dr. D. A.
			b. GARBC & the KJB/TR Textual Controversy	
1075	C	$4.00	Dangerous Drift In The GARBC	Waite, Dr. D. A.
0974	C	$4.00	GARBC & Bible Text Isssues	Waite, Dr. D. A.
2321	9	$1.50	GARBC 'Fundamentalists' Guilty? Exposure of Party	Spitsbergen, Rev. T.

Item ##	P/C	Gift	Title	Author
0992	7	2/$1.50	Is The GARBC Keeping Bible Authority?	VanKleeck, Rev. Wm.
2237-P	2	5/$1.50	Meaning Of Biblical Inspiration	Waite, Dr. D. A.
0985	10	$1.50	New Fundamentalism? Or A Moving Foundation–Which?	Steward, Rev. Bob
0993	22	$2.00	Textus Receptus–Is Our KJB Outdated?	Steward, Rev. Bob
			c. Defending the King James Bible as the Best	
			(1) Seminars in Defending the KJB	
1942VC1-2	C	$25.00	Bible Preservation & KJB Superiority + An Evangelist	Waite, Dr. D. A./Tully
1942/1-2	C	$7.00	Bible Preservation And The KJB's Superiority	Waite, Dr. D. A.
1989/1-2	C	$7.00	Bible Preservation, 40 Doctrinal Errors In Versions	Waite, Dr. D. A.
0938	C	$4.00	Bible Texts & Translations–Pro-KJB	Waite, Dr. D. A.
1432/1-3	C	$9.00	Bible Texts And Translations (3 Cassettes)	Waite, Dr. D. A.
1968/3	C	$4.00	Bible Versions & KJB Superiority + Giving & Grace	Waite, Dr. D. A.
1594/1-5	C	$15.00	Church Seminar On Bible Texts And Translations	Waite, Dr. D. A.
1594VC1-2	C	$25.00	Church Seminar On Bible Texts And Translations	Waite, Dr. D. A.
2568/1-6	C	$18.00	Contending for the Bible–Utah Bible Conference	Waite, Dr. D. A. + 7 othe
2568VC1-2	VC	$25.00	Contending for the Bible–Utah Bible Conference	Waite, Dr. D. A. + 7 othe
1848/5	C	$4.00	DAW's Michigan KJB Defense Meetings–At Dalton	Waite, Dr. D. A.
1848/18	C	$4.00	DAW's Michigan KJB Defense Meetings–At Farwell	Waite, Dr. D. A.
1848/4	C	$4.00	DAW's Michigan KJB Defense Meetings–At Greenville	Waite, Dr. D. A.
1848/9	C	$4.00	DAW's Michigan KJB Defense Meetings–At Manton	Waite, Dr. D. A.
1848/8	C	$4.00	DAW's Michigan KJB Defense Meetings–At Mio	Waite, Dr. D. A.
1848/1	C	$4.00	DAW's Michigan KJB Defense Meetings–At Roscommon	Waite, Dr. D. A.
1848/6	C	$4.00	DAW's Michigan KJB Defense Meetings–Dalton Lunch	Waite, Dr. D. A.
1848/10	C	$4.00	DAW's Michigan KJB Defense Meetings–Harrison (Q & A)	Waite, Dr. D. A.
1848/11	C	$4.00	DAW's Michigan KJB Defense Meetings–Harrison (Q & A)	Waite, Dr. D. A.
2709/1-2	C	$7.00	Defending the King James Bible (at Riverside, NJ Church)	Waite, Dr. D. A.
2660	C	$4.00	Defending the King James Bible at a Chinese Church	Waite, Dr. D. A.
2660VCR	C	$15.00	Defending the King James Bible at a Chinese Church	Waite, Dr. D. A.
2660	C	$4.00	Defending the King James Bible at a Chinese Church	Waite, Dr. D. A.
2661	C	$4.00	Defending the King James Bible in NY Chinatown	Waite, Dr. D. A.
2698/1-2	C	$7.00	Defending the King James Bible in two Sessions	Waite, Dr. D. A.
2698/1-2	C	$7.00	Defending the King James Bible in two Sessions + Q&A	Waite, Dr. D. A.
2496VCR	C	$15.00	Defending the King James Bible Seminar	Waite, Dr. D. A.
2579/1-5	C	$15.00	Defending the King James Bible–9 Sessions	Waite, Dr. D. A.
2579VC1-2	VC	$25.00	Defending the King James Bible–9 Sessions	Waite, Dr. D. A.
1594-P	340	$12.00	Defending The King James Bible–Four Superiorities	Waite, Dr. D. A.
2569/1-3	C	$9.00	Defending the King James Bible–Six Sessions	Waite, Dr. D. A.
2569VCR	VC	$15.00	Defending the King James Bible–Six Sessions	Waite, Dr. D. A.
2496/1-3	C	$9.00	Defending the KJB Seminar–Texts/Translators/Technique/	Waite, Dr. D. A.
2709/1-2	C	$7.00	Defense of the King James Bible in a New Jersey Church	Waite, Dr. D. A.
2663/1-5	C	$15.00	Defense of the KJB in South Dakota–5 Hours	Waite, Dr. D. A.
2663VC1-2	VC	$25.00	Defense of the KJB in South Dakota–5 Hours	Waite, Dr. D. A.
2005/1-3	C	$9.00	Doctrinal Errors In NIV/NASV/NKJB–70 Passages	Waite, Dr. D. A.
2005VCR	C	$15.00	Doctrinal Errors In NIV/NASV/NKJB–70 Passages	Waite, Dr. D. A.
2003	C	$4.00	Five New Version Viruses + Questions & Answers	Waite, Dr. D. A.
2003/VCR	C	$15.00	Five New Version Viruses + Questions & Answers	Waite, Dr. D. A.
2004	C	$4.00	Five Reasons For Version Inferiority	Waite, Dr. D. A.

BFT Brochure #1		8		KJB/TR Defense
Item ##	P/C	Gift	Title	Author
904/VCR	C	$15.00	Five Reasons For Version Inferiority	Waite, Dr. D. A.
TD/50-5	C	$7.00	Four Reasons for Defending KJB--Book Analysis (#1-2)	Waite, Dr. D. A.
2423	26	$2.00	Four Reasons for Defending the King James Bible	Waite, Dr. D. A.
2599	C	$4.00	Four Reasons for Defending the KJB for Senior Saints	Waite, Dr. D. A.
672/1-3	C	$9.00	Four-fold Superiority of the King James Bible--Petersburg,	Waite, Dr. D. A.
672VCR	VC	$15.00	Four-fold Superiority of the King James Bible--Petersburg,	Waite, Dr. D. A.
253TP	C	$4.00	Fourfold Inferiority Of The New King James Version, The	Waite, Dr. D. A.
253VCR	C	$15.00	Fourfold Inferiority Of The New King James Version, The	Waite, Dr. D. A.
2380	C	$4.00	Fourfold Superiority of The KJB (on "Let's Go Visiting")	Waite, Dr. D. A./Egan
227/1-2	C	$7.00	Fourfold Superiority Of The KJB--Bible Study	Waite, Dr. D. A.
738/1-4	C	$12.00	Fundamental Bible Institute--Seminar on the KJB	Waite, Dr. D. A.
738VCR	C	$15.00	Fundamental Bible Institute--Seminar on the KJB	Waite, Dr. D. A.
676/1-4	C	$12.00	King James Bible Defended--202 Overheads	Waite, Dr. D. A.
76VC1-2	C	$25.00	King James Bible Defended--202 Overheads	Waite, Dr. D. A.
609/1-3	C	$9.00	King James Bible Superiority In All Areas	Waite, Dr. D. A.
9VCR1-	C	$25.00	King James Bible Superiority In All Areas	Waite, Dr. D. A.
611/1-2	C	$7.00	King James Bible's Superiority In All Areas + Q & A	Waite, Dr. D. A.
2098	C	$4.00	King James Bible's Superiority To Spanish Audience	Waite, Dr. D. A.
1219	C	$4.00	King James Version-Superior Translators & Technique	Waite, Dr. D. A.
514/1-3	C	$9.00	KJB Seminar in MD Local Church--Four-Fold Superiority	Waite, Dr. D. A.
516VCR	C	$15.00	KJB Seminar in VA Local Church--Four-Fold Superiority	Waite, Dr. D. A.
516/1-2	C	$7.00	KJB Seminar in VA Local Church==Four-Fold Superiority	Waite, Dr. D. A.
44/VC1-	VC	$25.00	KJB Study--9 hours, 163 Overheads	Waite, Dr. D. A.
2108/1	C	$4.00	KJB Superiority--Bible Preservation/O.T. & N.T. Text	Waite, Dr. D. A.
2108/2	C	$4.00	KJB Superiority--Translation Technique & Theology	Waite, Dr. D. A.
2044	C	$4.00	KJB Superiority--Trust/Texts/Translators/Technique+	Waite, Dr. D. A.
0977	C	$4.00	KJB Translators, & KJB/Textus Receptus Revision	Waite, Dr. D. A.
2389	C	$4.00	KJB's Preservation & Superior Hebrew & Theology (IN)	Waite, Dr. D. A.
2390	C	$4.00	KJB's Superior Greek & Theology (Greek Class at Heritage	Waite, Dr. D. A.
1255/2	C	$4.00	KJB's Superior O.T. & N.T. Original Language	Waite, Dr. D. A.
648/1-8	C	$24.00	KJB's Superiority--Text/Translators/Technique/Theology	Waite, Dr. D. A.
648/1-8	C	$24.00	KJB's Superiority--Text/Translators/Technique/Theology	Waite, Dr. D. A.
48VC1-3	C	$35.00	KJB's Superiority--Text/Translators/Technique/Theology	Waite, Dr. D. A.
722/1-3	C	$15.00	KJB--Superior Texts, Translators, And Technique	Waite, Dr. D. A.
722VCR	C	$15.00	KJB--Superior Texts, Translators, And Technique	Waite, Dr. D. A.
2046	C	$4.00	KJB--Trust/Texts/Translation/Technique/Theology	Waite, Dr. D. A.
3VC1-4	CR	$50.00	Messages in the NC Seminar Defending the KJB	Waite, Dr. D. A./Hooper
2140	C	$4.00	One Hour Summary For Pastors Of KJB Superiority	Waite, Dr. D. A.
2001	C	$4.00	Our Superior KJB + 20 Easter Passages & Versions	Waite, Dr. D. A.
1255/1	C	$4.00	Revelation,Inspiration,Preserv.,Translation & Super.KJB T	Waite, Dr. D. A.
000/1-5	C	$15.00	Seminar #2 On Six Superiorities Of The KJB--N.Y.	Waite, Dr. D. A.
712/1-7	C	$21.00	Seminar Defending the King James Bible (at NC Church)	Waite, Dr. D. A.
12/VC1-2	C	$25.00	Seminar Defending the King James Bible (at NC Church)	Waite, Dr. D. A.
722/1-3	C	$9.00	Seminar Defending the King James Bible at Johnson City,	Waite, Dr. D. A.
722VCR	VC	$15.00	Seminar Defending the King James Bible at Johnson City,	Waite, Dr. D. A.
775/1-6	C	$18.00	Seminar Defending the KJB in a NY Bible Conference	Waite, Dr. D. A.
78VCR	C	$15.00	Seminar in Cape Cod Defending the King James Bible	Waite, Dr. D. A.
3VC1-4	C	$50.00	Seminar in NC Defending the King James Bible (48 hours)	Waite, Dr. D.A.&Dr. J.

Item ##	P/C	Gift	Title	Author
1250/1-19	C	$60.00	Seminar On Bible Texts & Translations	Waite, Dr. D. A.
2741/1-4	C	$12.00	Seminar on KJB & John 3:16 & DAW's Testimony	Waite, Dr. D. A.
2741VCR	C	$15.00	Seminar on KJB &John 3:16 & DAW's Testimony	Waite, Dr. D. A.
2764VC1-4	CR	$45.00	Seminar on KJB at BFT Headquarters–420 Overheads, 23	Waite, Dr. D. A.
2764/1-11	C	$33.00	Seminar on KJB at BFT Headquarters–420 Overheads, 23	Waite, Dr. D. A.
2756/1-4	C	$12.00	Seminar on KJB in Brantford, Ontario, Canada	Waite, Dr. D. A.
2756VCR	C	$15.00	Seminar on KJB in Brantford, Ontario, Canada	Waite, Dr. D. A.
1979/1-4	C	$12.00	Seminar On Six Superiorities Of The KJB (6 hours)	Waite, Dr. D. A.
1979VCR	C	$15.00	Seminar On Six Superiorities Of The KJB (6 hours)	Waite, Dr. D. A.
2796/1-3	C	$9.00	Seminar on Superiority of the King James Bible in a NJ Ch	Waite, Dr. D. A.
2543/1-5	C	$15.00	Seminar on the K.J.B.–9 hours, 163 Overheads	Waite, Dr. D. A.
2543/VC1-	VC	$25.00	Seminar on the K.J.B.–9 hours, 163 Overheads	Waite, Dr. D. A.
2744VC1-3	C	$35.00	Seminar on the KJB in Chinese Bible Institute–English	Waite, Dr. D. A.
2742/1-10	C	$30.00	Seminar on the KJB in Chinese Bible Institute–English &	Waite, Dr. D. A.
2742VC1-4	C	$45.00	Seminar on the KJB in Chinese Bible Institute–English &	Waite, Dr. D. A.
2745/1-2	C	$7.00	Seminar on the KJB in Connecticut	Waite, Dr. D. A.
2745VCR	C	$15.00	Seminar on the KJB; in Connecticut	Waite, Dr. D. A.
2679	C	$4.00	Superior King James Bible Theology	Waite, Dr. D. A.
1104/1-2	C	$7.00	Superior KJB & Bible Version Confusion Today	Waite, Dr. D. A.
2155/2	C	$4.00	Superior N.T. Text/Translators For King James Bible	Waite, Dr. D. A.
2155/3	C	$4.00	Superior Technique & Theology For King James Bible	Waite, Dr. D. A.
2155/1	C	$4.00	Superior Trust & O.T. Text For King James Bible	Waite, Dr. D. A.
1022/1-2	C	$4.00	Superiority Of KJB At Pastors' Conference (2 cass.)	Waite, Dr. D. A./Pifer
1026/1-3	C	$9.00	Superiority of KJB For Local Church (3 Cassettes)	Waite, Dr. D. A.
BFT/30	C	$4.00	Superiority Of KJB Translators (Radio #117-120)	Waite, Dr. D. A.
1155	C	$4.00	Superiority Of The King James Version	Waite, Dr. D. A.
1444TP	C	$4.00	Superiority of The King James Version & Questions	Waite, Dr. D. A.
1444VCR	C	$15.00	Superiority of The King James Version & Questions	Waite, Dr. D. A.
1597/1-2	C	$7.00	Superiority Of The King James Version–3 Sermons	Waite, Dr. D. A.
1597VCR	C	$15.00	Superiority Of The King James Version–3 Sermons	Waite, Dr. D. A.
1449	C	$4.00	Superiority Of The KJB, Texts/Translators/Techniques	Waite, Dr. D. A.
0935/1-2	C	$7.00	Superiority Of The KJB, The-Superior Texts, Translators	Waite, Dr. D. A.
1595/2	C	$4.00	Superiority OfThe King James Bible	Waite, Dr. D. A.
1848/3	C	$4.00	Textual & Translational Apostates–At Gaylord,MI	Waite, Dr. D. A.
1077/1-2	C	$7.00	Textual/Translator/Translation Superiority. of KJB	Waite, Dr. D. A.
1368	C	$4.00	Textus Receptus & KJB Defense + A Present For God	Waite, Dr. D. A.
2554	C	$4.00	The Doctrinal Superiority of the King James Bible	Waite, Dr. D. A.
2672	C	$9.00	The Four-fold Superiority of the King James Bible–Petersb	Waite, Dr. D. A.
2672VCR	C	$15.00	The Four-fold Superiority of the King James Bible–Petersb	Waite, Dr. D. A.
2566	C	$4.00	The King James Bible's Superiority	Waite, Dr. D. A.
2566VCR	VC	$15.00	The King James Bible's Superiority	Waite, Dr. D. A.
1942/3	C	$4.00	Threefold Superiority Of The KJB–A Plea To Pastors	Waite, Dr. D. A.
1551VCR	C	$15.00	Why I Believe The KJB Is 'God's Word Kept Intact'	Waite, Dr. D. A.
2020/1-2	C	$7.00	Why KJB Is Superior To All The Modern Versions	Waite, Dr. D. A.
2403/1-2	C	$7.00	Why Not Use That Version–Sierra Leone '93 Bible Confere	Waite, Dr. D. A.
2133	C	$4.00	Why The King James Bible Is Superior To All Others	Waite, Dr. D. A.
1926	C	$4.00	Why The KJB Is Superior To All Others–A Synopsis	Waite, Dr. D. A.

Item ##	P/C	Gift	Title	Author
			(2) Radio Defense of KJB	
TD/90-9	C	$9.00	BFT Radio Contemporary English Version (C.E.V.) Refute	Waite, Dr. D. A.
TD/83-8	C	$7.00	BFT Radio Dean Burgon's Confidence in the King James Bi	Waite, Dr. D. A.
TD/88-8	C	$7.00	BFT Radio King James Bible's Readability Vindicated, (#1-	Waite, Dr. D. A.
T/129-13	C	$30.00	BFT Radio Refuting Central Baptist Seminary on KJB/MT/	Waite, Dr. D. A.
T/124-12	C	$15.00	BFT Radio Refuting DTS Teacher, Dan Wallace on KJB/T	Waite, Dr. D. A.
T/119-12	C	$15.00	BFT Radio Refuting Two Biblical Seminary Men on TR &	Waite, Dr. D. A.
TD/85-8	C	$9.00	BFT Radio Westcott & Hort's Bad Text & Theory Refuted,	Waite, Dr. D. A.
2497	C	$4.00	Defending the KJB on Radio—One on One over Radio KXE	Waite, Dr. D. A./Pinalto
2792	C	$4.00	Halloween '97—Still the Devil's Birthday, on SW Radio Net	Waite, Dr.&Hutchings
2718	C	$4.00	Interview over NC Radio WOTJ about KJB Meetings	Waite, Dr. D. A./Gibbs,
2012	C	$4.00	King James Bible—Our Authority (Radio Talk)	Fuller, Dr. David Otis
1753	C	$4.00	Ministry of The Bible For Today—On Family Radio	Waite, Dr. D. A.
2247	C	$4.00	Radio Debate Championing The KJB Over WCVO In Ohio	Lenhart,Gregg
2151	C	$4.00	Radio Debate On King James Bible & The T.R. (KFAX)	Waite, Dr. D. A.
494/1-2	C	$7.00	Radio Debate on the King James Bible with James White	Waite, Dr. D. A./J. Whit
2621	C	$4.00	Radio Defense of KJB & Mark 16:9-20 (Texe Marrs)	Waite, Dr. & Texe Marr
2667	C	$4.00	Radio Defense of KJB & TR on "Frankly Speaking"	Waite, Dr. D. A. & Chev
2504	C	$4.00	Radio Defense of KJB in Utah	Waite, Dr. D. A./Tanner
2505	C	$4.00	Radio Defense of KJB in W. VA	Waite, Dr. D. A./Everna
503/1-2	C	$7.00	Radio Defense of KJB Over SW Radio Church Network	Waite, Dr. D. A.
2620	C	$4.00	Radio Defense of Mark 16:9-20—on 'Let's Go Visiting'	Waite, Dr. & Barb. Ega
2620	C	$4.00	Radio Defense of Mark 16:9-20—on 'Let's Go Visiting'	Waite, Dr. & Barb. Ega
2720	C	$4.00	Radio Defense of the King James Bible & Texts	Waite, Dr. D. A./Sparga
2720	C	$4.00	Radio Defense of the King James Bible & Texts	Waite, Dr. D. A./Sparga
2740	C	$4.00	Radio Defense of the King James Bible—WGTG	Waite, Dr. D. A.
2542	C	$4.00	Radio Defense of the KJB over KXEG	Waite, Dr. D. A./Pinalto
2542	C	$4.00	Radio Defense of the KJB over KXEG	Waite, Dr. D. A./Pinalto
795/1-2	C	$7.00	Radio Exposure of Halloween on 'Let's Go Visiting'— 1997	Waite,Dr.& Egan,Barb
2791	C	$4.00	Radio Exposure of the NIV's Inclusive Language Edition ov	Waite, Dr.&Hutchings
2550	C	$4.00	Radio Interview (Q & A) on the King James Bible	Waite, Dr. & Mr. Brock
2580/1	C	$4.00	Radio Interview on the King James Bible	Waite, Dr. & Dr.Chamb
2580/2	C	$4.00	Radio Interview on the King James Bible	Riplinger, Gail &Cham
2677	C	$4.00	Southwest Radio Church Interview on KJB, Westcott/Hort	Waite, Dr. D. A.
701/1-2	C	$7.00	Southwest Radio Church Interview on the KJB	Waite,Dr.D.A/Hutchings
2429	C	$4.00	SW Church Interviews Mrs. Riplinger on KJB (Wrote #233	Riplinger, Mrs.Gail A.
2677	C	$4.00	SW Radio Church Interview on KJB, Westcott/Hort & Text	Waite, Dr. D. A./Hutchi
507VDW	C	$15.00	SW Radio Church PA Conference Defending KJB	Waite, Dr. D. A.
2723	C	$4.00	SW Radio Exposure of the Contemporary English Version	Waite, Dr. D. A./Hutchi
2800	C	$4.00	The Evils of Halloween—on Radio WKDN, 1997	Waite, Dr. D. A.
			(3) Miscellaneous Materials Defending KJB	
			(a) Defense of Particular Verses or Sections	
2249	15	$1.50	1 John 5:7-8 Defended As Genuine—Part Of #1617	Moorman, Dr.Jack
2008	382	$32.00	1 John 5:7-8—History of the Debate Over These Verses (Har	Maynard, Michael
2651	C	$4.00	1 Timothy 3:16 Defended—"God was Manifest in the Flesh"	Drexler, Pastor Carl J.
2392	C	$4.00	23 Verses on Theologica! Version Viruses & 10 Devotional it	Waite, Dr. D. A.
2002/4	C	$4.00	Answer To Price Attack + 1 John 5:7-8 Defense +	Barnett +

Item ##	P/C	Gift	Title	Author
2793	20	$2.00	Bible Versions Compared on 18 Crucifixion & Resurrection	Aaordkian, Dr. Sol.
1654	75	$3.50	God Manifest In The Flesh–1 Timothy 3:16 Defended	Burgon, Dean John W.
2704	C	$4.00	Vindication of Mark 16:9-20 to Senior Saints	Waite, Dr. D. A.
1988VCR	C	$15.00	Why Calvary + Youth + Version Deviations + KJB Best	Waite, Dr. D. A.
1624	8	$1.50	Woman Taken In Adultery (John 8:1-11) Text Defended	Alexander,C.D.
			(b) The 1611 King James History, Translators, etc.	
1757	347	$17.00	Authorized Edition (1611)–History Of & Changes In	Scrivener, Dr. Frederick
1060	32	$1.50	Bible Word List (Difficult KJB Words Made Clear)	TBS Staff
1737	38	$4.00	Conies, Brass, And Easter–KJB Problems Answered	Moorman, Dr.Jack
2182/3	C	$4.00	Inspiration & KJB's Rythms For Easy Memorization	Hollowood/Champeon
0759	47	$3.00	King James Fans (?) John R. Rice Answered	Bynum, Pastor E. L.
1579	4	2/$1.50	King James I–Background Of The King & His Version	MacOnaghie,D.
2758	412	$17.00	King James I–Unjustly Accused?–a Defense	Costen, Stephen
1364	4	3/$1.50	King James Or Saint James	Bynum, Pastor E. L.
1419	260	$13.00	King James Translators Revived–Biographical Notes	McClure, Alexander
1102	999	$37.00	King James Version–1611 Edition	KJB Translators
2026	C	$4.00	KJB Alleged Translation Errors–Refuted With Facts	Waite, Dr. D. A.
BFTD/63	C	$4.00	KJB Meter & the Contemporary English Version	Waite, Dr. D. A.
1294	25	$2.50	KJB Of 1611 Compared To KJB Of 1917 Old Scofield	Waite, Dr. D. A.
1121	45	$3.00	KJB Translators' Preface To Readers–With Glossary	Sasse (ed)
0890	12	$1.50	Learned Men,The–Biography Of KJB Translators	TBS Staff
2822	5	3/$1.50	Marginal Notes in the Original A.V. 1611–11 N.T. Textual	Waite, Dr. D. A.
1633/4	C	$4.00	Memorizing The KJB & Dangers Facing Fundamentalism	Champeon,Al.
0584	212	$11.50	Men Behind The King James Version, The	Paine, G.S.
2811	183	$18.00	The King James Bible Translators	Opfell, Mrs. Olga S.
2700	464	$23.00	The Private Devotions of Lancelot Andrewes	Andrewes, Lancelot
2326	166	$22.00	Translating for King James–Notes by Translator Rev. J. Bo	Bois, John
BFTD/60-6	C	$9.00	Twenty-One KJB Bible Problems Answered (#1-3)	Waite, Dr. D. A.
			(c) Readability of the King James Bible	
1060	32	$1.50	Bible Word List (Difficult KJB Words Made Clear)	TBS Staff
1517/1	C	$4.00	KJB–Is It Too Hard To Understand?	Steward, Rev. Bob
2486	277	$27.50	Reading Ease of the King James Bible–Six Versions Compa	Waite, Mr. D. A., Jr.
2671	84	$5.00	The Comparative Readability of the Authorized Version–7	Waite, Mr. D. A., Jr.
			(d) Dr. Fuller's Defense of the King James Bible	
2341	45	$3.00	A Tribute to David Otis Fuller (Memorial for KJB Soldier)	Cloud, Rev. David
0637	8	2/$1.50	Battle For Word Of God–Answer To Dr. Kenneth Brown	Fuller, Dr. David Otis
0322	217	$13.00	Counterfeit Or Genuine–Mark 16? John 8?	Fuller, Dr. David Otis
1402VC/2	C	$15.00	Dean Burgon Soc: Fedena, Questions, Fuller & Waite	Waite, Dr. D. A., et al.
1637/2	C	$4.00	Dr.Fuller's Help To KJB & Future Defense Of KJB	Hollowood, Dr. M. J.
1169	C	$4.00	Fuller's 50-Year Fruitfulness	Fuller,Dr./DAW
1151	C	$4.00	Fuller's Fight For The Faith–Dr.D.O.Fuller's Life	Fuller,Dr./DAW
0086	6	2/$1.50	I wouldn't Dare Treat the Bible That Way!	Fuller, Dr. David Otis
0085	8	2/$1.50	Is the King James Version Nearest the Originals?	Fuller, Dr. David Otis
2012	C	$4.00	King James Bible–Our Authority (Radio Talk)	Fuller, Dr. David Otis
1820	7	2/$1.50	Life's Fabric–Testimonial To Dr.David Otis Fuller	Hollowood, Dr. M. J.
0109	16	$1.50	On Your Guard! God's Word Uderminded (NASV)	Fuller, Dr. David Otis
1210	8	$1.50	Position Paper On The Versions Of The Bible	Fuller, Dr. David Otis

| BFT Brochure #1 | | | 12 | KJB/TR Defense | |

Item ##	P/C	Gift	Title	Author
1210	8	$1.50	Position Paper On The Versions Of The Bible	Fuller, Dr. David Otis
0183	C	$4.00	Summary of Which Bible and True Or False	Fuller, Dr. David Otis
0157	295	$13.00	True Or False--Westcott-Hort Theory Examined	Fuller, Dr. David Otis
0169	318	$13.00	Which Bible?	Fuller, Dr. David Otis
			(e) Answering "B" & "Aleph" & Westcott & Hort	
1868	7	2/$1.50	Are The Oldest Manuscripts Automatically The Best?	Graham,Dr.M.A.
BFT/15	C	$4.00	Case For KJB ("B" & "Aleph" Vs. T.R.) (Radio #57-60)	Waite, Dr. D. A.
BFT/13	C	$4.00	Case For KJB (Defects Of "B" & Aleph) (Radio #49-52)	Waite, Dr. D. A.
1825	157	$15.00	Early Manuscripts And The A.V.--A Closer Look	Moorman, Dr.Jack
1612	135	$7.00	English Revised Version Text Is "Un-Authorized"	Samson,G.W.
1848/14-15	C	$7.00	External & Internal Evidence Against "B" & "Aleph"	Waite, Dr. D. A.
2002/2	C	$4.00	History Of Westcott/Ht.Heresy + KJB Verse + NKJB Defect	Sightler +
2432	138	$7.00	Manuscript Evidence of the N.T., Right Estimation	Birks, Thomas
2039	224	$11.00	Plea For Received Greek Text & KJB Against Alford	Malan,Rev.S.C.
2262	C	$4.00	Westcott & Hort's Heresies Vs. Superior KJB Text	Waite, Dr. D. A.
			(f) Other Titles on This Theme	
2710	23	$2.00	An INDEX of Scriptures for New Age Bible Versions	Waite, Dr. D. A. & DiVi
2002/3	C	$4.00	Atonement & Preservation/Spanish TR/Doctrinal Heart #2	VanKleeck +
1986	7	2/$1.50	Austialian Missionary Writes About The Bible Battle	Bennett, Dr. David
1297	C	$4.00	Authority Of The King James Version	Baker,Rev.T.
2189	6	5/$1.50	Authorized Version As A Translation, The	STRO
2500	C	$4.00	Beautiful Thee's & Thou's vs. the Version Changes	Waite, Yvonne S.
1164	C	$4.00	Beauty Of KJB & Word Of Truth	Brackstone,Dr.
1572	C	$4.00	Behold The Lamb!--Exalting KJB & Blood Of Christ	Jones, Dr. Bob, Jr.
1803	7	2/$1.50	Beware Of The 'Revised' Gary Hudson--Traitor To KJB	Barnett, Dr. Robert
0510	156	$4.50	Book, The--Which Bible Does God Use?	Cimino, Rev.D.
2730	C	$4.00	By the Word & Coming to the Lord Without Repentance	Webb, Dr. Gary
1167	C	$4.00	Can You Trust Your Bible?	Waite, Dr. D. A.
BFT/11	C	$4.00	Case For KJB (Sources, MSS, Trad., Txt) (Radio #41-44)	Waite, Dr. D. A.
BFT/12	C	$4.00	Case For KJB (TR History, West. Text) (Radio #45-48)	Waite, Dr. D. A.
BFT/14	C	$4.00	Case For KJB (W/H&Translators Of ERV) (Radio #53-56)	Waite, Dr. D. A.
2515	17	$2.00	Case for New Age Bible Versions: Response to Morey's Revi	Williams,Sharleen V.
2399	2	6/$1.50	Chart of Early KJB Greek MSS & N.T. MS Line of the Ver	Various
1643	924	$46.00	Codex B & Its Allies--A Study & An Indictment	Hoskier,H.C.
1562	34	2/$1.50	DBS Tract--How We Got Our Bible--Preservation	Waite, Dr. D. A.
1738	40	$1.50	DBS Tracts--Awana Churches, Keep Using The "Old" KJB	Waite, Dr. D. A./Barnett
1402/1-5	C	$15.00	Dean Burgon Society '86 Meetings (Michigan)	Waite, Dr. D. A., et al.
1402VC1-3	C	$35.00	Dean Burgon Society '86 Meetings (Michigan)	Waite, Dr. D. A., et al.
1403/1-3	C	$9.00	Dean Burgon Society '86 Meetings (Michigan)(Ladies)	Waite, Yvonne S. +
1850/1-6	C	$18.00	Dean Burgon Society '90 Meetings (Maine)	Waite, Dr. D. A., et al.
1850VC1-2	C	$25.00	Dean Burgon Society '90 Meetings (Maine)	Waite, Dr. D. A., et al.
2022	161	$16.00	Dean Burgon Society '91 Meetings (CANADA)--Book	DBS Men,9
2002/1-6	C	$18.00	Dean Burgon Society '91 Meetings (Illinois)	Waite, Dr. D. A., et al.
2002VC1-2	C	$25.00	Dean Burgon Society '91 Meetings (Illinois)	Waite, Dr. D. A., et al.
2242	251	$25.00	Dean Burgon Society '92 Meetings (Canada)--Book	DBS Men,13
2591	36	$3.00	Dean J. W. Burgon's CONFIDENCE in the KJB	Waite, Dr. D. A.
2711/1-5	C	$15.00	Defending the King James Bible and Text	Hooper, Dr. Jerry

BFT Brochure #1   13   KJB/TR Defense

Item ##	P/C	Gift	Title	Author
2286/1-7	C	$21.00	Defending The King James Bible--Bible Institute Course	Waite, Dr. D. A.
2286VC1-3	C	$35.00	Defending The King James Bible--Bible Institute Course	Waite, Dr. D. A.
BFTD/31-4	C	$57.00	Defending the King James Bible--Book Analysis (#1-19)	Waite, Dr. D. A.
2498	C	$4.00	Defending the KJB on Radio--Texe Marrs Show	Waite, Dr./Texe Marrs
1517/2	C	$4.00	Defense Of KJB + Where Do Schools Stand On KJB?	Fedena, Pastor Paul
2457	C	$4.00	Defense of KJB on 'CROSSTALK' Radio WVCY	Waite, Dr. D. A.
2804	C	$4.00	Defense Summary of the King James Bible in NJ	Waite, Dr. D. A.
1855	6	2/$1.50	Departure From Traditional Text By GARBC's Gromacki	Steward, Rev. Bob
1192	8	$1.50	Desecrating God's Word--Defense Of The KJB	DeJonge, W.A.
2707	53	$5.50	Did Jesus and the Apostles Quote the Septuagint (LXX)?	DiVietro, Dr. Kirk
0874	39	$4.00	Difference Between KJB & Modern Versions	Whiddon, Bill
2182/4	C	$4.00	Doers Of The Word & God's Infallible Word	D.Hol/Barnett
1187	15	$2.00	Dr. Paisley Thunders Out For The King James Bible	Paisley, Dr. Ian R. K.
2688	C	$4.00	Dr. Tow of Singapore Defends the KJB + Mrs. Tow's Testi	Tow, Dr. & Mrs. S. H.
2688VCR	VC	$15.00	Dr. Tow of Singapore Defends the KJB/Mrs. Tow's Testimo	Tow, Dr. & Tow, Mrs.
2688TP	TP	$4.00	Dr. Tow of Singapore Defends the KJB/Mrs. Tow's Testimo	Tow, Dr. & Tow, Mrs.
2069	13	$1.50	Dr.Edward Freer Hills' Position On The KJB	Barnett, Dr. Robert
1109	C	$4.00	Dr.Lester Roloff's Stand For KJB-Mountains Of Bible	Roloff, Dr.L
2182/6	C	$4.00	Dr.Logsdon's Change From NASV & Devotional Talks	Waite, Yvonne/Hollow.
2428	35	$3.50	Early Church Fathers' Witness to Antiquity of Traditional	Burgon, Dean John W.
1595/1-4	C	$12.00	Easter Bible Conference in W. Sumner,Maine	Waite, Dr. D. A.
1352	1	5/$1.50	Eight Propositions Favoring The KJB N.T. and T.R.	Lutheran,Ill.
2490/4	C	$4.00	Erasmus/T.R. & Computers & Testimonies	Hollowood/DiVietro
2386	53	$5.00	Essays on Bible Translation. (Good historical data.)	Sightler, Dr. James
1087	C	$4.00	Every Word Of God & KJB Superiority	Waite, Dr. D. A.
2182/5	C	$4.00	False Prophets & KJB Refutation Of Dr. E. Pickering	DeWitt/Waite
2374	403	$15.00	Final Authority--A Christian's Guide to the KJB	Grady, William P.
2578	467	$40.00	For the Love of the Bible--Catalog of Bible Defenders	Cloud, Rev. David W.
1428	217	$21.00	Forever Settled--Bible Documents & History Survey	Moorman, Dr.Jack
2226	14	$1.50	From The NASV To The KJB--Dr. Frank Logsdon's Story	Logsdon, Dr. S. Frank
1854	16	$1.50	GARBC Agency Abandons Bible Stand--Gromacki Answer	Barnett, Dr. Robert
1630	22	$2.50	GARBC's Removing The Ancient Landmarks--4 KJB vv.	Steward, Rev. Bob
2484VCR	C	$15.00	God Keeps His Word	DeWitt, Dr. Edward E.
1061	122	$7.50	God Wrote Only One Bible	Ray,Jasper J.
0725	77	$3.50	God's Inspired Preserved Bible	Rockwood, Dr. Perry F
1762	12	$1.50	God's Invisible Hand On The King James Version	Steward, Rev. Bob
2235	100	$6.00	Guide To Bibliology--The Lord God Hath Spoken	Strouse, Dr. Thomas M
2440	73	$3.50	Heinsius & His Contrib. to Elzeviers' Textus Receptus	DeJonge, H. J.
2465	C	$4.00	Holding to the King James Bible--Bible Institute Graduatio	Waite, Dr. D. A.
1850/6-P	7	2/$1.50	How "Ye" And "Thee" Help Me--A Worksheet	Waite, Yvonne S.
1850/6	C	$4.00	How "Ye" And "Thee" Help Me--Pesky Thee's & Thou's	Waite, Yvonne S.
2119	C	$4.00	How I Got Into The KJB Defense Battle And How Going	Waite, Dr. D. A.
1228/1-2	C	$7.00	How We Got Our Bible (4 Days With H.S.Seniors)	Waite, Dr. D. A.
1247	22	$2.00	How We Got Our Bible--Outline Lectures	Waite, Dr. D. A.
2144	C	$4.00	How We Got Our Bible--Talk To A Christian School	Waite, Dr. D. A.
2168	9	2/$1.50	In Defense of The Traditional Text	Waite, Dr. D. A.
1304	604	$30.00	Inquiry Into The Integrity Of The Greek Vulgate (T.R.)	Nolan, Rev. Frederick
1857	240	$12.00	Inside Story Of The Anglo American A.S.V. & R.S.V.	Coy,George H.

BFT Brochure #1			14	KJB/TR Defense

Item ##	P/C	Gift	Title	Author
1848/13	C	$4.00	Inspiration & Our 17th Century Baptist Heritage	Steward/Barn.
2047	6	2/$1.50	Inspiration Of The Hebrew Letters And Vowel-Points	Bishop,G.S.
2002/1	C	$4.00	Inspiration/Every Word Of God/Doctrinal Heart #1	Hollowood,D.+
2084	C	$4.00	Interview With Rev. David Cloud (KJB/TR/Ruckmanism)	Cloud & Waite
BFT/02	C	$4.00	Introduction To The Bible Text Issue (Radio #5-8)	Waite, Dr. D. A.
2173	26	$3.50	Is The English Language Provincial?--Custer Answer	Cloud, Rev. David
1628	10	$1.50	Joseph--A Type Of The Bible	Paisley, Dr. Ian R. K..
2749/1-2	C	$7.00	King James Bible Defended for BBF Ministers in Kansas	Waite, Dr. D. A.
2750/1-2	C	$7.00	King James Bible Defended in Kansas Church	Waite, Dr. D. A.
2751	C	$4.00	King James Bible Defended in Kansas Church	Waite, Dr. D. A.
0084	280	$16.00	King James Version Defended, The	Hills, Dr. Edward
2223	26	$2.00	King James Version Of The Bible, The	Houck,Rev.S.
1496	37	$4.00	King James Version--America's Priceless Heritage	Walmert,John
2297	12	$1.50	King James Version--Our Version & God's Version	DeWitt, Dr. Edward E.
1238	44	$4.00	KJB & Luther's Bible vs NIV & New World Translation	Seeger,Paul
2002/5	C	$4.00	KJB Errors (18) Of MacArthur's Man + Bible Basics	Waite, Dr. D. A., et al.
1517/3	C	$4.00	KJB Q.& A./Textual Criticism Made Easy/New Scofield	Barnett,R.+
BFT/40	C	$4.00	KJB's Superiority #10--Question & Ans. (Radio #157-160)	Waite, Dr. D. A.
BFT/41	C	$4.00	KJB's Superiority #11--Question & Ans. (Radio #161-164)	Waite, Dr. D. A.
BFT/42	C	$4.00	KJB's Superiority #12--Question & Ans. (Radio #165-168)	Waite, Dr. D. A.
BFT/43	C	$4.00	KJB's Superiority #13--Question & Ans. (Radio #169-172)	Waite, Dr. D. A.
BFT/32	C	$4.00	KJB's Superiority #2--O.T.Heb. Text(Radio #125-128)	Waite, Dr. D. A.
BFT/33	C	$4.00	KJB's Superiority #3--O.T. & N.T. Text (Radio #129-132)	Waite, Dr. D. A.
BFT/34	C	$4.00	KJB's Superiority #4--N.T. Greek Text (Radio #133-136)	Waite, Dr. D. A.
BFT/35	C	$4.00	KJB's Superiority #5--Translators+ (Radio #137-140)	Waite, Dr. D. A.
BFT/36	C	$4.00	KJB's Superiority #6--Tr. Technique (Radio #141-144)	Waite, Dr. D. A.
BFT/37	C	$4.00	KJB's Superiority #7--Dynamic Equivalent (Radio #145-148	Waite, Dr. D. A.
BFT/38	C	$4.00	KJB's Superiority #8--Dynamic Equivalent (Radio #149-152	Waite, Dr. D. A.
BFT/39	C	$4.00	KJB's Superiority #9--Dynamic Equivalent (Radio #153-156	Waite, Dr. D. A.
1047	C	$4.00	KJB--King OF English Versions	Waite, Dr. D. A.
1526-P	12	$1.50	KJB--Why It's God's Word Kept Intact (Outline)	Waite, Dr. D. A.
1526TP	C	$4.00	KJB--Why We Believe It's God's Word Kept Intact	Waite, Dr. D. A.
0692	19	$1.50	Like A River Glorious (Pro-KJB)	Nettleton, Dr. David
2182/1	C	$4.00	Living Bible's Author/Correcting The Uncorrectable	LaMore/Steward
1968VCR	C	$15.00	Lordship/Blood/Remarriage/Alcohol/KJB/Giving/Separatio	Waite, Dr. D. A.
1726	83	$8.00	Missing In Modern Bibles--Nestle-Aland & NIV Errors	Moorman, Dr.Jack
2378	C	$4.00	More Questions and Answers on the KJB (Murfreesboro, T	Waite, Dr. D. A.
2448	34	$3.50	Myths About the King James Bible--Myth 1 Erasmus a Hu	Cloud, Rev. David
2449	16	$2.00	Myths About the KJB--Myth 2 Reformers Lacked MS Evid	Cloud, Rev. David
2452	34	$3.50	Myths About the KJB--Myth 5 True Scholars Reject Receiv	Cloud, Rev. David
2335	696	$17.00	New Age Bible Versions--Exposes Men/Messages/Manuscri	Riplinger, Mrs.Gail A.
1517/4	C	$4.00	New Age Movement & The Bible + KJB Quest. & Answers	Hollowood, Pastor Dave
1739/3	C	$4.00	No Hebrew Or Greek--Who Do I Believe? & Problem Passa	Hendricks + Sr
2711/1-5	C	$15.00	Observations and Applications of a NC Pastor on the KJB	Hooper, Dr. Jerry
2393	C	$4.00	Occult Origins of New Bible Versions	Moore, Dr. Frank
1332	6	3/$1.50	One God--One Bible!	Life Tract
1170	C	$4.00	Paisley Thunders Out For The T/R And KJB!	Paisley, Dr. Ian R. K..
2536-P	240	$24.00	Patterns #1 for Overhead Transparencies Defending the KJ	Waite, Dr. D. A.

BFT Brochure #1			15 KJB/TR Defense	
Item ##	P/C	Gift	Title	Author
2760	210	$21.00	Patterns #2 For Overhead Transparencies Defending the K	Waite, Dr. D. A.
2040-P	60	$6.00	Pickering, Dr. Ernest—Answered On Bible Texts/Translatio	Waite, Dr. D. A.
2040/1-2	C	$7.00	Pickering, Dr. Ernest—Answered On Bible Texts/Translatio	Waite, Dr. D. A.
1085	33	$3.00	Position Of 24 Schools On The KJB	Fedena, Pastor Paul
1418/1-3	C	$9.00	Preservation Of The Written & Living Word	Waite, Dr. D. A./Doom
2377	C	$4.00	Questions & Ans. on KJB & KJB Defended (at Murfreesbo	Waite, Dr. D. A.
1739/4	C	$4.00	Questions & Answers & The Bible And I & Testimonies	Randolph/Etc.
2377TP	C	$4.00	Questions on the KJB and KJB Defended (Murfreesboro, T	Waite, Dr. D. A.
2377VCR	C	$15.00	Questions on the KJB and KJB Defended (Murfressboro, T	Waite, Dr. D. A.
2212	6	5/$1.50	Remove Not The Ancient Landmark!—Why Use The KJB?	Franklin,Mark
0611	640	$25.00	Revision Revised, The (hardback)	Burgon, Dean John W
2159	39	$4.00	Ripped Out Of The Bible	Jones, Dr. Floyd
1639	1	7/$1.50	Schools—Their Position On King James Bible & T.R.	Fedena, Pastor Paul
2565-P	247	$25.00	Sixteen Printed Messages from the Canada 1995 DBS	DBS speakers
0375	18	$1.50	Sixty-Six Reasons For Keeping Our Protestant Bible	DeJonge, W.A.
2702	211	$21.00	*Sola Scriptura*— A New Call to Biblical Authority	Watson, Dr. J. D.
2382	8	3/$1.50	Some Problems With Bible Translations	Daniel, Grady
1517/6	C	$4.00	Stick To KJB + God Has Written To Us (Ladies' Meet)	Hollowood/YSW
2167	4	3/$1.50	Straining At Gnats?—The Bible Is Vital	Robinson, Dean
2424	15	$1.50	Sunday School Lessons Defending the King James Bible	Rusnacko,Rev.
2015	11	$1.50	Superiority Of The King James Bible	Wolfe,Mathew
1850/5	C	$4.00	Ten Reasons For The DBS Name & 1 Walk By Faith With	Waite, Dr. D. A./Stew
2545/1-2	C	$7.00	Testimony, Answers, & Interview	Riplinger, Gail & Y.
2545VCR	VC	$15.00	Testimony, Answers, & Interview	Riplinger, Gail & Y.
1739/2	C	$4.00	Text Problem Causes	Hollowood, Dr. M. J.
1850/4	C	$4.00	Textual Criticism And Preaching & Q & A On KJB	Gibson/Et.AL
1850/4-P	11	$1.50	Textual Criticism, Its Impact On Faithful Preaching	Gibson, Pastor Denis
1360	10	$2.00	Textus Receptus—A Timely Re-Evaluation Of It	Kober,Dr.M.
2456	12	$1.50	That Rascal Erasmus—Defense of his Greek Text	Coats,Daryl R.
2375	164	$5.00	The Authorized King James Bible Defended	Murray, Chester
2565/1-6	C	$18.00	The Dean Burgon 1995 Conference in Toronto, Canada	DBS speakers
2565VC1-2	VC	$25.00	The Dean Burgon 1995 Conference in Toronto, Canada	DBS speakers
2385	22	$2.00	The Epistle of Polycarp to Philippi—Supports the TR	Polycarp
2820/1-7	C	$21.00	The King James Bible's Manuscript Evidence	Waite, Dr. D. A.
2820VC1-2	C	$25.00	The King James Bible's Manuscript Evidence	Waite, Dr. D. A.
2703	20	$2.00	The King James Version Debate: A Plea for Authority	Watson, Dr. J. D.
2626	55	$4.00	The King James Version On Trial	Winter, Dr. Mickey
2704	C	$4.00	The Vindication of Mark 16:9-20 Explained for Senior Sain	Waite, Dr. D. A.
2166	2	5/$1.50	The Word Of The Living God (The King James Bible)	Dickerson, Dr. Alan
2296	18	$2.00	There Can Only Be One True Guide—King James Bible	DeWitt, Dr. Edward
1188	19	$2.50	They Are Changing Our Bible!	Von Rohr,Jr.,Rev.O.
1517/5	C	$4.00	Translation Confusion In Churches + New KJV Defects	Pangburn/DAW
1856	22	$2.50	Trinitarian Bible Society—Changing Back? We Hope!	TBS/Browns
1659	6	5/$1.50	Use The Bible God Uses—The King James A.V. 1611	Bynum, Pastor E. L.
2263	42	$4.00	Waldenses' Bible And The Old Latin—The Real Truth	Johnson,Dr.K
2511	486	$35.00	Way of Life Encyclopedia of the Bible & Christianity	Cloud, Rev. David
1848/12	C	$4.00	When Will Alterations Of Our Bible Stop?	Waite, Dr. D. A.
0980	24	$2.00	Where Is The Word Of God Today—KJB Controversy	Massey,Rev.H

BFT Brochure #1   16   KJB/TR Defense

Item ##	P/C	Gift	Title	Author
2518	118	$10.00	Which Bible is God's Word?--Answers to Version Question	Riplinger, Mrs.Gail A.
0532	2	5/$1.50	Which Bible Should the Bible-Believer Believe?	Shaturvedi
1174/01	C	$4.00	Which Bible Stands Like A Rock, Undaunted?	Waite, Dr. D. A.
2160	184	$18.50	Which Version Is The Bible?	Jones, Dr. Floyd
1850/1	C	$4.00	Why Churches Should Support DBS & Hills' On The KJB	Champeon/Barn.
1739/1	C	$4.00	Why I Believe As I Do & Betrayal Of The Word Of God	Steward +DH
1878/1-2	C	$7.00	Why We Defend The K.J.B. And The Textus Receptus	Moorman/Waite
2203	8	5/$1.50	Why We Hold To The Authorized King James Bible	Paisley, Dr. Ian R. K..
2517	8	3/$1.50	Why We Use the King James Version	Sorenson,Pastor David
			d. Errors of the So-Called "Majority" Greek Text	
1739/5	C	$4.00	Baptist 17th Century Heritage & Why Reject "Majority Te	Barnett/Waite
2490/2	C	$4.00	Critical Problems & Benefits of KJB & Preservation	Krinke/Reno/Branine
1448	16	3/$1.50	DBS Tracts--Defects In So-Called "Majority Text"	Waite, Dr. D. A.
1727	12	3/$1.50	DBS Tracts--Why Reject The So-Called "Majority Text"	Waite, Dr. D. A.
1617	160	$16.00	Hodges/Farstad 'Majority' Text Refuted By Evidence	Moorman, Dr.Jack
1617	160	$16.00	Hodges/Farstad 'Majority' Text Refuted By Evidence	Moorman, Dr.Jack
2490/3	C	$4.00	KJB's Reading Ease & French vs. T.R. & Alexandrian Trail	Waite, Jr./Champeon/ +
BFT/21	C	$4.00	Majority Text Error (Defense Of 1 Jn 5:7-8) (Radio #81-84)	Waite, Dr. D. A.
BFT/21	C	$4.00	Majority Text Error (Defense Of 1 Jn 5:7-8) (Radio #81-84)	Waite, Dr. D. A.
BFT/16	C	$4.00	Majority Text Error (Intro. To Argument) (Radio #61-64)	Waite, Dr. D. A.
BFT/16	C	$4.00	Majority Text Error (Intro. To Argument) (Radio #61-64)	Waite, Dr. D. A.
BFT/20	C	$4.00	Majority Text Error (Proofs On Jn 8--1 Jn) (Radio #77-80)	Waite, Dr. D. A.
BFT/20	C	$4.00	Majority Text Error (Proofs On Jn 8--1 Jn) (Radio #77-80)	Waite, Dr. D. A.
BFT/19	C	$4.00	Majority Text Error (Proofs On Mt-Jn 8:10) (Radio #73-76)	Waite, Dr. D. A.
BFT/19	C	$4.00	Majority Text Error (Proofs On Mt-Jn 8:10) (Radio #73-76)	Waite, Dr. D. A.
BFT/18	C	$4.00	Majority Text Error (Review & Summary) (Radio #69-72)	Waite, Dr. D. A.
BFT/18	C	$4.00	Majority Text Error (Review & Summary) (Radio #69-72)	Waite, Dr. D. A.
BFT/17	C	$4.00	Majority Text Error (Von Soden Refuted) (Radio #65-68)	Waite, Dr. D. A.
BFT/17	C	$4.00	Majority Text Error (Von Soden Refuted) (Radio #65-68)	Waite, Dr. D. A.
1088	C	$4.00	Meet Dean Burgon & Burgon Evaluated Nelson's Majority	Waite, Dr. D. A.
2490/1	C	$4.00	Robinson Majority Text & Thy Word is Truth	Champeon/Barnett
2174	18	$1.50	Slipping Away--Examining Hodges-Farstad "Majority Text	Cloud, Rev. David
BFT/22	C	$4.00	When/How Burgon Revise TR/KJB?--#1 (Radio #85-88)	Waite, Dr. D. A.
BFT/23	C	$4.00	When/How Burgon Revise TR/KJB?--#2 (Radio #89-92)	Waite, Dr. D. A.
BFT/24	C	$4.00	When/How Burgon Revise TR/KJB?--#3 (Radio #93-96)	Waite, Dr. D. A.
BFT/25	C	$4.00	When/How Burgon Revise TR/KJB?--#4 (Radio #97-100)	Waite, Dr. D. A.
BFT/26	C	$4.00	When/How Burgon Revise TR/KJB?--#5 (Radio #101-104)	Waite, Dr. D. A.
BFT/27	C	$4.00	When/How Burgon Revise TR/KJB?--#6 (Radio #105-108)	Waite, Dr. D. A.
BFT/28	C	$4.00	When/How Burgon Revise TR/KJB?--#7 (Radio #109-112)	Waite, Dr. D. A.
BFT/29	C	$4.00	When/How Burgon Revise TR/KJB?--#8 (Radio #113-116)	Waite, Dr. D. A.
			e. Questions & Answers on Textual Criticism	
2392	C	$4.00	23 Verses on Theological Version Viruses & 10 Devotional	Waite, Dr. D. A.
1251	200	$20.00	Answer To Stewart Custer's Booklet--KJB Controversy	Waite, Dr. D. A.
2564/1-4	C	$12.00	Bible Answers to Current Questions	Waite, Dr. D. A.
2564VCR	VC	$15.00	Bible Answers to Current Questions	Waite, Dr. D. A.
2480/1-2	C	$7.00	Bible Answers to Questions on Various Subjects	Waite, Dr. D. A.
2480VCR	C	$15.00	Bible Answers to Questions on Various Subjects	Waite, Dr. D. A.

BFT Brochure #1   17   KJB/TR Defense

Item ##	P/C	Gift	Title	Author
2581	C	$4.00	Bible Q. & A. & Paul's Checklist for Departure (2Tim.4)	Waite, Dr. D. A.
2692/1-3	C	$9.00	Bible Questions & Answers at Bible Conference	Waite, Dr. D. A.
2774/1-3	C	$15.00	Bible Questions & Answers at Washington Bible Conferenc	Waite, Dr. D. A.
2774VCR	C	$15.00	Bible Questions & Answers at Washington Bible Conferenc	Waite, Dr. D. A.
1089/1-3	C	$9.00	College Classroom Q & A ON KJB And Underlying Texts	Waite, Dr. D. A.
1727	12	3/$1.50	DBS Tracts--Why Reject The So-Called "Majority Text"	Waite, Dr. D. A.
1594-P	340	$12.00	Defending The King James Bible--Four Superiorities	Waite, Dr. D. A.
1957	2	6/$1.50	Evolution's Influence On Biblical Studies/Criticism	Strouse, Dr. Thomas M.
2003	C	$4.00	Five New Version Viruses + Questions & Answers	Waite, Dr. D. A.
2003/VCR	C	$15.00	Five New Version Viruses + Questions & Answers	Waite, Dr. D. A.
2380	C	$4.00	Fourfold Superiority of The KJB (on "Let's Go Visiting")	Waite, Dr. D. A./Egan
1997	5	3/$1.50	Gnosticism And The N.T. Text--Heresies In Westcott/Ht.Te	Strouse, Dr. Thomas M.
1611/1-2	C	$7.00	King James Bible's Superiority In All Areas + Q & A	Waite, Dr. D. A.
0918/1-2	C	$7.00	King James Version Q & A--(3 hrs. 2 cassettes)	Waite, Dr. D. A.
2482	C	$4.00	KJB Questions & Answers & 23 Errors of Versions on the S	Waite, Dr. D. A.
2482VCR	C	$15.00	KJB Questions & Answers & 23 Errors of Versions on the S	Waite, Dr. D. A.
2389	C	$4.00	KJB's Preservation & Superior Hebrew & Theology (IN)	Waite, Dr. D. A.
2390	C	$4.00	KJB's Superior Greek & Theology (Greek Class at H.B.U.)	Waite, Dr. D. A.
2717/1-2	C	$7.00	KJB/TR Questions & Answers With Three Young Men	Waite, Dr. D. A.+ 3 you
2717VCR	C	$15.00	KJB/TR Questions & Answers With Three Young Men	Waite, Dr. D. A. + 3 you
1523VC3	C	$15.00	Lordship Of Christ & Bible Questions & Answers	Waite, Dr. D. A.
1523/5	C	$4.00	Questions & Answers On Bible Subjects	Waite, Dr. D. A.
0978/1-3	C	$9.00	Questions & Answers on Bible Texts & Translations	Waite, Dr. D. A.
0763/1-8	C	$22.00	Questions And Answers On Burgon's Views Of Textual Crit	Waite, Dr. D. A.
2657	C	$4.00	Questions and Answers on the King James Bible	Waite, Dr. D. A.
0988	C	$4.00	Questions From A Fund.Bapt. Ch. on Texts,Translators, etc	Waite, Dr. D. A.
2499	C	$4.00	Talking with Senior Saints--Questions and Answers	Waite, Dr. D. A.

                      f. Refutation of Works Against the KJB & T.R.

                      (1) Radio Refutations on Audio Cassette

BFT/62-80	C	$57.00	Answer to Dr. Stewart Custer on KJB (#1-19)	Waite, Dr. D. A.
BFT/83-86	C	$9.00	Answer to Dr. Wisdom's "Bible Text Debate" (#1-3)	Waite, Dr. D. A.
BFT/87-91	C	$15.00	Answer to Radio Bible Class on the KJB (#1-5)	Waite, Dr. D. A.
BFT/94	C	$4.00	Back to the Bible Refuted on Bible Versions	Waite, Dr. D. A.
FT/129-13	C	$30.00	BFT Radio Refuting Central Baptist Seminary on KJB/MT/	Waite, Dr. D. A.
FT/124-12	C	$15.00	BFT Radio Refuting DTS Teacher, Dan Wallace on KJB/T	Waite, Dr. D. A.
FT/119-12	C	$15.00	BFT Radio Refuting Two Biblical Seminary Men on TR &	Waite, Dr. D. A.
BFTD/85-8	C	$9.00	BFT Radio Westcott & Hort's Bad Text & Theory Refuted,	Waite, Dr. D. A.
BFT/60	C	$4.00	Dr. RobertL.Sumner Refuted On KJB--#2 (Radio #237-240	Waite, Dr. D. A.
BFT/57	C	$4.00	Dr. Ernest Pickering Refuted On KJB--#5 (Radio #225-228)	Waite, Dr. D. A.
BFT/58	C	$4.00	Dr. Ernest Pickering Refuted On KJB--#6 (Radio #229-232)	Waite, Dr. D. A.
BFT/59	C	$4.00	Dr. Robert L.Sumner Refuted On KJB--#1 (Radio #233-236	Waite, Dr. D. A.
BFT/61	C	$4.00	Dr. Robert L.Sumner Refuted On KJB--#3 (Radio #241-244	Waite, Dr. D. A.
BFT/62	C	$4.00	Dr. StewartCuster Refuted On KJB--#1 (Radio #245-248)	Waite, Dr. D. A.
BFT/71	C	$4.00	Dr. StewartCuster Refuted On KJB--#10 (Radio #281-284)	Waite, Dr. D. A.
BFT/63	C	$4.00	Dr. StewartCuster Refuted On KJB--#2 (Radio #249-252)	Waite, Dr. D. A.
BFT/64	C	$4.00	Dr. StewartCuster Refuted On KJB--#3 (Radio #253-256)	Waite, Dr. D. A.
BFT/65	C	$4.00	Dr. StewartCuster Refuted On KJB--#4 (Radio #257-260)	Waite, Dr. D. A.

Item ##	P/C	Gift	Title	Author
BFT/66	C	$4.00	Dr. StewartCuster Refuted On KJB--#5 (Radio #261-264)	Waite, Dr. D. A.
BFT/67	C	$4.00	Dr. StewartCuster Refuted On KJB--#6 (Radio #265-268)	Waite, Dr. D. A.
BFT/68	C	$4.00	Dr. StewartCuster Refuted On KJB--#7 (Radio #269-272)	Waite, Dr. D. A.
BFT/69	C	$4.00	Dr. StewartCuster Refuted On KJB--#8 (Radio #273-276)	Waite, Dr. D. A.
BFT/70	C	$4.00	Dr. StewartCuster Refuted On KJB--#9 (Radio #277-280)	Waite, Dr. D. A.
BFT/54	C	$4.00	Dr.Ernest Pickering Refuted On KJB--#2 (Radio #213-216)	Waite, Dr. D. A.
BFT/55	C	$4.00	Dr.Ernest Pickering Refuted On KJB--#3 (Radio #217-220)	Waite, Dr. D. A.
BFT/56	C	$4.00	Dr.Ernest Pickering Refuted On KJB--#4 (Radio #221-224)	Waite, Dr. D. A.
BFT/46	C	$4.00	Inspiration--Gromacki Answered--#1 (Radio #181-184)	Waite, Dr. D. A.
BFT/47	C	$4.00	Inspiration--Gromacki Answered--#2 (Radio #185-88)	Waite, Dr. D. A.
BFT/48	C	$4.00	Inspiration--Gromacki Answered--#3 (Radio #189-92)	Waite, Dr. D. A.
BFT/49	C	$4.00	Inspiration--Gromacki Answered--#4 (Radio #193-196)	Waite, Dr. D. A.
BFT/95-98	C	$12.00	John Ankerberg Refuted on Bible Versions (#1-4)	Waite, Dr. D. A.
BFTD/68-7	C	$9.00	Last 12 Verses of Mark Defended--Burgon's Book(#1-3)	Waite, Dr. D. A.
BFT/44	C	$4.00	MacArthur's Man Answered On KJB--#1 (Radio #173-176)	Waite, Dr. D. A.
BFT/45	C	$4.00	MacArthur's Man Answered On KJB--#2 (Radio #177-180)	Waite, Dr. D. A.
BFT/04	C	$4.00	Methods Of Burgon Vs. Westcott/Hort (Radio #13-16)	Waite, Dr. D. A.
BFT/99-10	C	$9.00	Refuting D. A. Carson on "KJB Controversy" (#1-3)	Waite, Dr. D. A.
BFT/102-10	C	$7.00	Refuting Dr. Alan MacRae's "Facts on T.R./KJV" (#1-2)	Waite, Dr. D. A.
BFT/104-10	C	$18.00	Refuting James White's "KJVO Controversy" (#1-6)	Waite, Dr. D. A.
FT/110-11	C	$27.00	Refuting John Ankerberg's Telecast (KJB)(#1-9)	Waite, Dr. D. A.
BFT/53	C	$4.00	Version Error/Pickering Answer--#4 (Radio #209-212)	Waite, Dr. D. A.
			(2) Other Audio or Video Refutations	
2821	C	$4.00	Answer to Canada's Seminary President Marvin Brubaker	Waite, Dr. D. A.
1031/1-5	C	$15.00	Answer To John MacArthur's Paper On Bible Versions	Waite, Dr. D. A.
1031/1-5	C	$15.00	Answer To John MacArthur's Paper On Bible Versions	Waite, Dr. D. A.
2002/4	C	$4.00	Answer To Price Attack + 1 John 5:7-8 Defense +	Barnett +
2002/4	C	$4.00	Answer To Price Attack + 1 John 5:7-8 Defense +	Barnett +
1049/1-7	C	$20.00	Answer To Stewart Custer's 'Truth About KJB' Controvers	Waite, Dr. D. A.
0758/06	C	$4.00	Carson, D.A., Refuted At DBS Meeting (Wisconsin)	Waite, Dr. D. A. et al.
0758/1-7	C	$19.00	Dean Burgon Society '79 Meetings (Wisconsin)	Waite, Dr. D. A. et al.
2490/7	C	$4.00	Dean Burgon's Vindication of Mark 16:9-20	Waite, Dr. D. A.
2286/1-7	C	$21.00	Defending The King James Bible--Bible Institute Course	Waite, Dr. D. A.
2286VC1-3	C	$35.00	Defending The King James Bible--Bible Institute Course	Waite, Dr. D. A.
2182/5	C	$4.00	False Prophets & KJB Refutation Of Dr. Ernest Pickering	DeWitt/Waite
1939TP	C	$4.00	MacArthur's Man Answered On 18 Errors On The KJB	Waite, Dr. D. A.
2040/1-2	C	$7.00	Pickering, Dr. Ernest--Answered On Bible Texts/Translatio	Waite, Dr. D. A.
2247	C	$4.00	Radio Debate Championing The KJB Over WCVO In Ohio	Lenhart,Gregg
1099/1-2	C	$4.00	Refutation Of Custer's Position On 'Heres.Of W & H'	Waite, Dr. D. A.
2429	C	$4.00	SW Church Interviews Mrs. Riplinger on KJB (Wrote #233	Riplinger, Mrs.Gail A.
2704	C	$4.00	The Vindication of Mark 16:9-20 Explained for Senior Sain	Waite, Dr. D. A.
BFT/81-82	C	$7.00	Westcott's Denies Christ's Bodily Resurrection (#1-2)	Waite, Dr. D. A.
			(3) Written Refutations of Individuals	
0955	7	$1.50	Answer To 'Textus Receptus: Is It Fund. To Our Faith'	Waite, Dr. D. A.
2681	7	2/$1.50	Answer to Professor Ron Minton on the KJB	Waite, Dr. D. A.
1251	200	$20.00	Answer To Stewart Custer's Booklet--KJB Controversy	Waite, Dr. D. A.
0637	8	2/$1.50	Battle For Word Of God--Answer To Dr. Kenneth Brown	Fuller, Dr. David Otis

Item ##	P/C	Gift	Title	Author
0325	10	$2.00	Critique Of Custer's Paper Against TR	Clarke, D.T.
0819	21	$2.50	Critique Of D.A. Carson's 'KJB Debate'	Strouse, Dr. Thomas M.
0324	16	$2.00	Critique Of MacRae & Newman's Paper Against KJB, TR	Clarke, D.T.
2777	164	$9.00	Foes of the King James Bible Refuted—Ankerberg Show	Waite, Dr. D. A.
2173	26	$3.50	Is The English Language Provincial?—Custer Answer	Cloud, Rev. David
1939-P	20	$2.00	MacArthur's Man Answered On 18 Errors On The KJB	Waite, Dr. D. A.
2040-P	60	$6.00	Pickering, Dr. Ernest—Answered On Bible Texts/Translatio	Waite, Dr. D. A.
2039	224	$11.00	Plea For Received Greek Text & KJB Against Alford	Malan,Rev.S.C.
0587	8	$1.50	Remarks On 'TR & KJB' By MacRae & Newman (Tr.Bib.S	TBS Staff
1668	21	$2.00	Response To An Attack On The King James Bible	Johnson,Dr.K.
0798	6	$1.50	Review Of 'KJB Debate' By Carson	Fowler,Ev.W.
0783	11	$2.00	Review Of D.A.Carson's 'KJB Debate'	Brown,A.J.
1477	25	$2.50	Stewart Custer Answered—Is English Provincial?	Cloud, Rev. David
2727	2	5/$1.50	Time Given to KJB and Anti-KJB on the Ankerberg TV Se	Waite, Dr. D. A.
2562	90	$9.00	Why Not the King James Bible!—Answer to KJVO Book	DiVietro, Dr. Kirk D.

(4) Other Miscellaneous Refutations

Item ##	P/C	Gift	Title	Author
2249	15	$1.50	1 John 5:7-8 Defended As Genuine—Part Of #1617	Moorman, Dr.Jack
2513	147	$7.00	1 John 5:7-8—1822 Defense of the Trinitarian System	Harrowar,David
2008	382	$32.00	1 John 5:7-8—History of the Debate Over These Verses (Har	Maynard, Michael
1823	24	3/$1.50	Awana's Errors In Leaving Their K.J. Bible Stand	Barnett, Dr. Robert
1727	12	3/$1.50	DBS Tracts—Why Reject The So-Called "Majority Text"	Waite, Dr. D. A.
2022	161	$16.00	Dean Burgon Society '91 Meetings (CANADA)—Book	DBS Men,9
2242	251	$25.00	Dean Burgon Society '92 Meetings (Canada)—Book	DBS Men,13
2506	36	$3.00	Dean Burgon's Vindication of the Last 12 Verses of Mark	Waite, Dr. D. A.
2245	20	$1.50	Defending God's True Words Until Christ Returns	Proper,Gordon
1762	12	$1.50	God's Invisible Hand On The King James Version	Steward, Rev. Bob
2509	8	2/$1.50	Hebrew Defense for KJB Reading of 'Lucifer'(Isaiah 14:12)	Waite, Dr. D. A.
1364	4	3/$1.50	King James Or Saint James	Bynum, Pastor E. L.
2026	C	$4.00	KJB Alleged Translation Errors—Refuted With Facts	Waite, Dr. D. A.
2002/5	C	$4.00	KJB Errors (18) Of MacArthur's Man + Bible Basics	Waite, Dr. D. A., et al.
1726	83	$8.00	Missing In Modern Bibles—Nestle-Aland & NIV Errors	Moorman, Dr.Jack
1733	65	$6.50	Oldest And Best Manuscripts—How Good Are They?	Carter, Cecil
2524	51	3/$1.50	Psalm 12:6-7 And Bible Preservation	Moorman, Dr.Jack
0611	640	$25.00	Revision Revised, The (New HARDBACK Book!)	Burgon, Dean John W.
1845	66	$6.50	Theological Errors In Westcott/Hort Texts—158 vv.	Waite, Dr. D. A.
2263	42	$4.00	Waldenses' Bible And The Old Latin—The Real Truth	Johnson,Dr.K
2518	118	$10.00	Which Bible is God's Word?—Answers to Version Question	Riplinger, Mrs.Gail A.

g. Textual Criticism of the Bible

(1) Major Works on Textual Criticism

Item ##	P/C	Gift	Title	Author
0875	40	$4.00	Ancient Text Of The N.T.	VanBruggen,Dr.
BFT/62-80	C	$57.00	Answer to Dr. Stewart Custer on KJB (#1-19)	Waite, Dr. D. A.
1031/1-5	C	$15.00	Answer To John MacArthur's Paper On Bible Versions	Waite, Dr. D. A.
1049/1-7	C	$20.00	Answer To Stewart Custer's 'Truth About KJB' Controvers	Waite, Dr. D. A.
1251	200	$20.00	Answer To Stewart Custer's Booklet—KJB Controversy	Waite, Dr. D. A.
0986	84	$8.50	ASV, NASV & NIV Departures from Traditional Heb./Gree	Waite, Dr. D. A.
2528	47	$4.50	Background Information on N.T. Syriac Manuscripts	Hatch,William Henry
0598	258	$16.00	Believing Bible Study	Hills, Dr. Edward

Item ##	P/C	Gift	Title	Author
1324/1-4	C	$12.00	Bible Versions—The Basics For A Local Church	Anderson,Rev.
0083	112	$7.00	Case for the King James Bible, the & Its Texts	Waite, Dr. D. A.
1160	316	$14.00	Causes Of Corruption Of The Traditional Text (hardback)	Burgon, Dean John W.
1594/1-5	C	$25.00	Church Seminar On Bible Texts And Translations	Waite, Dr. D. A.
0322	217	$13.00	Counterfeit Or Genuine—Mark 16? John 8?	Fuller, Dr. David Otis
1239	91	$9.00	Credibility Of The Majority Text	Williams, Dr. J. B.
2124	96	$5.00	Dabney's 19th Century Defense Of T.R. Against W & H	Dabney,Rev.R.
FTD/31-4	C	$57.00	Defending the King James Bible—Book Analysis (#1-19)	Waite, Dr. D. A.
1594-P	340	$12.00	Defending The King James Bible—Four Superiorities	Waite, Dr. D. A.
2707	53	$5.50	Did Jesus and the Apostles Quote the Septuagint (LXX)?	DiVietro, Dr. Kirk
2136	63	$6.00	Early Church Fathers & The A.V.—A Demonstration	Morman,Rev.J.
1612	135	$7.00	English Revised Version Text Is "Un-Authorized"	Samson,G.W.
2777	164	$9.00	Foes of the King James Bible Refuted—Ankerberg Show	Waite, Dr. D. A.
1428	217	$21.00	Forever Settled—Bible Documents & History Survey	Moorman, Dr.Jack
2380	C	$4.00	Fourfold Superiority of The KJB (on "Let's Go Visiting")	Waite, Dr. D. A./Egan
2532	176	$17.50	Greek Manuscripts of the N.T. at Mount Sinai	Hatch,William Henry P.
2531	144	$14.50	Greek Manuscripts of the N.T. in Jerusalem	Hatch,William Henry P.
0743	162	$7.00	Guide To Textual Criticism Of N.T.	Miller,Edward
1617	160	$16.00	Hodges/Farstad 'Majority' Text Refuted By Evidence	Moorman, Dr.Jack
0556	253	$12.00	Identity Of The New Testament Text, The	Pickering, Wilbur
1304	604	$30.00	Inquiry Into The Integrity Of The Gr. Vulgate Or T/R	Nolan, Rev. Frederick
1857	240	$12.00	Inside Story Of The Anglo American A.S.V. & R.S.V.	Coy,George H.
1220	567	$25.00	Inspiration & Interpretation	Burgon, Dean John W.
1303	530	$25.00	Intro. To Revised Greek Text (an erroneous theory)	Hort, Fenton John A.
0084	280	$16.00	King James Version Defended, The	Hills, Dr. Edward
1139	350	$15.00	Last 12 Verses Of Mark—perfect bound	Burgon, Dean John W.
1726	83	$8.00	Missing In Modern Bibles—Nestle-Aland & NIV Errors	Moorman, Dr.Jack
0836	16	$1.50	Modern Versions & 19th Century Critics	Ecob,J.R.
0876	16	$1.50	Modern Versions & Ancient Manuscripts	Ecob,J.R.
0470	85	$8.50	New Testament Majority Greek Text Defended	Waite, Dr. D. A.
1123	263	$13.00	Our Authorized Bible Vindicated (Re-Print Edition)	Wilkinson, Benjamin
2536-P	240	$24.00	Patterns #1 for Overhead Transparencies Defending the KJ	Waite, Dr. D. A.
2760	210	$21.00	Patterns #2 For Overhead Transparencies Defending the K	Waite, Dr. D. A.
1285	920	$45.00	Plain Intro. To The Criticism Of The New Testament	Scrivener, Dr. Frederick
2529	190	$19.00	Principal Minuscule Manuscripts of the N.T.	Hatch,William Henry P.
2530	215	$21.50	Principal Uncial Manuscripts of the N.T.	Hatch,William Henry P.
2492	75	$4.00	Proper Perspective on the PSEUDOSCIENCE of Biblical C	Graham, Rev. Carl
0639	44	$4.00	Providential Preservation Of Greek Text Of N.T.	McLean
0611	640	$25.00	Revision Revised, The (hardback)	Burgon, Dean John W.
1670	668	$35.00	Scrivener's Greek New Testament—T.R. & Westcott & Ht.	Scrivener, Dr. Frederick
250/1-19	C	$60.00	Seminar On Bible Texts & Translations	Waite, Dr. D. A.
764VC1-4	CR	$45.00	Seminar on KJB at BFT Headquarters-420 Overheads, 23	Waite, Dr. D. A.
764/1-11	C	$33.00	Seminar on KJB at BFT Headquarters-420 Overheads, 23	Waite, Dr. D. A.
0734	14	$2.00	Syllabus Of Textual Criticism	Strouse, Dr. Thomas M.
2527	264	$13.00	Text of the Greek Bible: A Students Handbook	Kenyon,Frederic G.
1159	350	$15.00	Traditional Text Of The Holy Gospels Vindicated (hardbac	Burgon, Dean John W.
2326	166	$22.00	Translating for King James—Notes by Translator Rev. Joh	Bois, John
0157	295	$13.00	True Or False—Westcott-Hort Theory Examined	Fuller, Dr. David Otis

Item ##	P/C	Gift	Title	Author
2708	48	$5.00	Where the King James Bible Leaves Beza 1598 Greek Text	DiVietro, Dr. Kirk D.
0169	318	$13.00	Which Bible?	Fuller, Dr. David Otis
2562	90	$9.00	Why Not the King James Bible!—Answer to KJVO Book	DiVietro, Dr. Kirk D.
			(2) Minor Works on Textual Criticism	
2651	C	$4.00	1 Timothy 3:16 Defended—þGod was Manifest in the Fleshþ	Drexler, Pastor Carl
1416	2	5/$1.50	Ante-Nicene Patristic Witness To The Textus Receptus	Strouse, Dr. Thomas M
0534	10	$1.50	Authenticity Of Last 12 Verses Of Mark-Trinitarian Bib.So	TBS Staff
0771	16	$2.00	Bible A Sure Foundation, The—Trin. Bible Society	TBS Staff
1266	C	$4.00	Bible Preservation Defended-17th Century Puritan John O	Letis, Ted
1103	C	$4.00	Bible Preservation Of Words—Not Just 'Message'	Waite, Dr. D. A.
1432/1-3	C	$9.00	Bible Texts And Translations (3 Cassettes)	Waite, Dr. D. A.
1025	60	$6.00	Bible—Our Book—Study Guide	Pangburn, Dr.F.
1174/02	C	$4.00	Bible—Preserved For Our Grandchildren	Waite, Dr. D. A.
0582	4	3/$1.50	Broken For You—Trinitarian Bible Society	TBS Staff
0049	33	$3.50	Christian Approach to the Evaluation of English Versions	Fowler, Ev. W.
0557	20	$2.00	Contending For Or Departing From The Faith	Klahr, H.E.
1353	55	$3.50	Controversy on the Last 12 Verses of Mark (Mk. 16:9-20)	Thompson, Bishop
1175/VCR	C	$15.00	Debate On Westcott/Hort vs Textus Receptus Greek Texts	Waite, Dr. D. A./Custe
1175TP	C	$4.00	Debate On Westcott/Hort vs Textus Receptus Greek Texts	Waite, Dr. D. A./Custe
2286/1-7	C	$21.00	Defending The King James Bible—Bible Institute Course	Waite, Dr. D. A.
2286VC1-3	C	$35.00	Defending The King James Bible—Bible Institute Course	Waite, Dr. D. A.
0597/1-2	C	$7.00	Defense Of Hebrew & Greek Text Underlying KJB	Waite, Dr. D. A.
0238	16	$3.50	Defense of N.T. Majority Text, The	Waite, Dr. D. A.
2726VCR	C	$15.00	Doctrinal Heart of the Bible—Removed from Modern Versio	Moorman, Dr. Jack A
2135	135	$13.50	God Keeps His Word—Outline Studies	DeWitt, Dr. Edward F
0588	C	$4.00	God Perserved The Bible	Waite, Dr. D. A.
0676/1-3	C	$9.00	God's Word—Important, Written, Inspired, Infallible	Waite, Dr. D. A.
1165	C	$4.00	How Far Inerrancy?	Waite, Dr. D. A.
1094	8	3/$1.50	How Shall Child Of God Know Which Is Word Of God?	Madden, D.K.
1247	22	$2.00	How We Got Our Bible—Outline Lectures	Waite, Dr. D. A.
0793	14	$1.50	If The Foundations Be Destroyed—Higher Criticism Danger	TBS Staff
0824	C	$4.00	Importance Of Determining The Text Of Scripture	Waite, Dr. D. A.
1038/1-2	C	$7.00	Importance Of Which Translation Of The Bible	Waite, Dr. D. A.
1078	C	$4.00	Important Books Defending The KJB Superiority	Waite, Dr. D. A.
2047	6	2/$1.50	Inspiration Of The Hebrew Letters And Vowel-Points	Bishop, G.S.
1205	3	2/$1.50	Is The New KJV The Fundamentalist's Bible?	Strouse, Dr. Thomas
1173/1-3	C	$9.00	KJB's Superior Texts, Translators, And Translation	Waite, Dr. D. A.
1180	95	$6.00	Let's Weigh The Evidence-Which Bible Is Word Of God	Burton, Barry
0976	C	$4.00	N.T.Textual Criticism For Women	Waite, Dr. D. A.
1062	8	$1.50	New Eye Opener	Ray, Jasper J.
0973	C	$4.00	O.T. Textual Revisions of ASV,NASV, & NIV	Waite, Dr. D. A.
1418/1-3	C	$9.00	Preservation Of The Written & Living Word	Waite, Dr. D. A./Doo
0802	4	3/$1.50	Prove All Things—N.I.V. Critique	Start, Rev.D.T
1057/1-8	C	$24.00	Seminar On KJB Superiority (8 cassettes)	Waite, Dr. D. A.
0183	C	$4.00	Summary of Which Bible and True Or False	Fuller, Dr. David Oti
0218	10	$1.50	Tampering With The Truth	DeJonge, W.A.
1756	143	$7.00	Textual Commentary On Mathew 1-14—MSS Evidence	Miller, Edward

Item ##	P/C	Gift	Title	Author
1850/4	C	$4.00	Textual Criticism And Preaching & Q & A On KJB	Gibson/Et.Al.
1850/4-P	11	$1.50	Textual Criticism, Its Impact On Faithful Preaching	Gibson, Pastor Denis
1360	10	$2.00	Textus Receptus--A Timely Re-Evaluation Of It	Kober,Dr.M.
0472	C	$4.00	Translations Of The Bible-Critique Of Westcott-Hort	Logsdon, Dr. S. Frank
1166	C	$4.00	Trustworthiness Of Byzantine Tradition Greek Text	Waite, Dr. D. A.
1258	C	$4.00	Trustworthiness Of Traditional Text; 11 Rules For Debatin	Waite, Dr. D. A.
1168	C	$4.00	Westcott-Hort Capture Of Fundamental Seminaries	Bergman,Eric
0542	14	$1.50	What Is Wrong With Modern Versions-Trininitarian Bible	TBS Staff
1157	C	$4.00	Why I Left The False Westcott & Hort Greek Text	Rasmussen, Dr. Roland
0925/1-5	C	$14.00	Wonderful Word Of God-5 cassettes, 9 hours	Waite, Dr. D. A.
0901	37	$3.00	Word of God on Trial, The	Barnett, Dr. Robert
			h. Theories & Heresies of Westcott & Hort	
1251	200	$20.00	Answer To Stewart Custer's Booklet--KJB Controversy	Waite, Dr. D. A.
1100	C	$4.00	Apostasy & More Apostasy Of Westcott & Hort	Rasmussen, Dr. Roland
1101	C	$4.00	Approval of Westcott & Hort's Apost. By BJU	Woodbridge, Dr. Charle
2461	3	5/$1.50	Chronological Significance of Westcott & Hort's Heresy	Anonymous
2182/2	C	$4.00	Critical Text & W/H's Tie With Greek Philosophy	Gibson/S'tler
175/VCR	C	$15.00	Debate On Westcott/Hort vs Textus Receptus Greek Texts	Waite, Dr. D. A./Custer
1175TP	C	$4.00	Debate On Westcott/Hort vs Textus Receptus Greek Texts	Waite, Dr. D. A./Custer
BFT/05	C	$4.00	Doctrines Changed By Westcott/Ht.Text (#1) (Radio #17-20)	Waite, Dr. D. A.
BFT/06	C	$4.00	Doctrines Changed By Westcott/Ht.Text (#2) (Radio #21-24)	Waite, Dr. D. A.
1997	5	3/$1.50	Gnosticism And The N.T. Text--Heresies In Westcott/Ht.Te	Strouse, Dr. Thomas M.
1850/2	C	$4.00	Heresies Of Westcott/Hort & Testimonies On KJB	Sightler/Al.
BFT/07	C	$4.00	Heresies Of Westcott/Ht.(#1) (Bible, God, Man) (Radio #25-	Waite, Dr. D. A.
BFT/08	C	$4.00	Heresies Of Westcott/Ht.(#2) (Satan, Church) (Radio #29-32	Waite, Dr. D. A.
BFT/09	C	$4.00	Heresies Of Westcott/Ht.(#3) (Christ's Person) (Radio #33-3	Waite, Dr. D. A.
BFT/10	C	$4.00	Heresies Of Westcott/Ht.(#4) (Christ's Work) (Radio #37-40	Waite, Dr. D. A.
1889	C	$4.00	History Of Biblical Deviations From T.R.--Anti-W/H	Sightler, Dr. James
2031	15	$1.50	Importance Of Hodge/Warfield In Accepting Westcott/Ht.E	Sightler, Dr. James
1303	530	$25.00	Intro. To Revised Greek Text (an erroneous theory)	Hort, Fenton John A.
1866	928	$45.00	Life And Letters Of Brooke Foss Westcott--Data	Westcott, Arthur
1867	997	$48.00	Life And Letters Of Fenton John Anthony Hort--Data	Hort, Arthur F
1156	C	$4.00	Peril of Following Wrong Leaders & David and Goliath	Waite, Dr. D. A.
0611	640	$25.00	Revision Revised, The (New HARDBACK Book!)	Burgon, Dean John W.
250/1-19	C	$60.00	Seminar On Bible Texts & Translations	Waite, Dr. D. A.
2788	8	2/$1.50	The Green Eggs & Ham False Theory of Westcott & Hort	Smith, O. Ray
2574	14	$1.50	The Westcott and Hort Text Under Fire	Everts, William Wallace
1845	66	$6.50	Theological Errors In Westcott/Hort Texts--158 vv.	Waite, Dr. D. A.
0595	38	$3.00	Theological Heresies Of Westcott & Hort	Waite, Dr. D. A.
BFT/03	C	$4.00	Theological Heresies Of Westcott/Hort (Radio #9-12)	Waite, Dr. D. A.
2695	36	$3.00	Westcott & Hort's Greek Text & Theory Refuted--from Rev	Waite, Dr. D. A.
2262	C	$4.00	Westcott & Hort's Heresies Vs. Superior KJB Text	Waite, Dr. D. A.
TD/55-5	C	$15.00	Westcott & Hort's Theological Heresies (#1-5)	Waite, Dr. D. A.
2610	5	2/$1.50	Westcott Denied `Flesh' Resurrection	Lake, Dr. Kirsopp
1131	38	$4.00	Westcott's Clever Denial Of Christ's Bodily Resurrection	Waite, Dr. D. A.
			i. Old Testament Textual Defense	
2696	225	$11.00	A Scientific Investigation of the Old Testament	Wilson, Dr. Robert Dick

Item ##	P/C	Gift	Title	Author
			BFT Brochure #1 23 KJB/TR Defense	
			15. Reading of the Bible (Cassette Commentaries)	
0999/1-31	C	$75.00	Yearly Bible Reading Brief Commentary (31-2hr.Cass)	Waite, Dr. D. A.
			16. Reading of the Bible (Cassette Reading)	
BFTD/88-8	C	$7.00	BFT Radio King James Bible's Readability Vindicated, (#1-	Waite, Dr. D. A.
0777/1-43	C	######	Yearly Bible Reading On Cassettes-(43 2-hr.cass.)	Waite, Dr. D. A.
			17. Reading of the Bible (Yearly Reading Schedule)	
1024	C	$4.00	Bible Read And Preached, The (2 Tim. 3:16-4:5)	Waite, Dr. D. A.
0179	2	0/$1.5	Yearly Bible Reading Schedule-85 verses per day	Waite, Dr. D. A.
			18. The Bible as the Rule of Faith & Practice	
0008	16	$1.50	Bible—Baptists' Only Rule of Faith & Practice, The	Fleming, M.D.
			19. Texts of the Bible (English/Hebrew/Greek, etc.)	
2757	830	$6.00	An Award King James Bible	Jubilee Publishers
2733	253	$25.00	Codex Vaticanus—Edited Edition—Warning! Danger!	Maius, Angelus
2707	53	$5.50	Did Jesus and the Apostles Quote the Septuagint (LXX)?	DiVietro, Dr. Kirk
0339	90	$2.00	Gospel of John, The—Special Edition by E.R. Taylor	Taylor, E.R.,Ed
0471	487	$14.00	Greek New Testament, The—Received Text	TBS Staff
0382	1	4/$1.50	Indian Version Of Psalm 23	Crawford, I.
0186	811	$26.00	Interlinear Greek/English New Testament (Flexible Cover)	Berry, George
1102	999	$37.00	King James Version—1611 Edition	KJB Translators
2432	138	$7.00	Manuscript Evidence of the N.T., Right Estimation	Birks, Thomas
1427	32	$3.00	Noah Webster's Bible Translation & Testimony	Webster,Noah
0239	29	$2.50	Selected Proverbs	Taylor, E. R.
2488	20	$3.00	Spanish (1960) N.T.'s Departures from the Greek T.R. (Mat	Waite, Dr. D. A.
2731	44	$4.50	Spanish N.T. (1960) 45 Departures from Textus Receptus	Waite, Dr. D. A.
2161	58	$6.00	The Septuagint—A Critical Analysis	Jones, Dr. Floyd
2779VCR	C	$15.00	The Spanish Bible Is the 1602 Valera Version—	Park, Rev. Wm. A.
2708	48	$5.00	Where the KJB Leaves Theodore Beza 1598 Greek	DiVietro, Dr. Kirk
			20. Versions & Translations of the Bible Analyzed	
			a. Introductory Material on Bible Translations	
			(1) Doctrines Affected by New Versions	
2715	18	$2.00	Another Bible—19 Doctrines Compared in Five Versions	Baker, Robert M.
2002/3	C	$4.00	Atonement & Preservation/Spanish TR/Doctrinal Heart #2	VanKleeck +
0670	19	$3.00	Bible Doctrines Affected By New Versions	Freeman,Rev.P
2286/1-7	C	$21.00	Defending The King James Bible—Bible Institute Course	Waite, Dr. D. A.
2286VC1-3	C	$35.00	Defending The King James Bible—Bible Institute Course	Waite, Dr. D. A.
BFTD/01	C	$4.00	Doctrinal Defects In Greek Texts—#1 (Daily #1-20)	Waite, Dr. D. A.
BFTD/02	C	$4.00	Doctrinal Defects In Greek Texts—#2 (Daily #21-40)	Waite, Dr. D. A.
BFTD/03	C	$4.00	Doctrinal Defects In Greek Texts—#3 (Daily #41-60)	Waite, Dr. D. A.
BFTD/04	C	$4.00	Doctrinal Defects In Greek Texts—#4 (Daily #61-80)	Waite, Dr. D. A.
1595/4	C	$4.00	Doctrinal Defects In The NASV/NIV/RSV—14 Of Them	Waite, Dr. D. A.
1613-P	7	$1.50	Doctrinal Deviations (14) In New Versions—outline	Waite, Dr. D. A.
1988/3	C	$4.00	Doctrinal Deviations (40) In NIV/NASV/NKJB Versions	Waite, Dr. D. A.
2005/1-3	C	$9.00	Doctrinal Errors In NIV/NASV/NKJB—70 Passages	Waite, Dr. D. A.
2005VCR	C	$15.00	Doctrinal Errors In NIV/NASV/NKJB—70 Passages	Waite, Dr. D. A.
2726VCR	C	$15.00	Doctrinal Heart of the Bible—Removed from Modern Versio	Moorman, Dr. Jack
1923	2	5/$1.50	Doctrinal Terms (44) Missing/Reduced In N.I.V.	Waite, Dr. D. A.

BFT Brochure #1   24   KJB/TR Defense

Item ##	P/C	Gift	Title	Author
BFT/05	C	$4.00	Doctrines Changed By Westcott/Ht.Text (#1) (Radio #17-20)	Waite, Dr. D. A.
BFT/06	C	$4.00	Doctrines Changed By Westcott/Ht.Text (#2) (Radio #21-24)	Waite, Dr. D. A.
BFT/54	C	$4.00	Dr.E.Pickering Refuted On KJB--#2 (Radio #213-216)	Waite, Dr. D. A.
2386	53	$5.00	Essays on Bible Translation. (Good historical data.)	Sightler, Dr. James
2002/1	C	$4.00	Inspiration/Every Word Of God/Doctrinal Heart #1	Hollowood,D.+
2482	C	$4.00	KJB Questions & Answers & 23 Errors of Versions on the S	Waite, Dr. D. A.
2482VCR	C	$15.00	KJB Questions & Answers & 23 Errors of Versions on the S	Waite, Dr. D. A.
2108/2	C	$4.00	KJB Superiority--Translation Technique & Theology	Waite, Dr. D. A.
2450	39	$4.00	Myths About the KJB--Myth 3 No Doctrinal Differences in	Cloud, Rev. David
2335	696	$17.00	New Age Bible Versions--Exposes Men/Messages/Manuscri	Riplinger, Mrs.Gail A.
2679	C	$4.00	Superior King James Bible Theology	Waite, Dr. D. A.
2429	C	$4.00	SW Church Interviews Mrs. Riplinger on KJB (Wrote #233	Riplinger, Mrs.Gail A.
2554	C	$4.00	The Doctrinal Superiority of the King James Bible	Waite, Dr. D. A.
2126	C	$4.00	Theological Error's In Versions & Faith's Fight	Waite, Dr. D. A.
BFT/50	C	$4.00	Theological Errors In Versions--#1 (Radio #197-00)	Waite, Dr. D. A.
BFT/51	C	$4.00	Theological Errors In Versions--#2 (Radio #201-204)	Waite, Dr. D. A.
BFT/52	C	$4.00	Theological Errors In Versions--#3 (Radio #205-208)	Waite, Dr. D. A.
1845	66	$6.50	Theological Errors In Westcott/Hort Texts--158 vv.	Waite, Dr. D. A.
2522	C	$4.00	Theological Superiority of the KJB + Bible Q. & A.	Waite, Dr. D. A.
BFT/53	C	$4.00	Version Error/Pickering Answer--#4 (Radio #209-212)	Waite, Dr. D. A.
2518	118	$10.00	Which Bible is God's Word?--Answers to Version Question	Riplinger, Mrs.Gail A.

(2) General Concepts About Translations

1968/3	C	$4.00	Bible Versions & KJB Superiority + Giving & Grace	Waite, Dr. D. A.
1545	32	$3.00	Bible Versions And Perversions--Warning By DeHaan	DeHaan,Dr.M.R.
1324/1-4	C	$12.00	Bible Versions--The Basics For A Local Church	Anderson,Rev.
1814	35	$3.50	Bibles--And Bibles, Why Bible Versions Multiply	Von Rohr,Jr.,Rev.O.E.
0428	C	$5.00	Biblical Translations Tape (c 1.5 hrs.)	Waite, Dr. D. A.
0427	49	$5.00	Biblical Translations--Introductory Study	Waite, Dr. D. A.
1267	35	$3.50	Biblical Translations-Defects Of NIV-Part 1	Waite, Dr. D. A.
0820	14	$2.00	Brief Hist. Survey Of Impact Of Modern Versions	King,C.P.
0049	33	$3.50	Christian Approach to the Evaluation of English Versions	Fowler, Ev. W.
2286/1-7	C	$21.00	Defending The King James Bible--Bible Institute Course	Waite, Dr. D. A.
2286VC1-3	C	$35.00	Defending The King James Bible--Bible Institute Course	Waite, Dr. D. A.
1255/3	C	$4.00	Diabolical Curse Of 'Dynamic Equivalency' Translation	Waite, Dr. D. A.
1337/1-3	C	$9.00	Dynamic Equivalency--The "Translation" Plague!	Waite, Dr. D. A.
1337VCR	C	$15.00	Dynamic Equivalency--The "Translation" Plague!	Waite, Dr. D. A.
0621	117	$5.00	Eeny/Meeny/Miny/Mo--To Which Translation Shall I Go	Paulson,R.
2386	53	$5.00	Essays on Bible Translation. (Good historical data.)	Sightler, Dr. James
0952	72	$5.00	Evaluating Versions Of The N.T.	Fowler,Rev.W.
1256	192	$10.00	Future Of The Bible	VanBruggen,Dr.
2191	12	$1.50	Modern Bible Translations--Should We Trust Them?	Hamilton,Ste.
0836	16	$1.50	Modern Versions & 19th Century Critics	Ecob,J.R.
0876	16	$1.50	Modern Versions & Ancient Manuscripts	Ecob,J.R.
0936	12	$1.50	NCC Moves To Put Women's Lib Above Bible	Stang, Alan
1210	8	$1.50	Position Paper On The Versions Of The Bible	Fuller, Dr. David Otis
2558	375	$19.00	Roman Catholic and Protestant Bibles Compared	Jacobus, Dr. M. W.
1250/1-19	C	$60.00	Seminar On Bible Texts & Translations	Waite, Dr. D. A.

Item ##	P/C	Gift	Title	Author
2081	6	5/$1.50	Should Churches Be Concerned On Bible Translations?	Graham,Dr.M.
2382	8	3/$1.50	Some Problems With Bible Translations	Daniel, Grady
0207	8	2/$1.50	Translation Or Paraphrase?	Steele, Dr. F. R.
1848/12	C	$4.00	When Will Alterations Of Our Bible Stop?	Waite, Dr. D. A.
2160	184	$18.50	Which Version Is The Bible?	Jones, Dr. Floyd
			(3) Paraphrases of the Bible (General Concepts)	
1255/3	C	$4.00	Diabolical Curse Of 'Dynamic Equivalency' Translation	Waite, Dr. D. A.
1337/1-3	C	$9.00	Dynamic Equivalency--The "Translation" Plague!	Waite, Dr. D. A.
1337VCR	C	$15.00	Dynamic Equivalency--The "Translation" Plague!	Waite, Dr. D. A.
1256	253	$12.00	Future Of The Bible	VanBruggen,Dr.
0535	10	2/$1.50	Paraphrase Is Not The Bible	Woychuk,Dr. N.
2382	8	3/$1.50	Some Problems With Bible Translations	Daniel, Grady
2488	20	$3.00	Spanish (1960) N.T.'s Departures from the Greek T.R. (Mat	Waite, Dr. D. A.
			(4) Various Translations Analyzed in One Study	
0348	154	$12.00	Bible Version Manual	Clarke, D.T.
1324/1-4	C	$12.00	Bible Versions--The Basics For A Local Church	Anderson,Rev.
0908	16	$2.00	Critique On Bible Translations	Ditty, Dr. William
2286/1-7	C	$21.00	Defending The King James Bible--Bible Institute Course	Waite, Dr. D. A.
2286VC1-3	C	$35.00	Defending The King James Bible--Bible Institute Course	Waite, Dr. D. A.
0313	44	$3.50	Is Your Bible Really The Word of God?	Starr, Rev. Roland
1238	44	$4.00	KJB & Luther's Bible vs NIV & New World Translation	Seeger,Paul
0583	4	3/$1.50	Modern Bible Versions Are Dangerous	Reynolds, Dr. Marion
2623	48	$3.00	Modern Bibles--the Dark Secret	Moorman, Dr. Jack
0209	27	$2.00	Modern Versions of the Bible	Rockwood, Dr. Perry F.
2335	696	$17.00	New Age Bible Versions--Exposes Men/Messages/Manuscri	Riplinger, Mrs.Gail A.
1008	30	$3.50	Perfected Or Perverted?-Exposure of Modern Versions	Ward,Norman
0312	8	3/$1.50	Should You Choose The Bible Of Your Choice?	Clarke, D.T.
2194	67	$5.00	The Old Is Better--Some Bible Versions Considered	Levell,Alfred
0160	8	2/$1.50	Today's Modern Versions	Cook, C.W.W.
0781	6	2/$1.50	Translations Trap, The	Keener,Rev.F.
2485	C	$4.00	Unholy Bible Versions of the New Age	Marrs,Texe
2518	118	$10.00	Which Bible is God's Word?--Answers to Version Question	Riplinger, Mrs.Gail A.
			(5) Errors of Dynamic Equivalency in Versions	
2286/1-7	C	$21.00	Defending The King James Bible--Bible Institute Course	Waite, Dr. D. A.
2286VC1-3	C	$35.00	Defending The King James Bible--Bible Institute Course	Waite, Dr. D. A.
1594-P	340	$12.00	Defending The King James Bible--Four Superiorities	Waite, Dr. D. A.
1255/3	C	$4.00	Diabolical Curse Of 'Dynamic Equivalency' Translation	Waite, Dr. D. A.
2176	52	$4.00	Dynamic Equivalency--Death Knell Of Pure Scripture	Cloud, Rev. David
1337/1-3	C	$9.00	Dynamic Equivalency--The "Translation" Plague!	Waite, Dr. D. A.
1337VCR	C	$15.00	Dynamic Equivalency--The "Translation" Plague!	Waite, Dr. D. A.
1256	253	$12.00	Future Of The Bible	VanBruggen,Dr.
1548	4	3/$1.50	GARBC--Problems With 'Bibles International'/Dynamic Eq	Pifer,Rev.W.
1554	6	$1.50	GARBC--Translation Questions To 'Bibles International'	Cloud, Rev. David
			b. Specific Bible Translations Analyzed	
			(1) The American Standard Version (ASV)	
0986	84	$8.50	ASV, NASV & NIV Departures from Traditional Hebrew/G	Waite, Dr. D. A.
2335	696	$17.00	New Age Bible Versions--Exposes Men/Messages/Manuscri	Riplinger, Mrs.Gail A.

Item ##	P/C	Gift	Title	Author
1494-P	187	$15.00	New American Standard Version Analyzed & Refuted	Waite, Dr. D. A.
1123	263	$13.00	Our Authorixed Bible Vindicated (Re-Print Edition)	Wilkinson, Benjamin
2518	118	$10.00	Which Bible is God's Word?--Answers to Version Question	Riplinger, Mrs.Gail A.
			(2) The Amplified Bible (AB)	
0892	4	2/$1.50	Amplified New Testament Critique	TBS Staff
			(3) The English Revised Version--1881 (ERV)	
1492	32	$3.00	Case Against The English Revised Version Of 1881	Hoste,Wm.
1612	135	$7.00	English Revised Version Text Is "Un-Authorized"	Samson,G.W.
1123	263	$13.00	Our Authorixed Bible Vindicated (Re-Print Edition)	Wilkinson, Benjamin
1560	32	$3.00	Remove Not The Ancient Landmark--Case Against E.R.V.	Hoste, William
			(4) Good News for Modern Man (TEV)	
0001	6	2/$1.50	American Bible Society & The Blood of Jesus Christ	Waite, Dr. D. A.
2519	27	$2.50	Good News Bible & Translator Bratcher--Deception	Cloud, Rev. David
0675	19	$2.00	Good News Bible--Analysis (8 Test Texts)	Paisley, Dr. Ian R. K..
1491	8	2/$1.50	Good News For Modern Man (T.E.V.)--Bratcher Exposed	Cloud, Rev. David
0982	4	3/$1.50	Southern Bapt. Translator Fired--Robert Bratcher	Bynum, Pastor E. L.
			(5) The Living Version (LV)	
0289	C	$4.00	Finding The Needle In The Haystack--Living Bible Exposed	Waite, Dr. D. A.
0086	6	2/$1.50	I wouldn't Dare Treat the Bible That Way!	Fuller, Dr. David Otis
0386	47	$3.00	King James Version, The vs Taylor's Paraphrase	Greene, Dr. Oliver B.
0199	92	$3.00	Livid Libel of the Scriptures of Truth, The	Paisley, Dr. Ian R. K..
2182/1	C	$4.00	Living Bible's Author/Correcting The Uncorrectable	LaMore/Steward
0663	8	$1.50	Living Bible, The--Critique (Trin. Bible Soc.)	TBS Staff
0127	344	$9.00	Paraphrased Perversion of the Bible, Living Bible	Nowlin, Dr. Gene
FTD/64-6	C	$9.00	The "Living Version" Exposed (#1-3)	Waite, Dr. D. A.
			(6) The New American Version (NASV)	
0986	84	$8.50	ASV, NASV & NIV Departures from Traditional Hebrew/G	Waite, Dr. D. A.
0755	6	3/$1.50	Correction Or Corruption--NASB & NIV Critique	Mosley,Bill
0484	24	$2.50	Critical Examination Of NASB	Madden,D. K.
0483	31	$3.00	Critique Of The New American Standard Bible	Falnigan, R.W.
1518	38	2/$1.50	DBS Tracts--Defects In The "NASV" (Cf. #1494-P)	Waite, Dr. D. A.
2245	20	$1.50	Defending God's True Words Until Christ Returns	Proper,Gordon
2459	C	$4.00	Dr. Frank Logsdon's NASV Part & Friendship with Dewey	Logsdon, Dr. S. Frank
2226	14	$1.50	From The NASV To The KJB--Dr. Frank Logsdon's Story	Logsdon, Dr. S. Frank
0688	8	3/$1.50	N.A.S.V., The--Can It Be Trusted?	Reynolds, Dr. Marion
0656	4	3/$1.50	N.A.S.V.--A Critique, The (Trinitarian Bible Soc.)	TBS Staff
0512	6	3/$1.50	NASV & The Deity Of Christ, The	Carter, Cecil
1494-P	187	$15.00	New American Standard Version Analyzed & Refuted	Waite, Dr. D. A.
494/1-11	C	$30.00	New American Standard Version--2,959 Comments	Waite, Dr. D. A.
1399	2	4/$1.50	New American Standard Version--A Critique	TBS Staff
0109	16	$1.50	On Your Guard! God's Word Uderminded (NASV)	Fuller, Dr. David Otis
0735	16	$2.00	Review Of NIV & NASV	Rockwood, Dr. Perry F.
1027	C	$4.00	They Have Taken Away My Lord--NIV,NASV Easter Perv.	Waite, Dr. D. A.
			(7) The New English Version (NEV)	
0251	C	$4.00	Critique of New English Bible & RSV's Common Bible	Paisley, Dr. Ian R. K..
0262	72	$3.50	New English Bible Exposed, The	Paisley, Dr. Ian R. K..

Item ##	P/C	Gift	Title	Author
0851	5	2/$1.50	New English Bible, The—Critique Against It	Carter, Cecil
1394	8	2/$1.50	New English Bible—An Ecumenical & Heretical Bible	Westminster
			(8) The New International Version (NIV)	
2768	56	$4.00	A Brief Analysis of the NIV Inclusive Language Edition (NI	Waite, Dr. D. A.
0393	150	$15.00	Analysis Of The New International Version	Nowlin, Dr. Gene
0986	84	$8.50	ASV, NASV & NIV Departures from Traditional Hebrew/G	Waite, Dr. D. A.
1267	35	$3.50	Biblical Translations-Defects Of NIV-Part 1	Waite, Dr. D. A.
2032	22	$3.50	Can The New International Version Be Trusted?	Carter, Cecil
0755	6	3/$1.50	Correction Or Corruption—NASB & NIV Critique	Mosley,Bill
1801	4	3/$1.50	Critique Of The New International Version(NIV)	Green,Jay
2054	38	2/$1.50	DBS Tracts—Defects In The "NIV" (Cf. #1749)	Waite, Dr. D. A.
2245	20	$1.50	Defending God's True Words Until Christ Returns	Proper,Gordon
1255/3	C	$4.00	Diabolical Curse Of 'Dynamic Equivalency' Translation	Waite, Dr. D. A.
1923	2	5/$1.50	Doctrinal Terms (44) Missing/Reduced In N.I.V.	Waite, Dr. D. A.
1337/1-3	C	$9.00	Dynamic Equivalency—The "Translation" Plague!	Waite, Dr. D. A.
1337VCR	C	$15.00	Dynamic Equivalency—The "Translation" Plague!	Waite, Dr. D. A.
1256	192	$10.00	Future Of The Bible	VanBruggen,Dr.
2640	107	$8.00	If the Foundations Be Destroyed—N.I.V. Against Jesus	Salliby, Chick
2490/8	C	$4.00	Lesbian Virginia Mollenkott Exposed & Her Part on the NI	Waite, Yvonne S.
2491	C	$4.00	Lesbian Virginia Mollenkott—Her Lesbianism & Part in the	Waite, Yvonne S.
1726	83	$8.00	Missing In Modern Bibles—Nestle-Aland & NIV Errors	Moorman, Dr.Jack
0924	21	$2.00	N.I.V.-Paraphrased Perversion, Not Accurate Trans.	Waite, Dr. D. A.
2670	8	2/$1.50	New International Version (NIV) vs. the King James Bible	Smith, Rev. O. Ray
0754	14	$1.50	New International Version Critique	Brown,Rev.T.H.
1801	4	3/$1.50	New International Version Is Not A Reliable Version	Green,Jay
1322	70	$7.00	New International Version Under Suspicion	Seeger,Paul
1749/1-16	C	$40.00	New International Version—4,607 Translation Errors	Waite, Dr. D. A.
1749-P	284	$25.00	New International Version—6,653 Defects Documented	Waite, Dr. D. A.
0548	13	$1.50	New International Version—Critique	Carter, Cecil
2033	36	$3.00	New International Version—What We Need To Know	Anderson,G & E
1112/1-16	C	$40.00	NIV Critique From Orig.Lang.–A Paraphrased Perverion	Waite, Dr. D. A.
1268	3	4/$1.50	NIV Downgrades Our Lord Jesus Christ	Fowler,Ev.W.
BFTD/05	C	$4.00	NIV—A Perverted Paraphrase—#1 (Daily #81-100)	Waite, Dr. D. A.
BFTD/14	C	$4.00	NIV—A Perverted Paraphrase—#10 (Daily #261-280)	Waite, Dr. D. A.
BFTD/15	C	$4.00	NIV—A Perverted Paraphrase—#11 (Daily #281-300)	Waite, Dr. D. A.
BFTD/16	C	$4.00	NIV—A Perverted Paraphrase—#12 (Daily #301-320)	Waite, Dr. D. A.
BFTD/17	C	$4.00	NIV—A Perverted Paraphrase—#13 (Daily #321-340)	Waite, Dr. D. A.
BFTD/18	C	$4.00	NIV—A Perverted Paraphrase—#14 (Daily #341-360)	Waite, Dr. D. A.
BFTD/19	C	$4.00	NIV—A Perverted Paraphrase—#15 (Daily #361-380)	Waite, Dr. D. A.
BFTD/20	C	$4.00	NIV—A Perverted Paraphrase—#16 (Daily #381-400)	Waite, Dr. D. A.
BFTD/21	C	$4.00	NIV—A Perverted Paraphrase—#17 (Daily #401-420)	Waite, Dr. D. A.
BFTD/22	C	$4.00	NIV—A Perverted Paraphrase—#18 (Daily #421-440)	Waite, Dr. D. A.
BFTD/23	C	$4.00	NIV—A Perverted Paraphrase—#19 (Daily #441-460)	Waite, Dr. D. A.
BFTD/06	C	$4.00	NIV—A Perverted Paraphrase—#2 (Daily #101-120)	Waite, Dr. D. A.
BFTD/24	C	$4.00	NIV—A Perverted Paraphrase—#20 (Daily #461-480)	Waite, Dr. D. A.
BFTD/25	C	$4.00	NIV—A Perverted Paraphrase—#21 (Daily #481-500)	Waite, Dr. D. A.
BFTD/26	C	$4.00	NIV—A Perverted Paraphrase—#22 (Daily #501-520)	Waite, Dr. D. A.

Item ##	P/C	Gift	Title	Author
BFTD/27	C	$4.00	NIV–A Perverted Paraphrase–#23 (Daily #521-540)	Waite, Dr. D. A.
BFTD/28	C	$4.00	NIV–A Perverted Paraphrase–#24 (Daily #541-560)	Waite, Dr. D. A.
BFTD/29	C	$4.00	NIV–A Perverted Paraphrase–#25 (Daily #561-580)	Waite, Dr. D. A.
BFTD/07	C	$4.00	NIV–A Perverted Paraphrase–#3 (Daily #121-140)	Waite, Dr. D. A.
BFTD/08	C	$4.00	NIV–A Perverted Paraphrase–#4 (Daily #141-160)	Waite, Dr. D. A.
BFTD/09	C	$4.00	NIV–A Perverted Paraphrase–#5 (Daily #161-180)	Waite, Dr. D. A.
BFTD/10	C	$4.00	NIV–A Perverted Paraphrase–#6 (Daily #181-200)	Waite, Dr. D. A.
BFTD/11	C	$4.00	NIV–A Perverted Paraphrase–#7 (Daily #201-220)	Waite, Dr. D. A.
BFTD/12	C	$4.00	NIV–A Perverted Paraphrase–#8 (Daily #221-240)	Waite, Dr. D. A.
BFTD/13	C	$4.00	NIV–A Perverted Paraphrase–#9 (Daily #241-260)	Waite, Dr. D. A.
0802	4	3/$1.50	Prove All Things–N.I.V. Critique	Start,Rev.D.T
2791	C	$4.00	Radio Exposure of the NIV's Inclusive Language Edition ov	Waite, Dr.&Hutchings
0735	16	$2.00	Review Of NIV & NASV	Rockwood, Dr. Perry F.
0225	8	5/$1.50	Should We Trust The New International Version?	Bynum, Pastor E. L.
2298	14	$1.50	Sodomy And The NIV–Proper Persp.On Bible	Graham, Rev. Carl
TD/67,71-	C	$21.00	The New International Version Exposed(#1-7)	Waite, Dr. D. A.
BFTD/67	C	$4.00	The New International Version Exposed–Introductory	Waite, Dr. D. A.
1027	C	$4.00	They Have Taken Away My Lord–NIV,NASV Easter Perv.	Waite, Dr. D. A.
2082	12	2/$1.50	What Is The Difference Between The KJB And The NIV?	Martin,R.W.
			(9) The New King James Version (NKJB)	
2111	24	$2.50	Brief Refutation Of The New King James Version Ads	Waite, Dr. D. A.
1355	8	3/$1.50	Careful Look At The 'New King James Bible'	Reynolds, Dr. Marion
1547	2	7/$1.50	Church Resolution Against New King James Version	Calvary Bp.Ch.
1465	28	2/$1.50	DBS Tract–Defects In The "New KJV" (Cf. #1442)	Waite, Dr. D. A.
1738	40	$1.50	DBS Tracts–Awana Churches, Keep Using The "Old" KJB	Waite, Dr. D. A./Barnett
2245	20	$1.50	Defending God's True Words Until Christ Returns	Proper,Gordon
2075	11	$1.50	Evaluating The New King James Version	VanKleeck, Rev. Peter
2002/2	C	$4.00	History Of Westcott/Ht.Heresy + KJB Verse + NKJB Defect	Sightler +
1347	6	3/$1.50	Is The "New King James Bible" The Word Of God?	Sargent,Rob.
0858	7	3/$1.50	Is The New KJV Just Another Translation?	Bero,Rev.Chas
1507	10	$1.50	New King James Version & Revised Authorized Version	Brown,T.
1442	95	$10.00	New King James Version Analyzed (Cf. #1465 Tract)	Waite, Dr. D. A.
0818	8	2/$1.50	New KJV N.T., The–A Critique (Trin. Bible Society)	TBS Staff
1739/6	C	$4.00	New KJV–A Danger To Our Children & Devotions	Waite, Yvonne S.+GH
1367/1-9	C	$25.00	New KJV–Detailed Critique With 2,675 Comments	Waite, Dr. D. A.
1348	24	$1.50	Remarks On New King James Version & Rev.Auth. Vers.	Madden,D.K.
1120	6	3/$1.50	Should Bible-Loving Christians Us The New KJV?	Oldfield,Rev.
1517/5	C	$4.00	Translation Confusion In Churches + New KJV Defects	Pangburn/DAW
1349	6	3/$1.50	Why I Reject The New King James Version	Cimino,Rev.D.
			(10) The New Scofield Reference Version (NSRV)	
1517/3	C	$4.00	New Scofield/Textual Criticism Made Easy/Q & A	Van §Kleeck,Wm
0517	11	$2.50	Plague Of Egypt, The–Critique of New Scofield Bible	Estep, Rev.G.
			(11) The Reader's Digest Version (RDV)	
1107	15	$1.50	Reader's Digest Bible Critique–Don't Face-Lift	McIntire,Rev.
			(12) The Revised Standard Version (RSV)	
0251	C	$4.00	Critique of New English Bible & RSV's Common Bible	Paisley, Dr. Ian R. K.
0138	14	$2.00	One Hundred One Arguments Against the NCC's RSV	Waite, Dr. D. A.

Item ##	P/C	Gift	Title	Author
0852	11	$1.50	Revised Standard Version--Critique Against It	Carter, Cecil
1900	30	$2.00	RSV, The--A Friend or a Traitor to the Truth?	Gray, Dr. Clayton H.
2313	7	$1.50	Why I Cannot Accept The RSV	MacRae, Dr. Allan
			(13) The King James Bible--1611 (KJB--1611)	
1495	12	3/$1.50	DBS Tracts--KJB 1611 Compared To The Present KJB	Waite, Dr. D. A.
1294	25	$2.50	KJB Of 1611 Compared To KJB Of 1917 Old Scofield	Waite, Dr. D. A.
			(14) The New Jerusalem Version (NJV)	
1506	12	$1.50	New Jerusalem Bible--Critique Of NJB	TBS Staff
			(15) The New Revised Standard Version (NRSV)	
1859	5	2/$1.50	New R.S.V. Critique--"Your Comrades The Prophets"	Strouse, Dr. Thomas M.
			(16) The Dake's Version (DV)	
2285	5	3/$1.50	Dake's Bible Exposed--The Pentecostal Study Bible	Fisher, Rev. Richard
			(17) The Contemporary English Version (CEV)	
2724	8	2/$1.50	An Evaluation of the Contemporary English Version	Doom, Dr. Robert
BFTD/90-9	C	$9.00	BFT Radio Contemporary English Version (C.E.V.) Refute	Waite, Dr. D. A.
2721	36	$3.00	Contemporary English Version (CEV)--AntiChrist Version	Waite, Dr. D.
BFTD/63	C	$4.00	KJB Meter & the Contemporary English Version	Waite, Dr. D. A.
			(18) The "Politically Correct" N.T. (PCNT)	
2594	C	$4.00	The `Politically Correct N.T. Version' Refuted	Waite, Dr. D. A.
			(19) The 21st Century King James Version (KJ21)	
2668	12	$1.50	21st Century King James Version--Brief Critical Review	Madden, Mr. D. K.
			21. Word Lists for KJB (Key Words Defined Briefly)	
2719	591	$20.00	Archaic Words and the Authorized Version (1,015 words)	Vance, Dr. Laurence M.
1060	32	$1.50	Bible Word List (629 Difficult KJB Words Made Clear)	TBS Staff
2669	8	2/$1.50	Dictionary of Obsolete King James Bible Words	Smith, Rev. O. Ray
			22. Bible Societies--(United, American, Trinitarian)	
0001	6	2/$1.50	American Bible Society & The Blood of Jesus Christ	Waite, Dr. D. A.
1660	27	$3.00	Ecumenism & The United Bible Societies--Compromise	TBS Staff
1256	192	$10.00	Future Of The Bible	VanBruggen,Dr.
1561/1-2	C	$7.00	Trinitarian Bible Society's Andrew Brown Answered	Waite, Dr. D. A.
1856	22	$2.50	Trinitarian Bible Society--Changing Back? We Hope!	TBS/Browns
2170	84	$6.00	Unholy Hands On God's Holy Book--United Bible Society	Cloud, Rev. David
1516	60	$6.00	Unholy Hands on God's Holy Word--United Bible Society	Cloud, Rev. David
2179	25	$2.00	Wycliffe Bible Translators--Whither Bound?	Cloud, Rev. David
			23. Old Reprints on the KJB & Textus Receptus	
1757	347	$17.00	Authorized Edition (1611)--History Of & Changes In	Scrivener, Dr. Frederick
1160	316	$14.00	Causes Of Corruption Of The Traditional Text (hardback)	Burgon, Dean John W.
1643	924	$46.00	Codex B & Its Allies--A Study & An Indictment	Hoskier,H.C.
2124	96	$5.00	Dabney's 19th Century Defense of T.R. Against W & H	Dabney,Rev.R.
1619	801	$40.00	Dean John Burgon's Biography	Goulburn,Dr.E.
1612	135	$7.00	English Revised Version Text Is "Un-Authorized"	Samson,G.W.
2042	608	$30.00	Greek Text Of Stephens 1550 (1872, With Footnotes)	Scrivener, Dr. Frederick
0743	162	$7.00	Guide To Textual Criticism Of N.T.	Miller,Edward
1304	604	$30.00	Inquiry Into The Integrity Of The Gr.Vulgate Or T/R	Nolan, Rev. Frederick
1857	240	$12.00	Inside Story Of The Anglo American A.S.V. & R.S.V.	Coy,George H.
1220	567	$25.00	Inspiration & Interpretation	Burgon, Dean John W.

| BFT Brochure #1 | | 30 | | KJB/TR Defense |

Item ##	P/C	Gift	Title	Author
1303	530	$25.00	Intro. To Revised Greek Text (an erroneous theory)	Hort, Fenton John A.
1419	260	$13.00	King James Translators Revived--Biographical Notes	McClure, Alexander
1139	350	$15.00	Last 12 Verses Of Mark--BFT reprint	Burgon, Dean John W.
1123	263	$13.00	Our Authorized Bible Vindicated (Re-Print Edition)	Wilkinson, Benjamin
1285	920	$45.00	Plain Intro. To The Criticism Of The New Testament	Scrivener, Dr. Frederick
2039	224	$11.00	Plea For Received Greek Text & KJB Against Alford	Malan,Rev.S.C.
1626	9	$1.50	Spurgeon's Quotations Against The E.R.V. Of 1881	Gibson, Pastor Denis
1756	143	$7.00	Textual Commentary On Mathew 1-14--MSS Evidence	Miller,Edward
1159	350	$15.00	Traditional Text Of The Holy Gospels Vindicated (hardbac	Burgon, Dean John W.
			24. Obsolete or Archaic KJB Words	
2719	591	$20.00	Archaic Words and the Authorized Version (1,015 words)	Vance, Dr. Laurence M.
1060	32	$1.50	Bible Word List (629 Difficult KJB Words Made Clear)	TBS Staff
2669	8	2/$1.50	Dictionary of Obsolete King James Bible Words (490 words	Smith, Rev. O. Ray
2671	84	$5.00	Readability of the Authorized Version--7 Versions Compare	Waite, Jr., Mr. D. A.
			25. Bible Readability	
2486	277	$27.50	Reading Ease of the King James Bible--Six Versions Compa	Waite, Mr. D. A., Jr.
2671	84	$5.00	The Comparative Readability of the Authorized Version--7	Waite, Mr. D. A., Jr.
			26. Translators of the KJB and Others	
2109	8	2/$1.50	Bible Translator--An Ordained Adulterer (Lutheran)	News,Christ'n
2519	27	$2.50	Good News Bible & Translator Bratcher--Deception	Cloud, Rev. David
1419	260	$13.00	King James Translators Revived--Biographical Notes	McClure, Alexander
1121	45	$3.00	KJB Translators' Preface To Readers--With Glossary	Sasse (ed)
0890	12	$1.50	Learned Men,The--Biography Of KJB Translators	TBS Staff
0584	212	$11.50	Men Behind The King James Version, The	Paine, G.S.
0982	4	3/$1.50	Southern Baptist Translator Fired--Robert Bratcher	Bynum, Pastor E. L.
2811	183	$18.00	The King James Bible Translators	Opfell, Mrs. Olga S.
2700	464	$23.00	The Private Devotions of KJB Translator Lancelot Andrew	Andrewes, Lancelot
2326	166	$22.00	Translating for King James--Notes by Translator Rev. J. Bo	Bois, John
2179	25	$2.00	Wycliffe Bible Translators--Whither Bound?	Cloud, Rev. David

Q. Greek & Hebrew Language Texts & Studies

0471-G	269	$18.00	Beginner's Greek Grammar Of The New Testament	Davis, Dr. William H.
1163/1-8	C	$24.00	Bib. Hebrew Vocabulary & Exercises (Lambdin's Text)	Waite, Dr. D. A.
1162/1-40	C	######	Biblical Hebrew Course (40 Cassettes; 80 Hours)	Waite, Dr. D. A.
2474	430	$43.00	Complutensian Polyglot--Greek T.R. & Latin Vulgate	Ximenes,Cardinal
2469	170	$17.00	Dead Sea Qumran Scrolls--Isaiah, Order of Community etc.	Shrine of Book
2476	95	$9.50	Diatessaron (in English)--Harmony of Four Gospels	Tatian
1055/1-4	C	$12.00	English & Greek Reading Verse by Verse-Gosp.of John	Waite, Dr. D. A.
0060	53	$5.00	Granville Sharp's Rule--Proving Deity of Christ	Durham, Dr. Richard D.
2487	129	$13.00	Greek N.T. Text Underlying the KJB (Matt./Rom./Gal.)	DiVietro, Dr. Kirk D.
0471	487	$14.00	Greek New Testament, The--Received Text	TBS Staff
0471	487	$14.00	Greek New Testament, The--Received Text	TBS Staff
2042	608	$30.00	Greek Text Of Stephens 1550 (1872, With Footnotes)	Scrivener, Dr. Frederick
1142/1-2	C	$7.00	Heb.Verbs & Nouns By Their Frequency--Heb.To Eng.	Waite, Dr. D. A.
2064	1384	$50.00	Hebrew Masoretic O.T. Underlying KJB (Parallel KJB)	Ben Chayyim
1141	C	$4.00	Hebrew Words By Frequency In Bible	Waite, Dr. D. A.
2047	6	2/$1.50	Inspiration Of The Hebrew Letters And Vowel-Points	Bishop,G.S.
0186	811	$25.00	Interlinear Greek/English New Testament (Flexible Cover)	Berry, George

Item ##	P/C	Gift	Title	Author
1287	20	$1.50	Isaiah 9:6–Proof Of 'Wonderful,Counselor'Reading	TBS Staff
2477	290	$14.50	Manuscript 666 of the Four Gospels–The Harvard Manusc	Unknown Scribe
1753	C	$4.00	Ministry Of The Bible For Today–On Family Radio	Waite, Dr. D. A.
1260-P	270	$18.00	N.T. Greek Course–Davis Beginners' Grammar (1st ⅔Year)	Davis, Dr. William H.
0998/1-40	C	######	N.T. Greek Course–8 Sem. Hrs. (40-2hr.Cass;Grammar)(A)	Waite, Dr. D. A.
1260/1-37	C	######	N.T.Greek Course–8 Sem.Hrs. (40-2hr. ⅜Cass.;Grammar)(B	Waite, Dr. D. A.
2483	242	$24.00	Novi Testamenti–The Latin Vulgate New Testament	Jerome
2475	152	$15.00	Papyrus 66 in Greek–Parts of the Gospel of John	Unknown Scribe
0141	19	$2.00	Salvation By Grace Through Faith (Eph. 2:1-10)	Waite, Dr. D. A.
1670	668	$35.00	Scrivener's Greek New Testament–T.R. & W & H Texts Se	Scrivener, Dr. Frederick
1064/1-30	C	$80.00	Second Year Greek–Trans.Of John & Exegesis-30 cass.	Waite, Dr. D. A.
0159	93	$9.00	Successful Church–Exegesis of Titus, The	Waite, Dr. D. A.
2462	383	$38.00	Washington Manuscript of the Four Gospels	Danders,Henry A.

251 STUDY QUESTIONS
FOR *DEFENDING THE KING JAMES BIBLE*

*[The following questions were asked of his students by Dr. Waite when he taught a class using DEFENDING THE KING JAMES BIBLE as a textbook. It was a fourteen-week course, taught in the Spring of 1993. Each class was fifty minutes in length and covered about fourteen pages of the book. The classes were taught at the Bible Baptist Institute in Philadelphia, Pennsylvania. The questions were written down during the class by Mrs. Waite. The entire semester course is available on either 7 audio or 3 video cassettes. The audio is **B.F.T.** #2286/1-7 @ $21.00 + P&H. The video is **B.F.T.** #2286VC1-3 @ $35.00 + P&H]*

A. INTRODUCTORY QUESTIONS

1. In how many ways is the KING JAMES BIBLE superior to other books that are called "Bibles" or "Versions"? (See cover)
2. Name the KING JAMES BIBLE "superiorities." (See cover)
3. What do we mean when we say something is "superior" to something else?
4. Do you think we should "DEFEND" the KING JAMES BIBLE? Why, or why not?
   ### B. QUESTIONS FROM THE FOREWORD (pp. xi-xii)
5. Compared to the "Textus Receptus" (TR) Greek text that underlies the KING JAMES BIBLE, how many New Testament Greek words have been either ADDED, SUBTRACTED, or CHANGED in the so-called "Westcott and Hort" (WH) Greek text? (p. xii.2)
6. The differences between the Textus Receptus (TR) Greek New Testament text that underlies the KING JAMES BIBLE and the Westcott and Hort (WH) Greek text involve how many PAGES in the Greek text? (p. xii.2)
   ### C. QUESTIONS ON THE INTRODUCTION (pp. 1-5)
7. When we say that the KING JAMES BIBLE is "God's Words Kept Intact," what does the word "intact" mean? (p. 1.3)
8. What three things does DYNAMIC EQUIVALENCY do to the Words of God? (p. 1.6)
9. Out of the some 791,328 English words in the KING JAMES BIBLE, how many of them have changed their meaning a little since 1611 A.D.? (p. 1.8)

10. How many examples of DYNAMIC EQUIVALENCY did I find in the NEW KING JAMES VERSION? (p. 3.4) Over _____. In the NEW AMERICAN STANDARD VERSION? (p. 3.2) Over _____. In the NEW INTERNATIONAL VERSION? (p. 3.7) Over _____.

11. Comparing the 791,328 English words in the KING JAMES BIBLE, how many changes in SOUND does the AV 1611 have compared with the present KING JAMES BIBLE? (p. 3.9)

D. QUESTIONS ON CHAPTER I--BIBLE PRESERVATION (pp. 6-19)

12. What does it mean to believe in "BIBLE PRESERVATION"? (p. 6.4) What languages are referred to in the Biblical sense of this term? (Bible "Preservation" with a capital "P")

13. What are two reasons why we should believe in "BIBLE PRESERVATION" today? (p. 6.5)

14. How does Psalm 12:6-7 promise BIBLE PRESERVATION? (p. 6.7)

15. How does Psalm 105:8 promise BIBLE PRESERVATION? (p. 7.6)

16. What is the meaning of "IT IS WRITTEN" in Matthew 4:4? How does this meaning show BIBLE PRESERVATION? (pp. 9.1--9.9)

17. In how much detail did Christ promise BIBLE PRESERVATION of the Old Testament in Matthew 5:17-18? (p. 10.5)

18. To what extent does Matthew 24:35 promise BIBLE PRESERVATION? (pp. 11.2--13.2)

19. How does 1 Peter 1:23-25 promise BIBLE PRESERVATION? (pp. 14.1--14.6)

20. Does God keep His promises? (p. 14.8)

21. How does Romans 4:20-21 show that God keeps His promises? (p. 15.5)

22. What is a historic creed? (pp. 15.9--16.1)

23. Did the historic creeds say anything about a belief in BIBLE PRESERVATION? (p. 16.3)

24. What words in the historic creeds were used to indicate their belief in BIBLE PRESERVATION? (p. 16.4)

25. What did the historic creeds say about the need for translation of the original Hebrew and Greek languages? (p. 16.8)

26. What are four reasons why we can say that the KING JAMES BIBLE has "preserved" (with a small "p") the Words of God in English? (p. 17.2)

E. QUESTIONS ON CHAPTER II--SUPERIOR OLD TESTAMENT TEXT (pp. 20-61)

27. What is meant by the KING JAMES BIBLE's having "superior original language texts" when compared to the modern versions? (p. 20.4)

28. What Old Testament original language text was the source of the KING JAMES BIBLE? (p. 20.7)

29. What were some of the sources that were used to CORRECT the KING JAMES BIBLE'S Old Testament original language text for the New American Standard Version (NASV)? (p. 20.9)

30. What were some of the sources for the New International Version? (NIV) (pp. 21.5--22.5)

31. What were some of the sources for the New King James Version (NKJV)? (pp. 22.8--23.8)

32. What Bible verse would you use to prove that the Bible was accumulated and guarded by the Jews. What is involved in this? (pp. 23.8--24.6)

33. What were some of the methods used by the Jews to guard the Old Testament Hebrew Scriptures. (pp. 24.6--26.5)

34. What does "Masoretic" mean? (p. 26.6)

35. What did the Masoretes do with the Hebrew Scriptures? (p. 26.6)

36. Which Masoretic Hebrew text was used by the translators of the KING JAMES VERSION? (p. 27.5)

37. What was the date of this text? (p. 27.6)

38. Who was the editor of this text? (p. 27.6)

39. What is the name of the edition of this text? (p. 27.6)

40. What is the name of the Hebrew text used by the modern versions of the Bible since 1937? (p. 27.9)

41. What is the name of the Hebrew Bible used by these versions? (p. 27.9)

42. Who was the editor of this Hebrew text? (p. 27.9)

43. What is the manuscript that was followed in this Hebrew text? (p. 28.1)

44. What is the date of this manuscript? (p. 28.1)

45. What reason is given for using this ONE Hebrew manuscript instead of the entire mass of Masoretic Hebrew manuscripts as used in the KING JAMES BIBLE? (p. 28.3)

46. About how many changes does Kittel's *BIBLIA HEBRAICA* suggest in the footnotes? (p. 28.2)

47. What Hebrew Bible and text do the vast majority of colleges and universities use today? (p. 28.3)

48. What is the name of the most recent Hebrew Bible which is used

most frequently today? (p. 28.7)

49. What is the date of this Hebrew Bible? (p. 28.7)

50. What are some of the nineteen erroneous documents that are used by the NIV, NASV, NKJV, and others to allegedly "CORRECT" the Masoretic Hebrew text that underlies the KING JAMES BIBLE. Why are they erroneous? (pp. 28.7--31.8)

51. What should be our attitude toward the Masoretic Hebrew text that underlies the KING JAMES BIBLE? (p. 32.4)

52. What do we mean when we say that the Old Testament Masoretic Hebrew Text was "authorized by Jesus"? (p. 32.7)

53. How does Matthew 4:4 show that the Old Testament Masoretic Hebrew Text was "authorized by Jesus"? (pp. 32.9--33:1)

54. How about Matthew 5:17-18? (p. 33.2)

55. In His references to the Old Testament, was the Lord Jesus Christ referring to the so-called "Septuagint"? Why or why not? (p. 34.4)

56. What did Dr. Edward Hills have to say about Christ's reference to the Hebrew Old Testament? (p. 34.6)

57. What was Dr. Robert Dick Wilson's view of our Hebrew text of today? (p. 35.2)

58. What is the alternative of holding to the traditional Masoretic Old Testament Hebrew text that underlies our KING JAMES BIBLE? (pp. 35.8--36.3)

59. What was Rudolf Kittel's theological orientation? (p. 36.9)

60. What did Zondervan's interlinear Hebrew Old Testament do to some of the Hebrew verses? (p. 37.3)

61. Again, what was the Old Testament basis of our KING JAMES BIBLE? (p. 37.8)

F. QUESTIONS ON CHAPTER II--SUPERIOR NEW TESTAMENT TEXT (pp. 38-61)

62. What are the two lines of proofs that the Greek New Testament "Textus Receptus" that underlies the KING JAMES BIBLE's New Testament is superior to all other Greek texts? (p. 38.2)

63. What is meant by *"Textus Receptus"*? (p. 39.9)

64. What Greek text is the chief opponent of the Greek *Textus Receptus* today? (p. 38.3)

65. In the 81 years, from 1898 until 1979, how many revisions has this opposition Greek text gone through? (p. 38.4)

66. This is an average of one revision in how many years? (p. 38.6)

67. What can be said about the theological position of the editors of this opposition Greek New Testament? (p. 38.9)

68. What modern New Testament versions make use of this false, opposition Greek New Testament text? (p. 39.1)
69. What can be said as to the assurance this opposition Greek text has that it has the exact words of the original New Testament? (p. 39.4) Why do you say this?
70. What group has printed the exact Greek text that underlies our KING JAMES BIBLE? (p. 39.6)
71. Who originally got this Greek text together? (p. 39.7)
72. On what edition of the Greek text did the KING JAMES BIBLE translators rely for the vast majority of their Greek words? (p. 39.8)
73. In how many places did the KING JAMES BIBLE translators depart from this one Greek text? (p. 39.8)
74. Has this Greek text that underlies the KING JAMES BIBLE changed in the last approximate 400 years of its existence? (p. 39.9)
75. As asked before, what two reasons are there for holding the *Textus Receptus* that underlies the KING JAMES BIBLE superior to all others? (p. 40.2)
76. What two men were leaders in abandoning the *Textus Receptus* that underlies our KING JAMES BIBLE? (p. 40.6)
77. What year did their revised Greek New Testament text appear? (p. 40.7)
78. What can be said of their theological position? (p. 40.7)
79. In how many places in the Greek New Testament did they make alterations, either by ADDITIONS, SUBTRACTIONS, or CHANGES? (p. 40.8)
80. How many Greek WORDS in total are involved in these places? (p. 40.8)
81. If all of these words were placed in one place, how many pages of their alterations in the Greek New Testament would there be in total? (p. 40.8)
82. What book gives many examples of the heresies of these men? (p. 40.8)
83. Why are their false theories about the Greek New Testament accepted by so many today? (p. 41.2)
84. By actual count, how many Greek words did Pastor Jack Moorman find that the false Greek text had dropped out of the *Textus Receptus*? (p. 42.2)
85. If you put this number of Greek words into English words, this would be the equivalent of dropping out what books of the New Testament? (p. 42.3)

86. Many say that the alterations in the Greek New Testament text don't make any difference. Is this correct? Why or why not? (p. 43.3)

87. Some say if a doctrine is left out of the false Greek text in one or more places, but is found in some other place, that this is all right. What do you think of this? (p. 43.9)

88. Why can you NOT say that the NIV, NASV, or other modern versions are the "Words of God in English" as you can of the KING JAMES BIBLE? (p. 44.2)

89. Which Greek text was the author of *Defending the King James Bible* influenced to accept as true from his teachers? (p. 44.5)

90. In stating that the *Textus Receptus* was "ACCEPTED BY THE CHURCHES," the textbook lists 37 historical evidences that support that text. How would you sum up the argument of these 37 links? (pp. 44.9--48.1)

91. What is the author's conclusion about the Hebrew Words and Greek Words that underlie the KING JAMES BIBLE which are presently available to us today? (p. 48.2)

92. What year did the false Westcott and Hort Greek New Testament text first make its public appearance? (p. 48.6)

93. What was the first English New Testament version that was based on this false Greek text? (p. 48.6)

94. What are some of the recent English New Testament versions that are based on this same false Greek text? (pp. 49.1--49.7)

95. What does the "RIGHT WRITER" computer program tell us about the "READABILITY INDEX" of various portions of the KING JAMES BIBLE? (p. 49.9)

96. No matter how simple and "READABLE" the Bible is, what does the Bible Itself say about the only way to UNDERSTAND the Scriptures? (p. 50.7)

97. What do you think will be the result of the controversy over different Bible versions versus the KING JAMES BIBLE? (pp. 51.9--52.1)

98. What are the three kinds of evidence available for us to judge the reliability of any text in the Greek New Testament? (pp. 52.4--58.5)

99. As of 1967, about how many Greek New Testament manuscripts have been preserved for us? (p. 52.4)

100. What are the four kinds of Greek New Testament manuscripts? (pp. 53.9--54.9)

101. About how many Greek New Testament **papyrus** manuscripts have been preserved to date? (p. 54.1)

102. What percentage of these side with the Westcott-Hort-type of text

and what percentage side with the *Textus Receptus* type? (p. 54.2)

103. About how many Greek New Testament **uncial** manuscripts have been preserved to date? (p. 54.3)

104. What percentage of these side with the Westcott-Hort-type of text and what percentage side with the *Textus Receptus* type? (p. 54.4)

105. About how many Greek New Testament **cursive** manuscripts have been preserved to date? (p. 54.6)

106. What percentage of these side with the Westcott-Hort-type of text and what percentage side with the *Textus Receptus* type? (p. 54.7)

107. How many Greek New Testament **lectionary** manuscripts are there? (p. 54.8)

108. What percentage of these side with the Westcott-Hort-type of text and what percentage side with the *Textus Receptus* type? (p. 54.8)

109. What book defends the authenticity of the last 12 verses of Mark (Mark 16:9-20)? (pp. 55.2--55.8)

110. What are some of the **ancient versions** that support the Greek text underlying the KING JAMES BIBLE? (p. 56.3)

111. Who were the "Church Fathers"? (p. 56.5)

112. How can they help establish the true Greek text of the New Testament? (p. 56.6)

113. What are some of the titles of books by Dean John William Burgon that have been reprinted by the BIBLE FOR TODAY which defend the traditional Greek text and the KING JAMES BIBLE? (p. 56.7)

114. How many quotations by the Church Fathers did Dean Burgon index? (p. 56.8)

115. How many volumes are included in these indexes? (p. 56.8)

116. How many Church Fathers wrote extensively from 100 A.D. to 600 A.D.? (p. 56.6)

117. What did Dean John William Burgon find regarding the Church Fathers' support of the traditional Greek text that underlies the KING JAMES BIBLE? (pp. 57.7--58.2)

118. What did Dr. Jack Moorman find out about the same question? (p. 58.3)

119. To what Greek New Testaments do the letters "B" and "Aleph" refer? (p. 58.6)

120. What did Westcott and Hort say about "B" and "Aleph"? (p. 58.8)

121. What is the author's estimation of "B" and "Aleph"? (p. 58.8)

122. What two reasons are given to explain the preservation of "B" and "Aleph"? (p. 58.8)

123. Describe the finding of manuscript "Aleph." (pp. 59.1--59.6)

124. How many changes were made in "Aleph" by hands different from that of the original copyist? (p. 59.6)
125. How did Westcott and Hort use "B" and "Aleph" in the construction of their false New Testament Greek text? (p. 59.7)
126. What important information did Herman C. Hoskier's research bring to the light concerning manuscripts "B" and "Aleph" in the four Gospels alone? (p. 59.9)
127. How would you answer the present-day pastors and teachers who declare dogmatically that there are no traces whatsoever of *Textus Receptus* readings before about 400 A.D.? (pp. 60.1--60.7)
128. What was Hort's erroneous explanation as to why some early Church Fathers did quote from Bibles that had *Textus Receptus* readings? (p. 60.8)
129. What is the author's conclusion as to the New Testament Greek text that underlies the KING JAMES BIBLE? (p. 61.2)

G. QUESTIONS ON CHAPTER III--SUPERIOR TRANSLATORS (pp. 62-82)

130. Name two valuable books that speak about the KING JAMES BIBLE translators and their work. (pp. 62.3--62.5)
131. Many today are saying that the KING JAMES BIBLE translators perhaps were not saved, and had only a routine interest, but had little spiritual insight as to the need, value and urgency of reading and heading the Scriptures. How would you begin to answer this? (pp. 62.8--66.1)
132. How many companies were there that translated the KING JAMES BIBLE? (p. 66.4)
133. Where did these companies meet to do their work? (p. 66.4)
134. Even though it was at first included in the KING JAMES BIBLE, did the translators or the Church of England believe that the Apocrypha was canonical Scripture? (p. 66.7)
135. Who first requested of King James that the translation of the KING JAMES BIBLE be undertaken? (p. 66.8)
136. When was the translation begun? When was it completed? (p. 67.2)
137. How many men, at various times, helped in translating the KING JAMES BIBLE? (p. 66.4)
138. Give a few highlights about the translating superiority of Dr. Lancelot Andrews. (pp. 67.5--68.2)
139. Give a few highlights about the translating superiority of Dr. William Bedwell. (pp. 68.2--69.9)
140. Give a few highlights about the translating superiority of Dr. Miles

Smith. (pp. 69.9--70.5)

141. Give a few highlights about the translating superiority of Sir Henry Savile. (pp. 70.7--71.7)

142. Give a few highlights about the translating superiority of Mr. John Bois. (pp. 71.7--75.8)

143. What are seven of the reasons why the Apocrypha should not be regarded as the Words of God or canonical Scripture. (pp. 72.3--73.1)

144. What types of Greek did the author study at the University of Michigan? (p. 74.3)

145. Of the 24 other names mentioned in the book, select 6 and tell how they were qualified to be a translator of the KING JAMES BIBLE. (pp. 76.1--79.9)

146. What was McClure's opinion of the superiority of the translators of the KING JAMES BIBLE? (pp. 79.9--80.8)

147. What was McClure's opinion about the inferiority of others compared to the KING JAMES BIBLE translators? (pp. 80.8--81.5)

148. Sum up the opinion of Dr. Alexander Geddes concerning the excellencies of translation found in the KING JAMES BIBLE. (pp. 81.8--82.1)

H. QUESTIONS ON CHAPTER IV--SUPERIOR TECHNIQUE (pp. 83-130)

149. What do we mean by the word, "technique"? (p. 83.2)

150. In what two types of techniques was the KING JAMES BIBLE superior, and the other versions inferior? (p. 83.3)

151. What was a requirement for every translator of the KING JAMES BIBLE, among other conditions? (p. 83.6)

152. What was the translation assignment of the Westminster Old Testament group? (p. 84.3)

153. What was their assignment in the New Testament group? (p. 84.6)

154. What was the translation assignment of the Oxford Old Testament group? (p. 84.9)

155. What was their assignment in the New Testament group? (p. 85.2)

156. What was the translation assignment of the Cambridge Old Testament group? (p. 85.3)

157. What was the assignment of the other Cambridge group? (p.85.5)

158. How would you answer those who criticize King James in order to criticize the KING JAMES VERSION? (p. 85.8)

159. Summarize Rule #8 for the KING JAMES BIBLE translators. (p. 86.5)

160. Summarize Rule #9 for the KING JAMES BIBLE translators. (p.

86.7)

161. Summarize Rule #10 for the KING JAMES BIBLE translators. (p. 87.1)

162. Summarize Rule #11 for the KING JAMES BIBLE translators. (p. 87.5)

163. Summarize Rule #12 for the KING JAMES BIBLE translators. (p. 87.7)

164. What is the most significant difference between the KING JAMES BIBLE team technique of translation and that of the modern versions like the NASV, NIV, or NKJV? (p. 88.5)

165. What were the two kinds of superior translation techniques used in the KING JAMES BIBLE? (p. 89.3)

166. What inferior translation technique was used, to a greater or lesser degree, in the modern versions like the NASV, NIV, or NKJV? (p. 89.8)

167. What is dynamic equivalence? (p. 89.9)

168. What is verbal equivalence? (p. 90.3)

169. What is formal equivalence? (p. 90.3)

170. Why does the author think that dynamic equivalence is diabolical? (p. 90.7)

171. Where did the technique of dynamic equivalence begin? (p. 90.9)

172. How can you illustrate the diabolical principle of subtraction? (p. 91.2)

173. How many complete English Bibles have been published during the last 612 years through 1991? (91.7)

174. How many complete English New Testaments have been published during the last 612 years through 1991? (p. 91.7)

175. How many examples of addition, subtraction, or change did the author find in the New King James Version? (p. 92.1)

176. How many in the New American Standard Version? (p. 92.2)

177. How many in the New International Version? (p. 92.3)

178. How can you illustrate the diabolical principle of change? (p.92.6--92.9)

179. How can you illustrate the diabolical principle of addition? (pp. 93.1--93.6)

180. Who is the man who began "dynamic equivalence"? (p. 93.6)

181. What is the three-fold definition of dynamic equivalence? (p. 93.8)

182. During what years was the modern day "founder" of dynamic equivalence writing much of his articles and books on the subject of Bible translation? (pp. 94.1--94.7)

183. Give an example of the dynamic equivalence in the *TODAY'S ENGLISH VERSION* known as *GOOD NEWS FOR MODERN MAN?* (p. 94.9)

184. What apostate-led group has sanctioned dynamic equivalence for all their approved Bibles? (p. 95.3)

185. What modern version boasts of using dynamic equivalence? (p. 95.5)

186. What publication signaled the adoption of dynamic equivalence by so-called Fundamentalists? (p. 95.6)

187. What mission field did this booklet describe? (p . 95.6)

188. What mission board was involved? (p. 95.6)

189. What did the native Christians who were helping with the paraphrase think about the "liberties" they were taking with the words of the Bible? (pp. 96.9--97.1)

190. What other so-called Fundamental Baptist mission has adopted some of the principles of dynamic equivalence? (p. 97.7)

191. If you adopt dynamic equivalence, how would you evaluate the importance of the wording of the original language texts? (p. 98.2)

192. How many changes in sound were found in present day King James Bibles compared with the original Authorized Version of 1611 (that is, the King James Bible of 1611)? (p. 99.2)

193. Describe the findings of the analysis of the New King James Version. (p. 99.3)

194. Describe the findings of the analysis of the New American Standard Version. (p. 99.7)

195. Describe the findings of the analysis of the New International Version. (p. 100.1)

196. What kinds of "Bibles" does the United Bible Society plan to continue to produce almost entirely? (p. 101.2)

197. How would you define "dynamic equivalence" briefly? (p. 101.7)

198. What does "dynamic" mean? (p. 101.8)

199. How can things change and still remain the same? (Your own ideas)

200. What does "equivalent" mean? (p. 102.7)

201. What does "idiomatic" mean? (p. 103.3)

202. What is wrong with an "idiomatic" version of the Bible? (p. 103.5)

203. What is a brief definition of "translation"? (p. 103.6)

204. What is a brief definition of "paraphrase"? (p. 104.3)

205. What should the Bible be in the various languages of the world, a genuine translation, or an idiomatic paraphrase? Why? (pp. 103.7--104.3)

206. How many examples of paraphrase or dynamic equivalence, or adding to, subtracting from, or changing God's Words did the author find in the New King James Version? In the New American Standard Version? In the New International Version? (p. 104.8)

207. Sum up some of the main points of Dr. Francis Steele's detailed definition of a translation. (pp. 105.8--106.8)

208. What do we mean when we say that dynamic equivalency is diabolical? (p. 107.7)

209. What do we mean when we say that dynamic equivalency is deceptive? (pp. 107.9--108.5)

210. What do we mean when we say that dynamic equivalency is determined? (p. 108.6)

211. What do we mean when we say that dynamic equivalency is dishonest? (p. 109.4)

212. What do we mean when we say that dynamic equivalency is deifying of man? (p. 109.5)

213. What do we mean when we say that dynamic equivalency is disobedient? (p. 109.7)

214. What do we mean when we say that dynamic equivalency is disapproved by God? (p. 109.8)

215. What do the following verses have to say about dynamic equivalence as it ADDS TO God's Words? (pp. 110.1--110.7) Deuteronomy 4:2; Deuteronomy 12:32; Proverbs 30:6; Revelation 22:18.

216. What do the following verses have to say about dynamic equivalence as it SUBTRACTS FROM God's Words? (pp. 110.8--111.1) Deuteronomy 4:2; Deuteronomy 12:32; Jeremiah 26:2.

217. What do the following verses have to say about dynamic equivalence as it CHANGES God's Words? (pp. 111.3--113.1) Deuteronomy 5:32-33; Deuteronomy 17:18-20; Deuteronomy 28:13-14; Joshua 1: 7-8; 2 Kings 22:2.

218. Of the 13 verses given that show the importance of God's "WORDS" instead of merely His "THOUGHTS" or "IDEAS," explain how any 6 of these verses illustrate this: (pp. 113.7--116.1)

219. How does the book, *THE FUTURE OF THE BIBLE*, help us against dynamic equivalence? (p. 117.1)

220. What are the two reasons given in *THE FUTURE OF THE BIBLE* which tend to prove that the Bible as we know it in the King James Bible has a dim future? (pp. 117.5--117.8)

221. What does Van Bruggen mean when he wrote that translations must be "respectful of the form" in which God gave us His Words? (p.

118.2)

222. What does dynamic equivalence do with the FORMS of words? (p. 118.4)

223. What does Van Bruggen mean when he wrote that *"Obedience in Bible translating means a careful transmission of what God caused to be written"*? (p. 118.7)

224. What book is called the "bible" for modern Bible translators? (p. 119.2)

225. What does "implicit" mean? (p. 119.3)

226. What does "explicit" mean? (p. 119.3)

227. How does this book for Bible translators violate true principles by suggesting their method of how translators should handle "IMPLICIT" information in the following verses? (pp. 119.5--121.2): 1 Thessalonians 4:14; 2 Timothy 1:7; Luke 4:29-30.

228. How does this book for Bible translators violate true principles by suggesting their method of how translators should handle "EXPLICIT" information in the following verses? (pp. 121.3--123.8): Luke 1:18; Luke 8:35-38.

229. What are some of the things you would say to a person who asked you what you thought about the value of using the New King James Version? (pp. 124.1--125.6)

230. Why does the author say that the New Testament section of the New King James Version offers the reader a "smorgasbord of textual variance" in the footnotes? (p. 125.5)

231. Where would you find detailed information about the defects in the New American Standard Version? (p. 125.8)

232. Where would you find detailed information about the defects in the New International Version? (pp. 125.8--126.3)

233. Give 5 examples of how one of the modern versions (NKJV, NASV, or NIV) differs from the King James Bible and its underlying Hebrew and Greek texts in various places: (pp. 126.8--128.4)

234. What are at least 6 out of the 8 words that are found in the King James Bible, but are omitted from the New International Version? (p. 128.7)

235. Explain the nature of the theological changes in the new versions in the following verses (pp. 128.9--130.9): 1 Timothy 3:16; Mark 16:15; Luke 2:33; Luke 24:51.

I. QUESTIONS ON CHAPTER V--SUPERIOR THEOLOGY
(pp. 131-183)

236. What false statement did the following men make about DOCTRINE

or THEOLOGY not being affected either in any Greek variant reading, or in the various Bible versions?: Dr. Philip Schaff; Dr. Arthur T. Pierson; Dr. Louis T. Talbot; Dr. John R. Rice; Dr. Robert L. Sumner; Dr. Robert L. Thomas; Dr. H. S. Miller; Dr. Stanley Gundry; Dr. Ernest D. Pickering. (131.1--135.5)

237. Who is the modern-day researcher who found many doctrinal differences between the Westcott and Hort-type of Greek New Testament text, and the Textus Receptus-type of Greek New Testament text? (p. 135.6)

238. What was the name of his book? How many doctrinal passages did he find where these above two Greek New Testament texts differed? (p. 135.7)

239. How many Greek words did he find omitted in the Nestle-Aland 26th edition (the Westcott and Hort-type of Greek text) as compared with the Textus Receptus Greek New Testament text? (p. 135.9)

240. If all of these Greek words were placed together in one place, what two books in the New Testament would be eliminated (in terms of the total number of Greek words they contain)? (p. 136.1)

241. What method did the author use to check out the theological errors in the various modern versions? (pp. 136.2--136.9)

242. Give an example of how the new versions question the Trinity. (pp. 137.9--138.1)

243. Give an example of how the new versions question Christ's giving orders to Satan. (p. 139.1)

244. Name the two largest sections of the New Testament that are questioned by the New Versions. What is the importance of each? (pp. 139.3--141.6)

245. How do the new versions question the ministry and prophecy of Daniel? (p. 141.6)

246. How do the new versions deal with Peter's authorship of 2 Peter? (pp. 141.9--142.5)

247. How do the new versions deal with the Bible's Words as being important? (p. 142.5)

248. What fulfilled prophecies do the new versions question? (pp.143.2--145.8)

249. Of the 15 passages dealing with eschatology, or the doctrine of future things, select 7 and explain how each of them is weakened or denied in the new versions. (pp. 145.8--151.5)

250. Of the 19 passages dealing with soteriology, or the doctrine of salvation, select 10 and explain how each is weakened or denied in

the new versions. (pp. 151.6--158.4)

251. Of the 86 passages dealing with Christology, or the doctrine of Christ, select 20 and explain how each is weakened or denied in the new versions. (pp. 158.4--183.9)

the
BIBLE
FOR
TODAY

900 Park Avenue
Collingswood, NJ 08108
Phone: 856-854-4452
www.BibleForToday.org

LaVergne, TN USA
17 February 2011
216803LV00005B/7/P